Futures and Options Markets

An Introduction

Colin A. Carter

Cover and book design by Olesya Carter

ISBN: 979-8397871662

Manufactured in the USA
Published by Kindle Direct Publishing
Davis, California

To Noreen, Dakota, and Olesya

Contents

Preface

*F*utures and Options Markets: An Introduction provides an economics understanding of the history, importance, and operations of global futures and options markets, where everything from coffee to gold to crude oil is publicly traded. Starting with the fundamentals of commodity futures, this book advances the reader through the exciting and ever changing world of financial futures and options, including currencies, interest rates, and equity indexes like the S&P 500 Index. Utilizing real-world examples, this text brings the markets to life by explaining how and why these markets function, how they establish prices for things like copper and orange juice, how they affect us in our daily lives, and how they are used by firms to manage price risk.

Futures markets are viewed by business managers as leading economic indicators. They are essentially a "crystal ball" for the global economy, because futures markets are ground zero where prices of commodities and financials pick up shifts in supply and demand fundamentals. In other words, futures markets are forward looking. For instance, some economists use ocean freight rate futures as a leading indicator of global business cycles. Freight rate futures are based on an index of shipping costs for commodities such as iron ore and grain. Through establishing the price of basic raw materials, futures markets also influence economic outcomes such as economic growth in China, a very large importer of commodities such as crude oil and copper. Prices in futures markets are very responsive to changes in the market's outlook. For example, when the 2008 financial crisis began to halt global economic growth, oil prices dropped quickly, from $145 per barrel in July to $30 per barrel by December 2008. When Russia invaded Ukraine in February 2002, wheat and corn futures prices rose sharply because Ukraine is one of the breadbaskets of the world.

Some features of this book include:

- Explanation of fundamental versus technical trading analysis
- Real-world examples, providing practical applications of the com-

plicated theory of how futures and options markets establish near and distant prices —the futures curve

- Market efficiency section explaining the debate regarding market efficiency and providing empirical evidence from economic research on this question
- Discussion problems and questions reinforcing concepts learned in each chapter
- A balanced coverage of material on both commodity and financial futures and options markets

Futures and options markets are globally linked through round-the-clock computerized trading, and they lead the world in price discovery for commodities and financial assets. This book explains the economic role of futures and options markets in the modern global economy and explains how these markets evolved to better serve a more integrated world economy. The agricultural commodity contracts have historical significance and provide a foundation for understanding price formation in the modern financial futures and options markets—the center of the industry today.

Futures and options markets are the epitome of the global competitive marketplace. I have been interested in futures and options markets for many years and I have studied and traded these markets with enthusiasm and respect for the benefits of the competitive marketplace. Futures and options markets provide a wonderful laboratory to allow students to witness economics in action. The markets swiftly react to world news events that serve as either supply or demand shocks, such as a drought in Australia hitting the cotton market or a political coup in Venezuela rattling the crude oil market. The importance of futures and options markets in the global economy has grown remarkably and the industry remains dynamic and responsive to changing times. Bitcoin futures are a relatively new set of contracts, for example, and they give traders an opportunity to short the market, if they believe bitcoin prices are heading down.

Despite the economic importance of futures and options markets, there is a surprisingly high level of unfamiliarity among the public and the media regarding the functioning and economic benefits of these markets. Myths abound regarding the riskiness and undesirability of trading futures and options contracts, yet the volume of trade on these markets continues to expand year after year. As a result of the growth in this industry, more and more universities are beginning to introduce courses on futures and options markets. With this book, I hope to make a contribution to furthering the understanding of these markets so vital to our economy. This book is written as a textbook for an upper level course in futures and options markets taught in schools of business, economics, or agricultural and applied economics. Students in an MBA program are also a target audience as are professional financial planners, and money managers. The objective of this book is to provide an economic understanding of the development and operation of futures and options markets, using economics logic rather than complex mathematics. This book presents an integrated explanation of the market institutions, economic theory, and empirical evidence. It provides the reader with an intuitive explanation of the complicated nature of futures and options markets. The material in this book is presented in a way that is accessible to students with training in economics, mathematics, and statistics at the principles level. Mathematics and formulas are kept to a minimum in this book because this is introductory material. The illustrative examples and text boxes are aimed to make the material user friendly to readers new to this topic.

This book is designed for a one-semester course. Although some of the concepts are intellectually challenging, I hope you find the material to be interesting, relevant, and worth the effort.

Colin A. Carter
Davis, California
June 2023

Acknowledgments

I am grateful to Daniel Scheitrum and Armando Rangel Colina, who provided valuable research assistance on this book and very helpful editing suggestions for improving the manuscript. I also thank the many students at UC Davis who have taken my futures and options undergraduate course over the years. They have given me the incentive to stay current on the markets and to keep improving this book.

1.

The Markets

*Ken Roberts says the commodities markets are a blast! There is too much fun and
too much profit for anyone with a dream not to grab a share.*
—Worth magazine

I have never, ever been in the futures market myself; I don't have the skill for it.
—Philip Johnson, quoted in the Wall Street Journal

Who are these two guys, Ken Roberts and Philip Johnson? Well, Ken
Roberts is a former Amway home product salesman who turned to futures
markets and then started selling a mail order book called *The World's Most
Powerful Money Manual*, describing how to trade commodity futures with
the use of Roberts' trading secrets. Ken Roberts claimed you could make a
small fortune by jumping into the futures market, starting with as little as
$1,000. Roberts' book promotes simple trading strategies and trading sys-
tems to investors new to futures trading, and he reportedly made over $50
million selling his book and support materials online and through the mail.
The Federal Trade Commission found that Ken Roberts' trading materials
were misleading to the public investor.

In contrast, Philip Johnson is a former chairman of the Commodity Futures Trading Commission (CFTC), the U.S. government agency that regulates and oversees the futures industry in the United States. Johnson is a
lawyer and an expert on commodity law who wrote a treatise on commodities regulation. Johnson clearly disagrees with Roberts' wild claim that it is
easy to make money speculating in the futures market.

Diverse attitudes like those of Roberts and Johnson make futures and
options markets a colorful and interesting industry. Someone as knowledgeable as Johnson believes that speculating, or trading in the futures market with the sole intention of making a profit, is too risky (we discuss speculating in a later chapter). In all likelihood, Johnson knows that the futures

market is close to being informationally efficient and it is foolish to believe there is easy money to be made in trading futures, because new information is quickly absorbed into the market price and it is difficult for a small trader armed with public information to be ahead of the market fundamentals. As an example, Philip Johnson might remind you that finding a $100 bill lying on the sidewalk is a very rare experience. How many times has it happened to you? Not very often because anyone who is paying attention will pick up the money as soon as they see it. Professional futures traders behave in a similar manner; that is, they will take the opportunity to make money if presented with it. Therefore, scenarios where there is "too much profit", as Ken Roberts would put it, are actually scarce or nonexistent.

Box 1.1 In plain English, what are futures and options?

In the financial industry, derivatives have become more and more important, and the derivative business has flourished. Both futures and options are financial derivatives, but what exactly does that mean? In plain English, a derivative is a financial contract the value of which is derived from or linked to the value of an underlying asset or security. The underlying asset could be a commodity such as gold or rice, a foreign currency, an equity such as a common stock, or a financial asset such as a U.S. Treasury note. A derivative is nothing more than an agreement (i.e., a contract) between two parties, and the value of the contract varies with the price of the underlying asset. The buyer and the seller of derivatives could be speculating or hedging on future price moves of the underlying asset or security.

A futures contract is an obligation to buy or sell a specific quantity and quality of a commodity or financial instrument at a certain price on a specified future date. Futures contracts are standardized and traded on organized exchanges. Options, on the other hand, give the buyer the right to buy or sell futures contracts, but unlike futures, there is no obligation.

Nevertheless, Roberts throws caution to the wind and tells his clients that there is a lot of money to be made trading futures, with minimal effort and little or no expertise required. Roberts sold thousands of books because the industry attracts certain small time investors who believe in "too-good-to-be-true" schemes, like the Ken Roberts trading formula. The truth is that most of these naïve investors ultimately lose money speculating in the futures markets. At the same time, people like Roberts become wealthy from selling "get rich quick" money making schemes to novice traders. It is unlikely that Roberts became rich from trading according to his own trading systems. The U.S. Federal Trade Commission went after Roberts for improperly advertising his books and videos, because he over-stated the profit potential of his trading techniques.

The "get-rich-quick" gurus are a fringe group in the industry and they are the only collection of traders who claim to hold the secrets of how to beat the market gods. The majority of traders in the industry make no such claims. This majority includes agricultural producers, such as farmers; processors of primary products, such as mining companies, oil companies, and food and beverage manufacturers; users of natural resources (e.g., fuel) like airline companies; and multinational commodity merchants, such as Cargill based in the U.S., or COFCO based in China. Today, financial derivative contracts (e.g., interest rate, and equity index futures and options) account for the largest share of trading volume in the market and traders in that part of the market include global investment banks, insurance companies, mutual fund managers, hedge funds, pension funds, and multinational firms trying to manage price risk, interest rate risk, exchange rate risk, or other forms of financial risk.

Unlike *speculators*, many individuals or firms participate in the futures market as *hedgers* in order to shift some of the risk of asset price fluctuations onto other traders in the market. It is not unusual for these types of firms to take opposite positions from one another in the market; for instance, an oil company may be selling oil futures while at the same time an airline company is buying oil futures. One company may be seeking insurance against a price fall and the other against a price rise. In the course of everyday business, oil companies lose money if oil prices fall and, at the same time, airline companies lose money if oil prices rise. Their motives for trading are dissimilar to those of Ken Roberts' disciples, who basically seek to profit from price fluctuations and are not looking for a way to reduce their portfolio risk.

This book devotes very little attention to the colorful fringe of small speculators who believe in get-rich-quick schemes. Instead, it presents the institutional background on futures and options markets and focuses on the economics of the markets and the economics of hedging, which entails participating in the futures or options market to reduce the effects of commodity or financial price risk. Hedging is an essential topic that we discuss in later chapters. The topics presented in this book were chosen with the objective of providing the reader with an understanding of and appreciation for the economic principles, the benefits that underlie futures and options markets, and the objectives and goals of market participants. This book does not survey in detail the extensive academic literature on futures and

> **Box 1.2 What is the probability of turning $1,000 into $100,000 in just 10 months of futures trading?**
>
> The correct answer to the above question is that this feat is virtually impossible, unless you are Hillary Clinton, the former US secretary of state. When she was young, Clinton made international headlines with her amazing speculative profits in cattle futures contracts. Her ability to trade futures contracts became an issue when her husband was running for president of the United States. According to press reports, Mrs. Clinton started trading commodities in 1978 on the Chicago Mercantile Exchange (CME). Somehow, she was able to turn her initial investment of $1,000 into $100,000 after just 10 months of trading.
>
> A study by Anderson, Jackson and Steagall (1994) investigated the odds of generating a 100-fold return in the cattle futures market. They found the probability is one in approximately 31 trillion. Clinton's cattle futures trades were also studied by Leo Melamed, a former chairman of the CME. He found that in all likelihood most of her profits came from larger trades ordered by someone else and then shifted to her account. It is possible that her broker had two "mirrored" accounts, with one account buying cattle futures and the other selling cattle futures. After the trades were completed, the profitable trades could be credited to one account and the losses to the other. No matter which way the market moved, one of the mirrored accounts would make money.

options markets, but Carter (1999) and Williams (2001) each provide such a survey.

Growth of Exchange Traded Derivatives: Futures and Options

It is an understatement to say that futures and options are an increasingly important set of derivative markets in the U.S. and global economy. These markets are a segment of the financial industry that is always changing with the introduction of new exchanges, technologies, and contracts. Futures and options are contracts that derive their value from different underlying assets (more on this in Chapter 2) such as equities, interest rates or commodities. On a global scale, futures and options trading volume grew close to fourfold from 2010 to 2022 (see Figure 1.1), from approximately

22 billion contracts traded in 2010 to over 84 billion in 2022.[1] But despite its size and growing economic importance, the futures and options industry remains poorly understood. Many view futures and options as a set of derivative markets that are far too complicated to understand and in which participation is too risky. The general public sometimes mistakenly views derivatives such as futures and options as legalized gambling. This is unfortunate because derivatives provide the commodity and financial world a relatively inexpensive and very efficient way of discovering prices and controlling risk. These markets are centralized, which means they collect and aggregate information from traders around the globe. Speculators provide liquidity to the markets and non-speculators use these markets to manage price risk. Derivatives are not a new idea. In fact, one of the earliest derivatives was money, which for many centuries was tied to the value of gold.

Figure 1.1: Growth in Global Futures and Options Trading

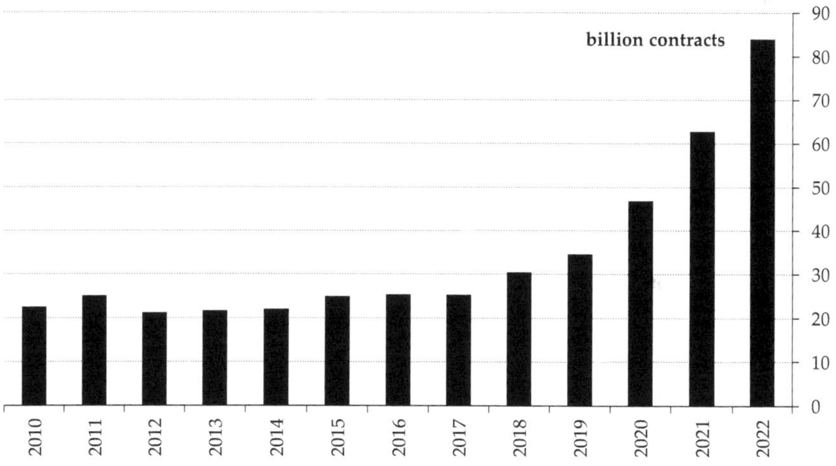

Source: *Futures Industry Association. Note: Includes single equity options.*

Derivatives have become very important in the financial world and the derivative business has flourished, but not without controversy, as witnessed by the 2008 financial crisis. Strictly speaking, a derivative is a financial contract (an agreement between two parties), the value of which is derived from or linked to the value of an underlying equity (e.g., a common

---

[1]According to Etula (2013) exchange traded derivatives account for less than 10% of the total global market for commodity derivatives. However this comparison is based on adding up the notional value of outstanding OTC derivatives and is not the notional value of the derivatives' underlying assets, and thus may be over counting the importance of the OTC markets.

stock), a Treasury bond, a financial index (e.g., S&P 500 stock index), or a commodity such as corn. Both futures and options contracts are considered derivatives and they are traded on public exchanges with industry and government oversight. Other types of derivatives, such as swaps (e.g., credit default swaps), are not typically traded on exchanges. These instruments are mainly traded "over the counter" (OTC) and they were only loosely regulated by government agencies until the 2008 financial crisis. Credit default swaps, an instrument providing credit insurance, played an important role in the 2008 financial crisis, beginning with the collapse of Bear Stearns and Lehman Brothers. It is now believed they should have been regulated like most agricultural swaps are. Globally, policy makers are requiring that credit default swaps be better regulated in order to reduce systemic risk (more on this in Chapter 2). In particular, regulators are trying to run swap trades through *Clearinghouses*, to make sure that either party in the transaction cannot easily default on their obligation.

Students are sometimes confused as to the difference between the "stock market" and the "futures and options market." There is a big difference between the two. Shares (or equities) that are traded on stock markets such as the New York Stock Exchange or the NASDAQ are assets, and buyers of stock (say in Tesla Motors (TSLA) or Apple (AAPL)) are actually acquiring a percent of ownership of the company. In other words, the investor acquires equity interest in a company, which gives them a "share" of the company's profits. If the shares appreciate in value, all those investors who have bought shares will enjoy profits. When the Tesla Motors stock price increased from $20 in 2011 to $350 in 2017, all owners of the stock benefited and were happy. Unlike the futures market, the stock market is not a *zero sum game* because a gain to a holder of the stock is not always balanced by a financial loss of another stock market participant.

Alternatively, futures and options are derivative contracts, and they are not shares of a company. Unlike in the stock market, a gain or loss to a futures or options contract holder is exactly offset by a loss or gain to another trader, therefore, it is a *zero sum game*. A futures or options contract is a standardized agreement between two parties–a buyer and a seller–to buy or sell a certain underlying asset (e.g., gold or crude oil) at a certain date in the future, at a mutually agreeable price. For every buyer of a futures contract there has to be a seller, and vice versa. If futures prices appreciate, those who "bought" futures will earn a profit and, at the same time, those who "sold" futures will experience a loss on their futures position. This is why we describe futures and options trading as a zero-sum game. We will soon explore the contract make-up in more detail.

Futures and options markets have many characteristics in common with other financial markets. Using a broad definition, a *market* is a place or

Box 1.3 World's Top Derivative Markets

The United States once dominated the exchange traded derivatives industry, but this is no longer true because of a tremendous boom in trading on foreign markets, especially in Asia, Latin America, and Europe. The growth in overseas derivative markets was due largely to the initial success of similar markets in the United States. Electronic trading has facilitated trading in foreign markets. The list of global markets below is based on number of contracts traded.

Top 10 Exchanges in the world by trading volume in 2022

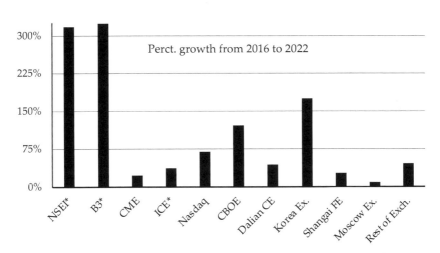

* NSEI: National Stock Ex of India, BE: Brazilian Ex.,& ICE: Intercontinental Ex.

Source: Futures Industry Association, annual surveys.

situation that puts sellers and buyers in communication with each other, discovers prices, and facilitates ownership transfer. This applies to street markets in Buenos Aires, Beijing, or San Francisco as well as to futures markets in Chicago, New York, London, Shanghai, or Tokyo. However, one key feature of the futures and options markets is that they allow the participants to enter into a transaction today that will be *fulfilled in the future*. For instance, a cane sugar farmer in Florida can price his sugar crop before harvest by selling a sugar futures contract. Similarly, a sugar refiner in Louisiana can price its major input, raw sugar, in advance of harvest by purchasing a sugar futures contract.

A key feature of the futures and options markets is that they are traded on *exchanges*. With exchange-traded derivatives like futures and options, very specific rules and regulations govern trading, and these rules are laid down by the exchange bylaws. These rules, the exchange's centralized location, and the standardized characteristics of futures and options contracts make futures and options markets unique compared to other markets.

Prices in the futures and options markets that we study in this book are driven by supply and demand fundamentals. Think about the impact on the price of crude oil if there is growing political instability in the Middle East or Eastern Europe. That is a potential supply disruption. Russia was the world's second largest exporter of crude oil in 2021 and when Putin invaded Ukraine in early 2022, the price of oil on the futures market spiked from $80 to about $120 a barrel over concerns of a supply disruption. In Europe, natural gas futures prices rose from 100 to 350 euros (€) per megawatt hour after the invasion, as Western Europe is very dependent on Russia for supplies of natural gas. Electricity is generated by natural gas and electricity prices skyrocketed so much in Europe that some folks on fixed incomes stopped using household appliances. At the same time, the price of Chicago wheat and corn futures increased sharply as Russia cut off Ukraine's ability to export grain via the Black Sea.

What will happen to the value of the U.S. dollar if inflation heats up in the American economy? Will growing incomes and changing diets in China along with urbanization in that country continue to push the global price of soybeans higher, due to rising demand for meat in Chinese diets? At the next scheduled meeting of the U.S. Federal Reserve Bank will short-term interest rates be raised, lowered, or kept unchanged? What are the chances of a late summer hurricane battering Florida's orange groves and driving up the price of orange juice? If there is a drought in Texas, will this drive up the price of beef in the future? If there is a cold snap in the Northeastern United States, how much will the price of natural gas jump due to increased demand for heating homes? On a daily basis, the futures and options markets around the globe are implicitly searching for answers to these types of supply and demand questions and the answers are revealed in the futures contract prices for nearby and distant contract months. These markets represent the ultimate form of real-world supply and demand dynamics.

As mentioned above, the material in this book is focused primarily on "exchange traded" futures and options contracts–a specific class of derivatives. In the United States and elsewhere there is also extensive derivative trading in
non-standardized "over-the-counter" derivative contracts (mostly swaps), which are given less attention in this book. Over-the-counter (OTC) trades are traditionally outside of any specific formal exchange or marketplace, often trading through a network of dealers or brokers who negotiate directly with one another. For instance, many financial instruments such as bonds are not traded on formal exchanges and as such are called "over-the-counter" contracts. However, it is becoming more common for exchanges to facilitate OTC trading to reduce the risk of default.

An important aspect of OTC trades is that the buyer and the seller face *counterparty risk*. That is, each participant runs the risk that the other party will fail to abide by the contract. Instead, central *counterparty clearing* reduces this risk, and is a service that is typically offered at exchanges. The largest U.S. clearinghouses are CME Clearing, ICE Clear U.S., and LCH Clearnet Group. Central clearing is believed to make the financial system safer, which is true only if the clearinghouse can withstand a financial crisis.

According to the Bank for International Settlements (BIS), the notional value of outstanding global derivatives exceeded $630 trillion in a typical week in 2022. Roughly 85% of these derivatives were traded OTC versus 15% on exchanges. Following the 2008 world financial crisis, the G-20 Finance Ministers (from the top 20 major economies) called for the standardization of OTC derivatives so that central counterparties "clear" all trades, similar to derivatives traded on exchanges such as futures and options contracts. In the United States, this was called the "Dodd-Frank" financial reform, named after legislation passed in 2010 and drafted by two members of Congress, Chris Dodd and Barney Frank. The Dodd-Frank bill is generally recognized as the most sweeping set of U.S. financial regulatory reforms since the Great Depression in the 1930s, and it was introduced to try and avoid a repeat of the 2008 financial crisis by increasing the regulation of OTC derivative trading.

The Market Fundamentals

Forward (or deferred delivery) contracts are probably familiar to most readers of this book but you may not recognize the formal definition of these contracts. A forward contract calls for the future delivery of an item or a service at a specified price and at a set time period. If you plan ahead and buy an airline ticket for travel to see your family over Thanksgiving, this is a forward contract between you and the airline. You agree on a price today, but the transportation service and peanuts will not be provided until some future specific date. An apartment lease is another type of forward contract. In most college towns, the student tenant signs a one-year lease with the landlord, and this constitutes a forward contract. As with an airline ticket, it will cost the tenant some money if the contract is broken for some reason. If your roommate moves out you may have to break the apartment lease and there will be a financial penalty for doing so. Thus, you may have entered into a forward contract even though you were unaware of the formal definition of the contract.

In the financial and commodity world, forward contracts are also very common. These contracts are typically traded over-the-counter (OTC), and the underlying item can range from interest rates and currencies to commodities such as crude oil. Additionally, the size of the contract can vary quite significantly. For example, the notional value of the forward could range from thousands of dollars to hundreds of millions.

A futures contract shares several similarities with forward contracts, so much so that a futures contract can be thought of as type of forward contract that happens to be standardized and traded on an organized exchange. The way in which the futures contracts are standardized consists of a fixed number of units to be exchanged, at a specific date, and at a given price. For example, the parties may agree to exchange 100,000 barrels of crude oil (the standardized size of one contract is 1,000 barrels), in three month's time at $95 per barrel. The futures contract for U.S. crude oil calls for physical delivery to be made in Oklahoma.

Some of the details of futures trading may be confusing at first because with futures contracts, you can actually sell something that you do not own. This is possible because when you "sell" a futures contract you are only promising to sell the underlying asset at some point in the future (during the futures contract expiry month, such as December). With futures contracts, the sell position can be reversed at any time before the contract expires by simply taking an opposite "buy" position to make the reversal. Likewise, an original "buy" position can easily be reversed by selling a contract for the same expiry month.

When you trade in the futures market, even if you do not own the actual crude oil, you can sell crude oil futures contracts as a speculator. You might do so if you thought the price of oil was going to decline. Even if you do not own orange juice, you can sell orange juice futures contracts, and so on. This is called going *short* in the market. Whereas the opposite trade, buying a futures contract, is called going *long*.

While most people may not be aware of the existence of futures markets, futures' trading affects those who are at "arms length" from the actual futures market. This means that firms or individuals affected by price activ-

Box 1.4 Markets Influencing Daily Lives

Futures markets influence our daily lives in many different ways. For instance the following is a list of commodities and financial instruments, the prices of which are established on global futures markets. We all recognize these items and at some point in time we have probably commented on their prices to our friends or family. If you are planning a foreign trip in the summer, the currency market will impact the cost of your trip in U.S. dollars. If you filled up your car with petro in the past few weeks, the price you paid at the pump is heavily influenced by the futures market, and so on.

- Coffee
- Cocoa
- Sugar
- Orange Juice (FCOJ)
- Milk and Cheese (Dairy)
- Cooking oil (Soybeans and Canola)
- Toast (Wheat)
- Bacon (Lean Hogs)
- Oats (Breakfast cereal)
- Petro (Crude Oil, RBOB, Heating Oil)
- Natural Gas (electricity generation, heating & cooking)
- Corn (hundreds of Corn products, Ethanol at the gas pump)
- Beef
- Cotton (textiles)
- Currencies
- Interest rates

ity in the underlying cash market are indirectly affected by price activity in the futures (and options) market. This results because day-to-day changes in futures prices affect day-to-day changes in cash (or spot) prices and *vice versa*. This is true whether or not these firms or individuals use the futures and options market directly. On a small scale, if the price of coffee futures increases sharply then you may end up paying more for your daily favorite cup of coffee at Starbucks, because the futures market is the primary price discovery point for coffee in the global market. You can rest assured that Starbucks is a trader in the coffee futures market and therefore significant futures price changes may impact what you pay for a cup of java in the local Starbucks.

On a larger scale, farmers in many regions (e.g., the United States, New Zealand, Canada, Australia, and Europe) have become more reliant on underlying supply and demand changes in the commodity markets (and therefore in the futures markets) because their governments no longer prop up the market price for all farm commodities. Even if a farmer does not trade directly on the futures market, the cash price in the local market that he or she sells into fluctuates daily along with the price changes in the futures market. There is often a high degree of correlation between local cash prices and futures prices. For example, over time the price of rice in Arkansas (the largest rice producing state in the United States) will rise and fall with the rice futures price in Chicago. Similarly, wheat farmers in western Australia pay attention to the Chicago wheat futures price because the Chicago market influences prices received by the Australian farmers.

Following deregulation in the electricity market in many parts of the United States and in other countries, utility companies have become more dependent and knowledgeable regarding electricity cash, forward, and futures markets. Trade in electricity derivatives took off with deregulation. This is also true of their input markets such as natural gas, which is used to generate electricity.

There are numerous electricity futures contracts traded on the New York Mercantile Exchange (CME Group), ICE, and the Nodal exchange. Nodal advertises that it offers over 1,000 futures and options contracts at hundreds of locations. One of the largest volume electricity futures is the ICE "PJM Western Hub Real Time Off-Peal Contract." This is a a cash settled futures contract based upon the average daily off-peak hourly electricity prices published by PJM.

The importance of contingent markets (i.e., futures and options markets) is spreading internationally. This means that prices determined by futures markets affect production and consumption decisions of individuals and firms in every corner of the world. For instance, even small farmers in places like India and China are beginning to trade forward contracts based on futures prices, and the price of soybeans, corn, or rice futures at planting time affects production and marketing decisions in these countries. These small and isolated farmers can access the latest market price information from global futures markets through their cell phones.

In the southern hemisphere, Brazil is a large coffee producer and exporter. If a surprise frost hits Brazilian coffee trees, the New York coffee futures market will react quickly and prices will rapidly adjust to this weather news. The world's coffee industry will gauge the severity of the frost by observing the price change in the coffee futures market. Starbucks may raise their retail prices if they believe the price effect will be long term. But for short-term price fluctuations, Starbucks may be hedged in the futures market (and therefore not have to raise their retail prices) because reportedly Starbucks hedges coffee eight to ten months forward.

These examples are meant to illustrate that a primary function of futures (and options) markets is the discovery of prices. These prices are signals for producers and consumers around the world to serve as a gauge as to how to ration available supplies. If the weather is expected to turn bad in northern China, the price of wheat on the Chicago futures market will most likely rise, based on this news. This price rise signals to the world a possible reduced supply of wheat. A higher price induces farmers in places like Argentina to produce more and buyers in places like Egypt to buy less, so that a new equilibrium can be reached. Wheat ranks up there in terms of being one of the most important grains in the world, along with rice. Wheat is one the oldest futures contracts and it is a commodity that is traded extensively in world markets because it cannot be grown everywhere–definitely not in the tropics. This means that wheat is grown in the southern hemisphere–say in Australia and Argentina–or in Canada, United States, China and Russia in the north. Given that international trade is a relatively large share of wheat production (about 17%), it is a market that is sensitive to world developments. And, supply shocks happen with some frequency in the wheat market. If there is a problem with the crop in Australia, the Ukraine, or Canada, the Chicago futures market reacts sharply. Futures and options markets permit this type of supply shock to be transmitted across both near-term and distant futures prices, and the information is instantaneously available to traders globally. For most futures and options contracts, supply and demand pressures originating from every corner of the globe are transformed into price levels on the futures and options exchanges.

Prices of products ranging from soybeans to gasoline to gold to foreign currencies are determined in futures and options markets. Contracts traded on the futures and options markets fall into four product categories: (a) agricultural commodities (e.g., corn and frozen concentrated orange juice-FCOJ), (b) metals (e.g., silver and gold), (c) natural resources (e.g., crude oil & lumber), and (d) financial instruments (e.g., the European Euro and the S&P 500 Index). Thousands of different futures and options contracts (representing hundreds of different commodities/financial instruments) are now actively traded on North American markets alone. Some of these contracts have relatively small trade volume, but close to 90 futures contracts in

Table 1.1: U.S. Futures Volume: 2022

Exchange	2022 Traded Volume (Millions of contracts)	
Chicago Mercantile Exchange (CME Group)	3,262.94	▬▬▬▬▬
Chicago Board of Trade (CME Group)	1,944.32	▬▬▬
New York Mercantile Exchange	514.19	▪
ICE Futures U.S.	393.72	▪
Commodity Exchange: COMEX (CME Group)	124.88	❙
Minneapolis Grain Exchange	3.29	
Total	6,243.35	

Source: Futures Industry Association Volume report 2022

the United States enjoy annual trade volume exceeding 1 million contracts.

In the United States there are presently about 6 different major exchanges that trade futures or options contracts (see Table 1.1). The largest United States exchanges are located in Chicago and New York. Outside the United States, there are as many as 40 exchanges, with several operating in Asia, Europe, and Latin America.

The four major exchanges in the United States are the Chicago Board of Trade (CBOT), the Chicago Mercantile Exchange (CME), the New York Mercantile Exchange (NYMEX), and the Intercontinental Exchange U.S. (ICE). CBOT is historically known for trading grains (such as corn and wheat) and interest rates (such as Treasury Bonds and Treasury Notes). The CME is known for equity indexes (such as the S&P 500 Index), foreign currencies, and livestock (such as live cattle and lean hogs). The NYMEX is famous for trading energy contracts (such as WTI crude oil and natural gas) and metals (such as gold and silver). Finally the ICE Futures U.S. focuses on the traditional "soft" commodities such as sugar, cotton, coffee, frozen concentrated orange juice, and cocoa. There has been massive consolidation in the U.S. futures and options industry and now the top three U.S. exchanges (CBOT, CME, and NYMEX) are controlled by just one publicly traded corporation, the CME Group Inc., headquartered in Chicago. As of 2022, the CME group handled about 10% of the world's trading volume in options and futures contracts. The largest exchange by volume, the National Stock Exchange of India accounted for about 19% of global trading, next was the Brazilian stock exchange (B3) with 13%. The Intercontinental Exchange accounted for about 6% of world volume–see Box 1.3. In North America alone, about 16.8 billion futures and options contracts were traded in 2022. About 15% of the global volume of exchange traded derivative financial instruments is accounted for by trading in single single equity futures and options. In this book we will focus on understanding the remaining 85% of the volume of trade, including the large markets in interest rate futures, equity index futures, equity index options, and commodity futures.

Futures traders can buy and sell silk futures in Japan, stock index futures in London or Chicago, white maize futures in South Africa, copper futures in London, coffee futures in New York, Treasury Bond futures in Chicago, canola (oilseed) futures in Canada, and cotton and sugar on the Zhengzhou Commodity Exchange in China. In addition, barge and tanker freight futures are traded in New York, London and elsewhere. Freight futures are one of the few active futures contracts based on a service, and are used as a hedging device by international commodity merchants. For example, the Baltic Exchange in London trades freight derivatives on ocean vessel shipping rates for bulk commodities such as coal, iron ore, and grain. In 2006 and 2007, freight futures prices rose by more than four-fold, reflecting the booming global demand for commodities and increased demand for freight services. In 2008, the BDI index peaked at close to 10,000 (see Box 1.5) and when the financial crisis hit, freight futures then plummeted down by over 90%. The BDI then remained low for several years due to excess capacity in the shipping industry. This changed in the latter part of 2021 when the BDI surged, see Box 1.5.

Figure 1.2: World Exchange Traded Derivatives: Options versus Futures 2022

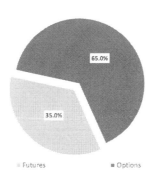

Source: *Futures Industry Association.*

From Figure 1.2 we see that options make up 65% of world exchange traded derivatives. To further understand the makeup of the total trading volumes shown in Figures 1.1 and 1.2, turn to Table 1.2 where the derivative trading by category is shown. Equity index futures and options are the biggest market in exchange traded derivatives with 27% of world futures volume and 74% of global options trading volume, in 2022. Following equity index contracts, the next largest market is individual equity index fu-

Box 1.5 Baltic Dry Index

The Baltic Exchange in London has been around since 1744. It trades ocean freight derivatives and publishes the daily Baltic Dry Index (BDI), an indicator of the price of shipping bulk dry raw commodities (such as iron ore, coal, and grain) by sea. The BDI is based on freight rates for different size ships on over 20 different shipping routes. The BDI index is shown in the figure below for the 1995 to 2022 time period. In early 2016, the BDI was at an historically low level (about 430 points), due to low commodity demand and a glut of ships at the time. In 2015-2016 the daily charter rate for Capesize vessels (large ships that can haul more than 100,000 dead weight tons) was as low as $3,000 per day, approximately one-half of the operating cost. Contrast that with daily charter rates of over $300,000 in 2008 for the Capesize vessels. The BDI reached over 9,500 points in 2008. The daily price to lease a Panamax ship was over $32,000 in 2008, compared to only $1,000 in 2015. A Panamax can carry 60,000 to 80,000 dead weight tons of cargo, and they are the largest ships allowed through the Panama Canal.

The BDI is recognized as a leading indicator of global economic growth. At any given point in time the supply of ships is fixed and given that fixed supply the price of shipping then depends on the global demand for raw materials. As the world demand for raw commodities increases, the BDI increases, and vice versa.

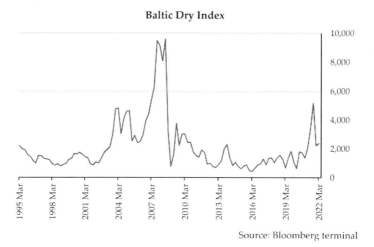

Baltic Dry Index

Source: Bloomberg terminal

Table 1.2: Global Exchange Traded Derivatives (Futures and Options) by Category: 2022

Category	2022 Volume (million contracts)	Percent of trade
Agriculture	2,394	2.9%
Currency	7,714	9.2%
Energy	2,067	2.5%
Equity Index	48,619	58.0%
Individual Equity	13,216	15.8%
Interest Rates	5,146	6.1%
Non-Precious Metals	1,630	1.9%
Other	2,498	3.0%
Precious Metals	564	0.7%
Grand Total	83,848	

Source: Futures Industry Association.

Figure 1.3: Global Exchange Traded Derivatives (Futures and Options) by Region, 2022

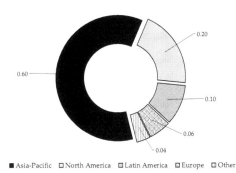

■ Asia-Pacific ☐ North America ☐ Latin America ☐ Europe ☐ Other

tures and options, making up 16% of world (exchange based) derivative trading. About two-thirds of this volume is in options, as opposed to futures. Interest rate futures and options account for 6% of the market, most of which is in futures. Currency futures and options account for 9.2% of global exchange traded derivatives, followed by agriculture, energy, and metals.

Regionally, the U.S. and Asia continue to dominate the derivatives industry as we see from Figure 1.3. The data for the U.S. in this figure are for North America, but Canada and Mexico comprise a very small share of the market. Exchanges in Asia-Pacific enjoy over 60% of global volume in exchange traded futures and options. The North American exchanges control about 20% of global derivative trading, ahead of Latin America with 10% and Europe with 5.7%.

If we considered only futures trading, then the regional market shares measured by number of contracts traded are as follows: Asia-Pacific (38.5%), Latin America (20.7%), North America (18.1%), Europe (12.9%), and other (9.7%). Keep in mind that these volume statistics are based on number of contracts traded, and not the notional value of the contracts traded.

Box 1.6 Relationships Across Markets

There is a strong inter-relationship across a number of commodity and financial markets. The boom or bust of the price in one market can cause a price rise or fall in another market. As discussed above, a rise or fall in the price of coal or grain due to shifting demand and supply, can heavily impact ocean freight rates and therefore freight futures. Another relationship exists between commodity prices and the currencies of those countries highly dependent on commodity exports–the so called *commodity currencies*–such as the Australian dollar. Consider just one important commodity, crude oil. The Norwegian Krone slumped in value in 2014-2015, due to the slide in oil prices. The figure in this box shows the price of crude oil versus the Russian Ruble and Canadian dollar, two other commodity currencies. Both of these currencies dropped sharply in 2008 when oil prices collapsed, and we see a similar pattern in 2014-2015 when oil lost 50% of its value. The Canadian dollar fell by about 15%, and the Russian Ruble declined by 50%. Both Canada and Russia are top oil exporters and oil accounts for a relatively large share of each country's total exports. This means that the price of oil impacts each country's *terms of trade*–the ratio of export prices to import prices.

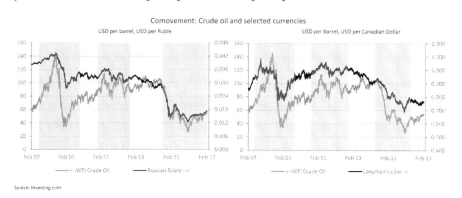

Comovement: Crude oil and selected currencies

Source: Investing.com

Market Participants: Hedgers, Speculators, and Arbitrageurs

Unlike a common stock (or equity), which can be held for decades, futures contracts have relatively short finite lives and most are traded for only one to two years before they expire. But there are exceptions with some contracts trading for multiple years. For instance, crude oil futures contracts can trade for eight or more years prior to their delivery (expiry) month. For example, in 2023, buyers and sellers were exchanging distant crude oil futures for delivery in December 2030. Natural Gas is another example with contracts actively trading about six years into the future. In contrast, corn futures contracts trade for about three years before expiry.

Futures and options are primarily used for offsetting price risks in the cash market or for taking advantage of price movements of the underlying asset, rather than an avenue for physically buying or selling the actual cash commodity. Many futures contracts require delivery of the commodity or financial instrument in a stated month in the future to ensure that futures prices conform to the value of the underlying commodity in the cash market. However, more often than not the contract is closed or offset before it expires. Some contracts do not even allow for physical delivery, but instead use a system of cash settlement in the delivery month. For example, you cannot physically deliver a "stock index" (because it is a theoretical construct) so settlement in the month of expiry takes place at the prevailing cash price.

There are two broad groups of participants in the futures and options markets. The first group is termed **hedgers**, and the second group **speculators**. Starting with hedgers, consider a firm or individual that holds a commodity such as orange juice or natural gas in inventory in a warehouse, pipeline, or terminal facility. They clearly want the price of that commodity to increase, or at least not decrease. In an attempt to reduce any loss in value of their asset, the company or individual may use the futures or options markets to take a derivative market "paper" position opposite to their cash position (meaning they would sell futures if they hold inventory) in order to minimize the risk of financial loss from holding the asset in question. This is called "hedging." The dictionary defines hedging as an "attempt to lessen loss by making a counterbalancing investment." The concept underlying most hedging objectives is that losses (or in the opposite case, profits) in the futures or options market are offset by gains (losses) in the cash market. Hedgers buy and sell futures and options contracts in order to facilitate business transactions and/or reduce exposure to risk associated with price fluctuations in underlying commodity and financial markets. One of the main economic reasons why futures and options markets are useful to society is that they provide hedgers with a mechanism for lowering the cost of business and managing price risk.

Another definition of a hedger is a firm or individual that transacts business in the same underlying commodity or financial instrument specified in the futures contract, and then simultaneously trades futures and/or options. For commodities, this classification includes oil and mining companies, energy companies, farmers, food and beverage companies, cattle feeders, and so on. Banks, trust companies, mutual funds, insurance companies, and construction companies are typical hedgers in the financial futures market. Hedgers trade futures and options in order to reduce exposure to cash price fluctuations. By taking a position in the futures or options market that is opposite their underlying cash position, they can reduce the risk of price variability. They take a position in the futures or options market in order to offset risk in their underlying business. Hedging is not necessarily conducted for profit from price fluctuations, but rather to reduce price risk. But sometimes there are profit opportunities available to hedgers when cash and futures markets are temporarily out of line with one another, and hedgers will take a cash and offsetting futures position in anticipation of the cash-futures price relationship returning to normal.

Hedging is not much different from buying other forms of insurance, such as health insurance or auto insurance. For example, a wheat farmer can purchase insurance against the loss of a crop due to a random hailstorm. In fact, almost every risky aspect of the farming business is privately insurable except product price risk. The reason for the "missing" insurance market is very simple. An insurance company could not afford to offer a price insurance policy to wheat farmers for a reasonable insurance premium because during a year of low prices, every client would make a claim. But if instead the farmer was hit by a freak hailstorm, a farmer in the next county may have been spared. From county to county, such storms are somewhat independent events.

The probability of a single wheat farmer being adversely affected by low prices is not independent from the same event affecting other wheat farmers. For the same reason, earthquake insurance is prohibitively expensive for residents of San Francisco. If there is one claim due to an earthquake loss, there will be hundreds of thousands of claims. The pooling of independent risks is not very effective (and is therefore costly) for earthquake insurance, but it is not even feasible for commodity and financial asset prices. However, futures and options markets serve this important function: they facilitate the transfer of price risk from hedgers to speculators.

There are many examples of hedgers. Cotton farmers in Australia who trade futures contracts are one such example. One characteristic about agricultural production in a sparsely populated country like Australia is that most of their agricultural commodities are sold into foreign markets and priced in U.S. dollars. If you study international trade in most commodities, for example in crude oil or in wheat or in cotton, you will find that almost all this world trade is conducted in U.S. dollars. Even if a third country is the importer, the exporter typically requests payment in U.S. dollars, because the U.S. dollar is a stable currency and viewed as a reserve currency worldwide. It is also the case that a number of the major commodity markets are based in the United States and this reinforces the tradition of denominating international commodity trading in U.S. dollars, irrespective of the origin and destination of the commodity flow. Did you know that of all the U.S. dollars in circulation globally, more are in circulation outside the United States than within the United States? It is truly a global currency. So, if you are an Australian cotton farmer, selling cotton on the world market, there are two main factors that affect you on the price side. One is supply and demand developments and their impact on the cotton futures market in New York, because that is the central marketplace where information comes in from around the world regarding cotton supply and demand. If there is a weather problem in any major cotton producing region, then the futures market in New York will respond to this news in a matter of minutes and the cotton price will quickly react to the news. So, that is one factor on the Australian farmer's computer screen. Another is the exchange rate, because the Australian growers have to convert their foreign cotton sales from U.S. dollars back into Australian dollars in order to pay their local costs. So, these farmers could be hedging both the price of cotton and the Australian dollar/U.S. dollar exchange rate. Here we have a nice example of why hedging is important.

Unlike hedgers who use futures and options primarily to counterbalance another position in the cash or spot market, "speculators" buy and sell futures and options in anticipation of profiting from changes in the price of the contract. This is often their sole objective, although futures and options also help speculators diversify their investment portfolios. One reason that hedge funds have been attracted to speculating in the futures market is that they believe commodities serve as a useful way to diversify their portfolio because commodity prices often move opposite to equity prices in the stock market. For instance, during inflationary periods the stock market typically does not perform well but commodity prices (e.g., gold) often increase. As with any investment, there is a risk return trade-off. Speculators are willing to expose themselves to financial risk in the commodity markets because diversifying into the futures market can serve to reduce their overall risk.

Gorton and Rouwenhorst (2006) and Bhardwaj, Gorton and Rouwenhorst (2016) studied monthly returns to commodity futures as an asset class.

Their data set went back as far as the 1950s. They conclude that commodity futures have offered the same return and as publicly traded U.S. stocks, adjusted for the risk free return equities. Furthermore commodity futures returns are negatively correlated with stock returns and bond returns. The negative correlation arises from commodity futures' different behavior over a business cycle because commodity futures are positively correlated with inflation. Implicit in this finding is the implication that speculators in commodity futures receive a return for providing price insurance to hedgers. However, this finding is not without controversy. The notion that commodities offer equity like returns (or even a portfolio of commodities) has been challenged by Erb and Harvey (2006). The interested reader might consult Barron's database on *Commodity Trading Advisers (CTA)* Performance at www.barrons.com, where the annual performance of major *long-only* CTAs is reported.

Futures and options market speculators do not normally buy or sell the underlying physical commodity or financial instrument during the normal course of their business activities. They assume the price risk from hedgers and seek to profit from price variability. It is a well known fact that a futures or options market would be very difficult (or even impossible) to operate without the risk-absorbing service (i.e., liquidity) that speculators provide. If a hedger wishes to buy or sell a futures contract, speculators are usually willing to take the other side of the transaction. The risk of price fluctuation is thereby transferred from the hedger to the speculator. The same is true with options on futures.

There are a large number of large, medium, and small speculative traders in these markets trying to make a profit. Speculators use one of two approaches to trade futures and options. The first approach is **fundamental** price analysis and the second is **technical** price analysis. Fundamental analysis studies supply and demand information and speculators attempt to forecast price changes based on the economic fundamentals. Alternatively, technical price analysis uses past price behavior in order to predict future price behavior. These two alternative schools of trading philosophies will be covered later in this book.

Technical analysis is a trading philosophy and a set of trading techniques borrowed from the stock market; however, the assumptions behind the logic of technical traders violate the basic laws of economics. Nevertheless, there is a large number of traders who use technical trading rules, including hedge funds and managed futures funds who rely on computerized algorithmic trading. These traders are often referred to as chartists. Basically, they use historical prices to forecast forthcoming prices. But in reality in these markets it is very difficult to forecast the future based on the past. What has happened in the market has happened–it is history. Sup-

Box 1.7 Betting on the Weather

In the business world, it is not uncommon for a firm to experience financial loss due to uncertain and adverse weather patterns. Losses can arise from a number of weather-induced developments, such as physical damage to assets, higher input costs, lower selling prices, or disrupted market conditions. Weather derivative contracts have arisen in an attempt to help businesses cope with such weather risks and the financial consequences of adverse weather. Weather risk contracts are tied to specific meteorological events that are easily measurable, such as snowfall in a certain location over a certain time period. Firms exposed to weather risk look to weather derivatives as a form of insurance. Besides exchange traded standardized weather derivatives, there is a large over-the-counter market in weather derivatives where the contracts are customized for firm specific needs.

Weather derivatives are still relatively new concepts in the futures and options industry, and some of these contracts have not survived. For instance, in the early 1990s, the Chicago Board of Trade (CBOT) introduced catastrophe options based on property claims due to hurricanes, tornadoes, and other climatic events. In the late 1990s, the Bermuda Commodities Exchange introduced similar options based on losses from hurricanes, tornadoes, thunderstorms, windstorms, hail, and winter storms. Both the CBOT and Bermuda catastrophe option contracts failed because of insufficient trading volume.

The most active exchange traded weather contracts are offered on the Chicago Mercantile Exchange (CME). The CME trades "heating degree-days" and "cooling degree-days" futures and options contracts based on temperatures in many different cities in the U.S., Canada, Australia and Europe. In addition there are contracts based on rainfall, snowfall and frosts.

Go to: *www.cmegroup.com/trading/weather/*

pose the price of oil has increased $20 per barrel in the last month. That does not tell us whether it is going up or down next week, but if a chartist walked into your life, they would try to convince you otherwise.

The *efficient market hypothesis* says investors cannot predict future prices with historical information. Despite the efficient market theory, *Momentum Trading* is popular with hedge funds and Commodity Trading Advisors (CTAs). The momentum trading philosophy believes that on average past winners outperform past losers over a trading horizon of less than one year, and due to long-term market reversals, on average past losers outperform past winners over a longer time horizon. Momentum traders in futures markets use buy (sell) signals for commodities that have performed well (poorly) over a certain time period. Momentum trading is also called *algorithmic trading*, and the traders running the computers are known as "algos." These computer automated traders account for a large share of transactions in futures markets.

In addition to outright speculators and hedgers, there is a subclassification of speculators called arbitrageurs. These individuals or firms often take very short-term positions in the market, seeking to take advantage of market anomalies. They simultaneously buy and sell futures (or options) contracts in order to profit from a discrepancy in price relationships. Arbitrageurs are invaluable in terms of "making" a market because they often provide needed liquidity and their buying and selling (i.e., arbitrage) activities enhance the pricing efficiency of the futures and options market. An arbitrage opportunity is a risk-free profit opportunity. It is often said that there is no "free lunch" in the markets. But arbitrageurs are constantly on the lookout for a "free lunch" (e.g., when relative prices for two different options contracts display an abnormal relationship), and if they find a "free lunch," they quickly exploit it. Three-way arbitrage opportunities also exist among the cash, futures, and options markets. Given that futures and options trading is a zero-sum game (i.e., aggregate profits equal aggregate losses), there is much debate as to whether speculators consistently earn profits from hedgers. Whether hedgers pay a significant insurance premium to speculators is very difficult to determine empirically. However, research has shown that, as a group, speculators do not earn a large insurance payment from hedgers. This is not to say that in certain markets and at certain times an insurance premium does not exist, but the general claim that speculators earn a premium in return for assuming the price risk has not been proven unequivocally.

What Exactly Are Futures and Options Markets?

As mentioned earlier, a futures market is an organized marketplace where buyers and sellers come together (in person through open-outcry, through brokers, or electronically) to establish prices for deferred delivery of a specific commodity (e.g., gold or coffee) or financial asset (e.g., a U.S. Treasury bond or the Japanese yen). It is called a futures market because the price established today is for future delivery (or future financial "settlement" for contracts that do not permit delivery). Supply, demand, and expectations interact to determine futures contract prices. The futures exchange sets all the specific rules and regulations governing trading, except for the price. Prices are established when futures contracts are bought and sold by hedgers and speculators. Futures traders originally bought and sold contracts through a public open outcry bid-and- offer system in a large trading *pit*, but most trading pits have gone dark in favor of electronic trading. In 2015, the CME decided to close most of its futures trading pits in Chicago and New York. The COVID-19 pandemic led to more trading floor closures.

Remember, it is not unusual for firms who are buying and selling futures (or options) contracts to have an opposite position in the cash market. To the extent that futures prices tend to be positively correlated with spot market prices over time, having opposite positions in these two markets tends to neutralize the effects of a price change in either direction, hence the term hedging. Gains (losses) in the futures market tend to offset losses (gains) in the cash market regardless of the direction of the price movement.

Consider the following hedging example. With growing political problems in the Middle East and strong growth in the global economy, the price of crude oil more than doubled from 2007 to 2008–rising on both cash and futures markets from about $70 per barrel to over $140. With the run-up in oil prices, suppose an oilman in Alberta, Canada, determines that it would be profitable to purchase and uncap old abandoned oil wells. The cost of pumping his oil is estimated to be about $100 per barrel, so $140 yields a handsome profit. However, the decision to uncap the well is somewhat irreversible in the short run, and it will take the oilman about three months to bring the well back into production. In the meantime, he runs the risk of the price of oil falling back below $100. The oilman desires some protection against a potential price drop, so he emails his futures broker and instructs him to sell a distant crude oil futures contract at $140 per barrel. Such a futures contract sale would obligate the oilman to deliver oil to the futures delivery point and receive $140 per barrel in return. But he knows that this obligation can be offset by reversing his futures position. The sale of the futures contract is a temporary substitute for the oilman's future sale of crude oil in the cash market.

The New York Mercantile Exchange (now part of the CME Group) futures contract calls for delivery of 1,000 barrels of crude oil: the contract size. Suppose the oilman chooses a contract specifying delivery in about five month's time, say, the December futures contract. Basic economics tells us that once the oilman decides to uncap the well and start pumping oil, he is exposed to the risk of a price decline. To reduce this risk, he sold a futures contract. He therefore would stand to gain from his futures position if prices were to fall because to liquidate (i.e., to close) his futures market position, he would buy back the futures contract at a lower price than he originally sold it for. Alternatively, if prices rise, he will gain in the oil spot market but lose in the futures market. The futures contract would then have to be "bought back" at a higher price than what it was sold for; hence, a futures loss would be incurred. The hedgers goal is to have the spot market gain/loss offset by the futures market loss/gain.

As in any other marketplace, for every seller of a futures contract there has to be a buyer. Continuing with our example, consider a trader on the opposite side of the market from the oilman. Suppose a major international airline company from Britain watches the price of oil rise to $140 and is worried that prices could go even higher if the United States steps up the war in the Middle East and invades Iran. The airline wants to attempt to lock in the current price of oil in order to protect itself against higher jet fuel prices in the future. Higher fuel prices could lead to large financial losses for the airline because fuel costs can typically account for one-fourth to one-third of airline operating costs. The airline company initiates an order with its futures broker to buy a December crude oil futures contract at $140 per barrel. Note that the purchase of the futures contract is a temporary substitute for the future purchase of jet fuel in the cash market. There are no "active" futures contracts for jet fuel so in this example the airline uses crude oil derivatives as a proxy for the price of jet fuel because the price of crude oil and jet fuel are highly correlated.

Technically, the use of crude oil to hedge jet fuel prices is called cross-hedging. Jet fuel is the cash commodity being hedged, but there is no active futures contract for jet fuel. Instead, the airline uses a different but related futures contract (i.e., crude oil futures). With cross-hedging, prices for the cash commodity being hedged and the related futures market should follow similar price patterns over time.

The British airline and the Canadian oilman are both hedgers. Their profits are affected by the price of crude oil in the daily course of their business because they either produce or consume oil, the underlying commodity. In this example, they are on opposite sides of the market and they both trade futures contracts in order to try and reduce price risk.

Suppose both futures contract orders–from the Canadian oilman and the British airline–reach the New York Mercantile Exchange at about the same time. The oilman's broker offers to sell December oil at $140, and the airline's broker bids (i.e., offers to buy) December oil at $140. Since the bid and offer prices match, the trade is immediately completed on the New York exchange. The price of December oil futures on the exchange is public information, and news of any price change on the exchange is quickly sent out to brokerage firms and other interested parties around the world.

Now, rather than the British airline buying the contract from the oilman, suppose a hedge fund from California anticipates that the price of oil will rise to $160. This hedge fund manager is a speculator–one who buys and sells futures contracts with the sole intention of making money. This is a much different objective for trading futures than was the case for the oil-man or the airline, both of which are hedgers. The hedge fund anticipates that an Iranian invasion by the United States would push the price of oil up from $140 to $160. The fund manager calls his futures broker and puts in an order to buy December crude oil futures at $140. Assume the oilman takes the other side of the position. The intention of the hedge fund is to wait for the price of oil to rise and then liquidate its futures position by entering into a reverse trade (i.e., it would later sell a December futures contract). If the price rises to $160 before December, the fund sells a December futures con-tract and earns a profit of $20,000: $20 per barrel times 1,000 barrels (which is the size of the futures contract). Of course, if oil futures prices fall instead of rise, the fund is forced to sell at a lower price than the original purchase price, and thus it loses money. In relative terms, the fund's position in the futures market is much riskier than is the case for the hedger because the fund does not hold an underlying position in the cash (spot) market. How-ever, maintaining a well-diversified portfolio would help reduce the fund's risk associated with any position in the futures market.

To illustrate some key features of a typical futures contract, refer to Fig-ure 1.4, which displays daily closing futures prices for (light, sweet) crude oil traded on the New York Mercantile Exchange (NYMEX). The unit of trade is 1,000 U.S. barrels (approximately 42,000 gallons), and the price on the vertical axis in Figure 1.4 is quoted in $U.S. per barrel. The futures price in Figure 1.4 ranged from approximately $40/bbl to over $75/bbl, over the seven years of price history shown. The $35/bbl price change (from $40 to $75) represents a change in contract value (i.e., notional value) of $35,000. Figure 1.4 shows that crude oil prices traded below $55/bbl for most of the COVID-19 period when demand was suppressed but then prices jumped to $75/bbl when Russia invaded Ukraine in 2022.

Crude oil is one the world's most actively traded "commodity" futures contracts and the NYMEX and the ICE oil contracts are used as interna-tional pricing benchmarks. The NYMEX contract is known as the West Texas Intermediate–WTI–contract, based on the price of oil in Cushing, Ok-lahoma. WTI crude largely reflects supply and demand fundamentals in the U.S. market but is closely linked with the global oil market ever since the U.S. 40 year ban on oil exports was lifted in 2016. In 2022, approxi-mately 206 million WTI crude oil futures contracts were traded on the New York Mercantile Exchange. On some days the WTI trades over a million contracts! The ICE contract specifies delivery of *Brent* crude and it repre-sents supply and demand for crude oil in the North Sea, primarily west of Scotland in deep water. Originally there was a oilfield named Brent in that

Figure 1.4: December 2025 Crude Oil Futures: NYMEX (CME Group)
Dollars per Barrel

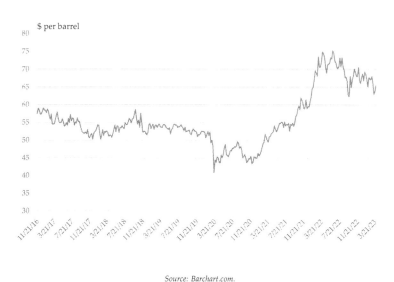

Source: Barchart.com.

region.

For the WTI price graph shown in Figure 1.4, the contract specifies December 2025 as the delivery month and Cushing, Oklahoma as the delivery point. The delivery month indicates the month during which the futures contract expires (in this case December). In fact the WTI contract expires near the end of the calendar month prior to the delivery month. For instance, trading in December WTI futures will cease near the end of November. More precisely, trading ends 3 business days prior to the 25th calendar day of the month prior to the contract month. Prior to expiry, the contract must be offset (sold if one was previously bought, or bought if one was previously sold), or settled by the exchange of the physical commodity. Crude oil futures are somewhat unique in that trading is conducted for all 12 calendar months. Most futures contracts have fewer than 12 standardized delivery months. For instance, live cattle futures on the Chicago Mercantile Exchange has six standardized trading months: February, April, June, August, October, and December.

As mentioned, an alternative benchmark, the Brent crude oil futures contract is traded on the ICE in Europe and it is very important as a global benchmark. About 75% of the world's oil is priced off the Brent. The WTI and the ICE crude oil markets are rivals as to which is the most globally relevant contract. Brent crude (mostly) reflects supply and demand fundamentals outside of the U.S. In 2022, volume in ICE Brent futures was 235.3

million contracts. Brent crude is considered slightly lower in quality than WTI because Brent has a higher viscosity and sulphur content which affects the cost of refining. Historically WTI traded at a premium of a few dollars per barrel to Brent but this has changed since the U.S. started producing more oil and exporting onto the world market. The shale revolution in the U.S. more than doubled production, and increased U.S. exports 12 fold from 2015 to 2023, after export restrictions were lifted. The U.S. is now the number one oil producer in the world and the third largest exporter. As a result, U.S. production is more and more influential over global oil prices. It is noteworthy that in 2023 the oil index publisher, S&P Global Platts, started to include U.S. WTI Midlands crude in the Brent oil benchmark because the supply of oil in the North Sea was declining. This means that Brent will now be partially influenced by the U.S. market.

Figure 1.5 charts the price of Brent vs WTI and the spread (Brent minus WTI) between them. The price spread between WTI and Brent is an important benchmark itself as the spread affects international trade in oil, refiner margins, and the price of refined products globally, see Scheitrum, Carter and Revoredo-Giha (2018). During the Jan 2021 to March 2023 time period Brent was trading above the WTI price by $4.41 per barrel, on average. The average spread widened to $5.80 in 2022 and early 2023 because European customers bid up the price of Brent in order to replace crude oil supplies they were importing from Russia before the Ukraine war (see Figure 1.5). Many traders try to profit from changes in the WTI-Brent price spread. In fact, the CME trades a WTI-Brent spread futures contract. The contract size is 1,000 barrels and the contract is financially settled. Brent is based on the price of North Sea crude oil and delivery is on the water. Supply and demand differences in the WTI versus the Brent market will impact the spread shown in Figure 1.5. For example, increased shale oil production in the United States in 2011 drove WTI to a discount under Brent.

Crude oil futures contracts have underlying cash markets in which trading of the physical commodity takes place. For instance, Cushing, Oklahoma, is the U.S. center of cash market trading in WTI oil and is also accessible to participants in the international spot market for crude oil. The spot price is called West Texas Intermediate (WTI) crude oil, a particular grade of crude oil. Trading in the cash market is much less standardized and less regulated than trading in the corresponding futures market. In the futures market, settlement of the contract is managed by the exchange's clearinghouse (unlike in the spot market). The clearinghouse is discussed in the next chapter.

If you read the *Wall Street Journal* or use the Internet to track futures prices, check out crude oil futures prices. You can trade for delivery more than eight years from now. It is interesting to look at the spectrum of prices

Figure 1.5: Brent versus WTI Crude Oil Futures:
Dollars per Barrel

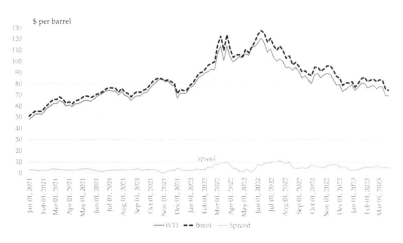

Source: U.S. Energy Information Administration (EIA).

that differs due to the specified time of delivery. Today, the price for crude oil is between 70 and 75 dollars a barrel, well below the $140 it reached in 2008. Guess what the oil price is for delivery in 2 years? Is it lower, higher or about the same? What about for delivery in 4 or 6 years time? Why do you suppose it would be higher than today? When this chapter was written, the futures price for delivery in 2 years was about the same as the current price. So, if you're running an airline and you look at this, you have little room for optimism because the futures market is not forecasting a drop in the price of oil. A relatively high price of oil can also slow global economic growth, which is an important factor for an airline, not to mention other businesses. How do we explain these price relationships? How do we explain the relationship between the price of December oil for delivery this year versus the price of December oil for delivery in two years time, or in six years time?

We can use the economics of storage theory to understand these price relationships. We can do the same for prices of financial futures. Some of the largest volume futures contracts are in U.S. Treasuries, especially Treasury Notes. And so, in this book we study financial price relationships for contracts for nearby and distant expiry. Every futures contract has an expiry month, so December 2025 oil means that if you buy or sell that contract, you are either agreeing to take delivery of oil or you are agreeing to deliver oil, one of the two, depending on whether you buy or sell in the month of December in the year 2025. So that is the delivery (or expiry) month, and the futures price is related to what the market judges might happen to the spot price between now and then.

Origins of Futures and Options Trading

The characteristics of commodity futures contracts that are traded on modern-day exchanges were largely developed during the 19th century. However, it is believed that futures markets had historical counterparts in Japan and Europe in the 18th century, as some form of a rice futures contract was traded on the Dojima Rice Exchange in Osaka, Japan, during that time. The Dojima Exchange traded rice for over 300 years, almost up until World War II. Around the same period, futures trading was apparently conducted in grains, brandy, whale oil, and coffee in Amsterdam.

Figure 1.6: Seasonal Price Swings

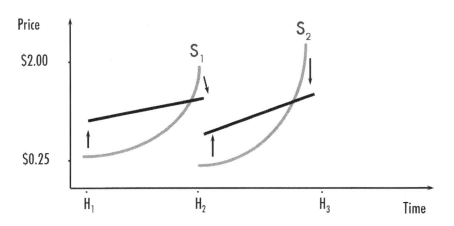

In 1848, the Chicago Board of Trade organized futures trading as it exists in principle today. Primarily because of its geographic location between the Great Lakes and the midwestern U.S. grain belt, Chicago had become the grain-marketing center of the United States. Futures and forward trading essentially arose out of the cash grain market in Chicago. At that time, Chicago futures markets evolved for two major reasons: a) to provide economic incentives to encourage grain storage, and b) to correct large seasonal cash price changes. Large volumes of both wheat and corn were marketed through Chicago. Wheat generally arrived at this terminal market immediately after harvest because most farmers were eager to sell and receive payment for their crops in order to pay their bills associated with producing the crop. This temporary oversupply of wheat at harvest time resulted in a seasonal price swing that tended to severely depress prices for a period of months. This issue regarding seasonal price swings is illustrated with the help of Figure 1.6. The figure displays representative cash price behavior over two full crop years (i.e., two seasons). In the figure, three hypothetical harvests are denoted as H_1, H_2, and H_3. Each harvest is depicted as a discrete point in time. The two curved lines, labeled S_1 and S_2, represent typical seasonal cash price patterns for wheat prior to the introduction of a forward market. Immediately following each harvest, cash prices were low (because supply exceeded demand), and then prices rose throughout the crop year as the fixed supply was continuously utilized. During the first season, starting from time H_1, the cash price followed along the S_1 curve upward, and then eventually the price came crashing down from $2.00 to $0.25 as soon as the next harvest was under way, at point H_2. As shown in Figure 1.6, in the mid-1800s, it was not unusual for grain prices to rise from as low as $0.25 per bushel following harvest to as high as $2.00 per bushel immediately prior to the next harvest.

This marketing problem of wide seasonal price swings led to the development of "forward," or "to arrive," contracts, which were essentially deferred delivery contracts. The seller agreed to deliver a specific amount of grain at a future period and for a pre-established price. And the buyer consented to accept delivery at the future point in time for an agreed upon price. These contracts provided economic incentives to store wheat (because the forward price was guaranteed), and this resulted in a more rational flow of the product to market over time by reducing supplies that were being dumped on the market at harvest time.

After the introduction of forward contracts, post-harvest prices were typically higher than before because some harvested grain was placed in storage rather than sold on the spot market. Much later in the crop year, pre-harvest prices were generally reduced because grain was removed from storage and sold onto the market. Seasonal price spreads were therefore reduced by arbitrage. Grain was taken off the cash market after harvest and sold forward, only to be placed back on the cash market later during the season. Removing grain from the cash market after harvest served to raise post-harvest cash prices. Subsequently, placing that same grain back on the market later served to lower the next season's pre-harvest prices. Again, consider the example in Figure 1.6. Recall that the graph is divided in three harvest periods: H_1, H_2, and H_3. The lighter nonlinear curves show the price movements that would take place without forward contracting throughout the first harvest season (S_1), the second harvest season (S_2), etc. The darker lines shows the price movement that takes place with forward contracting. Notice that the darker lines have become flatter than the lighter curves, reflecting less seasonal price swing in each harvest period. Producers and consumers benefit from less volatility since they have a higher degree of certainty of how much they would receive/pay for the product.

However, a major economic problem remained even after forward contracts were in place. Some traders were reluctant to trade these "forward" contracts because of their heterogeneity. For instance, delivery to certain areas might have been more difficult, and therefore more expensive than to others. Assessing how much more expensive it would be was quite challenging. Additionally, there were different qualities of grain, some better than others. So it became difficult to determine the correct price given that there was no market standard. The Chicago Board of Trade played a major role at this point by introducing standardized futures contracts. Each standardized contract guaranteed a pre-specified quantity, quality, and delivery at a specific location and time. These standardized contracts soon led to futures contracts, which were very similar to forward contracts except the futures contracts were homogeneous and more easily traded. The uniformity of futures contracts facilitated and added liquidity to the market. Instead of trading wheat in the physical marketplace, traders could trade a more liquid instrument based on the underlying physical commodity. Is it easier to buy and sell futures contracts, compared to buying and selling wagon loads of wheat. As a result, the futures markets added liquidity to the underlying physical market and that continues to be a benefit of futures trading today for hundreds of different markets.

Using the Chicago market as a model, standardized futures contracts subsequently developed in other cities in the United States and around the world. London and Winnipeg set up wheat futures trading, while cotton futures markets were established in New York and Bombay. These exchanges used the open outcry system to trade and large chalkboards near the trading pits kept track of price movements, which were sent by telex around the world. As a result of these historical developments, there are numerous futures exchanges around the world today. The Chicago and New York markets remain important, but most of the world's exchange trading is now done electronically and the physical location of the exchange is not that important, except for regulatory purposes.

To summarize, U.S. futures markets evolved over 180 years ago to remove agricultural marketing inefficiencies and to facilitate trading in agricultural commodities such as wheat and corn that had short harvest periods and required storage. More than a century later, in the 1960's, commodity exchanges started trading in nonstorable agricultural commodities such as livestock, and by the 1970's they were offering contracts for many nonagricultural commodities, such as lumber and gold. The 1980's and 1990's saw more dramatic innovation and growth in futures markets. Financial futures were introduced in the 1980's and electronic trading in futures began in the 1990's. In just twelve years time, from 2000 to 2012, electronic (i.e., "on the screen") futures trading grew from around 9% to over 95% of U.S. futures and options volume. Open outcry pit trading of futures and options has faded into obscurity.

Ongoing Evolution of Futures and Options Trading

Over the past few decades the futures and options industry has grown by such large proportions that it is difficult to overstate the phenomenal growth. From 2002 to 2022, global volume of (exchange based) trade rose from 6.2 to 83.9 billion futures and options contracts, according to Futures Industry Association statistics. Growth in the trading of non-agricultural contracts (primarily financial and equity futures and options) has vastly outstripped trade in the traditional agricultural commodities, but agricultural volume has regained some market share since the collapse following the 2007-08 commodity price boom and then bust.

Table 1.3 reports the most popular U.S. futures contracts, ranked by volume of trade in 2022. The largest volume contract is the E-mini S&P 500, a stock index futures contract, followed by the 3 Month Secured Overnight Financing Rate (SOFR). Crude oil and natural gas are in the top 10, as are a number of interest rate contracts (U.S. Treasuries). The highest volume agricultural contracts are soybeans (ranked number 19), followed by corn (ranked 20th.). Other notable agricultural contracts are soybean oil and soybean meal, CBOT wheat, and sugar #11 (which is the *world market* sugar price). The Euro and the Japanese Yen are the highest volume foreign currency futures, followed by the British Pound and the Australian and Canadian dollars.

Not only has the overall volume of trade increased steadily, but also many innovative contracts, such as Exchange Traded Fund (ETF) options, ethanol, and electricity swap futures such as the Midwest ISO Cinergy Hub 5 MW off-peak calendar month day-ahead swap futures (K2). There has also been a trend to more and more over-the-counter (OTC) trading, with "clearing" of trades provided by futures exchanges. For instance, the trading volume in OTC electricity forward contracts exceeds electricity futures volume on the NYMEX. Ethanol futures are also traded OTC.

RBOB gasoline futures have also been a success story. RBOB stands for "reformulated gasoline blendstock for oxygen blending," an unfinished gasoline product that serves as a pricing benchmark in the gasoline industry. In the U.S., crude oil is refined into blendstock, which is then blended with ethanol before shipment to retail gas stations. RBOB accounts for about 90% of the total volume of automobile gasoline at the pump, with ethanol making up the remaining 10%. Figure 1.7 shows the growth in RBOB open interest for futures. Unlike volume of trade, open interest reports the number of "open" contracts at any point in time.

Table 1.3: U.S. Futures Volume: Top Contracts, 2022

Contract	Exchange	2022 Volume (mil. Contracts)
E-mini S&P 500	CME	503.95
10 Year Treasury Note	CBOT	462.60
3 Month SOFR	CME	418.85
Eurodollar	CME	394.59
Micro E-mini Nasdaq 100 Index	CME	364.95
Micro E-mini S&P 500 Index	CME	343.97
5 Year Treasury Note	CBOT	326.81
WTI Light Sweet Crude Oil (CL)	NYMEX	206.00
E-mini Nasdaq 100	CME	176.87
2 Year Treasury Note	CBOT	169.86
North American Natural Gas	ICE	153.33
30 Year Treasury Bond	CBOT	97.40
Ultra 10 Year Treasury Note	CBOT	95.65
Henry Hub Natural Gas (NG)	NYMEX	85.88
Federal Funds	CBOT	83.83
Corn	CBOT	77.88
Euro FX	CME	61.53
E-mini Russell 2000 Index	CME	60.57
Ultra Treasury Bond	CBOT	59.94
Gold (GC)	COMEX	54.26
CBOE Volatility Index (VX)	CBOE	52.24
Soybeans	CBOT	51.72
E-mini $5 DJIA	CBOT	51.03
E-micro $5 DJIA	CBOT	44.93
Mini MSCI Emerging Markets	ICE	44.71
RBOB Gasoline Physical (RB)	NYMEX	41.04
NY Harbor ULSD (HO)	NYMEX	39.67
Japanese Yen	CME	39.57
Micro E-mini Russell 2000 Index	CME	32.83
Sugar #11	ICE	32.75
British Pound	CME	31.24
Micro WTI Crude Oil (MCL)	NYMEX	30.08
Soybean Oil	CBOT	30.05
Soybean Meal	CBOT	28.09
Chicago Soft Red Winter Wheat	CBOT	25.96
Australian Dollar	CME	25.50
1 Month SOFR	CME	23.15
Canadian Dollar	CME	22.77
Copper (HG)	COMEX	21.54
Brent Crude Oil Last Day	NYMEX	17.36
Silver (5,000 oz) (SI)	COMEX	17.08
Mexican Peso	CME	15.34
Mini MSCI EAFE Index	ICE	15.29
Live Cattle	CME	14.15
North American Power	ICE	13.68
Cocoa	ICE	13.23

Source: Futures Industry Association.

Figure 1.7: Open Interest in RBOB Gasoline Futures
Number of contracts

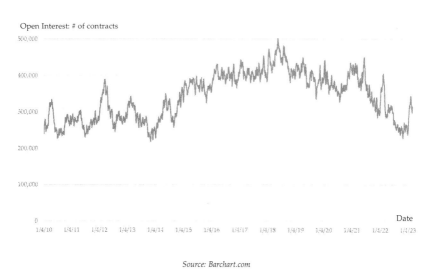

Source: Barchart.com

The E-Mini S&P 500 (on the CME)–an equity index futures–has the largest share of trading volume on U.S. exchanges. Roughly 504 million E-Mini S&P 500 contracts traded in 2022. The 10 year Treasury note is the most important interest rate contract in the U.S. measured by volume with about 463 million contracts changing hands in 2022.

Figure 1.8: Exchange Traded Financial Futures: U.S. & Non-U.S. Volume

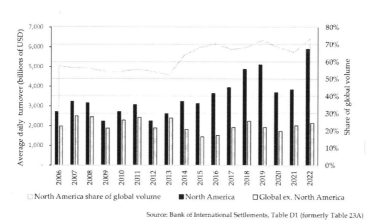

Source: Bank of International Settlements, Table D1 (formerly Table 23A)

Figures 1.8 and 1.9 report Bank of International Settlement statistics on exchange traded **financial** futures and options, which is largely interest rate

Figure 1.9: Exchange Traded Financial Options: U.S. & Non-U.S. Volume

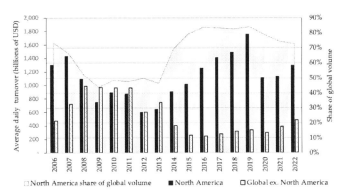

□ North America share of global volume   ■ North America   □ Global ex. North America

Source: Bank of International Settlements, Table D1 (formerly Table 23A). Does not include single equity contracts.

derivatives plus a relatively small share of foreign exchange derivatives. This trading is measured by the notional principal represented by the average daily turnover of contracts, in billions of US dollars. In many ways this is a more accurate measure of market rankings than contract volume data that was discussed above. Contract volume is impacted by the size of each contract and some exchanges trade contracts with a relatively small contract sizes. Figures 1.8 indicates that exchanges in North America accounted for about 73% of the notional value of financial futures and options contracts in 2022. Measured this way, Asia-Pacific exchanges are much less important as they accounted for just over 4% of the value of financial futures traded in 2022 and less than 1% of financial options traded (on exchanges). European exchanges accounted for around 23% of global financial futures and options trading, measure by the value of contracts traded.

The U.S. futures and options industry is concerned about this issue of global competitiveness, and some argue that the loss of market share is largely due to overregulation of U.S. exchanges. However, market share also depends on competition to introduce new contracts and the willingness of exchanges to be innovative and introduce new technology, such as electronic trading. The European competition for financial futures volume between the London International Financial Futures and Options Exchange (LIFFE) and the Eurex illustrates this point. LIFFE was the largest exchange in Europe, but in the late 1990's a large share of LIFFE's trading shifted over to the Eurex. LIFFE had a trading floor that lost out to the highly efficient electronic trading system introduced by the Eurex.

Another example of competing exchanges is the time the Intercontinental Exchange (ICE) announced plans in 2012 to trade five new U.S. grain and oilseed contracts (corn, wheat, soybeans, soybean oil, and soybean meal) in direct competition with the CBOT (CME Group) grain and oilseed contracts. These contracts are cash settled, unlike the CBOT grain and oilseed contracts which are settled through delivery. To date, these ICE grain and oilseed contracts have not generated much trading volume.

Stock index futures (such as the S&P 500 Index at the CME) became popular in the 1980's, during which there was heightened stock market volatility. However, these contracts suffered a setback as a result of the October 1987 stock market crash, when the Dow Jones Industrial Average (DJIA) fell by 22.6% in one day. Some argued that the futures index led the stock market to fall and was therefore responsible for the crash. How could an informationally efficient stock market fall by 22.6% in one day? It seems unbelievable that economic fundamentals could change that much in a single day. After exhaustive study, the futures market was exonerated, but nevertheless daily stock index futures contract volume declined by about 30% after the crash and remained well below pre-crash levels for a number of years. In 1997, the Chicago Board of Trade started trading the DJIA Futures Index in competition with the CME's S&P 500 index. The DJIA "mini" futures contract is valued at $5 times the Dow Jones Industrial Average Index (or about $165,000 per contract at 2023 stock market levels) is the most heavily traded index futures on the CBOT. In 2022, around 51 million mini $5 Dow contracts were traded. At the CME, the E-mini S&P 500 futures ($50 times the Standard & Poor's 500 Stock Index–or about $205,000 at the approximate 2023 S&P level) is the highest volume equity index and is much more popular than the Dow mini.

Given the long history of trading, there have been few recent innovations in agricultural futures (and options) contracts that have been successful. For example, the Chicago Mercantile Exchange initiated a cheddar cheese futures contract in 1997 in anticipation of attracting hedging interest from cheese producers and food processors; however, the this venture failed. The CME has replaced it with a revamped cheese futures contract based on the USDA average weighted price of U.S. cheese. The contracts are cash-settled, so actual delivery or taking of delivery is not possible. The contract size is 20,000 pounds. The CME also lists a butter futures contract and different milk futures contracts: Class III Milk, Class IV Milk, and Nonfat Dry Milk. Prior to WWII, the CME actively traded butter and egg futures. The CBOT introduced corn yield futures in 1995. The contracts were cash settled and the value of the contract was $100 times the average corn yield (in bushels) in a specific region. The corn yield futures contract eventually failed due to a lack of speculative and hedging interest. In recent years the CME has introduced three new wheat futures contracts: Black Sea

Table 1.4: Event Futures Contract: Will WTI Close Above $73?

Yes	$18.50	Max return: $1.50
No	$2.00	Max return: $18.00
time remaining		3:36:19 hrs

wheat, Australian, and Canadian wheat.

Potatoes provide another example of a commodity that has never been successfully traded on futures exchanges. A potato contract at the New York Mercantile Exchange failed in the 1970's. Subsequently, a new revised potato contract introduced on the New York Cotton Exchange in 1996 also failed. The reasons for these failures are not totally clear, and the explanations run from alleged manipulation by both buyers and sellers to quality problems with potatoes to concentration in the potato processing industry. Private contracts between growers and many processors, in addition to the market presence of large corporations, also preclude the need for traditional hedging instruments, such as futures contracts. At one time, onion and lard futures were traded successfully but they are no longer.

Recently, the CME introduced a number of *event* futures contracts. These are financially settled **daily** expiring contracts, which means the change in contract value depends on what happens to a daily price change relative to a certain price hurdle. For instance Table 1.4 shows an example of pricing of an event in the WTI contract. On this particular day, traders were evaluating the probability of WTI futures closing about $73. If you said "no" and paid $2, then you would receive a return of $20 if WTI did not close about $73. However if it did close above this specific hurdle then you would lose your $2.

The suite of CME event contracts include bitcoin, gold, silver, copper, crude oil, natural gas, E-mini S&P 500, E-mini Nasdaq-100, E-mini Dow Jones Industrial Average, E-mini Russell 2000 and euro-U.S. dollar forex futures. With these relatively small valued products the trader's loss is limited to the cost of placing the order. In Table 1.5 we report a sample day in the bitcoin event market. Will bitcoin close above $28,500? If you chose "yes" then you pay $8.75 per contract and if your prediction is correct you collect $20. If you are incorrect then you lose the $8.75.

Table 1.5: Event Futures Contract: Will Bitcoin Close Above $28,500?

Yes	$8.75	Max return: $12.25
No	$12.25	Max return: $7.75
time remaining		5:06:05 hrs

The basics of these event contracts is based on "prediction" markets such as the Iowa electronic market where contract payoffs are based on real-world events such as Joe Biden being re-elected as the US President. The PredictIt market at Victoria University of Wellington, New Zealand, offers similar contracts to those at the Iowa market.

The Commodity Futures Trading Commission (CFTC) approves new contracts. Like the corn yield contract, not all of these new contracts are success stories and in fact many new futures instruments fail to attract sufficient trading volume. For instance, the Coffee Sugar and Cocoa Exchange launched inflation futures in 1985, based on the consumer price index, but it failed miserably, and trading was discontinued in 1991. The municipal bond futures contract (introduced in the mid 1980's on the CBOT) failed in March 2003, as did the Municipal Note Index (CBOT) futures that replaced the municipal bond futures. But there are also many success stories such as equity Volatility Index (VIX) futures. The Chicago VIX futures are based on S&P 500 stock volatility and VIX futures volume grew from 1.4 million contracts in 2009 to 52 million contacts in 2022, on the Chicago Board Options Exchange (CBOE) Futures Exchange.

Some new contracts, such as the very successful crude oil futures contract, take several years before they blossom. When crude oil futures were introduced on the New York Mercantile Exchange in 1983, several industry analysts predicted that the contract would fail. It did take about four or five years before the contract attracted considerable trading interest, but it turns out that today crude oil ranks in the top ten largest U.S. futures contract measured by annual trading volume.

The discovery and introduction of a new futures contract with a very high volume happens only once or twice in a decade. In 1980, agricultural futures accounted for 64% of the total volume of U.S. futures contracts traded. By 2022, these contracts accounted for only about 6% of total volume. However, futures trading volume does fluctuate from year to year with changing market conditions and changing government commodity programs. For example, the volume of energy futures and options grew 21% year over year due to an almost 60% drop in crude oil prices from 2014 to 2015.

Like futures contracts, options on futures have a long history, although a more tattered one. A certain type of option, called privileges, was traded in grains from about the 1840's until the 1930's. These financial instruments were blamed for the excessive volatility of grain prices before the Great Depression and the eventual collapse of prices in the early 1930's.

At that time, the futures exchanges did not have strict control over options trading, which was often conducted away from the futures trading floor. As a result, the U.S. Congress banned options trading on agricultural

Box 1.8 Stock or Equity Futures

Futures contracts on individual stocks were proposed for trading in the United States in the early 1980s but the government regulatory agencies (the Commodity Futures Trading Commission and the Securities and Exchange Commission) would not approve them at that time. However, the U.S. government reversed policy in 2001 and approved single-stock futures.

In a single-stock futures transaction, the buyer and seller agree to purchase/sell a stock at a set price during a specified future month. For example, an investor might enter into a contract to buy 1,000 shares of Microsoft at $250 per share, one year from now, under the expectation that the share price will increase during that time. The Chicago Mercantile Exchange, the Chicago Board Options Exchange, and the Chicago Board of Trade formed a joint venture to offer single-stock futures. This joint-venture exchange was called One Chicago (www.onechicago.com). It offered trading on over 2,000 security futures and about 300 exchange-traded-funds (ETFs), but it closed in 2020.

In 2017 the ICE introduced *FANG+* Index futures, based on an index of stock prices of 10 modern tech firms, including Facebook, Apple, Amazon, Netflix, Alphabet's Google, Alibaba, Baidu, NVIDIA, Tesla and Twitter. The Micro NYSE Fang+ contract size is $5 times the NYSE FANG Index. Trading volume for this equity index topped 2 million contracts in 2022.

commodities in 1936. It was not until 1981 that the Commodity Futures Trading Commission (CFTC) approved options for a very limited number of futures contracts, including gold, sugar, and Treasury bonds. In 1984, several more agricultural options were introduced under a three-year pilot-trading project. This program included options on futures for corn, soybeans, live hogs, live cattle, wheat, and cotton. In January 1987, the CFTC judged the pilot trading successful and approved options trading on all futures contracts. Options have been a big part of the success story of U.S. derivative exchanges. Equity Index and volatility options are the most popular trading category within options, followed by the Eurodollar and 10 Year Treasury Notes.

The Chicago Mercantile Exchange (CME) and the Chicago Board of

---

Box 1.9 Rise in Futures Trading in China

Policy makers in China have started to recognize the importance of futures and options markets and they are encouraging the growth of trading in domestic markets in China, given China's significant buying and selling presence in the major commodity markets globally. By 2018 China was the world's largest metals consumer, responsible for over 50 percent of consumption. Global prices of commodities such as soybeans, cotton, and copper are increasingly influenced by market fundamentals in China. The marketization of China is also another driver behind the rise of futures trading in that country. Futures trading in China is only a few decades old, but China's three futures commodities exchanges, Dalian, Zhengzhou and Shanghai are becoming global leaders in futures trading and they have introduced some innovative contracts such as rebar (a form of steel bar), coke (an input in steel production) and PVC pipe. The Dalian exchange trades iron ore futures that are settled by physical delivery, which will better reflect the supply and demand fundamentals in the spot market for iron ore in China, compared to iron ore contracts that are cash settled in markets outside of China. This could shift trading from foreign markets (such as Singapore) to China's new futures and options markets. Shanghai is know for trading base metals, Zhengzhou for agricultural products, and Dalian for agriculture, chemical and energy products. China's role in the commodity futures market will no doubt continue to expand.

Trade (CBOT) merged in 2007 into a single entity–the CME Group–that is now the world's largest derivatives exchange. As part of the continued consolidation in the industry, in 2008 the CME Group purchased the New York Mercantile Exchange (NYMEX). As mentioned previously, the NYMEX trades crude oil, unleaded gas, heating oil, gold, silver, platinum, copper and palladium. In 2012, the CME group purchased the Kansas City Board of Trade (KCBT) which specializes in hard-red winter wheat. Besides the CME group, the other leading exchange in the United States is the Intercontinental Exchange (ICE), headquartered in Atlanta. ICE purchased the New York Board of Trade (NYBOT) in 2005 and the Winnipeg Commodity Exchange in Canada in 2007, solidifying its position as a major player in the North American futures and options industry. In 2013, the ICE acquired the NYSE Euronext stock exchanges.

What has happened in the last 30 years in the futures and options industry is phenomenal. There has been huge growth in financial futures, as the financial community has discovered what the agricultural community has known for 180 years, that a set of market determined contingent prices has economic value. These contingent, or intertemporal markets, establish a price for today, two months forward, six months forward, and one year forward, etc. For example, you can buy the right to obtain crude oil at a fixed price eight years from now in the futures market. Or, you can sell crude oil for delivery eight years from now in the futures market, so you know the approximate price that you will receive in eight years time. This pricing flexibility is very important to some businesses.

The airline industry is a good example of where firms that have used futures and options to manage price risk have fared much better than competitors that have shunned these markets. Considering the amount of fuel that an airline company burns in a day, the price of fuel has a tremendous impact on the bottom line of the airline industry. A single Boeing Dreamliner holds over 30,000 gallons of fuel. Do you think the profitability of airlines moves in the opposite direction of oil prices? Obviously the price of jet fuel moves in tandem fashion with the price of oil. The U.S. Air Transport Association (ATA) estimates that every dollar added to the cost of a barrel of oil adds $456 million a year in jet-fuel costs for U.S. airlines. As oil prices doubled from 2007 to 2008, the price of jet fuel went from one-third of total airline costs, to one-half of costs. Foreign airline companies have the added exchange rate risk because energy products- like jet fuel- are typically traded in U.S. dollars. For instance, the Brazilian airline GOL earns revenue in Brazilian Real, but its fuel costs are in U.S. dollars. Therefore, GOL faces currency risk in its operation. When the Real fell against the dollar from 2011 to 2014, GOL's fuel costs rose even though world crude oil prices remained relatively stable, as measured in U.S. dollars.

After the Brexit vote in 2016 signaled that the UK would be leaving the European Union, the British pound sterling (GBP or £) fell from about 1.43 £/$ to 1.22 £/$ in a very short time period. This was costly to British Air because jet fuel is priced in U.S. dollars and British Air's ticket revenue is primarily in pound sterling. Suppose jet fuel was priced at approximately $1.70 per gallon in 2016. At the pre-Brexit exchange rate the cost in GBP would have been £1.19 /gallon (=$1.7/£1.43) and at the post-Brexit exchange rate the cost would have risen to £1.39 (=$1.7/ £1.22), assuming the price of fuel in U.S. dollars did not change. For 33,000 gallons of fuel (enough to fill one Dreamliner for one trip) the cost to British Air would have risen from £39,270 to £45,870, a 17% increase in fuel costs. If fuel accounts for one-third of operating costs, then total costs would have increased by about 5.5% simply due to the currency move after the Brexit vote.

Most major airlines have now used the futures and options market to attempt to better manage the volatile price of jet fuel and exchange rates. Of course, they also use over-the-counter (OTC) swaps to manage fuel and currency price volatility. Generally speaking, swaps are derivatives that involve an exchange of cash flows between two counter-parties over a given time period. One party makes a payment to the other, based on whether an underlying asset price is above or below a fixed reference price. For example, if an airline company entered into a fuel swap with a hedge fund, the airline would collect payments on the swap if fuel prices rose above a reference price set at the time the swap was negotiated. Alternatively, if fuel prices declined below the reference price then the airline would be required to make a payment to its counter-party, the hedge fund.

Regulation

In the United States, the futures and options markets are regulated by a combination of industry/exchange self-regulation and formal government regulation. At the industry level each futures exchange self-regulates its registered traders and member firms. From the government side, the Commodity Futures Trading Commission (CFTC) is in charge of overseeing the correct functioning of the futures and options markets by promoting fair and competitive behavior. One important role of the CFTC is the regulation of firms (such as brokers) who place trades in the markets on behalf of retail customers (e.g., small hedgers and speculators). Market manipulation is prohibited, and rules are in place to prevent a trader from creating an artificial price movement (or "cornering" the market) in order to earn abnormal profits. The CFTC uses the court system to enforce the law. For instance, in 2008 the CFTC won a court ruling against a failed hedge fund, Amaranth, charged with attempted manipulation of the natural gas futures market and providing false information to the New York Mercantile Exchange (NYMEX). The Amaranth hedge fund lost about $6.6 billion in 2006 and some of its large investors, such as the San Diego Employees Retirement Association, lost hundreds of millions of dollars. One reason Amaranth went down is that it believed hurricanes would drive up natural gas prices in 2006 affecting the spreads between futures months, just like the 2005 hurricane season. But they were wrong as the storms did not materialize in 2006 and Amaranth reportedly lost $5 billion in one week alone. In 2011 the U.S. Federal Energy Regulatory Commission (FERC) fined Amaranth Advisor Brian Hunter $30 million for trying to manipulate the price of natural gas on NYMEX in 2006.

For the most part, self-regulation by the exchanges themselves is very effective in the futures industry because futures trading is a zero-sum game, which means that a profit earned by a trader must be matched by a loss by another trader. In a zero-sum game if a trader is trying to manipulate the market, then another trader on the other side of the market is getting hurt, financially, and it is in his or her best interest to file a formal complaint. Unlike the securities industry, insider trading is not a common problem in the futures industry. In the securities industry, insiders know when a company earnings report is to be released and its details, but no one has inside information as to the severity of the next hurricane and its impact on natural gas production in the Gulf of Mexico, and so on. So there is less need for government regulation in the futures and options industry. For a discussion of some of the issues surrounding self-regulation, see Pirrong (2017).

The National Futures Association (www.nfa.futures.org) is an industry funded independent self-regulatory organization, established in 1981. The National Futures Association (NFA) assumes some regulatory responsibility on behalf of the CFTC. One such responsibility is the registering of every firm or individual who conducts futures or options business with the public. This includes introducing brokers, futures commission merchants, forex dealers, commodity pool operators, commodity trading advisors, and swap dealers. The basic goal of the NFA is to protect all futures and options traders from fraudulent trading activities, and the NFA has an arbitration program that handles complaints against broker or trading firms. In addition, the NFA handles swap valuation disputes.

The NFA publishes the outcome of disputes on their website. You can read about these disputes at https://www.nfa.futures.org/news/. For instance in 2022, NFA fined Goldman Sachs & Co. $2.5 million for failing to submit accurate reports regarding certain swap transactions. Many of the disputes brought by NFA against one of its members have to do with record keeping deficiencies. Sometimes the NFA finds that registered brokers cheat or deceive customers over futures trading and these brokers are typically permanently banned from NFA membership. For instance, in 2022 the NFA determined that Rohit Chopra from Newport Beach, CA, "placed unauthorized trades in customers' accounts, misrepresented to customers about the trades placed in their accounts, made highly risky trades in a customer's account and manipulated allocation instructions to benefit Chopra to the detriment of customers." His company EV Capital was banned from NFA membership. In 2019, NFA went after a NFA Member commodity pool operator, Denari Capital LLC from Walnut Creek, CA, and its principal, Travis Capson, and suspended Denari from NFA membership. According to NFA, "This action was taken to protect the investing public, the derivatives markets and other NFA Members since Denari and Capson, among other things, commingled pool funds, improperly calculated the pool's rates of return, provided misleading information to their investors and NFA, and failed to cooperate in an investigation of the firm." The CFTC also sued Mr. Capson and his partner, Arnab Sarkar, in federal court for fraud and the CFTC won the case.

The CFTC was formed in 1974 to oversee the operations of the nation's futures and option markets. Regulation of the futures industry was revamped at that time to cover the growing futures trading in nonagricultural contracts, especially financials. Prior to 1974, U.S. futures trading was governed by the 1936 Commodity Exchange Act, which was administered by the U.S. Department of Agriculture. However, this task has been trusted to five commissioners, appointed by the U.S. President, to run the CFTC. In 2000, Congress passed the Commodity Futures Modernization Act (HR 5660), which reauthorized and amended the Commodity Exchange Act. The Commodity Futures Modernization Act created a new structure for regulation of futures and options trading and codified an agreement between the CFTC and the Securities and Exchange Commission (SEC) to allow trading of single-stock futures. The SEC regulates stock exchanges. The Commodity Futures Modernization Act freed up over-the-counter (OTC) derivative trading from much regulation. The deregulation of OTC trading of energy related derivatives was known as the "Enron" loophole, because supposedly Enron lobbyists drafted the legislation. Enron was a firm based in Texas and was one of the world's largest energy traders. The company went bankrupt in 2001, after extensive fraud and corruption at the firm was uncovered. In Europe, the Markets in Financial Instruments Directive (MiFID) has been rewritten to attempt to move towards harmonization with CFTC trading rules to ensure that trading in U.S. products on European based markets adhere to CFTC position limits. However there remains less than full harmonization.

The CFTC's main responsibilities are to protect the trading public from fraud and trading abuses on and off the exchange, to prevent price distortions and manipulations, and to encourage the overall competitiveness and efficiency of all U.S. exchanges. The CFTC posts pictures on its Web site (http://www.cftc.gov) of individuals wanted for financial crimes related to futures and options. In addition, the CFTC has video clips of "true fraud stories" available at www.smartcheck.gov/videos, and they have a list of advisories for the investing public. They also publish as RED list of fraudulent entities that are not registered with the CFTC, but they are acting as though they are registered. This is part of their educational program to help the public spot financial fraud.

As example of CFTC enforcement actions, in 2023, the CFTC brought legal action against Binance cryptocurrency exchange, which accounted for about 60% of world crypto trading at the time. The U.S. regulatory agency accused Binance of operating illegally in the United States. While much of Binance's business orginated in the U.S., it failed to register with the CFTC and ignored U.S. financial laws designed to protect investors. The CFTC noted that Binance illegally offered investors crypto derivatives, such as futures or options contracts, without registering as a futures commodity merchant (FCM) with the CFTC.

CFTC Monitoring of Large Traders

As part of its regular oversight of the futures and options industry, the CFTC monitors the trading of large speculators. The CFTC first classifies all large traders as speculators, hedgers, swap dealers, or money managers. Then for most markets it either establishes *position limits* or oversees exchange set position limits that apply to large speculators. *Position limits* define a maximum number of contracts that any one trader may hold. The purpose of these limits is to try to prevent speculators from manipulating prices. For example, on the CBOT, no speculator may hold or control positions, net long or net short, exceeding 33,000 contracts in corn or 15,000 contracts in soybeans. Large traders must report their position to the CFTC if they hold more than 250 corn contracts or 150 soybean contracts.

On the NYMEX, the position limit for crude oil is 20,000 net futures (any one month/all months) and must not exceed 3,000 contracts in the last three days of trading in the delivery month. As in this case for crude oil, position limits in other markets are typically reduced in size as the contract approaches maturity because there is greater potential for market manipulation near maturity, especially for deliverable contracts. Additionally, speculators are required to report their position if it exceeds a certain number of contracts. For example, the reporting level for crude oil (CL) in the NYMEX is 350 contracts. Note that these rules apply to speculators but not to hedgers. The various reporting levels by contract are found in CFTC Regulation 15.03(b).

One important service provided by the CFTC is publishing the weekly "Commitments of Traders" (COT) reports. The COT classifies traders into five groups: hedgers (commercial traders), swap dealers, managed money, large speculators, and small speculators. For the major markets, the COT's give a breakdown of which side of the market large traders (hedgers and speculators) are on and what percentage of the open interest they hold in that week. *Open interest* is the market total of all futures and/or option contracts that have been executed and not yet offset, which means they remain "open." Alternatively, it is the total number of futures that have not been offset or fulfilled by delivery. The reporting levels determining whether traders are classified as large or small are established by the CFTC.

As an illustration of the CFTC COT data, refer to Figure 1.10 which shows the net long (long minus short) weekly positions of commercial traders (i.e., large hedgers) in the NYMEX crude oil market, from 2000 to 2017. The net long line in Figure 1.10 (the gray line) is negative when the number of short hedge positions exceeds the number of long hedge positions. For most of the time period shown, the hedgers were net short in oil, hence the gray line is below the 0 horizontal line.

Figure 1.10: CFTC Commercial Trader Positions: Crude Oil

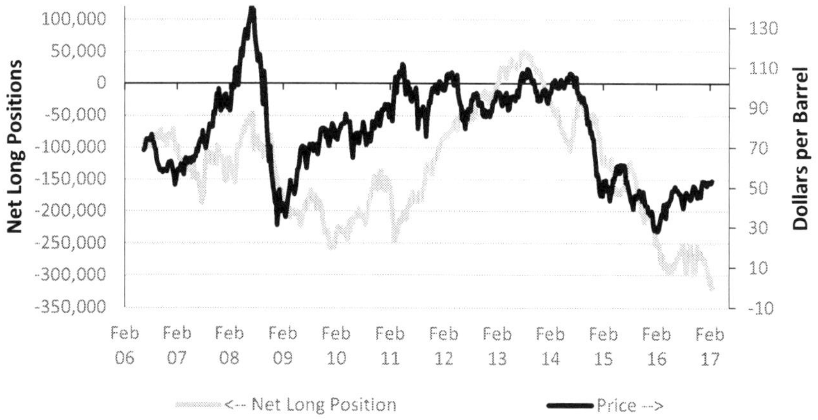

Source: U.S. Commodity Futures Trading Commission and U.S. Energy Information Administration.

The price of crude oil is also shown on the graph with the right hand axis and the solid black line. In this graph we see that early in the time period when oil rose and peaked at $140 per barrel, the commercial traders reduced the size of their aggregate net short position from about 190,000 net short contracts only 50,000 net short positions (shown as -190,000 and -50,000 respectively on the graph). When the price of oil then plunged to less than $40 per barrel, the net short positions grew rapidly to exceed 250,000 contracts.

Later in the time period shown in Figure 1.10 the commercials reduced their net short positions and they actually became net long for most of 2013 (shown as the gray line rising above the 0 horizontal axis). When crude oil prices started to fall in 2014, the net position of the commercial firms switched back to that of net short.

Of course, during these swings in net hedge positions, speculators would have to be willing to hold the other side of these contracts and be willing to be net long in order to absorb the persistent short hedging demand in the market. As hedge volume grew in the crude oil futures market, speculative volume would have grown by the same amount.

In recent years hedge funds, index traders, and investment banks have surged into commodity futures markets. The new role of these speculative traders in the futures industry has attracted considerable policy debate regarding the appropriate amount of government regulation of the industry. In 2008, U.S. Congress held several hearings in an attempt to determine whether or not the futures and options industry was properly regulated. The hearings were focused mainly on energy prices because oil peaked at $140 per barrel. However, foreign governments (especially in developing countries) were concerned about the role of speculation in the formation of commodity prices in general, due to rising food prices.

Partly in response to this controversy, the CFTC started publishing more detailed reports on trader positions. An example of the newer detailed "disaggregated" weekly CFTC Commitment of Traders (COT) data is shown in Table 1.6 for the week of February 14, 2017. These data show that total open interest (i.e., the number of contracts that have not been offset or fulfilled) in WTI crude oil was 2,183,943 contracts on Tuesday of that week. The data in Table 1.6 are for large traders only, as there is another group of small non-reportable traders that do not meet the CFTC reporting threshold and their positions are not shown in the Table here. The data shown here represent futures positions only. The CFTC publishes a separate report showing futures and options positions combined.

As the reader might remember, near the beginning of the Regulation section it was mentioned that whenever a trader has more than a certain number of contracts, she must report her positions to the CFTC. Although the threshold varies depending on the underlying asset, and the time to expiry of the contract, whenever it is exceeded, the participant is classified as a *large trader*, and must report their end-of-day aggregate position to the CFTC.

There are four categories of large traders categories whose positions are shown in Table 1.6. These categories include producers/merchants, swap dealers, managed money traders, and other reportables (large speculators). The CFTC provides information on the size and the positions taken (long, short, or spreading) across all maturities, by the four categories of futures traders.

Referring to Table 1.6, Producer/Merchants (i.e., large hedgers) were net short in the market; their long positions totaled 384,000 contracts, compared to 703,430 short contracts, for a net short position of 319,430 contracts. Swap Dealers held net short positions equal to 206,987. Swap Dealers also were active in "spreading" crude oil futures. Spreading involves simultaneously buying and selling different expiry months to try and take advantage of unusual pricing relationships across time horizons. Managed Money participants held net long positions equal to 383,532 (432,594 - 49,062) contracts.

Table 1.6: Sample CFTC Weekly Report on Trader Positions

Contract name: CRUDE OIL, LIGHT SWEET - NEW YORK MERCANTILE EXCHANGE				
Contract Size: 1,000 barrels				
Date:	February 14, 2017			
Trader Category	Position: Number of contracts		Change from Feb 16th, 2016	Number of traders
Producer/Merchant	Long	384,000	201,103	62
	Short	703,430	269,805	80
Swap Dealers	Long	159,104	(110,301)	24
	Short	366,091	178,419	23
	Spreading	191,066	3,809	38
Managed Money	Long	432,594	165,492	77
	Short	49,062	(160,179)	34
	Spreading	369,269	(1,855)	74
Other Reportables	Long	250,660	(178)	90
	Short	125,736	(23,976)	59
	Spreading	290,588	79,388	110

Crude Oil: Open Interest (number of contacts)

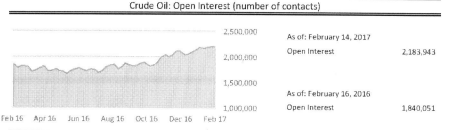

As of: February 14, 2017

Open Interest   2,183,943

As of: February 16, 2016

Open Interest   1,840,051

Source: U.S. Commodity Futures Trading Commision

At the same time, the large speculators were long 250,660 contracts versus short 125,736 contracts, for a total net long position of 124,924 contracts.

CFTC data for WTI crude oil similar to the data in Table 1.6 are shown in Figure 1.11 but for a longer period of time, from June 13th, 2006 through February 14th, 2017. The net number of contracts (excluding spreading) is shown on the left-hand axis in Figure 1.11 and the percentile associated with the number of contracts is shown on the right-hand axis.

Figure 1.11: Illustration of CFTC Data on Larger Trader Positions: Crude Oil

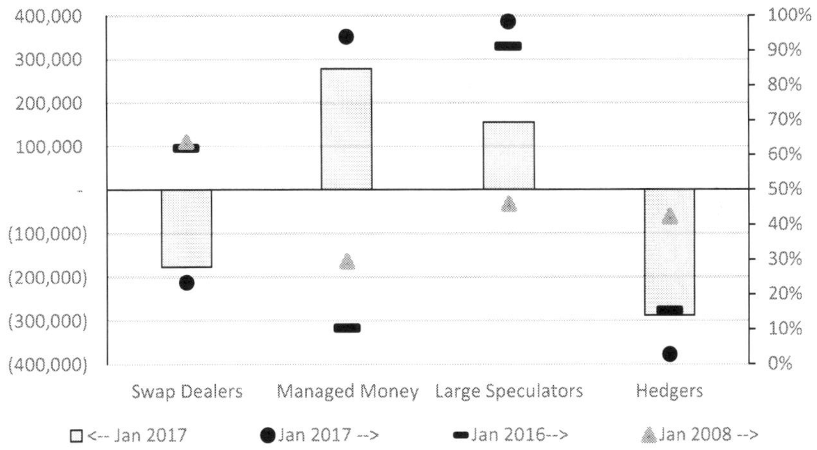

Source: U.S. Commodity Futures Trading Commision

*The range of the data for the percentiles is calculated from June 13th, 2006 to February 14th, 2017

**Each date corresponds to the close of the second trading week in each particular year

The shaded boxes represent the number of net contracts held by each group in January 2017. These three boxes show that swap dealers and hedgers were net short. The three symbols (bullet, dash, and triangle) represent each trading group's net position measured as a percentile in January 2008, January 2016, and January 2017. The percentiles of the distribution are based on data from 2006 through 2017.

During the time period shown in Figure 1.11, large hedgers increased their net long positions. In January 2008, hedgers were close to the historical average (50 percentile), as they were between the 40th and 50th percentile of the distribution. However, as the years passed and crude oil prices started to drop in 2014 (See Figure 1.10), hedgers continued to increase their net short position relative to the historical average. In January 2016, hedgers had moved close to the 20th percentile, and only one year later, in 2017, they reached the 3rd percentile. Recall that the time frame being analyzed is June 2006 to February 2017. Therefore, this means that in January 2017, oil hedgers reached the largest net short position recorded in more than 10 years.

Contrary to hedgers, speculators appeared to be thinking that the 2014 price drop from the 2008 peak was a good buying opportunity. Speculators went from being slightly net short (46th percentile) in January 2008 to having large net long positions by historical standards. On January 2017, speculators reached the 98th percentile of the position distribution.

From 2016 to 2017, swap dealers positions stayed within a relatively narrow range. On January 2016 they were slightly net long (62nd percentile) and on January 2017 they were net short (23rd percentile). This range of inter-percentile movement is much smaller compared to what was observed with managed money. Managed money were noticeably net short in January 2016 (10th percentile), but by January 2017 they had more than reversed that position to be on the 94th percentile of the distribution, being very long by historical standards. These data provide a nice overview of how the various large traders added to or subtracted from their futures positions as the price of oil rose, declined and then began to increase again, all over the space of 10 years.

The rise of commodity prices in 2007-2008 coincided with one view that commodity futures and options have become a new asset class, attracting investment from banks, hedge funds, etc. Hedge and index funds began investing billions of dollars in commodities. These investments were typically made through futures markets in the U.S., the EU and elsewhere. It has been argued that these institutional investors were responsible for a large share of the sudden commodity price increase through the summer of 2008. Masters (2009) suggested that the amount of money invested in futures markets by commodity index traders (such as those investing in the Goldman Sachs Commodities Index) rose from $13 billion to $260 billion between 2003 and 2008. He argued that index speculators are important, as they tend to be "long-only" which means they initially "buy" rather than "sell" futures contracts. They buy and hold their long positions but eventually have to sell the long positions before the contract expires. In order to maintain an investment in these commodities, they roll their long positions from the expiring contracts into more distant futures contracts.

In contrast the U.S. agency that regulates the commodity futures market (the CFTC) testified to Congress that "excess" speculation is unimportant as a factor explaining high commodity prices. The CFTC has pointed out that high prices have been achieved in commodity markets that have no futures trading (e.g., durum wheat) and in markets with little index trading. With regard to oil prices, the CFTC testified that speculation was not causing the price surge; instead prices were being driven by fundamental supply and demand factors. About two months later the CFTC reclassified one of the large oil traders from a hedger to a speculator and raised the percentage of open positions held by large speculators from 38% to over 50% of the market.

Citing CFTC data, a 2017 article in the *Financial Times*, Meyer (October 9, 2017), reported that algorithmic traders (*algos*) are becoming more and more important in the futures market. The article reported that automated trading systems account for 49% of transactions volume in grains and oilseeds, 54% in precious metals, and 63% in crude oil futures. In addition, the article mentioned that U.S. cattle ranchers have complained to the CME Group that algorithmic traders were causing unnatural and costly price gyrations in the cattle market.

Some U.S. policy makers argue that the CFTC provides lax oversight, and they would like to see greater controls over large speculators. For example, from 2000, the CFTC regulations granted some large investment banks an exemption from speculative position limits because they were trading on behalf of institutional investors. In reality these investment banks are middlemen who are hedging on behalf of large index traders–the investment banks enter into a "swap" with the large investors and in this way provide a trading filter that isolates the large traders from CFTC position limits. At the same time, the futures and options industry argues that markets in Europe and elsewhere operate with less regulation compared to the U.S. markets and that gives foreign exchanges a competitive advantage.

Starting in 2009, the CFTC started releasing data on index investment in commodity futures markets. This was in response to the rapid rise in commodity futures investing by index traders. These indexes include Standard & Poor's Goldman Sachs Commodity Index (SP-GSCI) and Dow-Jones UBS Commodity Index (DJ-UBS). Table 1.7 presents an example of the CFTC index investment data. According to these data, the index traders reportedly held in aggregate about a $144.4 billion net long position in commodity futures and options at the end of December 2014. Of this amount $110.8 billion was invested in U.S. futures and options markets. At this point in time, index traders were net long 428,000 corn contracts (see the last column in Table 1.7), 330,000 WTI crude oil contracts, 280,000 natural gas contracts, and so on. In 2015, the CFTC discontinued publishing these index investment data.

There is no question that regulation of futures and options markets is less stringent in other countries. For example, in the UK the markets are regulated by the Financial Services Agency (FSA), a broad-based agency that regulates the entire financial industry in that country. Futures and options have remained a bit of a backwater at the FSA. One high profile issue that emerged with the 2007-2008 global commodity boom was the so-called

Table 1.7: Sample CFTC Index Investment Data

Index Investment Data
In U.S. Dollars and Futures Equivalent Contracts

U.S. Futures Market[1]	October 30, 2015					
	Notional Value (Billions US$)			Futures Equivalent Contracts[3] (Thousands)		
(Notional Value > 0.5 billion US$)[2]	Long	Short	Net L (S)	Long	Short	Net L (S)
Cocoa	1.8	(0.7)	**1.1**	55	(22)	**33**
Coffee	3.1	(1.2)	**1.8**	67	(27)	**40**
Copper	6.7	(2.0)	**4.8**	116	(34)	**82**
Corn	10.8	(2.9)	**7.9**	556	(149)	**407**
Cotton	3.4	(1.0)	**2.4**	107	(31)	**76**
Feeder Cattle	1.1	(0.3)	**0.8**	12	(3)	**9**
Gold	17.1	(3.5)	**13.6**	149	(31)	**119**
Heating Oil	6.6	(1.5)	**5.1**	101	(23)	**78**
Lean Hogs	2.9	(0.9)	**1.9**	115	(39)	**76**
Live Cattle	6.4	(1.9)	**4.5**	113	(33)	**79**
Natural Gas	10.4	(3.2)	**7.3**	425	(128)	**297**
Platinum	0.7	(0.2)	**0.5**	14	(4)	**10**
RBOB Unleaded Gas	7.8	(1.4)	**6.4**	133	(23)	**110**
Silver	5.3	(1.3)	**4.0**	68	(17)	**51**
Soybean Meal	3.4	(0.9)	**2.5**	113	(31)	**82**
Soybean Oil	2.5	(0.9)	**1.6**	147	(52)	**95**
Soybeans	9.4	(2.6)	**6.8**	213	(60)	**153**
Sugar	6.3	(1.5)	**4.8**	389	(94)	**295**
Wheat (CBOT)	5.8	(1.8)	**3.9**	220	(70)	**150**
Wheat (KCBT)	2.0	(0.7)	**1.3**	78	(27)	**51**
WTI Crude Oil	32.7	(9.3)	**23.4**	673	(194)	**479**
Subtotal (>0.5 billion US$)	146.1	(39.7)	**106.5**			
Subtotal (<0.5 billion US$)	0.6	(0.2)	**0.4**			
Total Notional US Mkts	146.8	(39.9)	**106.9**			
Total Not'l Non-US Mkts	41.9	(10.4)	**31.4**			
Total All Markets	188.6	(50.3)	**138.3**			

[1] Each listed U.S. futures market includes index investment for all futures and OTC markets related to or referenced to that U.S. futures market. For example, the U.S. market listed as "WTI Crude Oil" includes (with the NYMEX's Light "Sweet" crude oil futures market) investments held in the NYMEX "Crude Oil Financial" market and the ICE Futures-Europe WTI Light Sweet crude oil market, because both of those contracts' settlement prices are determined by reference to the NYMEX Light "Sweet" crude oil futures contract.

[2] US Futures Markets with 0.5 billion US dollars or more in reported net index investment notional value on the report date.

"London loophole" which allowed U.S. traders to buy and sell on UK futures exchanges (such as ICE) without having to abide by CFTC regulatory guidelines such as position limits. This was complicated by the fact that ICE introduced futures contracts that mimicked those traded in the United States. One example is the ICE's West Texas Intermediate crude oil contract, the world's second most popular crude oil contract. A similar regulatory issue arose with respect to the Dubai Mercantile Exchange, whose traders are not subject to U.S. regulations, even though they may be trading contracts based on U.S. cash markets.

The Commodity Futures Modernization Act was passed in 2000 in an era of deregulation. The government at that time looked favorably on OTC derivatives and believed that more trade in OTC derivatives was preferable to less; consequently it saw no real need to regulate most of the expanding OTC derivatives market. At the time, Alan Greenspan (Federal Reserve Board) and Lawrence Summers (Treasury Secretary) testified to Congress that many OTC instruments should go unregulated. The Act established conditions under which derivatives–futures, options, or swaps–could be legally traded in the OTC market. The Act established three categories of derivatives: i) financials (e.g., interest rates, stock indexes), ii) agricultural, and iii) "all other" including metals and energy instruments. It was decided that OTC trading in "financials" required little regulation, most "agricultural" OTC trading had to be conducted on regulated exchanges, and "metals and energy" were exempt from regulation.

After the 2008 financial crisis, the government view of "no need to regulate" changed dramatically. The 2010 Dodd-Frank "Wall Street Reform and Consumer Protection Act" provides the CFTC new authority to regulate OTC derivatives. Dodd-Frank aimed to ensure central clearing and exchange trading of most derivatives but the CFTC has yet to fully determine which contracts should be cleared. These new regulations aimed to reduce risk, but costs of doing business may increase for many financial entities and their customers due to the new proposed regulations. Some *bona fide* hedgers may have some exemptions (e.g. airlines, electric companies) but their costs and risks could also increase.

Box 1.10 Attempts at Futures price manipulation

Given the competitive nature of the futures and options markets, there are relatively few attempts by traders to manipulate prices. However, some of the more famous examples of attempts at manipulation are as follows:

- Bunker, Herbert, and Lamar Hunt, members of a rich and colorful Texas oil and ranching family, were found to have manipulated the silver futures market during 1979 and 1980.

- Ferruzzi Finanziaria SpA, an Italian multinational agribusiness firm, was ordered by the CFTC to liquidate its soybean futures positions when it was found Ferruzzi had built up long positions of more than 50 percent of deliverable supply of soybeans in 1988-89. This case led to changes in the delivery points for CBOT soybeans and other grains.

- Merrill Lynch & Co. and Japan's Sumitomo Corp. allegedly worked together to manipulate the New York and London copper futures markets in 1995 and 1996. These two firms were found to have conspired to keep the price of copper high and to artificially force prices higher in late 1995.

- A Spokane energy company paid a $2.1 million fine to settle civil charges that its former employees tried to manipulate the electricity futures market in 1998. The CFTC found that on four occasions Avista Energy manipulated the settlement prices of electricity futures contracts. Avista had placed large orders for futures contracts that influenced prices on the entire Western market. Avista provides electric power for much of Eastern Washington and northern Idaho.

- Amaranth Advisers a firm that lost $6.6 billion in natural gas trades, paid $7.5 million in a settlement for attempting to manipulate the market. In 2006, the individual trader deemed responsible was issued a $30 million fine for his actions.

- Barclays was fined $200 million by the CFTC for manipulating and misreporting the LIBOR and Euribor rates over a four year period beginning in 2005. The CFTC found that Barclays was misrepresenting the benchmark interest rates to benefit its derivatives market and to protect its reputation during the global financial crisis.

- Two former executives of the Dairy Farmers of America settled for $12 million with the CFTC in 2008 for attempting to manipulate the milk futures contract and exceeding speculative position limits.

- In 2015, the CFTC sued Kraft Foods, alleging manipulation of CBOT wheat futures to try and lower the cash price of wheat, a major input used by Kraft. Kraft was apparently buying wheat futures with the express purpose of sending false market signals and lowering cash prices. Kraft's futures positions allegedly exceeded CFTC guidelines for the maximum size of speculative positions. CFTC claimed that Kraft illegally earned over $5.4 million.

The Exchange

Figure 1.12 schematically presents the major components of a futures and options exchange. Most exchanges are for-profit organizations, and a limited number of "members" have exchange trading privileges. For example, the Chicago Board of Trade has over 3,600 members under different categories, and membership significantly reduces the cost of trading through discounted rates. CBOT has full members, associate members, government instrument members, commodity options members, and so on. When this chapter was written full memberships at CBOT cost $300,000. The CME, CBOT, NYMEX, and COMEX memberships are separate from one another.

In 2002, the Chicago Mercantile Exchange Inc. became a for-profit corporation. The CBOT followed and went public in 2005. The merged company trades under the ticker symbol CME:NASDAQ. The Intercontinental Exchange (stock symbol is ICE:NYSE) is also publicly held. Memberships are sold through auction. As of 2023, full membership prices were about $350,000 on the CME, $300,000 on the CBOT, $150,000 on NYMEX, and $98,000 on the Comex. Traders can lease memberships on these exchanges.

Figure 1.12: Organization of a Typical Futures and Options Exchange

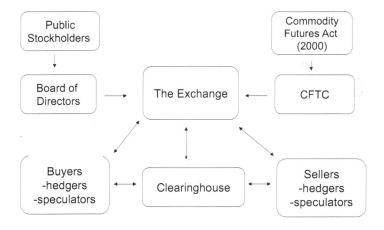

The exchange establishes all the rules of trading in accordance with government regulations, disseminates market information, and provides physical and/or computerized trading facilities. A board of directors, elected from the membership (or shareholders) manages the affairs of the exchange. It enforces the bylaws of the exchange and arrives at management decisions when necessary. The financing of an exchange's daily operating costs, such as rent, overhead, employees' salaries, and so on, is covered mainly by annual membership dues and a small transactions fee levied on each trade.

A clearinghouse consists of a subgroup of members from the exchange. It financially guarantees all contracts on the exchange and handles the financial settlement of all contracts. There has never been a default on U.S. exchanges because of the financial backing provided by the clearinghouse. The clearinghouse is discussed in more detail in Chapter 2.

Economic Functions of Futures and Options Trading

As explained previously, the futures market is a very old institution that (in its current form) developed largely in North America and originally served to correct marketing inefficiencies in commodity markets through the provision of inter-temporal prices. In more recent years, financial markets have also adopted the futures market for many of the same economic reasons that those in agriculture have used futures for about 180 years. The futures market serves several roles: it discovers prices, shifts price risk, disseminates information, and provides returns to hedgers for storage services (if they are hedging a storable commodity). One of the original reasons for the establishment of futures markets was to provide producers and merchants with a liquid market in which to shift the risk of price change onto others. Hedgers enter into both long (buy) and short (sell) positions, and as a consequence some of the risk is shifted to other hedgers. Speculators assume that amount of price risk that is not shifted to other hedgers. By reducing their exposure to price risk, producers are better able to make sound production and marketing decisions. For merchants, the opportunity to shift price risk through hedging means that their unit costs of marketing are lowered.

Prior to the introduction of futures markets, many markets were subject to large seasonal or cyclical price swings. A major reason for the large price changes was that merchants had no guarantee of earning an economic return for storing the commodity. As a result, less-than-optimal amounts of some products were put into storage. The futures market corrected this marketing anomaly and now ensures, through a set of intertemporal prices, that products such as oil or grain are placed in storage to be supplied to the market in a continuous fashion.

The informational role of futures prices is a public good in the sense that many people benefit from the service without paying the cost. Knowledgeable producers view futures prices as market signals that benefit them in the timing of sales and/or production decisions. Commercial interests who trade in the futures market reveal their market information through trading; thus, their information indirectly becomes public information. For instance, a commodity firm that makes a large sale to an overseas buyer may immediately turn around and hedge this sale on the futures market.

Therefore, futures markets serve to transfer information from those who have it to those who do not.

Summary

This introductory chapter has covered the basics of where and how futures and options contracts are traded. Futures exchanges are in the price discovery and risk transfer business, and trading started with agricultural commodities in the 19th century. Price discovery and risk transfer are both vital economic functions in any economy. The futures market creates hedging opportunities and enhances price discovery. A futures contract is an obligation to buy or sell a specific quantity and quality of a commodity or financial instrument at a certain price on a specified future date. Alternatively options on futures provide the buyer the right, but not the obligation, to buy (go long) or sell (go short) a specific futures contract at a specific price. The following six characteristics of exchange based futures and options trading have been discussed:

- Trading is conducted on organized exchanges.

- There are specific rules governing trading.

- Futures and options contracts are highly standardized.

- Futures contracts have symmetrical risks for the buyer and seller, and those risks are legally canceled by making offsetting trades.

- Options on futures contracts have asymmetrical risks for the buyer and seller, as the buyer has no obligation to fulfill the option. The option buyer's potential loss is limited but the seller's is not.

- The exchange clearinghouse guarantees all contracts.

The unique aspects of futures exchanges, as compared with other marketplaces, have been the focus of discussion in this chapter. These exchanges have not only an interesting history but also an exciting future. Their role of providing contingent markets in the economy is of utmost importance.

For the past 180 years, the futures industry has been the central point of price discovery for the food industry. Futures have simultaneously enabled producers, merchandisers, and processors of food to reduce their exposure to adverse price movements. In the past four or five decades, the futures industry has expanded to include many contracts for nonfood commodities, such as metals and energy products. In addition, contracts have been

developed to enable financial institutions to protect against currency fluctuations, equity index variations, and interest rate changes. The proven
usefulness of these derivatives has resulted in phenomenal growth in trading volumes. The number of contracts traded increased ten- or twenty-fold.
What does the next decade hold in store for this industry? After all, now
we have futures trading in bitcoin.

Discussion Questions

1. Discuss the economic importance of futures and options markets.

2. What role do market prices play in the economy, and how do they
   ration supply and demand?

3. Can a market be "efficient" if prices fall by over 20% in one day?

4. "Speculating in futures is no more risky than speculating in the stock
   market." Explain with the use of an example.

5. Discuss the various supply and demand factors behind the WTI versus Brent crude oil futures. Which is the true global benchmark? How
   has this changed since the shale revolution in the U.S.?

6. Why are the U.S. futures and options markets losing world market
   share to overseas markets?

7. What type of firms would use stock index futures (e.g., the E-mini
   S&P 500 index) as hedging devices? Explain with an example.

8. Explain the role of the Commodity Futures Trading Commission. Are
   they over-regulating OTC swaps?

9. How do the objectives of hedgers differ from those of speculators?

10. What are the key differences between futures and options?

11. Why do some futures contracts require delivery and others are closed
    by cash settlement?

Selected References

Anderson, Seth C, John D Jackson, and Jeffrey W Steagall. 1994. "A note on odds in the cattle futures market." *Journal of Economics and Finance*, 18(3): 357–365.

Bhardwaj, Geetesh, Gary B Gorton, and K Geert Rouwenhorst. 2016. "Investor Interest and the Returns to Commodity Investing." *The Journal of Portfolio Management*, 42(3): 44–55.

Carter, Colin A. 1999. "Commodity futures markets: a survey." *Australian Journal of Agricultural and Resource Economics*, 43(2): 209–247.

Erb, Claude B, and Campbell R Harvey. 2006. "The strategic and tactical value of commodity futures." *Financial Analysts Journal*, 62(2): 69–97.

Etula, Erkko. 2013. "Broker-dealer risk appetite and commodity returns." *Journal of Financial Econometrics*, 11(3): 486–521.

Gorton, Gary, and K Geert Rouwenhorst. 2006. "Facts and Fantasies about Commodity Futures (Digest Summary)." *Financial Analysts Journal*, 62(2): 47–68.

Masters, Michael W. 2009. "Testimony before the commodity futures trading commission."

Meyer, Gregory. October 9, 2017. "From ranchers to fund managers, "algos" cause a stir." *Financial Times*.

Pirrong, Craig. 2017. "The economics of commodity market manipulation: A survey." *Journal of Commodity Markets*.

Scheitrum, Daniel P, Colin A Carter, and Cesar Revoredo-Giha. 2018. "WTI and Brent futures pricing structure." *Energy Economics*, 72: 462–469.

Williams, Jeffrey C. 2001. "Commodity futures and options." *Handbook of Agricultural Economics*, 1: 745–816.

2.

Futures and Options
Market Mechanics

This chapter will explain the market mechanics and the jargon of futures and options markets. The options contracts discussed here are options written on underlying futures contracts. Hedgers and speculators trade options as either substitutes for, or in conjunction with, futures contracts. The chapter will emphasize futures more than options because options will be covered in greater depth in later chapters. In any case, an understanding of futures markets goes a long way towards an understanding of options on futures. The basic workings of the markets explained here cover both commodity (e.g., energy, precious metals, and agricultural) and financial (e.g., equity indexes, interest rates and foreign exchange rates) futures and options markets.

The Futures Contract

As explained in Chapter 1, a futures contract is very similar to either a deferred delivery contract or a forward contract. Traders buying or selling a futures contract establish a price for subsequent delivery (or cash settlement) of a certain type of a designated commodity, financial instrument, or financial index.

There are two ways that futures contracts are settled at contract expiry, through *delivery* or through *cash settlement* (sometimes called financial settlement). Table 2.1 lists the settlement procedures for U.S. based futures contracts. Delivery is a common settlement procedure for commodities (e.g., energy products like oil and agricultural products like corn) but it is a method also used for financial futures such as U.S. Treasuries (notes and bonds) and currencies. Cash (financial) settlement is used for indexes such as the E-mini S&P 500 stock index and the U.S. dollar index–because

Table 2.1: Settlement Procedures: U.S. Futures Exchanges

Deliverable	Cash (Financially) Settled
WTI crude oil, NYMEX	3 Month SOFR, CME
Corn, CBOT	E-mini S&P 500, CME
Soybeans, CBOT	E-micro $5 DJIA, CBOT
Wheat, CBOT	Federal Funds, CBOT
10 Year Treasury Note, CBOT	Lean Hogs, CME
5 Year Treasury Note, CBOT	N. American Natural Gas, ICE U.S.
30 Year Treasury Bond, CBOT	U.S. Dollar Index, ICE U.S.
Gold (GC), COMEX	Feeder Cattle, CME
Euro FX, CME	Black Sea Corn, CME
Henry Hub Natural Gas, NYMEX	Black Sea Wheat, CME
Sugar #11, ICE U.S.	Class III Milk, CME
Japanese Yen, CME	Australian Wheat, CME
Live Cattle, CME	E-mini Nasdaq 100 Index, CME
Cotton #2, ICE U.S.	E-mini Russell 2000 Index, CME
Canadian Dollar, CME	Canadian Wheat, CME

in practice these products cannot be physically delivered, or in some cases it would be extremely expensive to do so. For instance, it would be logistically very difficult and expensive to deliver 500 different stocks, each in relatively small amounts. In addition, some contracts that could in theory be physically delivered (e.g., lean hogs, feeder cattle, and Black Sea wheat) are settled financially.

For deliverables, the contract specifies a geographical area and a given time period for delivery. To serve as an example, Table 2.2 illustrates the specifications for the CME Group–New York Mercantile Exchange (NYMEX) WTI crude oil futures contract. The specifications in Table 2.2 cover the major terms and conditions of the contract. Units of 1,000 barrels of oil are traded and the contract specifies delivery of light "sweet" crude oil. Trading is conducted from 5:00 p.m. - 4:00 p.m. Chicago Time (Central Time) with a 60-minute break each day beginning at 4:00 p.m. in Chicago (see Table 2.2). Each crude oil contract can be traded for several years before its expiration date. For each contract the last trading day is the third business day prior to the 25th calendar day of the month preceding the delivery month. Trading in crude oil futures is conducted for twelve delivery months (i.e., for all twelve months of the calendar year). As explained in Chapter 1, twelve delivery months is unusual as most futures contracts have less than nine delivery months in any one calendar year. For example, lumber futures have only six delivery months in a given year.

Table 2.2: NYMEX WTI Crude Oil Contract Specifications

Exchange Symbol	CL
Contract	Crude Oil West Texas Intermediate (WTI)
Exchange	NYMEX
Tick Size	1 cent per barrel ($10.00 per contract)
Margin/Maintenance	$7,260/6,600
Daily Price Limit	15% above or below previous settlement
Contract Size	1,000 U.S. barrels (42,000 gallons)
Contract Months	All Calendar Months for up to 10 years forward
Trading Hours	5:00p.m.-4:00p.m. (Sun-Fri). Settles 1:30p.m. CST
Delivery	F.O.B Cushing, OK, at any pipeline or storage facility with pipeline access.
Speculator Position Limits	20,000 contracts, not to exceed 3,000 in expiry month or 10,000 in any month.
Last Trading Day	3rd business day prior to the 25th calendar day of the month preceding the delivery month

Source CME Rule Book, Ch. 200.

Upon entering a futures contract, the buyer and seller make equal and offsetting commitments. In the trade's terminology, a buyer of a futures contract enters into a "long" position, whereas the seller enters into a "short" position. The seller of one December crude oil contract, for example, is going *short* in the market by *agreeing to deliver* 1,000 barrels of light "sweet" crude oil to Oklahoma during the month of December. On the other side of the transaction, the buyer of the crude oil futures contract is going *long* in the market by *agreeing to accept delivery* in December and upon delivery to pay for the 1,000 barrels in full. Table 2.2 reports that the central delivery point for crude oil is Cushing Oklahoma, with several alternative delivery opportunities.

Table 2.3 categorizes various futures and options contracts into four broad categories: metals, natural resources and energy, financials, and agricultural. Globally, metals (including precious and non-precicous) volume of trade is approximately 2.2 trillion contracts per year, natural resources and energy about 2 trillion contracts/year, financials approximately 67 trillion contracts/year, and agricultural around 2.4 trillion contracts/year.

When entering into a futures contract, a trader can initially either sell or buy a futures contract. The initial trade must be subsequently offset by either taking an opposite position (e.g., the seller later buys) or through making or taking delivery (for deliverables). Many students may ask the obvious question - how can a trader first sell a futures contract before they actually buy one? How is it that I can sell a corn futures contract if I have not bought any corn and do not own any corn? The answer is that by selling

Table 2.3: Representative Categories of Futures/Options contracts

Metals	Natural Resources & Energy	Financials	Agricultural
gold	Brent crude oil	Eurodollar	corn
copper	WTI crude oil	SOFR (Overnight)	wheat
silver	ethanol	Treasury Notes	soybeans
steel	heating oil	Treasury Bonds	soybean meal
platinum	natural gas	Japanese ¥	soybean oil
aluminum	gasoline (RBOB)	Canadian $	cotton
steel	diesel	Euro	rice
iron ore	lumber	S&P 500 index	ethanol
palladium	rubber	U.S. $ index	cattle
lead	propane	Australian $	lean hogs
zinc	electricity	Mexican peso	coffee
	coal	British £	sugar
	DJ US Real Estate	Swiss franc	orange juice
	HDD Weather	NASDAQ 100 index	milk
	global emissions	single stocks	cattle
	fertilizer	Federal Funds	cheese
	CA carbon allowance	bitcoin	cocoa

a futures contract, the trader simply enters into an *agreement* to deliver (and thus eventually sell) the commodity or asset during the delivery month. Selling a futures contract is a promise to sell at a future date and for that reason a futures trader can "sell" an asset they may not even own. Even if I do not have a cattle ranch, I could promise to sell live cattle (i.e., sell live cattle futures) at a specific future time period, because I know that I can easily cancel that promise through buying back live cattle futures. In other words, traders either have to buy the physical asset before the delivery month and then deliver, or simply cancel their initial promise to sell by later buying a futures contract for the same delivery month. For non-deliverables such as *lean hogs* if you initially sell then you are committed to "buy back" a similar contract prior to expiry. If you wait until the final day, lean hog futures are settled at a cash price established by the U.S. Department of Agriculture. Most students are happy to learn that they don't have to touch hogs in order to trade them.

For deliverables, most futures contracts do not result in actual delivery, but this does not detract from their economic benefits. Unlike trading in most other markets (including the stock market) where equity ownership or ownership of physical assets changes hands with every trade, the execution of a futures market trade only involves future commitments on the part of the buyer and seller. These commitments are legally binding but can easily be offset, as described next.

A unique characteristic of a futures contract, and that which distinguishes it from a forward contract, is that it affords both the buyer and seller a continuing opportunity to avoid making or taking delivery. To avoid delivery any time after the initial transaction, traders execute an equal but opposite transaction in the same commodity (or asset) and futures month. For example, to absolve himself of the commitment to accept 1,000 barrels of crude oil in December, the original buyer of the futures contract could subsequently sell one December contract. This offsetting trade can be done at any time before the contract expires. For each trader, if the selling price of a futures contract is higher than the buying price, then a profit is recorded (ignoring transaction costs such as brokerage fees)–otherwise there is a loss.

For some futures contracts, the futures exchange establishes a limit on the extent to which futures prices may change during a single day. Prices are restricted from moving by more than some prescribed amount from the previous day's settlement price. If prices reach the upper or lower limit, then the market is "locked-limit" and trading is suspended for a period of time. For instance, for *lean hogs* the CME daily price limit move is 4.75¢ per lb. from the previous day's settlement price. This means that at all times during a given day, lean hog futures must be within 4.75¢ per lb. from the previous trading day's contract settlement price.

The reason for having daily price limits is to serve as a type of circuit breaker when trading becomes volatile. This reduces the risk of trader default and reduces the effects of emotional reactions to information that could threaten the financial foundation of the clearinghouse. The exchanges seek to avoid "panics" by forcing traders to stretch large price moves across days, thus giving everyone time to rationally evaluate new information. In cases where significant price changes are based on economic factors, the daily price limits are often increased by the exchange on a temporary basis. For example, in the case of Kansas City HRW wheat futures, if a "back month" futures contract price closes "at the limit" (all either up or down), the limit is increased from $0.65 to $1.00 per bushel. In this way, futures exchanges seek to maintain order in the pricing process while still allowing the markets to work and preserving the important role of the clearinghouse.

Each futures contract has a unique trading code. For instance the trading symbol for WTI crude oil futures is CL and the symbol for corn is C. This is an industry abbreviation and there is a separate symbol for each futures and options contract. The futures industry code for a particular futures contract employs abbreviations for both the contract and its expiration month and year. Typically, one or two letters represent the contract, one letter represents the contract expiration month, and a final number represents the last digit of the expiration year. For example, the December 2025 WTI Crude Oil futures contract is represented as CLZ25. CL represents crude oil, Z represents December, and 25 represents 2025. Contract month codes are listed in Table 2.4. Table 2.5 reports the contract symbol codes (first column), along with the contract (middle column) and the various months traded (last column).

Table 2.4: Futures Month Codes

Expiry Month Symbols Used for Futures Price Quotes					
Jan=F	Feb=G	Mar=H	Apr=J	May=K	Jun=M
Jul=N	Aug=Q	Sep=U	Oct=V	Nov=X	Dec=Z

A sample of daily futures price quotes is shown in Table 2.6. This table is for the copper futures market but the reporting framework is standard across all contract. Basic information reported for each contract includes the delivery month and year, the first (called the "open") and last ("settle") price at which each contract traded during the day, the highest ("high") and lowest ("low") prices at which transactions occurred during the day, and the change between the previous and current settlement prices. The "life-time high" and "lifetime" low is also reported, and this refers to the highest and lowest priced trades for that particular contract month/year since it was first traded. In this example, December copper futures prices opened on the day at $4.1165 per lb. and closed (i.e., settled) on the day at $4.1085 per lb. You can find this type of information online at barchart.com, investing.com, wsj.com, tradingcharts.com, admis.com, or specific exchange websites (such as CME and ICE).

Corn futures price quotations are shown in the top part of Table 2.7. Corn is the largest crop in the United States, measured either by value of production or planted acres. Corn accounts for over 96% of the total U.S. feed grain production and use. In recent years U.S. corn planted acreage has been approximately 90 million acres.

When viewed globally, U.S. corn farmers are among the most productive in the world and U.S. corn helps feed the world. For instance, in the 2020/21 September-August fiscal year, U.S. corn growers produced about 14.1 billion bushels of corn, worth approximately $64 billion. Corn is primarily used to provide the main energy ingredient in U.S. livestock feed - mostly cattle, hogs, and chickens (35% of the 2020/21 crop); for domestic food, alcohol, and industrial usage - including ethanol (40% of the 2020/21 crop); and for exports (17% of the 2020/21 crop).

The U.S. corn marketing (*i.e.*, fiscal) year runs from September 1st of one year through August 31st of the next - the beginning of which corresponds approximately to the timing of the annual U.S. corn harvest. In the United States, corn is planted each spring (mostly in April and May), and harvest normally starts during the months of September and October, al-

Table 2.5: Futures Months Symbols and Months Traded

Code	Contract	Months Traded
AD	Australian $	FHJMNUVZ
AG	Silver	GJMQVZ
BO	Soybean Oil	FHKNQUVZ
BP	British Pound	FHJMNUVZ
C	Corn	HKNUZ
CC	Cocoa	HKNUZ
CD	Canadian $	FHJMNUVZ
CL	WTI Crude Oil	All Months
CT	Cotton	HKNVZ
DX	U.S. Dollar Index	HMUZ
ED	Eurodollar, 90-Day	HMUZ
FC	Feeder Cattle	FHJKQUVX
FF	Fed Funds, 30-Day	All Months
FV	Treasury Notes, 5-Yr	HMUZ
TY	Treasury Notes, 10-Yr	HMUZ
GH	Gold	GJMQVZ
HG	Copper	All Months
HO	Heating Oil	All Months
JO	Frozen Conc. Orange Juice	FHKNUX
JY	Japanese Yen (¥)	FHJMNUVZ
KC	Coffee "C"	HKNUZ
KI	Gold	GJMQVZ
KV	Value Line Index	HMUZ
KW	Wheat	HKNUZ
LB	Lumber, Random Length	FHKNUX
LC	Live Cattle	GJMQVZ
LH	Live Hogs	GJMNQVZ
NG	Natural Gas	All Months
PM	Mexican Peso	FHJMNUVZ
RB	RBOB Gasoline	All Months
RR	Rough Rice	FHKNUX
S	Soybeans	FHKNQUX
SB	Sugar #11 (World)	HKNV
SI	Silver	HKNUZ
SM	Soybean Meal	FHKNQUX
SP	S&P 500 Stock Index	HMUZ
W	Wheat	HKNUZ
ZB	Treasury Bonds, 30-Yr	HMUZ

Note: Product codes may vary depending on where the contracts are cleared.

Table 2.6: Example of Daily Futures Price Quote: Copper Futures (CMX)-25,000 lbs.; $ per lb.

Contract	Open	High	Low	Settle	Change	Lifetime High	Lifetime Low
Dec	$4.1165	$4.1210	$4.0380	$4.1085	+$0.002	$4.1410	$4.0381

Table 2.7: Sample Futures Price Quotations

	SETTLE	CHG	OPEN	HIGH	LOW	VOLUME	LIFETIME HIGH	LIFETIME LOW	OPEN INT
			CORN (CBT)-5,000 bu.; cents per bu.						
Dec	638.75	-3.5	642.5	642.5	638.5	247,887	657.25	636.25	249,928
Mar	651.75	-3.25	654.75	655.25	651.25	299,633	656.00	648.75	771,092
May	660.00	-3.25	663.00	663.5	659.75	47,791	670.00	657.00	195,688
Jul	668.25	-3.00	671.25	671.5	667.75	25,337	674.25	655.00	199,694
			Canadian Dollar (CME)-100,000 Canadian Dollars; $ US per Can $						
Dec	0.7833	-0.0035	0.7869	0.7888	0.78315	65,234	0.8293	0.7286	138,168
Jan	0.78535	-0.00185	0.78715	0.7889	0.7842	256	0.8111	0.7753	1,012
Feb	0.78455	-0.0029	0.78625	0.78625	0.78445	196	0.8037	0.7760	242
Mar	0.78415	-0.00355	0.7878	0.7895	0.78415	468	0.8290	0.7301	3,817
			Japanese Yen (CME)-12.5 million yen; $ US per yen (.00)						
Dec	0.90155	0.00455	0.8969	0.90295	0.8961	162,834	0.936	0.8595	243,070
Jan	0.90335	0.00455	0.9000	0.90405	0.9000	370	0.905	0.875	2,145
Feb	0.9049	0.00455	0.9002	0.9049	0.9002	276	0.9032	0.8765	453
Mar	0.9063	0.0046	0.9016	0.9073	0.90095	916	0.9401	0.8685	5,019

though there is regional variation.

The United States' share of the global corn trade averages about 33%. Other major corn exporters include Argentina, Brazil, and Ukraine. The U.S. exports corn to more than 50 different countries and the largest international customers are China, Mexico, Japan, Colombia. S. Korea, Canada, Taiwan, Guatemala, Costa Rica and Honduras.

Corn futures contracts are traded on the Chicago Board of Trade (CBOT) in units of 5,000 bushels and prices are reported in cents per bushel. In Table 2.7, each row under the corn futures category reports information for a separate contract delivery month. Each column reports monetary units, except for the columns titled open interest and volume. Open interest is the number of open futures contracts for which a trader remains obligated to the Exchange's Clearing House because no offsetting sale or purchase has yet been made. Volume is the number of futures contracts traded that day. The December corn contract occupies the first row under "Corn" in Table 2.7 and it has an "opening" price of $6.3875 per bushel. The opening price is the average price generated through trading during the opening minutes of the trading day. If you look down to the second row you will see March contract listed under corn, and this contract is for the subsequent calendar year.

Referring to the nearby December corn contract occupying the top row (Table 2.7), the two columns on either side of the opening price report the "settle", "change", "high", and "low" prices. For December corn these prices are 638.75¢, -3.50¢, 642.50¢, and 638.50¢ respectively. The high and low prices are simply the highest and lowest prices at which a trade was conducted that day for December corn. The "settlement" (or closing) price is the average of prices at which the contract traded just before the close of trading at the end of the day. The settlement price is extremely important because it is the price used by the Clearinghouse to mark-to-market all outstanding positions at the end of the day. The "change" column is the change in the closing (or settlement) price from the previous day. On the right hand side of the corn table, we see the lifetime high and low prices, which are the highest (657.25¢) and lowest (636.25¢) prices ever recorded for that December contract over the duration of its trading life. Most corn contracts are traded for about two years or more before their expiry. The open interest column is reported in numbers of contracts. For the December corn contract, the open interest shown in Table 2.7 is 249,928 contracts.

Now consider the foreign currency futures prices shown in Table 2.7 under the heading "Currency Futures." These currency prices indicate the number of U.S. dollars it takes to buy one unit of foreign currency, for future delivery. In Table 2.7, the January Canadian dollar contract closed at U.S. $0.78535 per Canadian dollar. Canada's national currency also happens to

Table 2.8: CME Futures Trade Example: Rising $Cdn
100,000 $Cdn; U.S. $ Per Can $

Date of Futures Trade	Futures Trade	Delivery Month	Futures Price
Nov 1	Go Long	December	$0.78535 U.S
Dec 1	Go Short	December	$0.8173 U.S.
Profit (loss)			$0.03195 x 100,000 = $3,195 profit

Table 2.9: CME Futures Trade Example: Falling $Cdn
100,000 $Cdn; U.S. $ per Can $

Date of Futures Trade	Futures Trade	Delivery Month	Futures Price
November 1	Go Long	December	$0.78535 U.S
December 1	Go Short	December	$0.766 U.S.
Profit (loss)			$0.01935 x 100,000 = ($1,935) loss

be called the dollar, just like the U.S. national currency. A trader who purchased (i.e., went long) a December Canadian dollar contract would have agreed to purchase $100,000 Canadian dollars at a price of 78.535¢ U.S. per Canadian dollar.

Table 2.8 provides further information on this futures trade. Assume the Canadian dollar rose in value to 81.73¢ U.S., after the initial trade. Suppose that on November 1, the trader went long in December Canadian dollars and held that position open until December 1. On December 1 the trader in question liquidates his position by selling (i.e., going short) one December Canadian dollar contract at $0.8173. The profit from this transaction is $3,195 (= $0.03195 x $100,000) before transactions and brokerage fees.

Alternatively suppose the Canadian dollar fell in value after November 1. This outcome is shown in Table 2.9. In this case the Canadian dollar declined from $0.78535 U.S. to $0.766 U.S. A futures trader long Canadian dollars would experience a loss of $1,935 = $0.01935 x $100,000.

Now consider the Japanese yen (¥) futures contract in Table 2.7. Japanese yen are traded on the Chicago Mercantile Exchange in units of 12.5 million yen, and like all other currency futures, yen futures are quoted as U.S. dollars against the yen. One yen futures contract corresponds to 12.5 million yen. March Yen futures in Table 2.7 had a settle price of $.009063, which means that it cost less than one cent (0.9063¢) to buy one Yen for March delivery. If we take the inverse of this price (i.e., 1/.009063) this gives

Table 2.10: Futures Trade Example:
Japanese Yen (CME) 12.5 million ¥; U.S. $ per ¥

Date of Futures Trade	Futures Trade	Delivery Month	Futures Price
January 2	Go Short	March	$0.009063 U.S.
February 1	Go Long	March	$0.008865 U.S.
Profit (loss)			$0.000198 x 12,500,000 = $2,465 profit

110.34 Yen per U.S. dollar. This way of reporting the Japanese currency (as ¥ per $) might be more familiar to the reader, but the standard for CME currency quotation is in $ per ¥. Note the heading for Japanese Yen in Table 2.7 shows that prices are quotes in $ per yen (.00), which means the decimal place for the Yen prices in Table 2.7 must be moved two places to the left to calculate profit or loss. The March futures settlement price is printed in the table as $0.9063 and after we move the decimal place, this converts to $.009063. Moving the decimal place is the convention in newspapers and online websites that report futures prices.

Suppose a currency trader goes short (i.e., sells) one March yen futures contract calling for delivery of 12.5 million ¥, at a price of $.009063. This transaction is recorded in Table 2.10. The initial trade is entered into on January 2 and by February 1 the yen subsequently falls in value. When the yen falls in value, the $/¥ price decreases because it costs fewer $ to purchase one ¥. If the March futures price falls from $0.009063 to $0.008865, and the currency trader liquidates his position on February 1, a profit of $2,465 is earned before brokerage fees (= $0.000198 x 12,500,000 ¥ = $2,465 profit). Note that a futures price quote in $ per ¥ times a contract size in ¥ gives a profit or loss in $.

The Options Contract

Options on futures are contractual obligations that are traded on organized futures exchanges through an open outcry or electronic auction system. These characteristics they share in common with futures contracts, but there are some important differences between options on futures and futures contracts themselves. An option, as the name implies, gives its buyer the right, but not the obligation, to exercise the option and take possession of a futures contract at a predetermined price. For this right, the option buyer pays a *premium* to the option seller. Options on futures contracts specify delivery of either a long or short futures contract. A *call* option specifies that the seller must deliver a long futures position to the option buyer, and a *put* option specifies delivery of a short futures position. The seller of the option (i.e., the option's writer) has to provide the futures position to the option buyer if the option is exercised. This means that the buyer of an option has the right to either purchase (in the case of a call option) or sell (in the case of a put option) a futures contract at a pre-established price within a given period of time. The predetermined futures price is referred to as either the *strike price* or the exercise price; they are identical in meaning.

For example, in June a trader who expects crude oil futures prices to increase may decide to purchase a December crude oil call option at a strike price of $89 per barrel. If the current December futures price is trading in the $89 range, then the premium paid for this call option may be approximately $3.00 per barrel (or $3,000 per contract). If the December crude oil futures price rises above $89 before the option expires in December, then the holder of the option may exercise the option and take possession of a long December futures position at a price of $89. Alternatively, the holder of the option could reverse his position by selling an identical option contract and profit from the rise in the premium.

The financial obligations involved in options trading are different from those in futures trading. Futures traders have obligations to deliver (in the case of the seller) or accept delivery (in the case of the buyer) of a specified product or asset, at a specified price and time in the future. With options, in contrast, only the option buyer has the right to exercise the option, and the option seller is obligated to comply. When a call option is exercised, the holder of the option will acquire a long futures position at the option strike price. If a call option is exercised, the exchange (through the clearinghouse) assigns a short futures position to a trader who previously sold an identical call option. Alternatively, when a put option is exercised, the option holder acquires a short futures position at the option strike price and a long futures position is assigned to a trader who previously sold an identical put. An option can be exercised by its holder at any time before it expires.

The prices of options are reported publicly in the same manner as futures prices. One difference is that there is a much larger number of options, each of which is traded in relatively smaller volumes, so only the settlement price is typically reported to the public. Table 2.11 is an example of options (on futures) prices. The option price (i.e., the *premium*) is the price paid for the right to buy or sell a futures contract. For each commodity or asset, call and put options with different strike prices and (futures contract) expiration dates are listed. The strike price is the price at which the futures contract will be bought or sold.

Table 2.11 contains futures options prices for two different contracts. The upper rows Table 2.11 reports corn option prices. The far left-hand column shows the strike prices reported for corn options. The other columns

Table 2.11: Daily Options Prices Sample

STRIKE	CALLS-SETTLE			PUTS-SETTLE		
PRICE	MAY	JLY	SEP	MAY	JLY	SEP
Corn Options (CBT)-5,000 bu.; cents & eighths of a ¢per bu.						
640	25-0	25-0	16-3	4-4	29-0	78-2
645	21-2	23-0	-	5-6	31-7	-
650	17-6	21-0	14-3	7-3	34-7	86-1
655	14-7	19-2	-	9-3	38-0	-
660	12-0	17-4	12-5	11-4	41-3	94-2
Corn Futures $/bu; May $6.60-4, Jly $6.36-0, Sep $5.57-2						

STRIKE	CALLS-SETTLE			PUTS-SETTLE		
PRICE	MAR	JUN	SEP	MAR	JUN	SEP
Canadian $ Options (CME); $100,000 CDN; in $ US						
0.760	.0238	.0282	.0322	.0031	.0069	.0103
0.765	.0199	.0246	.0287	.0042	.0083	.0118
0.770	.0162	.0213	.0255	.0055	.0090	.0135
0.775	.0130	.0183	.0225	.0072	.0118	.0154
0.780	.0101	.0155	.0197	.0093	.0140	.0176
CAD Futures; Mar $0.78075, Jun $0.7815, Sep $0.7821						

show either the call option settlement prices or the put option settlement prices for the May, July, and September contracts. For instance, consider the third row under corn in Table 2.11. The strike price is 650, which means the buyer of option will have the right to obtain a futures position at a price of 650¢ per bushel. The premium for a May call is shown to be 17-6¢ per bushel. The "-6" represents 6/8 of one cent as corn options are quoted in units of 1/8 of one cent ($0.00125) per bushel. At this premium the buyer of the call would have the right to go long May corn at a price of 650¢ some time before May. The total premium would be $887.50 (= $0.1775 x 5,000 bu.). In addition there would be brokerage fees. Alternatively, the buyer of a 650 May put option would pay a total premium of 7-3 ¢ per bushel which equals $368 (= $0.07375 x 5,000 bu.). Recall that 7-3 is 7 3/8¢ for corn. The options buyer pays the premium to the writer (i.e., seller) of the option.

Consider the Canadian dollar March call option with a strike price of $0.77 U.S. dollars. This strike price indicates that the options buyer would obtain the right to a Canadian dollar futures contract that is priced at $0.77 U.S. dollars per Canadian dollar. The premium for this option is $0.0162 U.S. dollars per CAD and therefore for a single call option contract the premium equals $1,620 (= $0.0162 x $100,000).

The Clearinghouse

The *clearinghouse* is a corporation that is separate from, but associated with, the futures exchange. The clearinghouse is responsible for recording each futures transaction, reconciling all trades and assuring the financial integrity of each transaction. All futures trades must be "cleared" through the clearinghouse at the end of each trading day. Any member of the exchange who does not also hold a membership in the clearinghouse must have trades "cleared" through a member of the clearinghouse and pay a commission fee for this service. There is a separate clearing corporation for each futures exchange.

In addition to "clearing" trades, the clearinghouse is responsible for balancing the books of all outstanding futures accounts at the end of each trading day. The clearinghouse adjusts the monetary value of open positions (i.e., futures positions entered into and not yet liquidated) to reflect daily settlement prices. Daily *margin calls* (requests for additional capital) are made to clearing members whose balances show a loss as a result of daily price activity. Those members showing a gain due to the day's price moves can withdraw their funds on a daily basis.

Another important function performed by the clearinghouse is facilitation of delivery on futures contracts. If a seller of a futures contract chooses to settle contractual obligations by making delivery, the clearing corpora-

---

Box 2.1 Pit Trading versus Electronic Trading

Shouting buy and sell orders in the futures exchange trading pit was the traditional price discovery mechanism since the invention of futures trading. It was somewhat a crude system but it is one that worked well in the U.S. markets and elsewhere for more than 150 years. However, the traditional open-outcry trading has given way to computerized electronic trading. Foreign exchanges in London, Tokyo, Paris, and Frankfurt, were the first to fully move to electronic-futures screen trading. The exchanges in Europe and Asia are newer and compared to the U.S. exchanges, they originally met less member resistance to change towards computerized trading rather than have open-outcry pit trading.

There are pros and cons associated with *open outcry* versus *electronic* trading. The debate over which system is better has focused on cost, market liquidity, pricing transparency, speed, and regulatory issues related to minimizing trading abuse. The traditional open-outcry system was more expensive than computerized trading but some participants in the industry argue that human interaction among floor traders provided greater market liquidity and better revealed the psychology of the market. Electronic trading is faster, more efficient and easier to regulate. It may be difficult to determine which system is superior, but we do know one thing, the free market ultimately decided electronic trading would replace open-outcry as the dominant system.

---

tion selects the clearing member with an open long position who will receive delivery. The final invoicing and payment procedures are conducted between the buyer and seller under rules of the clearing corporation. In this way, individual traders need not be concerned about identifying or negotiating with other traders wishing to take the opposite side of delivery. In other words, there is no counterparty risk.

In essence, the clearinghouse becomes each buyer's seller and each seller's buyer. That is, the clearinghouse breaks each futures transaction apart after the initial trade. For example, if an individual enters into a long futures position, then the clearinghouse sold it to him or her for all further reference after the initial trade. Denoting this individual trader as person A, the initial position is shown in the first row of Table 2.12 as the buyer of one New York Mercantile Exchange gold futures contract valued at $159,000. Individual A has committed himself to buy 100 ounces of gold for $1,590 per ounce at some point in the future. On the other side of the market, indi-

Table 2.12: The Operation of the Clearinghouse: An Illustration from the NYMEX Gold Futures Market; 100 troy ounces per contract

Time Period	Futures Buyer	Futures Seller	Contract Value	Clearing-house Position	Open Longs	Open Shorts
1	A	B	$159,000	A's seller & B's buyer	A	B
2	C	A	$160,000	C's seller & A's buyer	C	B
3	B	C	$159,500	B's seller & C's buyer	–	–

vidual B has simultaneously agreed to sell to A one gold contract for $1,590 per ounce. After the initial futures trade is completed between individual A and B, the clearinghouse immediately becomes A's seller and B's buyer. Thus, the clearinghouse has a commitment to accept delivery from B and to deliver to A.

Suppose that on the following day individual A decides to liquidate his position by selling a gold futures contract for the same delivery month previously bought. Assume this contract is purchased by a third individual, C. If the price of gold increases from $1,590 to $1,600 per ounce before trader A sells, then after A sells the clearinghouse will pay individual A (through the broker) the difference between the selling and buying price times the number of ounces in question, or $1,000 in this case (ignoring commissions). However, because the clearinghouse *marks-to-market* all contracts at the end of each trading day, it will call on person B to deposit an additional $1,000 on day 2. Person B went short at $1,590 per ounce and then the market moved "against" him to $1,600. When his commitment is "marked to market" at the end of day 2, he is therefore required to put up $1,000 as a margin call, which in turn is paid to person A.

To complete this scenario in Table 2.12, assume that on day three the price of gold falls back to $1,595 from $1,600. If both individuals C and B liquidate their positions at $1,595, then the clearinghouse collects $500 net from person C. In addition, it returns $500 to individual B.

If no further trading takes place, the result is that A gained $1,000 and $500 was lost by both B and C. The clearinghouse never encounters a deficit or surplus because it "brings" each contract to the closing market price at the end of each day. This process is called "marking-to-market." The operating costs of the clearinghouse are covered by transaction fees levied on its members.

Margin Deposits

Futures trading does not involve the exchange of any physical assets or financial instruments unless delivery takes place during the delivery month. This means that buyers and sellers of a futures contract do not have to provide the full monetary value of their commitment at the time a trade is executed. Instead, they are only required to deposit a good faith or margin deposit. The *leverage* resulting from margin deposits is one reason speculators are attracted to futures trading. Leverage means the trader, with a relatively small deposit of capital, is able to control a contract with a relatively large total value. The clearinghouse (for each exchange) establishes minimum margin requirements (i.e., the deposit) for each particular contract. For example, for New York Mercantile Exchange (NYMEX) gold (symbol is GC), this is about $8,000 per 100-ounce contract, or roughly 5 percent of the total value if gold is trading at around $1,600 per oz. Margin requirements set by individual brokerage firms are often above this minimum and vary from firm to firm. With a 5 percent margin deposit, a 5 percent change in the futures price will result in a 100 percent change in the equity of a trader's account —this is leverage at work. Thus, futures trading is viewed as a risky venture for speculators. Yet, it is not only price volatility that makes trading risky, it is the leverage afforded a commodity futures trader.

Upon execution of a trade, a margin deposit is required by the brokerage firm (for non-member traders) and in turn, by the clearinghouse. In the case of cotton futures, for example, the required "initial" margin deposit for one contract is approximately $4,950 and the "maintenance" margin is about $4,500. Table 2.13 reports a sample of minimum margin requirements established by various exchanges. Margin requirements change quite often, with changing market conditions. Both the Chicago Board of Trade and Chicago Mercantile web sites report current margin requirements at http://www.cmegroup.com/clearing/margins/. Margin requirements differ among speculators and hedgers and there are special margin considerations for spread trading.

For public traders the margin requirements are set by brokerage firms and they will normally be above the minimum levels shown in Table 2.13. The *initial* margin is required on the day the futures trade in initiated, while the *maintenance* margin is the amount required to keep the trader's account in-the-black every day thereafter, so long as the futures position remains outstanding. As long as the market moves in favor of the trader, no additional margin money is required and, in fact, profits can be claimed and transferred to the trader at the end of each trading day. This is because the clearinghouse forwards any profit, realized or unrealized, to the broker and

Table 2.13: Sample of Minimum Margin Requirements

Contract	Initial Margin	Maintenance Margin
WTI Crude Oil (NYMEX)	$7,260	$6,600
Natural Gas (ICE)	$4,400	$4,000
RBOB Gasoline (NYMEX)	$8,250	$7,500
E-Mini S&P 500 (CME)	$11,660	$10,600
Cotton (NYCE)	$4,950	$4,500
Gold (COMEX)	$8,000	$7,400
Bitcoin (CME)	$33,500	$30,500
Corn (CBT)	$2,310	$2,100
Mini Corn (CBT)	$660	$ 420
Soybeans (CBT)	$3,630	$3,300
Wheat (CBT)	$3,300	$3,0009
One-Month SOFR (CME)	$1,050	$750
30 year T-Bonds (CBT)	$4,620	$4,200
Mini Dow Jones Index (CBT)	$8,250	$7,500
Japanese Yen (CME)	$4,092	$3,720
Copper (COMEX)	$6,325	$5,750
Lean Hogs (CME)	$1,925	$1,750

Source: https://www.tradestation.com/pricing/futures-margin-requirements/.

thus the client has the right to this money.

Margin requirements for options on futures are different. Unlike in the case with futures, the buyer of an option is not required to deposit margin money with the clearinghouse because the maximum risk exposure is the premium, which is paid in full at the time a position is taken. However, the seller of an option is exposed to significant risk and thus is required to deposit margin money in the same fashion as one who either bought or sold a futures contract outright. The seller (writer) of an option is normally required to deposit margin money equal to the margin on the underlying futures contract plus the current value of the option's premium.

Once the market moves against a trader, the brokerage firm, on behalf of the clearinghouse, will demand additional margin money from the trader. Table 2.14 provides an illustration of margin calls using the lean hog futures market as an example. If the individual in question goes long, then he is subject to margin calls if the price begins to fall. Suppose he goes long in lean hog futures at 96¢ per pound and the price subsequently falls to 94¢. The lean hog futures contract size is 40,000 pounds. Over this period he will be required to deposit a total of $625 in addition to the initial $1,925 margin. The 2¢ decline in price resulted in a loss of contract value equal to $800, so the initial margin of $1,925 was drawn down to $1,125. In order to

Table 2.14: Margin Calls: An Illustration of a Long Position in a Lean Hog Futures Contract

Time Period	Margin Deposit	Contract Price	Contract Size	Total Value	Margin Call
1	$1,925	$0.96	40,000 lbs.	$38,400	–
2	$1,925	$0.94	40,000 lbs.	$37,600	$625
3	$1,925	$0.88	40,000 lbs.	$35,200	$2,400

restore the margin money in the account to the maintenance margin level (of $1,750), the individual would receive a $625 margin call from his broker. The margin calls must be paid immediately. If the price continued to fall to 88¢, additional margin equal to $2,400 (6¢ × 40,000) would be required. Thus, it is often the case that margin calls equal to the full value of unrealized losses must be made by the futures trader. Margin money must be in the form of cash or near-cash instruments such as Treasury bills.

Volume and Open Interest

Volume is the number of contracts traded over a given time interval, and normally it is measured on a daily basis. Since for every buyer of a futures contract there must be a seller, volume is the total number of purchases or sales, but not the sum of the two. Volume is a useful indicator of market activity and market liquidity.

Open interest is the number of unliquidated contracts at any point in time; thus, it is a cumulative figure. It is measured by either the number of open long positions or the open short positions, but not the sum of the two. Table 2.15 illustrates how open interest and volume are calculated. Suppose that on day two a new futures contract begins trading and that individual A buys two contracts from B. At the end of the day, the clearinghouse records would indicate that individual A has two open long positions and individual B has two open short positions. Both the daily volume and open interest at the end of the day would be reported as two contracts.

On day three suppose that there is a sale of one contract by individual D (a "new" seller) to individual C (a "new" buyer). At the end of day three, the cumulative open interest will have increased from 2 to 3 and the daily volume will be recorded as one contract. Open interest rises to 3 contracts because trader A still has 2 open long contracts and now trader C also has 1 open long contract, for a total of 3 open interest. On the other side of the market, both trader B and D have open short positions and these positions also sum to 3.

Further illustration of how volume and open interest changes over time

Table 2.15: Illustration of Open-Interest and Volume Calculations for Future Contracts

Day No.	Buyer	Seller	Open longs	Open shorts	Daily Volume	Open Interest
1					0	0
2	A(2)	B(2)	A(2)	B(2)	2	2
3	C(1)	D(1)	A(2), C(1)	B(2), D(1)	1	3
4	B(1)	E(1)	A(2), C(1)	B(1), D(1), E(1)	1	3
5	D(1)	C(1)	A(2)	B(1), E(1)	1	2
6	E(1)	A(1)	A(1)	B(1)	1	1
7	B(1)	A(1)			1	0

Note: Number of contracts either bought or sold are in parentheses. Letters A, ..., E denote individual traders.

is provided in Table 2.15 for days four through seven. As can be seen from the table, if there is a purchase by an "old" seller from an "old" buyer, open interest declines. On the other hand if there is a purchase by a "new" buyer from an "old" buyer, open interest is unchanged. For instance, on day 5 if trader D buys one contract and trader C sells 1 contract, then both of these traders are exiting the market. Daily volume is 1 and open interest drops from 3 to 2 contracts.

Options Versus Futures

There are some important fundamental differences between futures and options. First, the obligation involved in buying an options contract is much different from that involved in buying a futures contract. For deliverables, the holder of a futures contract has the obligation to either deliver, or accept delivery, of the underlying asset or financial instrument. This obligation must either be "met" or "offset" by the holder of a futures contract. It is most often offset by the trader entering into an equal and opposite futures position, avoiding delivery. Alternatively, the holder of an option has the "right" but not an "obligation" to either buy or sell the underlying futures contract. For example, a buyer of a Treasury bond (or T-bond) futures contract must either accept delivery or sell an offsetting futures contract before contract expiration. On the other hand, a buyer of a T-bond "call" option can either exercise his right and obtain a long position in T-bond futures,

Table 2.16: Basic Differences Between Futures Contracts and Options on Futures

Alternative Position	Traders' Rights	Traders' Obligations	Margins Required
Futures contract buyer		Accept commodity at contract price*	Yes
Futures contract seller		Deliver commodity at contract price*	Yes
Put option buyer	Sell future contracts at strike price		No
Put option seller		Buy futures contract at strike price	Yes
Call option buyer	Buy futures contract at strike price		No
Call option seller		Sell futures contract at strike price	Yes

* For contracts that are not deliverable, the traders' obligation is to settle at the cash price before expiry of the contract.

or alternatively, choose not to exercise the option and simply let it expire. The basic differences between futures and options contracts are outlined in Table 2.16.

To reiterate, an option is a contractual agreement to either purchase or sell a futures contract at a pre-established price, and within a specified time period. As briefly explained early on in this chapter, there are two types of options: "puts" and "calls." A call option gives a buyer the right (but not the obligation) to purchase a futures contract at a specified strike price and during a specified period of time (before the expiry date). A put option gives a buyer of the option the right (but not the obligation) to sell a futures contract at a specified price and during a specified period of time. The seller (writer) of an option receives a premium, which is the amount paid by the buyer of the option in return for the right to control a futures contract. The premium is the price of the option, and thus it fluctuates with the supply and demand for the option itself. The holder can exercise an option at any time during the life of the option.

A few examples will help to illustrate these basic concepts. Consider Table 2.17 where representative futures options prices are reported for options written on wheat and gold futures contracts. The top panel of Table 2.17 reports wheat option prices. The wheat options prices have been converted from cents and eighths (i.e., the fractions used at CBOT, with 8 in the denominator) to decimals. For instance for the August call with an 875

Table 2.17: Wheat and Gold Futures Options

Strike Price	Calls-Settle			Puts-Settle		
	Aug	Sep	Dec	Aug	Sep	Dec
Wheat (CBT)-5,000 bu.; cents per bu.						
875	20.125	38.625	-	47.375	-	-
880	18.625	37	66.875	50.875	69.25	84.375
885	17.25	35.375	-	-	-	-
890	15.875	33.75	63.125	-	-	90.5
895	14.625	32.25	-	-	-	-
900	13.5	30.875	59.625	-	83.125	-
Gold (CMX)-100 troy ounces; $ per troy ounce						
1580	26.20	44.70	56.20	14.20	30.30	41.80
1585	23.10	41.80	53.50	16.10	32.40	44.10
1590	20.20	39.10	50.80	18.20	34.70	46.40
1595	17.70	36.50	48.30	20.70	37.10	48.90
1600	15.40	34.10	45.90	23.40	39.70	51.50
1605	13.30	31.80	43.60	26.30	42.40	54.20

strike price the premium on CBOT was quoted as 20-1 and this converts to 20.125 as the "1" behind the dash represents 1/8. On the day in question the options were trading, the purchaser of a call option in wheat would have numerous different strike prices to choose from. If the option buyer chooses $8.85 as the appropriate strike price, then he would pay 17.25¢ per bushel for the right to go long one August wheat futures contract at a strike price of $8.85 per bushel. He may exercise this right any time before the month of August. The total premium he pays to the seller of the option is $862.50 (17.25¢ per bushel times 5,000 bushels), and this is paid immediately at the time the option is purchased. If the price of wheat falls and he chooses not to exercise the option, then his total loss is limited to $862.50. However, if the price of wheat rises and he exercises his option, he will acquire a "long" futures position at the option strike price of $8.85. At the same time, the exchange clearinghouse will assign a "short" futures position to a trader who has previously sold an identical "call" option, with the same underlying futures contract and the same strike price.

Turning to the gold example in Table 2.17, consider the buyer of a put option. If the purchaser chooses a strike price of $1,600 per ounce and an August expiry date, the premium paid to the option seller is $23.40 per ounce, or $2,340 for one put option. The holder of this option has the right to acquire a short position in August gold futures at a price of $1,600. If the price of gold falls before the month of August and the option is exer-

---

Box 2.2 Bitcoin and Cryptocurrencies

In 2017 both the CME and Cboe Global Markets initiated trading in Bitcoin futures. This was a controversial move, because Bitcoin and other digital (crypto) currencies (also known as altcoins–alternatives to bitcoin) were initially associated with criminal activity, tax evasion, terrorist financing or money laundering. Furthermore, some futures industry participants expressed concern that the price volatility of bitcoin presents too much risk to clearing-houses. Bitcoin is a non-central bank digital currency. It was invented in 2009 by an unknown programmer who used the pseudonym Satoshi Nakamoto. Initially bitcoins traded for a few cents per coin and by 2023 they increased in value to over $28,000 per coin but remained extremely volatile. Bitcoin is like electronic cash, but it has the added characteristic of permitting transactions to be anonymous. The Bank of International Settlement's *Committee on Payments and Market Infrastructures* identified three key characteristics of cryptocurrencies: they are electronic; are not the liability of anyone; and feature peer-to-peer exchange.

---

cised, the holder obtains a short futures position from the exchange clearinghouse. She must then liquidate her futures position in order to capture the full profit available to her at the time. Alternatively, she may choose to sell her option for a profit before the expiry month. She will profit from selling the option because its premium will rise when the price of gold falls.

Why Speculate in Futures and Options Contracts?

It was established in Chapter 1 that hedgers trade futures for commercial reasons to manage the impact of price risk on the profitability of their business. Futures markets exist primarily to facilitate hedger interests but the speculator is also very critical to the functioning of the market. The volume of futures and options trading has grown rapidly in recent years due to both growing hedger and speculative interest. It is a fast moving industry and it offers a speculator certain advantages that are not available in more conventional investments.

One of the most attractive aspects of futures trading for speculators is the high leverage ratio they are afforded because futures contracts are bought and sold on margin money. Leverage means that you need only commit a small amount of money in order to control a futures contract that is highly valuable. Most contracts may be purchased or sold with only ten percent or less of the total value of contract initially invested (initial margin money). For instance, the initial margin on a short or long Canadian dollar futures position may be $7,500. The market value of the position may be $75,000, so the initial margin represents only 10% of the value of the futures position.

Whereas a $10,000 investment in the stock market would control $10,000 worth of securities, the same $10,000 investment in the futures market could control $100,000 worth of commodities or financial instruments. A ten percent change in the value of a stock would affect an investor's account by ten percent. Alternatively, a ten percent change in the value of a futures contract would result in a 100 percent change in an investor's account! Contrary to popular belief, futures prices are no more volatile than stock market prices, but trading in futures is riskier because accounts are highly leveraged.

Futures and options are very liquid forms of investments compared to many alternatives. At the other end of the spectrum is real estate, for example, a highly illiquid investment. Futures and options contracts can be easily bought and sold on a daily basis and the highly standardized nature of futures contracts contributes to market liquidity. An exchange's clearinghouse guarantees each contract and there is essentially no risk of default for an investor.

For the most part, brokerage fees for the purchase and sale of a futures contract are very low compared to many other forms of investment. The typical brokerage fee to initiate and then subsequently liquidate (i.e., complete a round-turn) is approximately $30 to $50 per contract. This amount is insignificant compared to the transactions fees on other investments, such as real estate.

There is a very diverse set of contracts traded on futures and options markets which not only provide many different trading opportunities but also provide diversification possibilities for the investor. Another attractive aspect of futures and options trading is that an investor can profit from price declines as well as price increases. Speculators can take a short (sell) position in the futures market as easily as they can take a long (buy) position. Spread or straddles–going long in one contract and short in another–also provide a unique investment strategy for speculators.

Options on futures are attractive to investors for many of the same reasons. The buyer of an option is required to pay a premium to the seller and in return the buyer gets a pre-determined level of risk. The potential return is high but the risk exposure is relatively small as long as the premium isn't excessive. Limited risk is the major advantage associated with speculating in options rather than futures.

Given the generally high level of risk associated with a leveraged fu-

---

Box 2.3 Portfolio Diversification Benefits of Futures and Options

Commodity futures and options contracts are becoming more and more desirable as a class of financial assets for purposes of portfolio diversification. Specifically, an investment in a commodity futures index may offer the diversifying properties that investors seek to balance their exposure to stocks and bonds. Despite the popular perception that commodity futures are highly risky, research supports the claim that the benefits of investing in commodity futures may be positive even for the more risk-averse investor. Commodity futures indexes have demonstrated significant positive correlation with the rate of inflation as well as changes in the rate of inflation. However, the benefits of investing in commodity futures for diversification purposes will be different for different investors. The actual level of investment for a risk-averse investor will depend on the investor's level of risk tolerance, and current portfolio composition. For further reading, see Boal and Wiederhold (2021).

---

tures investment, it is important to appreciate the risk-return tradeoff in futures and the merits of diversification. A high expected return from holding a futures contract as a speculator is normally associated with a high level of risk. Speculators often run the risk of losing more than their initial investment. However, risk exposure can be reduced if a speculator spreads their investment among different commodities and financial instruments. Generally speaking, the larger the number of different commodities and instruments held in a portfolio, the lower the risk exposure. This is a major reason the commodity futures funds have become so popular for investors.

While reducing the exposure to risk by investing in more than one commodity or financial instrument, a speculator will not necessarily forego potential returns. This is particularly true if the futures contracts chosen for the portfolio do not follow similar price patterns. The fundamental basis for diversification rests on choosing investments that are not closely correlated. For example, a portfolio comprised of one silver contract and one soybean contract is less vulnerable to risk than a portfolio comprised of two silver contracts; although the two portfolios may yield a similar expected rate of return.

Combining stock market investments with futures and options investments can also attain the merits of diversification. For example, stock and commodity futures prices are often negatively correlated. Futures tend to be good inflationary hedges while common stocks tend to be poor inflationary hedges. Research has shown that diversification in the stock and futures market can lower portfolio risk without affecting the expected return.

Summary

This chapter has provided an overview of the main characteristics of futures and options contracts. Differences between futures and options contracts were emphasized and the mechanics of trading in these contracts were explained with several examples. A futures contract is very similar to either a deferred delivery contract or a forward contract, except that each futures contract is standardized and is traded on an organized exchange. Both the buyer and seller of a futures contract enter into a binding commitment to exchange commodities or financial instruments at an agreed price at some future date. The risk and rewards for the buyer and seller of futures contracts are symmetrical. Alternatively, options on futures give the buyer the right (but not the obligation) to either buy or sell a futures contract at a specified strike price at some future date. The seller of the option is obligated to deliver the underlying futures contract at the strike price, if the option is exercised by its holder. For options on futures, the risk and rewards for the buyer and seller are asymmetrical.

Futures and options contracts can be easily bought and sold on a daily basis and the highly standardized nature of futures contracts contributes to market liquidity. A call option specifies that the seller must deliver a long futures position to the option buyer, and a put option specifies delivery of a short futures position. The financial obligations involved in options trading are different from those in futures trading.

The important role of the exchange clearinghouse was also covered in this chapter, with examples of how the clearinghouse "marks to market" each trade at the end of each trading day. Trading on margin is an important characteristic of futures markets, is vital for the investor to fully understand, and therefore was explained in this chapter.

For the reader interested in online video introductory material see cmegroup.com/education.html.

Discussion Questions

1. Why did electronic trading replace the open-outcry system of trading? What are the pros and cons of the two alternative systems?

2. How does the clearinghouse ensure the financial integrity of futures and options trading?

3. Explain why the risks for buyers and sellers of futures contracts are

symmetrical.

4. Explain why the risks for buyers and sellers of options on futures are asymmetrical.

5. Explain how margin trading provides leverage to speculators in the futures market.

6. Why are futures and options contracts attractive as a diversified investment for some wealthy traders?

7. "Daily trading volume was higher than normal but open interest remained unchanged." Explain this statement and the conditions under which open interest rises, remains unchanged, or falls.

Selected References

Boal, Fiona, and Jim Wiederhold. 2021. "Rethinking commodities." *The Journal of Alternative Investments*, 24(1): 136–147.

3.

Commodities

Commodity futures markets serve a very important role in the global economy, facilitating the trading of a wide variety of goods including soft commodities like rice, coffee, soybeans, and orange juice and hard commodities like oil, copper, iron ore, and gold.[1] These futures markets establish the price of many basic industrial raw materials, minerals, and food products. Commodity prices typically benefit from economic growth because they serve as raw materials for such things as commercial buildings, housing, ship building, autos and electronic devices. It is important to note that the commodity futures markets often reflect global shifts in supply and demand before the general economy is even aware of such developments and before the general economy has fully adjusted to the economic news. By the time that international agencies (such as the International Monetary Fund) predict stronger global economic growth, the commodity markets have usually started to rally. For instance, if copper and iron ore futures prices are on the rise, this may be a sign of a stronger economy and inflation around the corner. The lumber futures market has already priced in housing starts statistics before the government releases the numbers.

Prices on some commodity markets, such as gold, are also sensitive to geo-political turmoil in distant parts of the world. In a similar vein, certain commodity markets are quick to respond to abnormal weather patterns, foretelling supply shifts. Commodity markets are also a barometer of sup-

---

[1]Hard commodities are natural resources that are mined or extracted. This category includes commodities such as gold, silver, copper, iron ore, aluminum and oil. The supply of hard commodities is typically not influenced by the weather. Alternatively "softs" or soft commodities are agricultural products or livestock such as corn, wheat, coffee, sugar, orange juice, cotton, soybeans and pork. Sometimes agricultural commodities produced in the tropics are classified as "softs." The supply of softs is very much influenced by weather fluctuations.

ply and demand shifts in emerging markets, like China, For instance, China is a large importer of commodities such as base metals and energy products. When China's economy slows down this fact is quickly picked up by commodity prices.

A fundamental economic contribution of commodity futures and options markets is their role as a vehicle to establish prices across time (i.e., inter-temporal prices). For example, on any given trading day, the CBOT (CME Group) corn futures market establishes prices for five different "maturity" months in a given calendar year–March (H), May (K), July (N), September (U), and December (Z). Soybean futures trade for seven different months–January (F), March (H), May (K), July (N), August (Q), September (U), and November (X). Alternatively, coffee trades the same contract months as corn: March (H), May (K), July (N), September (U), and December (Z).

The basic economics of commodity inter-temporal price relationships is examined in this chapter. We focus on understanding inter-temporal price relationships such as the price differential between May and September soybean futures on a given date, or between May and September coffee futures. Is the September futures price normally above the May price, and if so by how much? What economic factors influence the inter-temporal price spread over time? A **futures curve** is a plot of futures prices against the month of maturity. In the crude oil market, what does it mean for the anticipated direction of the spot price when the futures curve is inverted (i.e., downward sloping)? In this chapter, we will learn that the slope of the futures curve is one indicator of whether market participants believe that spot prices are going higher or lower.

As explained by Anson, Fabozzi and Jones (2010) commodities have the following characteristics:

- Commodities are *real* (i.e., tangible) assets, providing an effective hedge against inflation.

- Commodity prices vary with the business cycle, rising during periods of economic growth, and vice versa.

- Commodity prices are predominantly denominated in U.S. dollars when traded globally. Therefore, a depreciating U.S. dollar leads to an increase in commodity prices, while an appreciating dollar leads to a decrease in commodity prices.

- Commodities are not income-producing assets and do not yield an ongoing stream of cash flows. Instead commodity prices depend on supply and demand.

Box 3.1 What Are Commodities?

A **commodity** is a homogeneous (i.e., uniform) good that is indistinguishable from another good of the same type (e.g., gold is gold and any troy ounce of gold is not specialized based on the firm that mined it or the location of the mine). Typically commodities are raw materials or agricultural products with no product differentiation. Commodities are often used as inputs in the production of finished goods.

Today, many commodities are traded on exchanges through standardized contracts. The contract specification attaches no premium to any particular producer. Most agricultural products like raw (i.e., unrefined) sugar are a "commodity" product. A refiner or user of sugar perceives supplies from different locations (domestic or foreign) as being physically identical. In other words, there is infinite supply side substitutability–one supplier's raw sugar (e.g., Australia) is a perfect substitute for another's (e.g., Brazil).

For example, if a sugar exporter tried to raise their price, the sugar importer would refuse to pay the higher price because it could buy identical sugar from another supplier. The reason is that in a commodity market competition is primarily based on the price.

This chapter examines the price relationship between cash and futures prices. How well does the cash price for U.S. crude oil track the Brent crude oil futures price, the European benchmark price for oil? How does the cash price for corn in New Orleans (at point of export through the Gulf of Mexico) relate to the Chicago corn futures price? Does a supply or demand shock have an equal impact on the New Orleans cash price and the Chicago futures price? The difference between the Chicago futures price and the New Orleans cash price is called a **basis**, a price spread between the futures and cash markets.

Knowledge of inter-temporal commodity market price relationships is essential for a full understanding of how cash, futures, and options markets interact. It provides insight into market sentiment, the role of inventories and price expectations, and whether the market is in a bullish or bearish situation. There are three dimensions to commodity price relationships: time, space, and product form. This chapter focuses on the **time dimension** of commodity markets, because futures and options markets provide a time dimension to commodity prices. Alternatively, the **basis** relates to the spatial dimension of commodity markets (e.g., price difference between corn ready for export in New Orleans versus the price of corn on a farm in central Illinois) and this chapter devotes some attention to the basis.

Box 3.2 What is El Niño and how could it affect the price of my morning coffee?

A weather pattern known as El Niño is often a topic of conversation in commodity blogs as traders are constantly trying to determine if and when the next big El Niño is forming. There is no exact cycle to recurring El Niños because it is a weather event that begins with a slight warming of the oceans. It is not unusual for an El Niño to occur, but the interval between significant El Niño events is unpredictable. Peruvian fishermen first named this weather pattern after the baby Jesus. An El Niño is associated with warm and heavy rain around Christmas time in South America, East Africa, and the southern part of North America. El Niño affects the typical weather around the globe, causing some areas in Central and South America to be wetter, some parts of Africa, South-East Asia and Australia to be drier, some parts of North America and Asia warmer, and parts of Central America cooler.

There have been more than 15 El Niños observed since 1970 and the strongest El Niño on record occurred in 1998. The 1972 El Niño was also very strong and it dramatically reduced the anchovy catch off the coast of Peru. The Peruvian fish harvest dropped by over 60%. This loss of protein-rich animal feed raised prices for soybean meal and other animal feeds. Combined with poor weather that reduced harvests of many crops in different parts of the world, these events led to a notorious commodity boom characterized by prices for many commodities increasing by 100%, peaking in 1973. El Niño were also recorded in 2014-16 and 2018-19.

El Niño causes above normal rainfall in certain areas of the globe and below normal rainfall in other areas. This impacts agricultural commodities like coffee, cocoa, soybeans, corn, cotton, rice, and wheat. For instance, coffee traders are constantly watching the weather forecast as El Niño can affect coffee harvests in Brazil, Vietnam, and Indonesia. The potential for major weather changes from El Niño could also affect natural gas and electricity prices, and even the price of minerals if mining is disrupted due to flooding.

The law of one price captures much of the economic theory of intertemporal commodity prices, especially for storable commodities like wheat or crude oil. In general, the **law of one price** says that there is one price for a commodity, the cash price of the underlying product, and all other prices are related to that price through storage and transport costs. Storage costs reflect the time dimension and transport costs reflect the spatial dimension. If inter-temporal and spatial price relationships do not reflect storage and transport costs, this may provide an arbitrage opportunity for traders. **Arbitrage** describes trading to make a profit by exploiting price differences within a market. In reality, it is arbitrage that keeps cash and futures prices in line with one another. Although the law of one price is not always empirically supported for international markets, due to international trade barriers and unanticipated exchange rate fluctuations, it accurately describes the workings of domestic commodity markets for storable commodities where arbitrage is less costly and therefore more effective. For instance, the price of gasoline in San Francisco is highly correlated with the price in Los Angeles due to arbitrage. The gasoline price in San Francisco is also correlated with the price in New York City, but the relationship is not as strong as between San Francisco and Los Angeles because arbitrage is more difficult when the spatial distance is 2,900 miles versus 380 miles. Furthermore, the state of California has very strict gasoline formulation rules for environmental reasons, and the extra costs associated with producing specially blended gasoline for the California market can also affect the price spread between California and other states that do not have such environmental requiremments.

The **price of storage** theory is consistent with the law of one price. In the discussion that follows, the price of storage theory is used to explain the pattern of inter-temporal price relationships among futures contracts for storable commodities. The price of storage theory predicts that inter-temporal price relationships are determined by the net cost of carrying inventory. For example, the theory suggests that in the presence of adequate supplies, the price of a futures contract for December delivery tends to be the price for October delivery plus the net cost of storing the commodity from October to December. This means that the futures price for any delivery month is equal to the current spot price plus the cost of storage.

As mentioned above, the basis is the linkage between cash and futures prices. Since there are numerous cash markets for any one futures market, there are numerous bases in any market. For every cash market, there is a unique basis associated with that market. If we consider corn, for example, there is a specific basis for Stockton California, Portland Oregon, New Orleans Louisiana, Central Illinois, Central Kansas, etc. From the hedger's perspective, the basis is one of the most important factors associated with cash, futures, and options markets. Inter-temporal price relationships are integrated into a simple spatial equilibrium model in this chapter, to help illustrate the important role of supply and demand for commodity storage in determining inter-temporal price spreads.

Understanding the economics of storage goes a long way towards understanding inter-temporal price relationships in futures markets. Various futures exchanges set maximum monthly storage rates and these rates give some indication of the full costs of storage. For instance, there are maximum storage rates set by the Chicago Mercantile Exchange (CME) and they apply to those who own grain (through purchasing a futures contract) that is in storage in a warehouse licensed by the CME. From Table 3.1 we see that these rates range from 7.95¢/bu. per month for soybeans to 12.6¢/cwt per month for rice—note that rice storage rates are per hundredweight (cwt), and per bushel (bu.) for soybeans. The storage rate for wheat was 8.25¢/bu. for most of 2014 and 2015, however this rate does change if the futures price spread increases to a certain threshold.[2] For instance, from September 2014 to March 2015, the maximum wheat storage rate was increased to 13.25¢/bu. In 2023 the rate was 5¢/bu. per month for wheat.

Table 3.1: CME Monthly Grain Storage Fees

Commodity	¢ per month
Corn	7.95¢ per bu.
Rice	12.6¢ per cwt
Soybeans	7.95¢ per bu.
Wheat	5.00-13.25¢ per bu.

Source: Chicago Mercantile Exchange Rulebook. http://www.cmegroup.com/rulebook/CBOT/ Note: Storage rates are not to exceed above rates, except for wheat which is subject to variable storage rate (VSR) mechanism.

Futures Contract Price Patterns over Time

For any futures contract, trading is conducted simultaneously for different delivery (or expiry) months. For example, Table 3.2 reports a sample of prices for alternative soybean futures contracts traded on the CME Group's Chicago Board of Trade (CBOT). These prices were recorded in March. The price for the nearby delivery month (March) is $10.57 per bushel and prices for the three subsequent delivery months are progressively higher. The U.S. soybean harvest normally begins in September and therefore September futures is a *new crop* contract. The distant September contract price is $10.52, and specifying delivery after harvest. The *old crop* year is separated from the new crop year by the annual harvest.

---

[2]The Variable Storage Rates (VSR) system for Chicago wheat futures was introduced in 2010. The VSR is the maximum allowable storage charges for outstanding wheat shipping certificates. VSRs increase above 5¢/bu. per month when inter-termporal wheat price spreads are near financial full carry.

Table 3.2: Delivery Months and Futures Prices for CBOT Soybean Futures Contracts

Crop Year	Delivery Month	Futures Price ($/bu)
Old	March (nearby month)	10.57
Old	May	10.68
Old	July	10.76
Old	August	10.77
New	September	10.52
New	November	10.38
New	January	10.41
New	March (distant month)	10.37

In Table 3.2, the inter-temporal price relationship for the "old" crop (nearby March through August) is in **contango**, a situation where futures prices are progressively higher for the more distant delivery months. Alternatively, the inter-temporal price relationships between the near (old crop) contracts and the distant (new crop) September and November contract represent an **inverted market** (or **backwardation**), as the nearer months are trading at price premiums to the more distant month. Specifically, July soybeans are trading at $10.76, a 38¢ per bushel premium over the more distant November price of $10.38 per bushel. Thus we can say that the July—November price spread is inverted. In addition, the old March—new November and old May—new November price relationships are also inverted. A contango is a more normal inter-temporal price relationship for storable commodities, although inverted markets are not uncommon, especially when there is a supply shortage.

In late 2011, the crude oil market entered into an unusual situation where the WTI crude oil futures curve was in contango, exhibiting steadily increasing prices at more distant delivery months, but, at the same time, the Brent crude oil futures curve, the European benchmark, was inverted. That is, Brent crude oil futures prices were declining for delivery months further in the future. The Brent benchmark was in backwardation in 2011 apparently due to the Libyan revolution at the time, causing Europeans to pay a premium for immediate delivery of oil. The same relationships occurred in 2017, with Brent in backwardation (i.e., downward sloping futures curve) and WTI in contango (i.e., upward sloping futures curve), however the discrepancy in 2017 was only for a very short time period. Both markets were in contango from January to September 2017, then they both moved into backwardation, with Brent moving from contango into backwardation a few weeks before WTI followed suit.

The 2023 Brent futures curve is shown in Figure 3.1. The nearby July futures was just over $85/barrel and the futures calling for delivery in 12 months time was trading at $78/barrel, with the spread was close to negative $7/barrel. At the time, Saudi Arabia was cutting back on production and the backwardation in the market was reflecting the temporary shortage of oil due to OPEC cutbacks.

Figure 3.1: Brent (CB) Futures Curve

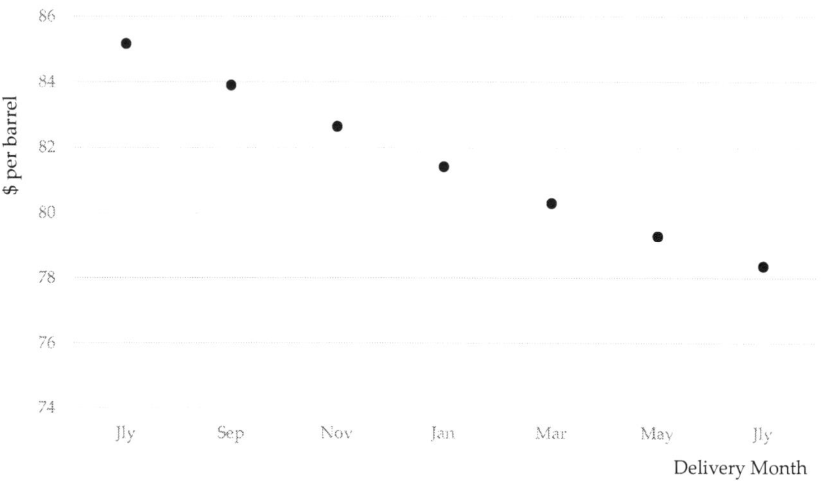

Source: Bloomberg.

In contrast the lumber futures curve is shown in Figure 3.2, representing a more normal situation with a market in contango. In Figure 3.2 nearby lumber futures are approximately $500 per thousand board feet, with the price one year forward at about $560, so the one year spread is about $60 per thousand board feet. From Figure 3.2 and Figure 3.1 we conclude there was an abundance of lumber in the market and at the same time tight supplies of crude oil in the North Sea (Brent). The lumber market was over-supplied as the construction industry was slowing down due to high interest rates and recession fears. The backwardation in Brent was signaling that the market needed the oil immediately and it would not pay for storage–in other words the market was telling traders not to store oil because nearby demand was strong relative to nearby supplies. Those holding physical crude in storage were being encouraged to sell barrels into the market because the negative returns to storage meant it would be unprofitable to keep the inventories. If they sold immediately they would earn a price premium. At the time we could interpret the backwardation as a sign that the market was fundamentally bullish. The data in 2023 reported that stocks in the North

Sea region were being drawn down due to the backwardation. At the time OPEC introduced production cuts in order to try and raise oil prices.

Figure 3.2: Lumber Futures Curve

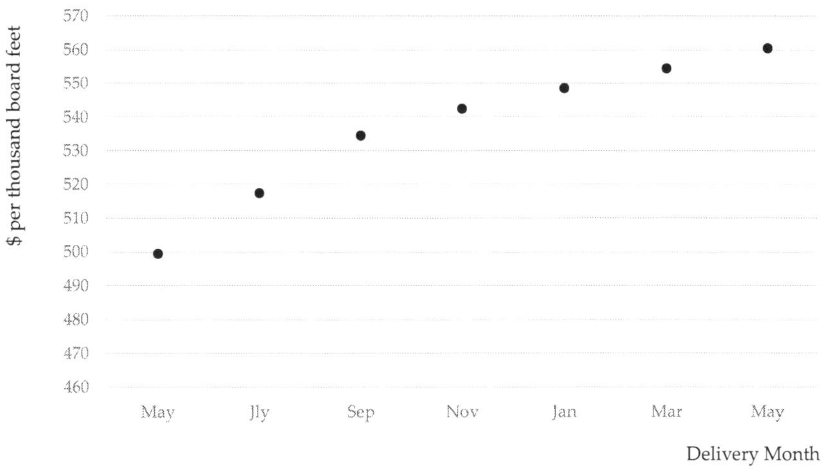

Source: Bloomberg.

Futures price patterns can be analyzed as relationships among contracts at a specific point in time (e.g., the November-January-March soybean price spreads as reported in Table 3.2) or as price changes of a specific futures contract over time (e.g., the behavior of January soybean futures prices over time). Typically, backwardation signals a shortage, while contango signals that there are adequate supplies of the commodity. This means that the slope of the futures curve is very informative. A curve in contango suggests a weak market and backwardation suggests a strong market.

The inter-temporal price pattern expected for a specific commodity is at least partially dependent on whether the commodity is classified as storable or nonstorable. Gold, silver, sugar, soybeans, wheat, corn, cotton, crude oil, heating oil, ethanol, and coffee are examples of storable commodities. Alternatively, electricity, live cattle, feeder cattle, and lean hogs are examples of nonstorable futures commodities. Storable contracts are in contango under normal conditions, reflecting the cost of storage. In contrast, nonstorables do not have a "normal" shape to the futures curve because different maturity months are not connected through storage.

Prices Between Time Periods for a Storable Commodity

Consider a simple economic model for allocating a storable commodity between two time periods–the present time period and a future time period.

Suppose the present time period is the summer season and the future time period is the winter season. In this example, the commodity is assumed to be heating oil, but the model can be applied to a broad range of storable commodities. Heating oil is refined from crude oil and is very similar to diesel. A barrel of crude oil typically yields about 20 percent fuel oil (i.e., diesel or heating oil). The demand for heating oil is highly seasonal because there is a large demand for use in furnaces to heat homes in the northeastern United States during the winter months. Heating oil is also used in large industrial furnaces to heat commercial buildings. As an interesting side note, heating oil prices are highly correlated with jet fuel prices and this allows airlines to use heating oil futures to manage price risk because there are no exchange traded futures contracts for jet fuel.

Figure 3.3: Heating Oil Price Relationship Between Two Time Periods

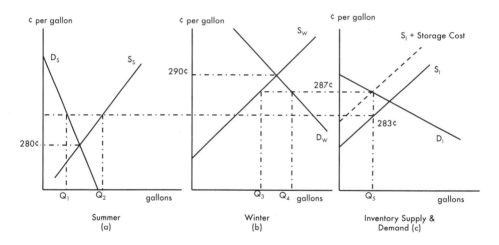

Assume that each of the two time periods (i.e., summer and winter) has a unique demand and supply curve (presented in Figure 3.3). The summer demand (D_S) and supply (S_S) schedules are known with certainty, and the winter demand (D_W) and supply (S_W) schedules are based on market expectations of what lies ahead for the upcoming winter months. The demand curve is a schedule indicating the quantity demanded of the commodity at each price level. Along the demand curve, only the commodity's price and the quantity demanded are allowed to change; all other factors such as income, expected winter weather patterns, and prices of other goods are assumed to remain constant. The supply curves in Figure 3.3 are assumed to be short-run supply curves, which imply that all factors of production are assumed variable except for industry capacity. The summer and winter supply curves are a summation of the supply curves for all firms producing heating oil. Each firm's supply curve is equal to the portion of its marginal cost curve at or above the minimum of the average variable cost curve.

A commodity such as heating oil will be stored from the summer into the winter as long as there is an economic incentive to store. One strong incentive that encourages storage is a price differential between the two time periods, a higher price in the winter. With the model presented in Figure 3.3, in order for storage to take place, a price differential must exist between the two periods that is sufficient to pay for full storage costs. Suppose at prevailing prices there is *excess supply* in the summer and *excess demand* in the winter. These conditions will generate a price differential between the winter and summer that will provide an incentive to store heating oil.

Figure 3.3 can be used to show that as long as storage costs are positive, then the price in the winter season must be higher than the price in summer season, if storage is to occur. The equilibrium cash price without storage is assumed to be $2.80 per gallon in the summer and $2.90 in the winter (Figure 3.3, panels (a) and (b)). The equilibrium price for each season (i.e., 280¢ in the summer and 290¢ in the winter) is determined by the intersection of the respective supply and demand curves. For example in panel (a)–the summer season–the intersection of D_S and S_S results in an equilibrium price of 280¢, in the absence of storage. In other words, if the market cleared in the summer season and there was no heating oil held in inventory at the end of summer, then the summer price would be 280¢ per gallon. In this case, no inventories would be carried into the winter season.

Given the 10¢ per gallon price differential between the winter and summer price, without storage, this condition indicates a "potential" case in which storage will occur. The term "potential" is used here because storage costs in relation to the price differential will determine if storage actually occurs. If full storage costs are less than the 10¢ price differential between the two seasons, storage is undertaken; otherwise, no economic incentive for storage exists.

Inventory Supply

In this simple model, how many gallons of heating oil will be stored from summer to winter and what is the equilibrium price spread between summer and winter? Even if storage costs were zero, all summer production would be sold during that season if the price of heating oil were expected to be equal to or below 280¢ per gallon in the winter. Demand during the summer is large enough to ensure that all summer production would be utilized in the summer if the summer price is 280¢ or less.

The potential inventory supply (S_I in panel (c)), before storage costs, is implicit in panel (a) of Figure 3.3, because the summer period is the most likely period to have excess supply that could be placed into storage. Demand for heating oil is relatively low in the summer, as shown by the positioning of D_S relative to D_W. The inventory supply schedule (S_I) is equal to the summer quantity supplied (S_S) minus the summer quantity demanded (D_S) at any price above 280¢ as shown in panel (c), as schedule S_I. If the price increases during the summer, the quantity demanded by consumers decreases and the quantity supplied by producers increases, so S_I is upward sloping.

Inventory Demand

Winter's heating oil inventory demand schedule (D_I) is determined relative to the equilibrium market price in the winter. For prices at or above 290¢ per gallon, the quantity supplied by producers in the winter is sufficient to meet demand during that season (Figure 3.3(b)). Inventory demand (D_I in panel (c)) equals winter quantity demanded (D_W) minus winter quantity supplied (S_W) at prices below 290¢ per gallon.

Inventory carried from the summer into the winter will result in lower prices in the winter, compared to a situation where no stocks are carried into the winter season. If prices decrease in the winter, consumers increase their quantity demanded and producers decrease their quantity supplied, *ceteris paribus*. As a result, inventory demand (D_I) is drawn as downward sloping in panel (c), because the lower the market price in winter, the greater the demand for inventory carried from the summer to the winter. Inventory demand is not simply the portion of the demand curve below the equilibrium price without storage; rather it is the horizontal difference between winter demand and supply in Figure 3.3, panel (b).

Storage costs

Positive storage costs are made up of the cost of operating physical storage facilities plus interest, insurance, and other expenses. Assume storage costs between the two time periods is equal to 4¢ per gallon of heating oil, independent of the quantity stored. In Figure 3.3 this is represented by a parallel upward shift in the inventory supply curve, S_I, to the dashed line denoted as S_I + Storage Cost (Figure 3.3(c)). These storage costs must be paid (through the market price) to reward those merchants who are willing to hold inventory from the summer until the winter.

The quantity of heating oil stored from summer to winter is indicated by the intersection of the inventory demand curve (D_I) and the inventory supply plus storage cost curve (S_I + Storage Cost in panel (c)). The equilibrium quantity stored from summer to winter is shown as Q_5 in panel (c), Figure 3.3. The price paid by consumers in the winter is 287¢, while

Figure 3.4: Change in Heating Oil Price Relationship After Forecast of Cold Weather

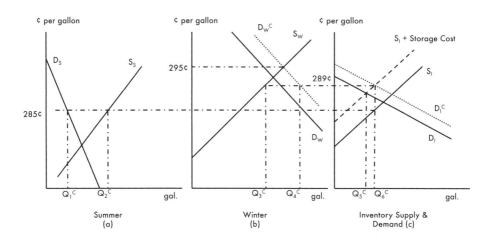

summer producers receive 283¢ (287¢ minus the 4¢ storage cost, which is captured by the merchants providing the storage services).

The storage activity links market clearing prices in the two seasons and therefore changes in the summer and winter heating oil prices will be highly correlated from day-to-day. This linkage becomes clear if there is an exogenous shock that shifts the demand or supply function in either season. Prices in both seasons will move in the same direction in reaction to such a shock. For instance, if OPEC countries agree to cut production, this would be a supply side shock that would drive prices higher in both seasons. Of course, this inter-temporal price relationship breaks down if the two seasons are not linked through storage.

No storage occurs between the two time periods in Figure 3.3 if storage costs exceed 10¢ per gallon. If storage costs were sufficiently high to preclude storage between two time periods, then lower correlations between prices for the different time periods would be expected. In other words, price changes in one time period would not be readily reflected in another time period.

To illustrate the effects of a potential market shock, refer to Figure 3.4 and suppose that during the summer there is a change in market expectations with a surprise weather forecast of an unusually cold winter ahead. The expectation of a very cold winter will shift demand in the winter (D_W) to a higher level, and of course the higher demand will raise expected prices in the winter. Suppose the demand curve in the winter period shifts upward to the dashed line D_W^C (in panel (b) of figure 3.4). If storage takes place, the new weather forecast would shift the inventory demand curve (D_I) rightward in panel (c) to D_I^C, expanding the volume of storage and resulting in a winter price of 289¢. The winter price increases from the 287¢ level in Figure 3.3, but the expanded volume of storage dampens the extent of this price rise.

Suppose the volume of storage expands from Q_5^C to Q_6^C in panel (c). This higher level of stocks takes additional heating oil off the market in the summer and places it into storage for use in the winter. So the heating oil price in the summer will also increase to 285¢ from the 283¢ level shown in Figure 3.3.

Using a simple two time period example, this section has demonstrated how the supply and demand for storage connects inter-temporal commodity prices and helps explain how a supply and/or demand shift in any time period can influence equilibrium prices, price spreads, and level of inventories. If the demand and/or supply in the next period shifts up or down, that market development will influence not only prices, but also supply, demand, and inventories in the current time period. Heating oil was used an an example but this framework is a good way to think of how prices, price spreads, and inventories behave in any storable commodity market.

Temporal Prices Within a Single Production Period

The previous discussion assumed two distinct production periods while describing the market linkage effects of carrying inventory between the two time periods. There was production in both the summer and winter seasons, and, of course, there was also consumption (utilization) in each season. However, an alternative temporal allocation situation exists within a single production period. For many agricultural crops there is only one harvest each year. The quantity supplied for a single season is fixed, based on current production plus inventories carried forward from the previous season. For example, grain markets (such as corn) have a relatively short harvest period (September-November in the Northern Hemisphere), but inventories are used and therefore drawn down throughout the year, until the next harvest.

Figure 3.5 depicts an expected price pattern within a single season for a commodity with a short and single harvest. The solid line in Figure 3.5 shows the expected path of the cash price over the "crop year." For agricultural commodities, a crop year (or marketing year) is a period from one year's harvest to the next. The lowest cash price occurs during harvest (August, in this example). Steadily increasing cash prices are expected until additional production becomes available during the next harvest period. This is a fairly typical seasonal cash price pattern for commodities. A sea-

Figure 3.5: Futures and Cash Price Pattern for a Storable Agricultural Commodity with Seasonal Production

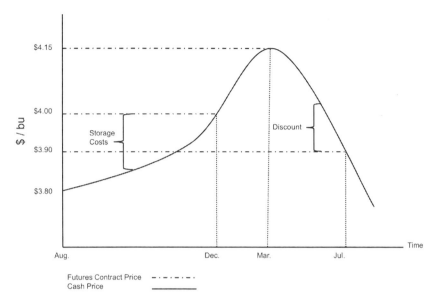

sonal pattern is any systematic fluctuation in prices within the marketing (or crop) year.

Figure 3.5 is drawn to depict the expected pattern of cash and futures prices, as of one point in time (i.e., in August). The cash price in Figure 3.5 is for the same location as specified in the futures contract. If the harvest was just completed, then Figure 3.5 captures the market's expectation of how the cash price will most likely behave over the full 12 months of the marketing year until the next harvest. Assume futures contract prices provide an accurate forecast of forthcoming cash prices. Also, assume that no "new" information becomes available which would alter the price forecasts–in other words, Figure 3.5 is a single "snapshot" in time of how the market expects the cash price to unfold over the marketing season. In addition to cash prices, the figure also shows futures prices. The futures prices in Figure 3.5 are represented as horizontal dashed lines. If the cash price were expected to rise from $3.80 in August to $4.15 by March, then the current March futures price would equal $4.15, and so on.

Convergence of the cash and futures contract prices in Figure 3.5 results from declining storage costs as the delivery month approaches. Storage costs are largely a function of time and the time factor becomes less and less important as the delivery month approaches. This means that futures and cash prices will be identical at the time of futures contract expiry. Situations where the cash and futures do not fully converge are explained later in this chapter.

Given that Figure 3.5 is a snapshot in time, the "expected" March futures contract price is constant, while the "expected" cash price increases from $3.80 in August to $4.15 by the following March. Futures contract prices therefore reflect expected cash price changes. On the other hand, when new information does come into the market (as it surely will), then the snapshot of prices changes and the entire spectrum of prices in Figure 3.5 will move up or down simultaneously with changing expectations. All prices in Figure 3.5 move up if the new information is **bullish**, prices are expected to rise, and they all move down if the news is **bearish**, prices are expected to fall.

If prices for futures contracts with later maturity dates are higher than prices for those contracts with nearer maturity dates, this typical inter-temporal price pattern is referred to as a positive carrying charge market, or a **contango**, as discussed above. The difference between the prices of alternative contracts indicates what the market is willing to pay inventory holders for storing the commodity: the price of storage. For example, referring to Figure 3.5, an inventory holder would expect to receive 15¢ per bushel ($4.15-$4.00=$0.15) for carrying stocks from December to March, an amount equal to the carrying charge reflected in the spectrum of futures prices.

If the price for contracts with more distant delivery dates is lower than that for contracts expiring earlier, the market is **inverted** or in backwarda-tion. As shown in Figure 3.5, the inventory holder would expect to suffer a 25¢ per bushel loss ($3.90-$4.15= -$0.25) between the March and July contract delivery dates. There is an economic incentive to deliver the commodity immediately (rather than store it) when a "negative" price for storage exists. Normally an inverted market arises when there is a relatively low carryover of stocks (and a normal harvest or production year coming up) or, alternatively, when there is a temporary shortage of stocks in a position to be delivered against futures contracts.

Inverted Carrying Charge Markets and Normal Backwardation

Actual price patterns between futures contracts and expected cash prices may deviate considerably from the theoretical patterns described in the previous section. Consider the inter-temporal price spreads for Brent crude shown in Table 3.3. Brent crude oil is a grade of light, sweet crude oil sourced in the North Sea that serves as the world benchmark for oil prices. On August 17, 2011, the closing price for the December 2011 Brent futures contract ($108.66) was 70¢ higher than the May 2012 futures contract price of $107.96 (Table 3.3). This inter-temporal price relationship indicates a tight

Table 3.3: Examples of Positive and Negative Inter-Temporal Carrying Charge Markets, NYMEX/ICE

Delivery Month	WTI Crude Oil, Positive Carry-on August 17, 2011 ($/bbl.)	Brent Crude Oil, Negative Carry-on August 17, 2011 ($/bbl.)
Dec. 2011	$87.58	$108.66
March 2012	$88.90	$108.02
May 2012	$90.23	$107.96

supply in the Brent market. The spread between the December and March futures was a negative 64¢ per bbl. At the time, the market was not paying a return for storage of Brent crude oil, and the market signal this sends to inventory holders is to sell in the spot market rather than carry Brent forward.

One explanation for the inversion in Brent crude shown in Table 3.3 is a temporary shortage of deliverable stocks, which would push up the nearby futures price relative to the distant contract prices. Traders with short positions would be unable to obtain stocks to deliver and therefore would be forced to bid up the price of the nearby contract in order to offset (or cover) their open short positions.

Another possible explanation of a market inversion is that the volume of trade in the distant months is relatively low–a thin market situation (see Box 3.3). In a **thin market**, a relatively large **risk premium** might explain the inversion. There might be an imbalance in the supply and demand for futures contracts and a shortage of speculators willing to hold long futures positions. While the Brent market is very active and is unlikely to experience inversion due to a thin market, low volumes are more likely for less active commodities like ethanol futures. In this case, long speculators would earn a financial reward (i.e., the risk premium) for holding futures contracts. To summarize, if the cash or nearby futures contract price is higher than prices for futures contracts with later delivery dates, then this is an inverted market. The market is not paying for storage, and this is reflected in the negative price difference when the nearer futures price is subtracted from the more distant futures price.

Refer again to the set of inter-temporal prices, shown in Table 3.3, for WTI and Brent crude oil futures on the NYMEX and ICE. A positive carry of $1.32 per bbl. existed between the December 2011 and March 2012 WTI crude oil contracts. Is this a "sufficient" price for storing crude oil over a three month time period? Along with insurance and warehousing charges, interest expense is a major cost in carrying inventory. An estimate of the in-

---

Box 3.3 Thin Markets

A thin market is synonymous with an inactive or illiquid market; a market where the volume of trading is small. In a thin market there are relatively few transactions per unit of time, and price fluctuations are high relative to the volume of trade. Since a small number of transactions establishes prices, this often results in large price swings. In financial markets, liquidity may be measured by the bid–ask spread (i.e., the amount by which the ask price exceeds the bid price), with a larger spread indicating market thinness. Actual market prices in a thin market may be biased indicators of the true supply and demand situation. Thin markets create liquidity risk–the inability to buy or sell an asset quickly with little or no price change from a previous transaction, assuming no new information has come into the market. As an example, the international rice market is often characterized as being a thin market because only a small portion (about 10%) of the total annual global production of rice is traded on the world market. In contrast, about 25% of the world's wheat supply is traded in any given year and this market is considered to be liquid.

---

terest expense can be calculated by multiplying the March futures contract price by the annual prime interest rate. The result is then multiplied by the fraction of a year the oil would be in storage. Using a prime interest rate of 5%, the interest component of the cost of carry would then be about 26¢ per barrel per month, (78¢ ≈ .05 × 3/12 × $88.90), or 78¢ from December to March. Therefore, the price spread shown in Table 3.3 seems sufficient to compensate the inventory holder, assuming the non-interest expenses did not exceed 18¢ per barrel per month, and it is doubtful that these other costs would push the total storage costs above 44¢ per month.

Even when a positive carrying charge exists, the price differences between futures contracts may be insufficient to cover all storage costs. Arbitrage opportunities would exist for oil traders if the carrying charge between futures contracts exceeded the storage costs; hence, storage costs typically represent the maximum price difference between delivery months that will be observed in an efficient market. However, there is no corresponding limit to the size of an inversion in the market.

When positive carry markets have price differences between the contracts that are insufficient to cover full costs of storage, this can be explained by the **theory of normal backwardation**. It says that hedgers must compensate speculators for assuming the price risk associated with holding futures contracts. However, the fact that storage occurs when negative carrying charge markets exist (such as the Brent oil example previously), continues to be a controversial economic phenomenon with alternative explanations. One possible explanation (not mentioned before) is that when current inventories are abnormally low, merchants are willing to hold inventories in the presence of an inverted market because the stocks provide a type of convenience yield. Convenience yield is best explained with an analogy. A **convenience yield** is a negative cost, hence the term yield which implies a return to the owner of inventory derived from the flow of services yielded by a unit of inventory over a given time period. The analogy is a person who walks around with large sums of cash in their pocket. Let's assume that this individual does not have a credit card. This may seem irrational because the individual is not earning interest on that money in his pocket and if he were rational he would keep the money in the bank rather than in his pocket. However, the cash on-hand may provide a convenience yield to the individual because it saves him the inconvenience of running back and forth to the bank. He may also encounter a situation where he needs a large sum of cash and foregoing the interest paid by the bank may be worthwhile. Cash in the pocketbook yields a flow of services not obtainable from money sitting in a bank account–hence there is a liquidity premium for holding money.

Theories of Inter-Temporal Prices: Storable Commodities

Over the years, economists have strived to explain inter-temporal price spreads in commodity markets. Some very famous economists examined this question. John Maynard Keynes (1923) is credited with the theory of normal backwardation, which emphasizes the financial burden posed by the necessity of carrying inventories, and he suggested futures markets exist to facilitate hedging. On the other hand, Holbrook Working (1949) promoted the idea that the primary function of futures markets is the provision of returns for storage services. The two theories of Keynes and Working are considered the most important contributions to the theoretical understanding of inter-temporal price spreads in commodity futures markets.

Theory of Normal Backwardation

The equilibrium futures price in relation to the expected spot price at expiry can be characterized by examining the net positions of hedgers and speculators. As discussed in Chapter 1, commercial hedgers are interested in entering into futures contracts in order to eliminate price risk. Commercial hedgers are typically net short indicating that at any given futures price, hedgers as a group want to sell more contracts than they want to buy as illustrated by the line WX in the left quadrant in Figure 3.6. The higher the futures price the more contracts they want to sell, and hence WX is downward sloping.

Speculators have no interest in entering into futures contracts as a way to reduce risk, instead they enter into futures contracts with the goal of profiting from expected price movements. When the futures price is equal to the expected spot price at expiry, E, speculators as a group will be neither short nor long as there is no potential profit since the expected price change in the futures contract is zero. When the futures price is below the expected spot price at expiry, (the right hand portion of the line YZ in Figure 3.6) speculators will be net long as they anticipate earning a profit from the expected increase in the futures price. Similarly, when the futures price is above the spot price "expected" at expiry, speculators as a group will want to be net short. This is shown by the top portion of the line YZ in Figure 3.6.

Figure 3.6: Net Hedger and Speculator Positions

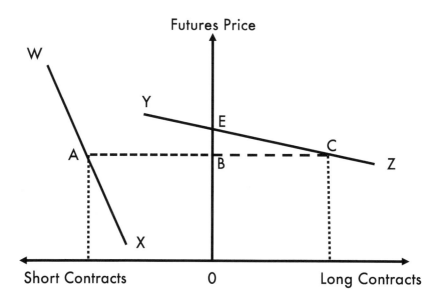

Source: Adapted from Hans Stoll. *Journal of Financial and Quantitative Analysis*, 14 (4) (1979), pp. 873-894.

The futures market will clear only when the total number of short contacts equals the number of long contracts. This market clearing condition along with the net short position of hedgers leads to the futures price equilibrium, B, at a price below the expected spot price (E) at expiry. In Figure 3.6, we can see that the equilibrium futures price is at point B and the volume of contracts represented by the net hedgers position, A, equals the speculators net long position, C.

In the view of John Keynes, futures prices are unreliable estimates of the cash price prevailing on the date of expiration of the futures contract. He believed it "normal" for the futures price to be a downward-biased estimate of the forthcoming spot price. This theory, in effect, argues that speculators sell "insurance" to hedgers and that the market is "normally" information-ally inefficient because the futures price is a biased estimate of the subsequent spot price.

The three critical assumptions of the theory of normal backwardation are: that speculators are net long, they are risk averse (i.e., they require positive expected profits to hold futures positions), and they are unable to forecast prices (i.e., all their profits can be viewed as a reward for risk bearing). Given these assumptions, two major implications are associated with the theory. The first is that over time speculators can earn profits by merely holding long positions in futures markets. The second implication is that there is an upward trend in futures prices, relative to spot prices, as the contract approaches maturity.

A graphical presentation of the **theory of normal backwardation** is presented in Figure 3.7. On the horizontal axis is the number of days until the first day of delivery for a specific futures contract (moving from left to right). The futures contract price and the cash price both converge to $4.00 on the delivery day in this example. In this example the cash price is for the same location as the futures delivery location. Assume full carrying costs are 10 cents per bushel for storing the commodity 100 days until delivery. This would imply a cash price of $3.90, 100 days out from delivery. If hedgers initially sell futures contracts to speculators (i.e., speculators are net long) , it is implied that speculators must later sell these contracts to offset their original long position. For speculators to profit from this transaction, the expectation must be that futures contract prices will increase, because they are holding long positions. For speculators to earn this compensation consistently with rising futures prices, a risk premium must exist. The risk premium would result in a reduction in the initial prices that speculators pay to purchase a futures contract from hedgers. For example, assuming the risk premium is 5 cents on day 100, the actual futures contract price would be only $3.95 rather than $4.00. The expected cash price upon delivery is $4.00, but the futures price trades for only $3.95 (100 days prior to delivery) because if speculators paid $4.00 their expected profit would be zero. For further discussion of futures risk premium see Carter and Revoredo-Giha (2023).

Figure 3.7: Backwardation and Risk Premiums in a Futures Contract Price

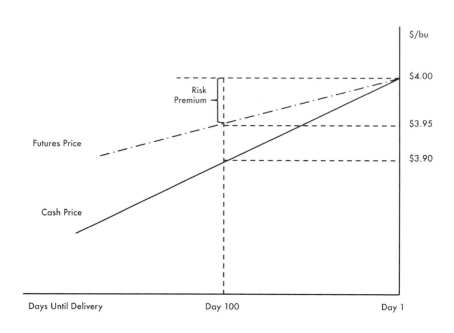

Theory of the Price of Storage

An important theoretical extension of the theory of normal backwardation was presented by Holbrook Working (1949). His theory was critical of the view that futures markets existed solely for the purposes of transferring risk from the hedger to the speculator. Additionally, he criticized the view that the cash and futures markets are autonomous. Working's theory of the price of storage hypothesized that inter-temporal price relationships are determined by the net cost of carrying stocks.

It should be noted that the *theory of price of storage* and the *theory of normal backwardation* are not mutually exclusive as the former adopted Keynes' notion of a risk premium as one component of the cost of holding stocks. However, the relative importance of the risk premium is greatly reduced by the theory of price of storage.

The theory of storage refers to the demand and supply of commodities as inventories. The term "storage" does not refer to the amount of available storage capacity or the price charged for such storage. Rather "storage" refers to the level of inventories.

According to the theory of the price of storage, the equilibrium relationship between the futures price and the spot price is as follows:

$$F_{t,T} = S_t \left(1 + r_{t,T}\right) + w_{t,T} + c_{t,T} \tag{3.1}$$

Where $F_{t,T}$ is the futures price at time t for delivery at a future time T, S_t is the spot price at time t, $r_{t,T}$ is the opportunity cost of tying up funds to finance inventory from time t through time T (i.e., the financing cost), $w_{t,T}$ is the total cost of carrying the inventory (i.e., warehouse costs, insurance, spoilage, etc), and $c_{t,T}$ is the convenience yield over the time interval t through T. Recall that convenience yield is the benefit associated with holding the underlying physical good, rather than holding a futures contract. If the equality in equation (3.1) is not satisfied (i.e., if $F_{t,T} > S_t(1 + r_{t,T}) + w_{t,T} + c_{t,T}$), then an arbitrage opportunity exists for merchants who are in a position to buy and hold inventory.

If a situation arises where $F_{t,T} < S_t(1 + r_{t,T}) + w_{t,T}$, then the theory suggests that the futures price contains an implicit convenience yield ($c_{t,T}$). Rewriting equation (3.1) provides a definition of convenience yield, a negative cost:

$$c_{t,T} = S_t \left(1 + r_{t,T}\right) + w_{t,T} - F_{t,T} \tag{3.2}$$

Working's theory predicts that the marginal convenience yield is decreasing in aggregate inventory and approaches zero for high inventory levels.

Fama and French (1987) found that marginal convenience yield varies seasonally for most agricultural commodities, but not for metals. Brennan, Williams and Wright (1997) studied precious metals, oil, lumber and plywood futures and they provided evidence that the convenience yield is inversely related to the level of inventories.

Fama and French (1987) argued that

> "there are two popular views of commodity futures prices. The theory of storage explains the difference between contemporaneous spot and futures prices in terms of foregone interest in storing a commodity, warehousing costs, and a convenience yield in inventory. The alternative view splits a futures price into an expected risk premium and a forecast of a future spot price. The theory of storage is not controversial."

The Formal Theory of The Price of Storage

We now turn to a complete and formal model of the theory of price of storage. The purpose of this section is to show that inter-temporal price spreads (e.g., the difference between the price of May wheat futures and the January cash price, during the month of January) are related to the level of stocks (i.e., inventories) that are carried from one period to the next (e.g., carried from January to May). This section demonstrates that the inter-temporal price spread is a market-determined price of storage that can be positive or negative. Normally, demanders of a commodity require a continuous quantity supplied throughout the year even though production may be seasonal and occur only once during the year. In this case, the (inverse) demand for a commodity in period t can be written as a function of consumption in period t (Brennan, 1958):

$$P_t = f_t(C_t) \tag{3.3}$$

where

$\partial f_t / \partial C_t = f'_t(C_t) < 0,$

P_t = price in period t, and

C_t = consumption in period t.

The total supply available in period t equals beginning stocks (S_{t-1}) plus quantity produced (X_t). Therefore, consumption in period t can be expressed as total supply available minus ending stocks (S_t). Equation (3.3) can be rewritten as:

$$P_t = f_t(S_{t-1} + X_t - S_t) \tag{3.4}$$

where

S_{t-1} = stocks at end of period t-1, which is equal to beginning stocks for period t,

X_t = production during period t, and

S_t = stocks at end of period t.

and note the identity, $C_t = S_{t-1} + X_t - S_t$.

To derive the demand for storage between two periods, consider the effect of an increase in ending stocks during period t (S_t) on the price of storage. The price of storage equals the price in period $t+1$ minus the price in period t, or $P_{t+1} - P_t$. This price spread, $P_{t+1} - P_t$, can be viewed as a nearby futures price (P_{t+1}) minus the current cash price (P_t). Alternatively, $P_{t+1} - P_t$ could represent the price spread between two different futures contracts with different delivery months. For the discussion that follows, think of $P_{t+1} - P_t$ as the spread between the nearby futures price and the current cash price.

Assume that incoming stocks (S_{t-1}), production levels (X_t and X_{t+1}), and outgoing stocks next period (S_{t+1}) are given so that only ending stocks (S_t) are allowed to change. In that case, the expression for the price of storage is:

$$P_{t+1} - P_t = f_{t+1}(S_t + X_{t+1} - S_{t+1}) - f_t(S_{t-1} + X_t - S_t) \qquad (3.5)$$

where $S_t + X_{t+1} - S_{t+1} = C_{t+1}$ and $S_{t-1} + X_t - S_t = C_t$.

Differentiating Equation (3.5) with respect to S_t and using the chain rule, gives

$$\frac{\partial(P_{t+1} - P_t)}{\partial S_t} = \frac{\partial f_{t+1}}{\partial C_{t+1}}\frac{\partial C_{t+1}}{\partial S_t} - \frac{\partial f_t}{\partial C_t}\frac{\partial C_t}{\partial S_t} < 0 \qquad (3.6)$$

The entire partial derivative in equation 3.6 is negative, because $\partial f_{t+1}/\partial C_{t+1} < 0$, $\partial C_{t+1}/\partial S_t > 0$, $\partial f_t/\partial C_t < 0$, and $\partial C_t/\partial S_t < 0$. This means that the first expression ($\partial f_{t+1}/\partial C_{t+1} \times \partial C_{t+1}/\partial S_t$) on the right-hand-side of equation 3.6 is negative. The second expression ($\partial f_t/\partial C_t \times \partial C_t/\partial S_t$) is positive but it is subtracted from the first expression, so the entire derivative expressed in equation 3.6 is negative.

If we examine the first expression on the right-hand-side of 3.6, we know that an increase in S_t, by definition, implies an increase in consumption in period C_{t+1}, so $\partial C_{t+1}/\partial S_t$ is positive. This follows because S_t becomes the beginning inventory in period $t + 1$, and S_{t+1} and X_{t+1} are assumed to be constant in equation 3.6, so consumption (C_{t+1}) must increase in period $t + 1$. There will be an increase in consumption (C_{t+1}) in period $t + 1$, if and only if there is a lower price in period $t + 1$, so $\partial f_{t+1}/\partial C_{t+1} < 0$, based on the law of demand (see equation 3.3).

Turning to the second expression on the right-hand-side of equation 3.6, $\partial f_t/\partial C_t < 0$, based on the law of demand. $\partial C_t/\partial S_t$ is also < 0, because an increase in S_t, by definition, implies declining consumption in period t (C_t), given that incoming stocks (S_{t-1}) and production (X_t) are assumed to be constant in equation 3.6.

Based on equation 3.6, the demand for storage is a downward-sloping curve, as in Figure 3.8. We see from Figure 3.8 that the expected price in the next period (P_{t+1}) minus the price in the current period (P_t) may be expressed as a decreasing function of stocks carried out of the current period (S_t).

There is an intuitive explanation for the downward-sloping demand curve in Figure 3.8. Suppose that firms decide to carry a smaller level of stocks out of period t and into period $t + 1$. This implies that more of the commodity is offered for sale in period t, and less is offered for sale in period $t + 1$. As a result, P_t falls and P_{t+1} rises. A decrease in stocks carried

Figure 3.8: The Demand for Storage

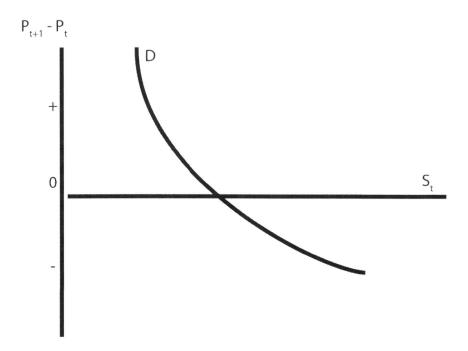

out of period t decreases the price in t relative to the price in period $t + 1$, which means a larger price spread, $P_{t+1} - P_t$.

Now lets turn to the supply side. The supply of storage arises from firms that carry stocks from period t to $t + 1$. The supply of storage refers to the supply of commodities as inventories, not to the supply of storage space. In a competitive market, firms will hold stocks (i.e., they will "supply" storage) from one period to the next if the net marginal cost of storage equals the expected change in price. Equilibrium requires that the net marginal cost of storage (positive or negative) must equal the price of storage. The total net cost of storage was specified by Brennan as a function of three components: physical costs of storage (o_t), a risk aversion factor (r_t), and convenience yield (c_t). The term net cost refers to the fact that convenience yield is subtracted from the two other components, because convenience yield is a negative cost. The total net cost of storage (m_t) can then be written as:

$$m_t (S_t) = o_t (S_t) + r_t (S_t) - c_t (S_t) \qquad (3.7)$$

where it is assumed when differentiating with respect to S_t that

$o'_t > 0$ and $o''_t \geq 0$ (physical costs)

$r'_t > 0$ and $r''_t \geq 0$ (risk aversion factor)

$c'_t \geq 0$ and $c''_t \leq 0$ (convenience yield)

Since supply curves are marginal cost curves above the minimum of average variable costs, differentiating the total net cost of storage gives the supply of storage. This means net marginal cost (m'_t) equals marginal outlay on physical storage (o'_t) plus the marginal risk aversion factor (r'_t) minus the marginal convenience yield on stocks (c'_t). Therefore, the net marginal cost of storage in period t is:

$$m'_t (S_t) = o'_t (S_t) + r'_t (S_t) - c'_t (S_t) \qquad (3.8)$$

Graphically, equation (3.8) can be represented by panel (d) in Figure 3.9. The three components of the equations are illustrated in panels (a) through (c) of the figure. The effects of each component are explained below.

Physical costs of storage include interest expense, insurance, handling, and other direct costs associated with storing a product. These costs are assumed to increase at a constant rate except at high levels of inventory. When inventory is high, physical costs of storage rise at an increasing rate because of capacity limitations. The marginal outlay on physical storage (o'_t) is presented in panel (a) of Figure 3.9.

The marginal risk aversion factor (r'_t) is positively related to stocks. The greater the level of stocks the greater will be the loss to the firm from an unexpected price fall (Figure 3.9(b)).

Marginal convenience yield (c'_t) is inversely related to the level of stocks. At low levels of inventories, merchandisers and processors potentially could experience stockouts. Stockouts may cause orders not to be filled or plants not to run at full capacity. Also, costs of obtaining the inventory later may be prohibitively high, which justifies carrying the inventory. Therefore, convenience yield becomes high with low stock levels because pipeline stocks are necessary for many firms processing raw commodities.

The beer industry provides an excellent example of where pipeline stocks are crucial and where convenience yield comes into play. Breweries in the United States (and around the world) produce a differentiated consumer product–a malt beverage that has a distinct taste. For example, a major U.S. brewery spends hundreds of millions of dollars each year advertising its distinct product. Their beer tastes different than their competitors' according to the ads. This brewery has a very large share of the U.S. beer market and its position in the market is highly dependent on the uniform quality of the barley that is used to produce its famous beer. The brewery is therefore susceptible to any problems with the barley harvest because in

Figure 3.9: Components of Net Marginal Cost of Storage and the Supply of Storage

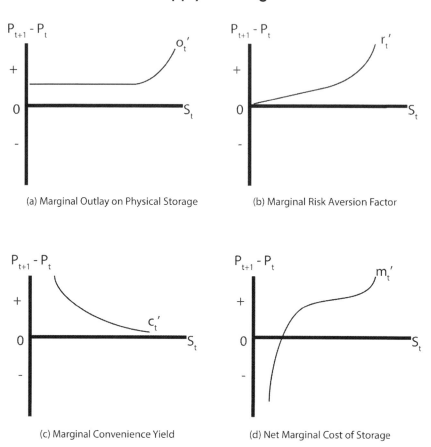

(a) Marginal Outlay on Physical Storage

(b) Marginal Risk Aversion Factor

(c) Marginal Convenience Yield

(d) Net Marginal Cost of Storage

the United States barley is harvested once a year, in the fall season. Furthermore, malting barley for beer is grown in a relatively small geographic region in the northern mid-tier states (i.e., North Dakota and Montana). The regional concentration of production adds additional harvest risk (i.e., loss of quality) due to unfavorable weather.

Beer has a rather short shelf life and it is produced throughout the year, so consumers can purchase a freshly brewed product at any time. If the brewery were to run out of good quality barley, it could not produce its beer with its distinct taste. This would be a disaster for the company. The quality of the barley crop varies from year to year due to weather conditions and, if there was a crop failure, this could jeopardize the supply of the company's leading beer. As a result, this brewery carries a very large inventory of barley, and the company places a high convenience yield on its barley inventories.

As another example, some of the world's finest racehorse stables are home to thoroughbred horses each worth millions of dollars. The horse trainers are very particular about the type of horse feed at the stable, as part of the exemplary care provided to the horses. The feed is grown under very specific conditions and sourced from the most reliable farms. Due to the importance of feed in the performance of the racehorse, the most exclusive racehorse stables will carry one year's feed supply to prevent a situation where the high quality feed they demand may not be available, to due adverse weather, disease, etc. In other words, the horse trainers place a high convenience yield on holding the very best feed for their champion horses.

Firms benefit from convenience yield; therefore, this component is a negative cost and is subtracted from other costs in Equations (3.7) and (3.8). At low levels of inventory, further reductions in inventory levels raises the convenience yield from holding inventory. Therefore, the marginal convenience yield is a decreasing function of the inventory level (Figure 3.9(c)).

Supply of Storage

The supply of storage, which is equal to the net marginal cost of storage, is presented in Figure 3.9(d), with the difference between the two price periods on the vertical axis and the horizontal axis representing the inventory level (S_t). Unlike a standard supply curve, storage is provided even with a negative price. A negative price for storage would occur when the futures price is less than the current cash price (i.e., an inverted market).

As inventory levels increase, convenience yield declines and the supply curve for storage flattens and approaches the full cost of storage (see Figure 3.9 (d)). For large inventories, the cost of carry will increase significantly. These increased costs for a merchandiser can result from inadequate storage space that, in turn, could cause higher levels of product deterioration for some commodities. Also, expensive temporary facilities may have to be built to store the inventory. In such a situation the price of storage must provide an incentive to merchants to carry the commodity.

Implications of the Theory

According to the theory of the price of storage, the set of inter-temporal prices established on the futures market provides a direct indication of the expected return from storage and provides a means of assuring receipt of storage returns. It is evident that storage is supplied even when the price of storage is zero or negative because of the importance of convenience yield.

The convenience yield offsets any loss associated with the sum of physical and risk costs.

In Figure 3.10, the demand and supply of storage are combined in order to demonstrate equilibrium conditions. With the aid of Figure 3.10, comparative static equilibrium points can be traced out. First, it can be assumed that the supply of storage is relatively stable. It is largely the demand for storage that shifts back and forth with changing market conditions, while the SS curve in Figure 3.10 does not move appreciably. But such factors as changing interest rates will shift the supply curve somewhat. However, normally the shifting demand gives rise to variations in the price of storage.

Figure 3.10: Supply and Demand for Storage

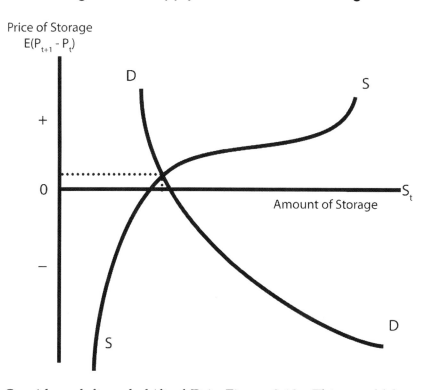

Consider a leftward shift of D in Figure 3.10. This would lower the price of storage and lower the equilibrium level of inventory carryout (S_t). A leftward shift in D could occur due to the following reasons:

- Production decreases in period t.
- Expected production in period t+1 increases.
- Expected carryout of stocks in period t+1 decreases.

Alternatively, consider what happens when D shifts to the right. In this case, the price of storage increases and S_t also increases. A rightward shift could arise if:

- Production increases in period t.
- Expected production in period t+1 decreases.
- Expected carryout of stocks in period t+1 increases.

In Figure 3.10, the dotted lines show a storage demand and supply equilibrium above the 0 horizontal line. This equilibrium represents a carrying charge market (or contango), where $P_{t+1} > P_t$. Alternatively, if the demand curve shifted leftward so that the supply and demand equilibrium was below the 0 horizontal line, then inter-temporal prices would be inverted (i.e., $P_{t+1} < P_t$).

Suppose that in the month of April the price of September wheat is trading at $0.15 below the price of May wheat futures. We know from the price differential that this is an inverted market, but what accounts for the price differential? According to the theory of storage, the amount by which the price of September wheat is discounted relative to the price of May wheat does not depend on the expected size of the wheat crop to be harvested between May and September. Rather, the expected size of the harvest (which occurs between May and September) will affect the price of the May futures contract by approximately the same amount as it will affect the price of the September futures price. The correct explanation of the inverted market is that the price of May wheat (in April) is above the price of September wheat because the previous crop was small. It is important to note that supplies already in existence have the most important impact on the current inter-temporal set of prices.

In summary, prices of storable commodities are linked over time through storage costs, and futures markets and futures price spreads (between different maturity months) play an important role in guiding inventory levels and forward pricing. Also, cash and futures prices are expected to be strongly related through time.

Inter-Temporal Prices of Nonstorable Commodities

The prices of "nonstorable" commodities are not linked over time through storage costs since, by definition, inventories cannot be carried from one period to the next because the commodity will deteriorate or spoil. Futures prices for these nonstorable commodities basically reflect market participants' current expectations with regard to supply and demand conditions likely to exist at the time of contract maturity. As a result, for nonstorable commodities, no strong relationship is expected to exist between current cash and distant futures prices, nor between prices of futures contracts with different maturity dates. In other words, the futures curves for nonstorable commodities do not convey the same information as futures curves for storable commodities.

Inter-temporal price patterns for nonstorable commodities (such as electricity, live cattle, feeder cattle, and lean hogs) do not adhere to the theory of price of storage. Due to the laws of physics (for electricity) and biology (for livestock), these commodities are "perishable" and therefore cannot be held in inventory from one futures maturity month to another. For example, once cattle or hogs reach their optimum weight they are ready for market and must be slaughtered. Once electricity is generated, it must be used or it soon dissipates traveling back and forth over the transmission lines. This means that in the short-run the supply of nonstorable commodities is price inelastic and can be represented as a vertical line.

The production period is continuous for most nonstorable commodities (that are traded on futures markets) and supply and demand expectations drive traders' price expectations. The cash price for nonstorables reflects current supply and demand conditions. Alternatively, the various futures prices reflect anticipated supply and demand conditions that will prevail during the maturity month. For instance, the U.S. Department of Agriculture's National Agricultural Statistics Service (NASS) releases quarterly reports on the hog market. These reports are called the *Hogs and Pigs Report*. It is not unusual for this government report to signal that the short-term price trend is down, while the long term trend is up, or vice versa. This means that the April lean hog contract is almost like a different commodity than the July lean hog contract, because you cannot arbitrage the two different maturity months through storage.

Given that different information sets affect cash versus futures prices, the cash and futures prices for non-storables are not necessarily highly correlated as they are for storable commodities. Furthermore, inter-temporal prices for nonstorable futures markets are as likely to be inverted as in contango. Price spreads may be in contango for some futures months and, at the same time, inverted for other months. For instance, the April-June spread in lean hogs could be in contango at 10 cents per pound, with June above April. At the same time, the June-August spread could be inverted by 5 cents per pound, while the August-December spread is in contango at 12 cents per pound.

However, cash and futures prices for nonstorables do converge as the maturity date approaches, assuming the cash price is the same price used to financially settle contracts. For deliverables, the possibility of delivery during the maturity month forces price convergence through arbitrage. If delivery is not a settlement option then cash settlement also forces converge.

As mentioned in Chapter 2, for many futures contracts, physical delivery is simply not possible or is not permitted by the exchange. For example, contracts such as Black Sea wheat, Class III milk, and Canadian Western Red Spring wheat are settled at the "cash value" on the last day of trading. Other contracts like lean hogs and live cattle are also settled at the cash price at the end of the trading period due to the considerable expense of transport and storage of live animals in addition to concerns of grading or quality variation from animal to animal. It is not a purely homogenous product.

The Basis

The principal measure for linking cash and futures prices for storable commodities is the basis. For most of this book, the basis is calculated as the futures price minus the cash price. However, it is also common (especially in the industry) to define the basis as the cash price minus the futures price. In domestic and international grain markets, traders have made the cash-minus-futures method the norm. The effect of using one definition versus the other is simply to reverse the sign of the difference between the two prices. Both methods appear in the futures literature and it makes no appreciable difference whether the basis is defined as futures minus cash or vice versa.

The price that farmers receive for their corn in central Illinois or Minnesota is made up of two components, the futures price and the basis. These components are separately identified and reflected in purchase contracts when farmers deliver corn to their local elevator facility. This means that if the CBOT futures price falls by 10 cents on a given day, the cash price will be 10 cents lower than it would otherwise have been (assuming no change in the basis). Thus, whenever the CBOT price for corn decreases, that decrease is *fully* reflected in the cash price that a local elevator company (i.e., grain buyer) pays farmers for their corn. This means that any change in CBOT corn futures is *fully* reflected in the local cash price.

Corn in the U.S. is a perfect example of an integrated market. When describing corn prices in his classic textbook, *The Economics of Futures Trading*, Professor Hieronymus characterized futures prices for corn in different time periods and spot prices across different geographic locations:

> These several prices are an integrated part of the price level of corn. They should be thought of as one price; the parts of which vary only with time and place of delivery. The system of price differences is intricate but simple in concept. There is one central price of corn; the multitudinous individuals prices over

> time, space, quality, and state of processing fall into place about the central price. The principle of one price within one market, in which the market is construed as the area of economic intercourse, applies to commodities traded in futures markets more than in any other area of the economic system. (Hieronymus (1977), p.152)

Commodity price quotes are frequently made in terms of the basis. The basis is an indicator of a broad range of factors affecting cash and futures markets. These factors include:

1. Availability and cost of transportation;
2. Supply and demand conditions in the cash market relative to delivery points for the futures market;
3. Quality differences between the cash commodity and the product specified in the futures contract;
4. Availability of storage space in the cash market;
5. Price and availability of substitute commodities; and
6. Price expectations in the futures and cash markets.

These factors can create numerous basis patterns over time, as illustrated in Figure 3.11. The left-hand-side of Figure 3.11 shows examples of a narrowing of the basis, where the cash and futures prices come together over time. Five possibilities (N-1 through N-5) of how the basis may narrow are shown on the left-hand-side of Figure 3.11. N-3 and N-4 are the most common scenarios, where both the cash and futures prices are moving in the same direction, but they are coming closer together, hence the basis is narrowing.

The right-hand-side of Figure 3.11, graphically shows five ways that the basis can widen (W-1 through W-5). W-3 and W-4 are the most likely because the cash and futures prices are either moving down together (W-3) or up together (W-4). In both W-3 and W-4, the cash and futures move in the same direction but they are diverging from one another and therefore the basis is widening. The importance of either a widening or narrowing of the basis becomes clear later in this book when we discuss hedging (in Chapter 7).

The basis can be used to understand spatial price relationships. For example, consider the following case where a CBOT September futures contract for corn is trading at $8.00 per bushel (Table 3.4). Market I is a cattle-producing region that is feed deficit and therefor imports corn from other

Figure 3.11: Scenarios of How the Basis May Change Over Time

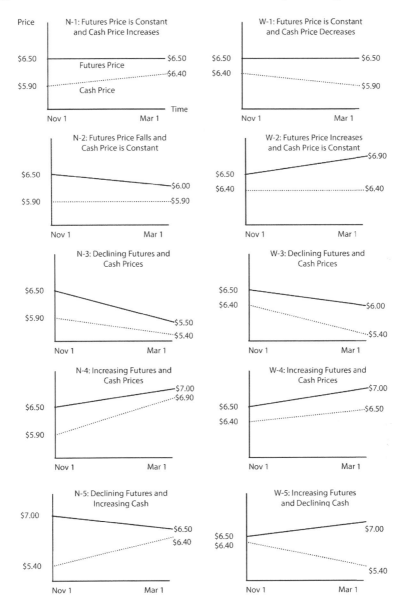

regions, and it has a corn cash price of $8.40 per bushel. Market E is a corn-exporting region, which has a cash price of $7.80 per bushel. Recall that we can define the basis as being equal to the cash price minus the specified futures contract price. Defined as cash minus futures, the basis for Market I equals +40 cents, while the basis is -20 cents for Market E. The positive basis for Market I can be stated as "40 cents over," because the cash price

Table 3.4: Basis and Spatial Price Difference Markets

Description of Market	Dollars per Bushel
Market I cash price for corn	8.40
Market E cash price for corn	7.80
Difference in cash market prices	0.60
CBOT September futures contract price for corn	8.00
Basis for Market I (cash minus futures)	0.40
Basis for Market E (cash minus futures)	-0.20
Difference in basis between cash markets	0.60

is "over" the futures contract price. Similarly, the basis for Market E can be described as being "20 cents under" for the opposite reason.

The difference between the two cash market prices (I and E) is equal to 60 cents per bushel, which is equal to the difference between the two bases. It may seem unnecessary to calculate the basis when absolute price levels can be reported instead. But commodity merchants and traders are interested in price relationships among or between markets. A common reference point for different cash markets is provided with the basis relative to the futures price. Table 3.4 can be used to make several preliminary conclusions based on simple spatial economics.

First, we know that corn will not be shipped from market I to market E, because market I is a relatively high priced market and market E is a relatively low priced market. Second, market E is a potential supplier of corn to market I, if transfer costs of moving corn from E to I are less than 60 cents per bushel.

Basis quotes are typically used in commodity trading rather than price quotes because market participants can more readily predict how the basis will change over time, compared to trying to predict absolute price levels. However, confidence in basis predictions depends on the type of cash market. For instance, the basis in the corn market is more stable than the basis in the natural gas market. It is also the case that the basis for non-storable commodities (such as lean hogs) is much more difficult to predict than for storable commodities (such as corn).

Cash markets can be categorized by their relationship to futures market delivery points. Some cash markets are viewed as terminal (i.e., central) markets if they are designated as either primary or alternate delivery points for futures contracts. Primary delivery points are locations designated as official delivery points under the futures contracts specifications, while alternative delivery points are locations where delivery make take place to fulfill a futures contract, through mutual agreement by the long and the short.

Box 3.4 Electricity Futures

Electricity futures are traded on the ICE, NYMEX, and the Nodal exchange. Each exchange offers trading in more than one electricity contract because the U.S. spot electricity market is physically broken into geographic regions, due to the complicated logistics of transmission over existing power lines. For instance, ICE has one contract which is based on delivery at the California/Oregon border.

Electricity is a commodity that flows across power lines, much the same as oil or natural gas flows through pipelines. However, unlike gas and oil, electricity cannot be stored and therefore electricity flows in a continuous circuit, sometimes flowing backward and forward until consumed.

Within a regional electricity transmission grid (e.g., the western grid) arbitrage is effective in this market. For example, if Los Angeles experiences a surge in demand due to a heat wave, the LA Department of Power and Water can import electricity from the Pacific Northwest (Washington and Oregon), a region that has less demand for electricity in the summer. By the same token, in the winter, when air conditioning demand lis low, California can sell excess power to the Pacific Northwest. Electricity can be in short supply in some regions and at the same time there may be a surplus in other regions.

Electricity is an important input cost for many industries and this gives rise to hedging demand from manufacturing firms. At the same time, suppliers of electricity are exposed to significant price risk and they also have a reason to hedge. The interest in electricity futures has risen because there have been some huge jumps in electricity prices with deregulation of the markets across the United States. An extreme incident occurred in California December of 2000, when the wholesale price of electricity surged to $1,400 per megawatt (MW) hour (a MW is one million watts), up from $30 a year earlier (a 4500% increase). 1 megawatt hour = 1,000 Kilowatt Hours (Kwh), the most common unit of electricity consumption for households. The average annual electricity consumption for a U.S. residential utility customer is 10,766 kWh.

Many commodity futures contracts enable a seller to make actual delivery of the commodity anytime during the delivery month, although delivery still accounts for a relatively small share of open interest in most "deliverable" futures markets. Corn is such a commodity where delivery is possible and is not uncommon. During the delivery month, the actual delivery of some corn will occur at one of the locations specified by the CBOT's contact specifications. The seller of the futures contract decides if delivery will be made and, if there is delivery, then the price received by the seller is that which the seller previously agreed to when the futures contract was initially sold.

Most traders have definite expectations concerning the behavior of the basis at a futures contract delivery point, because the cash price and the futures price will converge during the delivery month (even for non-storables). The reason for the convergence is the existence of arbitrage between futures and cash markets. Arbitragers will monitor the price relationships between the futures and cash markets to determine whether profitable transactions are possible. Producers, processors, merchandisers, and speculators will assume the arbitrage role.

Consider the case where an arbitrager is evaluating profit opportunities in a cash market, which is also a delivery point for a futures contract. Such an arbitrager has two basic strategies available. One strategy is to buy a nearby futures contract and sell forward the cash commodity at the delivery point. The arbitrager accepts delivery of the commodity specified in the futures contract, and then, in turn, uses the delivered commodity to make delivery on the forward cash transaction. The second strategy is to sell a futures contract, simultaneously buy the cash commodity, and then deliver on the futures contract.

The exact strategy that is selected by the arbitrager is determined by the futures contract price relative to the cash market price. The futures price is either (1) the price received by the arbitrager if she delivers (F_r), or (2) the price paid if she takes delivery (F_p). Also, the cash market price is either the price paid when buying the commodity (C_p) or the cash market price received when selling forward (C_r). If the net futures delivery price (after accounting for storage and transaction costs) is higher than the cash price, $(F_r > C_p)$, then the arbitrager buys the commodity in the cash market and delivers (sells) the commodity to the futures market. The arbitrager is buying "low" in the cash market and selling "high" in the futures market. If the futures price paid upon delivery is lower than the cash price received through a forward sale, $(F_p < C_r)$, then the arbitrager buys a futures contract and accepts delivery. After taking delivery, the arbitrager redelivers on the forward cash sale.

The futures contract price and cash prices are forced to converge through this type of arbitrage process. If the futures contract price is too high relative to the cash price, arbitragers will sell futures contracts and buy cash. As arbitragers sell futures contracts, the futures contract price will fall,

---

Box 3.5 Wheat Cash-Futures Convergence Controversy

In June 2009, the U.S. Senate Subcomittee on Investigations released a report describing excessive speculation in the wheat futures market. The report found that commodity index traders had been selling commodity indexes to hedge funds, pension plans, and other large investors. The commodity index traders then would directly purchase futures contracts that make up the indexes in order to offset their financial exposure to changes in commodity prices. Their purchase of offsetting futures contracts directly affected the futures market resulting in "abnormally high" futures prices for wheat compared to the cash price for wheat. At times this price disturbance resulted in the futures price and cash price for wheat failing to converge at expiration. The unpredictability and breakdown in relationship of cash and futures prices impaired farmers ability to use the futures market to reliably manage price risk, according to their report.

Source: "Excessive Speculation in the Wheat Market," Permanent Subcommittee of Investigations, United States Senate, June 24, 2009.

---

while increased buying in the cash market causes cash prices to rise. Decreasing futures contract prices and increasing cash prices cause the profit opportunity to disappear as the two prices converge to equal the costs of arbitrage. As explained in the next section, full convergence is not required to halt arbitrage trading. As soon as the two prices differ by an amount less than total transactions costs (brokerage fees, storage costs, transport costs, etc.), no arbitrage profit opportunity exists.

Basis convergence is affected by two factors: whether or not a cash market is a "par" delivery point and the delivery costs. A par delivery point is a cash market where no deductions (premiums) are taken from (added to) the futures contract price upon settlement for either grade or location reasons. A non-par delivery point would involve an adjustment to the futures price for a location differential. If the grade that is delivered is non-par, then a grade differential adjustment is also made to the price. If the delivery point has a premium, the buyer must pay the futures contract price plus the premium. If there is a discount for either location or grade, the discount is subtracted from the price received by sellers.

For example, the CBOT soybean futures contract specifies premiums and discounts according to the grade that is actually delivered and the delivery location. No. 2 yellow soybeans is delivered at par value, No. 1 yellow at 6 cents per bushel over contract price and No. 3 yellow at 6 cents per bushel under contract price. In addition, delivery in Chicago is at par,

Figure 3.12: Basis Convergence When Grade and Location Are at Par

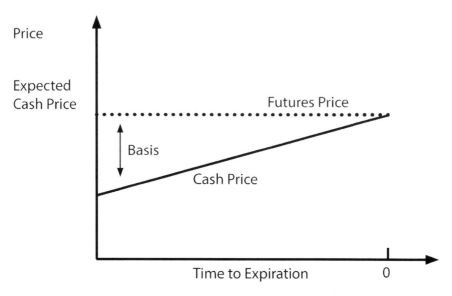

whereas delivery in St. Louis, Missouri, is at a premium of 6 cents per bushel over the contract price, subject to the grade differential. Delivery in St. Louis is at a premium because St. Louis is on the Mississippi river and therefore is closer to overseas markets than Chicago. Most U.S. soybeans are exported via the Mississippi and the Gulf ports.

The convergence of cash and futures prices is illustrated in Figure 3.12, assuming there is no location or grade discount. Time is measured on the horizontal axis and the commodity price is represented on the vertical axis. The delivery market is assumed to be a "par" delivery point. Therefore, the arbitrage process will ensure that the basis will converge to zero.

In Figure 3.12, the futures contract price is assumed to be an accurate forecast of the forthcoming cash price. If there is no new supply and demand information entering the market, then price expectations are unchanged and the futures contract price is constant, as represented by the horizontal dotted line in Figure 3.12. The cash corn price is assumed to increase steadily over time to compensate economic agents storing the commodity. However, as new supply and demand information comes into the market, the (horizontal) expected cash price will move up and down, as will the trajectory of the futures price. In all cases, the two prices will convergence during the delivery month.

For a par futures delivery point, the expected cash price pattern is straightforward. All other cash markets are related through a price grid, which reflects surplus and deficit regions. If a competitive situation exists,

Figure 3.13: Basis Convergence When Grade or Location Are Non-Par

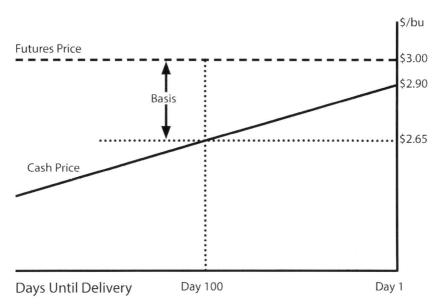

local cash market prices are expected to equal the futures delivery point cash price, plus or minus transfer costs. Figure 3.13 represents a situation where there is a discount on the cash price relative to the futures contract price at the time of delivery. This discount could be either due to a grade or location differential. In this case, the cash and futures prices will still converge over time as storage costs decline. However, the basis will not converge to zero because of the expected discount for grade or location.

Of course, there are cash markets that are not directly linked through commodity arbitrage with the market specified as the futures delivery point. In this case, the price transmission from one market to the other is more indirect and expectations concerning the basis are more unpredictable. This is true of some foreign cash markets vis-à-vis Chicago or New York futures markets. If a wheat grower in Australia is trying to hedge on the Chicago market, or a cocoa producer in Africa is trying to hedge on the New York market, then the basis in each case will be quite volatile. No direct arbitrage occurs to ensure a consistent convergence of cash and futures prices. The cash and futures markets are far apart spatially, there are rules affecting the international transport of commodities, and currency fluctuations will affect the basis. Marketing the cash commodity and using the futures market in such markets is more risky because of the weaker linkage between the cash and futures market.

Figure 3.14 displays daily basis data for corn for Kansas, Illinois, and the Gulf of Mexico ("The Gulf"), which is near the mouth of the Mississippi River, close to New Orleans (NOLA). Kansas and Illinois are farming regions, and corn produced in Kansas or Illinois will be sold into domestic markets for livestock feed and ethanol production, and it will be exported through ports like the Gulf to world markets. The Gulf is a key route for corn exports as around 60% of US corn exports are shipped down the Mississippi by barge and then loaded on ocean-going vessels. In Figure 3.14 it is shown that corn prices tend to be higher at the Gulf than in either Kansas or Illinois, due to the cost of transporting corn from the corn belt to the Gulf.

Figure 3.14: Corn Basis

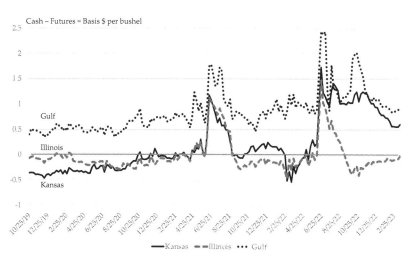

Note: The basis is calculated as the cash bid price minus the nearby futures price. Source: https://agtransport.usda.gov/Grain/Wheat-Basis-by-Location/uh4s-xysq.

The basis variability in noticeable in In Figure 3.14. Variability in the corn basis is partly driven by the regional demand for ethanol. This is evident if we compare the corn basis in Kansas versus Illinois in Figure 3.14. In the latter period shown in Figure 3.14 there was a drought in the Kansas region which led to strong prices for farmers at harvest. The ethanol plants and feedlots bid up the price of corn in Kansas as there was a regional shortage. Contrast this with Illinois basis at the same time period, which shows Illinois corn prices weakened relative to futures. This was partly due to the slowdown of barge traffic on the Mississippi River due to low water conditions.

Summarizing Figure 3.14, we conclude that the Illinois basis (cash - futures) was weak, meaning Illinois cash prices were low relative to the CME corn futures price. This was the case because supply in Illinois was large relative to demand in that region during the latter part of 2022 and early 2023.

Conversely, Figure 3.14 shows that the basis in Kansas was very strong in the latter part of 2022 (see right hand side of Figure 3.14) because the supply of corn in that region was low relative to demand.

Basis and International Trade

Basis risks and other complications increase rapidly with international trade, especially when foreign currency transactions are involved. Within the United States, commodities can generally move between regions without fees or restrictions. For example, corn moves freely from the Midwest to California and the price differential primarily reflects transfer costs. For most non-perishable commodities, price differences that exist between cash markets in the United States generally reflect supply and demand conditions and transfer costs. The existence of standardized grading systems enhances the spatial pricing efficiency of markets.

Alternatively, price differences between countries may be significantly impacted by border policies that restrict trade. Argentina's policy regarding crude oil from 2002 to 2017 is an excellent example of how a government can use policy to isolate domestic producers from changes in international prices. During that time period, oil producers in Argentina receive a fixed price per barrel of oil that was about 50 percent of the world's price. Argentina's policy was designed to shield domestic consumers from fluctuating global oil price. As a result, the production of oil in Argentina declined. Furthermore, "basis" was difficult, if not impossible, to predict for the oil industry in Argentina. They had little information as to the true value of their oil production over time. Furthermore, the usefulness of futures or options as means of risk transfer was dramatically reduced for Argentina's oil industry. The price caps were removed in 2018 after a change in government.

International exchange rate fluctuations can also affect price relationships between countries. As a result, international hedging of commodities has been less successful than domestic hedging programs. For example, currency fluctuations adversely affect the financial returns from hedging Australian cattle sales on U.S. futures exchanges because exchange rate movements reduce the degree of correlation between prices in the two countries. Haigh and Holt (2000) studied both commodity and freight futures contracts for their effectiveness in reducing uncertainty for international traders. They used various economic models to illustrate the importance of hedging volatile price and basis levels in international trade between the United States and Europe. They also illustrate the importance of hedging transportation rates and they show the benefits that an international trader realizes through hedging.

Box 3.6 Domestic vs. World Sugar Market

This chapter has emphasized how arbitrage links prices in markets separated by space or time. The sugar market is a counter-example to the law of one price, because world market–domestic U.S. market arbitrage is not allowed to work due to U.S. government policy on sugar. The U.S. government restricts imports of sugar from abroad in order to protect U.S. sugar farmers. Tariff-rate quotas (TRQs) are allocated annually to foreign suppliers of sugar. As a result, the price of domestic sugar in the U.S. is set at approximately two times world levels. U.S. production has increased in response to the high domestic price and imports have fallen. Soft drink manufacturers in the U.S. stopped using sugar a number of years ago and moved towards a sweetener substitute made from corn, because the U.S. trade restriction makes domestic sugar too expensive. Sugar is a primary example of how government policy can disrupt markets.

The ICE, trades both a domestic (No. 16) and world (No. 11) raw sugar futures contract. The domestic price is always above the world price because processing U.S. firms cannot freely import sugar outside the TRQ quantities.

Domestic (No. 16) versus World (No. 11) Sugar Futures Prices

Sugar future prices: U.S.A and the Rest of the World

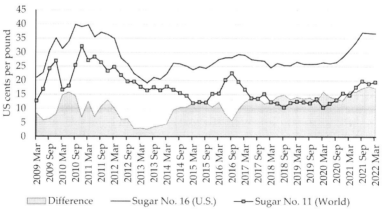

Source: Bloomberg

Price Relationships Across Product Forms

As commodities move through marketing channels, various types of processing change the commodity's form. Recall that time, space, and product form are the three dimensions associated with marketing. Processing of a raw commodity generally results in a number of products. For instance, a corn ethanol firm processes corn into ethanol for motor fuel and at the same time produces a by-product called Dried Distillers Grains with solubles (DDGS) used for animal feed.

In a competitive market structure, a processor plays a role that is analogous to that of a market arbitrager. A firm will engage in processing as long as its margin from processing equals at least its processing cost. Obviously, a firm will continue processing in the short run as long as its margin is enough to cover variable costs. In the long run, however, the firm will engage in processing only if the margin is enough to cover total costs, including fixed costs. The firm's margin is basically the value of processed products obtained from each unit of the base commodity, minus the base commodity's price.

Figure 3.15 illustrates the Iowa corn gross crush margin for an ethanol firm from March 2007 through March 2022. The crush margin serves as an indicator of the returns for corn as an input; however, this does not serve as a measure of profit. Here the crush is the difference in the value of corn as the input and ethanol and DDGS as the outputs.

The gross crush margin in Figure 3.15 is for a typical ethanol plant in Iowa. The data behind the figure show that the average margin from 2007 to 2022 was $1.93 per bushel of corn processed into ethanol. This calculation assumes that 1 bushel of corn yields 2.8 gallons of ethanol and 17 pounds of DDGS. Corn is traded in dollars per bushel, ethanol in dollars per gallon, and DDGS in dollars per short ton (2,000 lbs). Therefore the crush margin formula is as follows:

DDG price $\times$ (17/2,000) + (Ethanol Price $\times$ 2.8) - Corn Price

For the time period shown in Figure 3.15, ethanol contributed about 80 percent of the total output value and DDGs about 20 percent of the value. The ethanol value was $6.42 per bushel, on average. The price of corn averaged $4.49 per bushel. When the margin was relatively high in 2014 the price of corn had fallen but the price of ethanol remained relatively high. When the margin was relatively low during 2012 and 2013 in the figure, the high price of corn was pulling down the crush margin. During this period, corn prices rose to over $8 per bushel due to a drought in the U.S. corn belt.

For any processing technology, the cost of processing and yields of processed products obtained from a unit of base raw commodity are approximately fixed and predetermined. Given the information on processing yields and product prices, any trader can easily calculate the margin. By comparing this margin with processing costs, one can determine if processing volume is likely to rise or fall.

Figure 3.15: Iowa Corn Gross Crush Margin 2007-2022

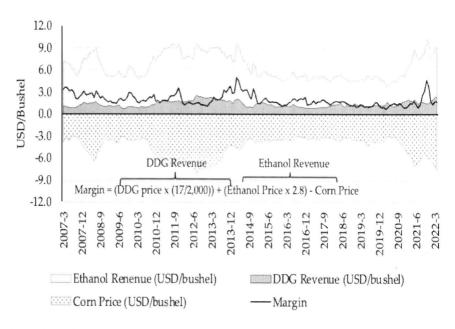

Ethanol Renenue (USD/bushel)   DDG Revenue (USD/bushel)

Corn Price (USD/bushel)   —— Margin

Source: Center for Agricultural and Rural Development at Iowa State University

Note 1: Calculations assume a yield of 2.8 gallons of ethanol per bushel of corn and 17 lbs of dried distiller grains with solubles (DDGs) per bushel.

Note 2: Recall that DDGs are traded in dollars per short ton (2,000 lbs).

Whenever market prices are such that processors' margins exceed processing cost, firms will enjoy a profit and will try to expand their operation. Their actions, however, will push the price of processed products down and/or the price of the raw commodity up, thereby decreasing processors' margins. This adjustment will continue until a new price relationship is established and the margin is just enough to cover processing costs. On the other hand, if the price relationship is such that processors' margins are less than costs, processing will entail a loss, and firms will reduce production. This will result in upward pressure on processed product prices and/or downward pressure on the base commodity's price

Processing usually does not stop after the raw commodity has been transformed into one or more products. The products obtained from processing a base commodity are generally intermediate products. These intermediate products are processed further before the final consumer good is produced. The correlation between the price of a raw commodity and the prices of processed products derived from it declines as the degree of processing increases.

Summary

This chapter has emphasized the economic principle that price patterns among futures contracts for storable commodities (such as corn or natural gas) are affected by inventory supply and demand. The theory of price of storage and the theory of normal backwardation were explained. For storable commodities, inter-temporal prices are highly correlated as they are linked through storage. In contrast, inter-temporal prices for nonstorable commodities (such as electricity or lean hogs) are not as highly correlated. For nonstorables, the price for each expiry month is somewhat independent from other months.

Using crude oil as an example, this chapter discussed the importance of the shape of the futures curve. The futures prices for each contract month are on the vertical axis and the maturity months are listed chronologically on the horizontal axis, tracing out the futures curve. If the curve is upward sloping, the market is said to be in contango. Alternatively, a downward sloping futures curve represents backwardation. If the market is in backwardation, the futures curve is reflecting a situation of commodity scarcity. This implies that market prices will strengthen in the coming weeks and months. Alternatively, a positive sloping futures curve (contango) signals that supply is adequate and prices may weaken. These generalizations regarding the shape of futures curves apply to all storable commodities.

The concept of the basis was introduced in this chapter and it was explained that the basis can be defined as the cash price minus the futures

---

Box 3.7 An Overlooked Model of Supply and Demand for Storage

In 1939, Jack Kenneth Eastham published a paper entitled 'Commodity Stocks and Prices' in *Review of Economic Studies*. He developed a model of commodity storage that accounts for demand to consume and hold as working stocks, D_C, as well as total demand, D_T, which includes demand to hold stocks speculatively. A probable mean output curve is represented by S_n and the anticipated price is P. However, in the case of a bumper crop, the quantity harvested shifts all the way out to Q_1 instead of Q resulting in a price drop to P_1. At this price, q_1 is consumed and held as working stocks and the remainder $(Q_1 - q_1)$ is held speculatively for the next year. This shifts the supply the next year out by the amount of stocks held speculatively giving the supply curve S_1. Stocks of the amount $(Q_2 - q_2)$ are held speculatively again giving the following year's supply curve of S_2.

Eastham's model presented many of the characteristics found in subsequent commodity storage models, yet his contribution was entirely overlooked. For further explanation, see Carter and Revoredo-Giha (2009).

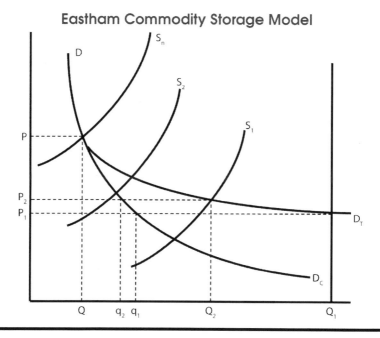

Eastham Commodity Storage Model

---

price, or vice versa. Arbitrage will cause futures and cash prices to converge to essentially zero at futures contract par delivery markets and to converge to transfer costs for other cash markets. Changes or movements in the basis are independent of movements in the futures price. The value to which the basis will converge is much more uncertain for some markets than others.

For a commodity to be physically transferred between regional markets, there must be some economic incentive to do so. For instance, the importing region will have a higher price than the exporting market. California imports corn from the U.S. midwest so the California price of corn is always higher than what it is in Illinois. If the price difference between markets is insufficient to compensate for transfer costs, trade is not expected between regions. The lack of physical arbitrage between markets will result in reduced correlation in prices between markets. This is particularly true for international trade, where exchange rates and trade barriers reduce the correlation in prices between countries. The same concept is true for inter-temporal transfer. For a commodity to be carried in inventory from one period to the next, there must be an economic incentive behind the storage decision.

Finally, it was stressed that processing changes the form of a product and, therefore, affects the price relationship between the raw commodity and products derived from it. In general, the greater the amount of processing, the lower the correlation between prices of related product forms. For instance, the use of natural gas to produce electricity transforms a storable commodity into a nonstorable commodity. Natural gas inter-temporal futures prices are highly correlated, but this is not the case for inter-temporal electricity prices.

Discussion Questions

1. Explain why the inventory supply from one time period to the next is not simply equal to the segment of the supply curve above the internal equilibrium price of the market.

2. Cash markets can be classified into three categories: a cash market designated as a futures contract delivery point, a cash market that can profitably deliver to the same location as a futures market delivery point, and a cash market that cannot profitably deliver to the delivery point. Explain and discuss the convergence of basis for each of these cash markets categories.

3. Define and explain how the basis terms "under" and "over" used in grain trading are different from "strengthening" and "weakening."

4. You have been requested by the secretary of agriculture of a Central American country to determine whether cattle produced in that coun-

try could be hedged using the Chicago Mercantile Exchange live cattle contract. What information would you need to collect to determine whether this is feasible? Also, what conditions could exist that would improve the probability of this activity being profitable?

5. Assume you are an analyst for an oil company that is hedging using crude oil futures. Your job is to forecast the basis for crude oil at a Midwest refinery. Assume the delivery point for the futures contract is in Texas. Discuss and explain whether the basis would strengthen or weaken in each of the following situations:

   (a) The major pipeline supplying your region has an oil spill and the EPA closes the pipeline for one month.
   (b) A major cold front decreases gasoline mileage and a gasoline shortage develops in your trade area.
   (c) OPEC embargoes oil shipments to the United States.
   (d) Local storage areas overestimated the demand for crude oil and now have excessive supplies of crude in storage.
   (e) A major supplier is only able to deliver a lower quality crude oil, which greatly increases the costs of processing.

6. You are given the following price information on December 21: CBOT July soybean futures contract price ($10.39), Market A cash ($9.92), Market B cash ($9.42), and Market C cash ($11.09). Calculate the basis for each cash market and discuss the relationships between markets. Assume Market A is a delivery market for the soybean contract. Also, transfer costs are 50 cents between Market A and B and 90 cents between Market A and C. Forecast and discuss the basis during the delivery month for each of the cash markets.

7. What is the difference between a "positive" and "negative" carrying charge market? What are the implications of this difference for commercial storage firms at a delivery market?

8. Draw the *futures curve* for Brent versus WTI crude oil and discuss reasons for the respective shapes of the curves.

9. Define "normal backwardation" and explain its expected effects on price relationships and risk premiums.

10. What is the *price for storage* and how does convenience yield affect this price? How is inventory level related to the price of storage?

Selected References

Anson, Mark JP, Frank J Fabozzi, and Frank J Jones. 2010. *The handbook of traditional and alternative investment vehicles: investment characteristics and strategies.* Vol. 194, John Wiley & Sons.

Brennan, Donna, Jeffrey Williams, and Brian D Wright. 1997. "Convenience yield without the convenience: a spatial–temporal interpretation of storage under backwardation." *The Economic Journal*, 107(443): 1009–1022.

Brennan, Michael J. 1958. "The supply of storage." *The American Economic Review*, 50–72.

Carter, Colin A, and Cesar L Revoredo-Giha. 2009. "Eastham's commodity storage model in a modern context." *Oxford Economic Papers*, 61: 801–822.

Carter, Colin A, and Cesar Revoredo-Giha. 2023. "Financialization and speculators risk premia in commodity futures markets." *International Review of Financial Analysis*, 102691.

Fama, Eugene F, and Kenneth R French. 1987. "Commodity futures prices: Some evidence on forecast power, premiums, and the theory of storage." *Journal of Business*, 55–73.

Haigh, Michael S, and Matthew T Holt. 2000. "Hedging multiple price uncertainty in international grain trade." *American Journal of Agricultural Economics*, 82(4): 881–896.

Hieronymus, Thomas A. 1977. *Economics of Futures Trading: For Commercial and Personal Profit.* Commodity Research Bureau.

Keynes, John Maynard. 1923. "Some aspects of commodity markets." *Manchester Guardian Commercial: European Reconstruction Series*, 13: 784–786.

Working, Holbrook. 1949. "The theory of price of storage." *The American Economic Review*, 39(6): 1254–1262.

4.

Financials

This chapter outlines the basic economics of financial futures and options markets, which are derivatives based on underlying equity (i.e., stock) indexes, foreign currencies (FX), and interest rates (i.e., based on financial instruments such as U.S. Treasury bonds, or the widely traded Secured Overnight Financing Rate (SOFR)). The fundamentals of financial futures and options markets are slightly different and perhaps more complicated than for commodity futures and options such as crude oil, coffee, or cattle. However, the core economic principles and financial theory applying to commodity and financial futures and options are similar, and these instruments are all traded for similar reasons. For instance, the inter-temporal prices of financial futures contracts are linked through a cost-of-carry relationship, much like the economic principles for storable commodities outlined in Chapter 3. Financing costs play a critical role in terms of influencing the contemporaneous determination of inter-temporal prices in the financial futures market. The most popular (measured by trading volume) financial futures are one-month and three-month SOFR futures, and all financial futures are actively traded by banks, hedge funds, and asset managers, among other traders.

This chapter on financials is particularly important because financial futures (and options) are clearly the booming segment of the futures and options industry, as explained in Chapter 1. There are three broad categories of financial futures and options traded at the present time:

1. Currencies (e.g., Japanese Yen; European Euro; British Pound; Canadian Dollar; Australian Dollar; Mexican Peso; US dollar index);

2. Debt Instruments–interest rates (e.g., U.S. Treasury Bonds and Treasury Notes; Federal Funds; SOFR Futures; European bonds); and

3. Equity Instruments (e.g., E-mini Standard & Poor's 500 Stock Index; E-mini Nasdaq 100; E-micro $5).

This chapter begins with a description of each of these three general categories, followed by a discussion of price formation within specific financial futures and options markets.

Foreign Currencies

The rate at which one country's currency can be converted into the currency of another country is called the exchange rate. The foreign exchange market is an international market, with active trading in New York, London, Tokyo and other financial centers. U.S. based trading desks handle about 20% of FX global trading, while the desks in the United Kingdom account for almost 40% of the trading. International banks buy and sell currencies twenty-four hours a day. These banks post their **bid** (the price they are willing to buy at) and **ask** (the price they are willing to sell at) prices for currencies so that they are available to traders around the globe. This market is known as the interbank market in foreign exchange. Bid and ask quotes are offered for both the spot and the forward market. Most foreign exchange interbank payments are handled by the Clearing House Interbank Payment System (CHIPS), an electronic system operated by a New York Clearing House. CHIPS links more than 130 banks to its central computer, and the average CHIPS transaction is more than $3 million. For more information on this market and how this clearing arrangement works, go to http://www.chips.org/.

An alternative currency market is non-bank online currency trading, such as FXCM, which offers an Internet trading platform for currencies (see http://www.fxcm.com/). This type of online FX trading is designed to give individuals and small institutional investors greater access to the FX market. Most of the over-the-counter trading (i.e., the inter-bank market) was previously controlled by the large international banks and it was difficult for the small investor to directly access this market. FXCM has lowered the difference between the buying price and the selling price of a currency pair, which is of benefit to the non-commercial trader. This price is known as the pip (i.e., percentage in point) spread.

According to the the Bank for International Settlements, the daily turnover in the global foreign exchange (FX) market is estimated to be around $7.5 trillion, on average, making it the world's largest market of any kind. In comparison, the daily average value of world trade in goods and services is less than $100 billion, which means the global currency market is more than seventy times larger than the global market for goods and services. Swaps are the most traded FX instrument with 51% of trades; followed by spot trades (28%), and forwards (15%). The U.S. dollar accounts for close to 90% of one side of all FX trades, followed in importance by the

Box 4.1 The Black Market for Foreign Currency

Anyone who has lived or traveled in a developing country has most likely had first-hand experience with the workings of the "black market" in foreign currency. Even though exchanging money on the black or "parallel" market is illegal in many developing countries, the local newspapers in these countries often quote black market rates! If you are a foreigner walking down a street in India or Argentina, chances are that strangers will approach you and ask you if you want to change money at a better rate than what the banks are offering. In some cases, they stand in front of the bank! In many developing countries, the government artificially fixes the price of the domestic currency by pegging the currency to a foreign exchange rate such as the U.S. dollar, or by restricting the range of values that the exchange rate may take on (i.e., a price band). This fictitious exchange rate becomes the official rate at which foreign currency transactions are to be conducted. Often times this policy creates a black market in the domestic currency because the economic fundamentals do not support the "pegged" rate and black market traders try and establish the real rate. Invariably, a price gap develops between the black market rate and the official rate, indicating there is excess demand for foreign currency. The relative value of foreign currency in the black market typically becomes higher than in the official market. Put differently, this signals that in these countries there is a scarcity of foreign "convertible" currencies such as the U.S. dollar.

Modern (young) tourists use app-based banks such as Monzo or Revolut, as both give good exchange rates without the hassle of converting on the black market.

Euro, the Japanese Yen, the British Pound Sterling, and China's Yuan.

The currency market is a large network of spot, forward, OTC, futures, and options markets and currency values in this network are established through supply and demand. The long run value of say, the U.S. dollar versus the Japanese yen, depends on economic fundamentals such as government budgets, the money supply, the balance of trade, economic growth rates, interest rates, international capital flows, and relative inflation levels. This means that merchandise trade flows (e.g., imports and exports of manufactured goods and food products), trade in services (e.g., transport, financial, and business services), and financial flows (e.g., foreign investment) jointly determine exchange rates. Of course, political uncertainty is also an important factor in the exchange rate market, especially for developing and emerging economies.

As an example of a currency realignment, over a period of several years in the early 2000s, the Canadian dollar (CAD) strengthened relative to the U.S. dollar by about 70 percent (see Figure 4.1). The Canadian currency rose from USD 62¢ in 2002 to USD $1.06 in 2007. This long-term currency realignment was largely based on the declining value of the U.S. dollar relative to currencies worldwide. The sharp increase in value in the Canadian dollar encouraged imports of U.S. goods into Canada and encouraged Canadian tourism in the United States. However, it also affected Canadian industries that export into the United States, who saw their output prices fall significantly when transferred from U.S. dollars back into Canadian dollars. The Canadian dollar then quickly fell in value for a period during the 2007-08 financial crisis, but it recovered in value by 2011. Subsequently the CAD fell again starting in 2013, down to less than 80¢ in 2022.

Figure 4.1: Canadian Dollar in USD/CAD: 1992-2022

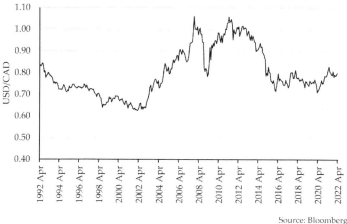

Source: Bloomberg

Globalization is a term that describes a growing trend towards internationally integrated markets and the free movement of goods, services, and factors of production. For instance, the North American Free Trade Agreement (NAFTA) was signed by the Government of Canada, the Government of the Mexico, and the Government of the United States in 1994. NAFTA (a regional trade agreement) helped globalize the three economies because the goal of NAFTA was to facilitate trade in goods and services in North America, by reducing trade barriers and promoting cross-border investment and fair trade in the area. NAFTA was very successful as regional trade expanded from $290 billion in 1993 to $1.1 trillion in 2021. In 2020, the United States-Mexico-Canada Agreement (USMCA) replaced NAFTA. Besides regional trade agreements, the World Trade Organization (WTO) facilitates increased international trade. China joined the WTO in 2001, boosting the importance of trade in the world economy. China is now of the top three largest trading partners of the United States, along with Canada and Mexico.

One byproduct of globalization is that exchange rates now play a greater role in the domestic economy. As more and more goods become tradable, through globalization and open economies, the prices of many domestic goods become heavily influenced by exchange rates. The average consumer may be unaware of this development, but nevertheless he or she is affected by exchange rates whenever they purchase food items, gasoline, sporting goods, clothing, large durables like automobiles or appliances, etc. This is true even if the goods are not actually traded, but are tradable. Goods are tradable if they can be consumed away from the point of production. Haircuts are not tradable but washing machines and refrigerators are.

Products such as lumber, beef, automobiles, steel, and fruits and vegetables are traded within USMCA and the prices of these goods are more closely linked to exchange rate fluctuations due to regional trade liberalization. For instance, Canada is a largest foreign supplier of petroleum, cars, lumber, steel, and aluminum to the United States. Canadian clothing factories responded to NAFTA's lower trade barriers and garments made in Canada made inroads into the U.S. market and captured a significant market share. Canadian manufacturers initially benefited from the steady weakening of the Canadian dollar from 85 cents (U.S.) in the early 1990's to only 62 cents (U.S.) in 2002. The weaker Canadian dollar effectively made Canadian labor and other costs cheaper in American-dollar terms. However, as discussed above, the Canadian dollar then rallied to trade on par with the U.S. dollar, a development that was not good for Canadian exporters.

As a result of globalization, many U.S. and foreign multinational companies now have a large share of their costs and revenues denominated in foreign currencies. For example, Callaway Golf, a U.S. manufacturer of golf clubs and golf equipment is dependent on Asia as an important market for golf supplies and Callaway's sales revenue is impacted by fluctuations in Asian exchange rates. Golf is popular in Japan and South Korea, and the demand for U.S. made golf clubs in those countries is affected by the international purchasing power of the Japanese Yen and the South Korean Won.

Callaway experienced a significant drop in both the volume and value of exports to Asia as a result of the 1997/98 Asian financial crisis, when the value of many Asian currencies plunged. Consumers in Asia pay for their Callaway golf equipment in their local Asian currency and the price in Asia therefore rose when the local currency fell. At the same time, consumer incomes were falling in Asia during the financial crisis. As a result of lower incomes, the Asian demand for imported golf clubs shrunk inward. At the same time, the supply of Callaway clubs (priced in the Asian currencies) shifted upwards and to the left because of the Asian currency devaluations.

Figure 4.2 shows the impact of the financial crisis on Callaway's international sales. The market equilibrium was at point A before the crisis and then it moved to point B (in Figure 4.2) during the crisis. Both the demand and supply curves (measured in the Asian currencies) shifted to the left. At point B prices were higher but the quantity of U.S. golf clubs purchased by Asian golfers was lower.

Figure 4.2: Supply and Demand of U.S. Made Golf Clubs After Devaluation of Asian Currencies

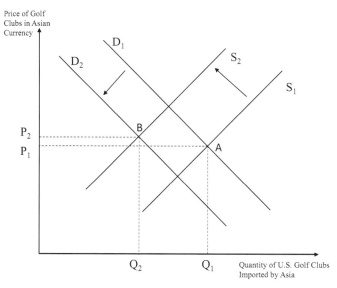

After it sells golf clubs in Asia, Callaway must exchange (i.e., repatriate) the Asian currency earned from the sale back into U.S. dollars. The Japanese Yen or S. Korean Won are exchanged for U.S. dollars in order to cover Callaway's manufacturing costs in the United States. During the period of the Asian crisis, revenue per unit exported fell, when measured by Callaway in U.S. dollars. Even though the golf club prices in the local Asian currencies rose, the increase in price did not match the rise in the value of the U.S. dollar.

In addition to the growing importance of FX earnings and receipts for multinational firms, there is massive foreign investment in many host countries and this has strengthened the linkage of global financial markets. For instance, in the United States the flow of incoming foreign direct investment totaled about $370 billion in 2021 (and there was a cumulative investment of about $4.98 trillion at the end of 2021). Japan, Canada, the Netherlands, the United Kingdom, and Germany are large investors in the United States.

How are Exchange Rates Determined?

Generally, the stronger a country's economy, the better its currency will perform and the more valuable it will become relative to other currencies. Typically, a certain currency will lose value if there is a high level of inflation in that country or if inflation levels are perceived to be rising. This is because inflation erodes purchasing power and demand for that particular currency. Inflation is an important factor in exchange rate determination because the exchange rate provides the link between a country's price and cost structures. Are hotel rooms expensive in London? Is Mexico a low cost producer of fruits and vegetables? Is it cheaper to take a golf vacation in Scotland (with the pound sterling) or in Ireland (with the euro)? From the U.S. perspective, these questions can only be answered by converting the foreign currency price into U.S. dollars, via the exchange rate.

Domestic firms and individuals demand foreign currency in order to purchase goods or services from a foreign country or to invest in that foreign host country. Foreigners supply foreign currency through their purchases of home goods or services or through investment in the home market. For example, as Japanese banks purchase U.S. financial assets they provide a supply of Japanese Yen, in exchange for U.S. dollars. At the same time, U.S. purchases of Japanese automobiles will result in a demand for Japanese Yen.

In international trade of goods, services, and financial assets, each participant measures the value of a transaction in terms of their own home currency. The linkage to all participants is through the exchange rate. For instance, in 2010 and 2011, the Swiss Franc gained sharply in value compared to the European euro (see Figure 4.3), largely due to significant financial flows out of the Euro zone and into Swiss Francs. Investors were afraid of the collapse of the Euro because of a debt crisis in Greece, Portugal, Spain, Italy and Ireland.

As another example, on June 23, 2016, geopolitics sent the British pound (GBP) down about 10 percent overnight as the Brexit vote delivered an "unexpected shock" to the market. The drop in the GBP is shown in Figure 4.4. Brexit is shorthand for the words "Britain" and "exit," a nickname for a British exit of the European Union (EU). In the 2016 referendum, the major-

Figure 4.3: European Euros per Swiss Franc

Source: Bloomberg

ity of the United Kingdom (UK) electorate voted to leave the EU, which came as a surprise. The British pound fell sharply because the consensus was that leaving the EU would lower economic growth in the UK. The falling GBP quickly drove up costs for UK manufacturing firms dependent on the Euro area or other foreign suppliers for inputs. Supply chain costs rose for all globalized firms operating in the UK because of the pound's post-Brexit fall.

For the most part, developed countries such as the U.S., the United Kingdom, and Japan have had floating or flexible exchange rates since the early 1970s. Under floating rates, supply and demand are allowed to determine the value of the currency and the currency's value fluctuates accordingly. In contrast, many developing and transition countries (such as China, Argentina, and India) have experimented with fixed exchange rates; although, they are slowly experimenting with floating rates. A fixed exchange rate means the exchange rate is rigid relative to the value of outside currencies. For example, following the Asian financial crisis in 1997/1998, Malaysia shifted from a flexible to a fixed exchange rate and imposed foreign exchange controls that "pegged" the Malaysian Ringgit at RM3.80 to the U.S dollar. The purpose of this move was to control capital flowing out of the country and to halt any further devaluation of the Ringgit, brought about during the Asian financial crisis. In July 2005, Malaysia returned to the flexible exchange rate. China has been very slow to liberalize its currency (yuan or renminbi), which would allow the market to fully determine

Figure 4.4: British Pound falls on 2016 Brexit vote

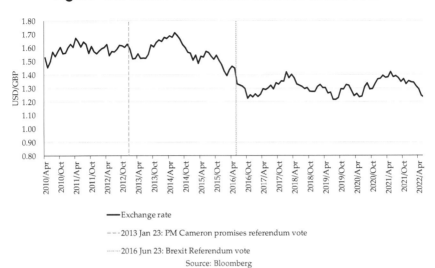

Exchange rate

- - - 2013 Jan 23: PM Cameron promises referendum vote

······ 2016 Jun 23: Brexit Referendum vote

Source: Bloomberg

the exchange rate.

Currency pegs cannot last forever (with Hong Kong a perhaps an exception) and in many developing countries the currency eventually becomes overvalued (see Box 4.1), which affects a country's international competitiveness relative to competing nations. For example, in 1991 Argentina pegged its currency (the peso) to the U.S. dollar in order to control hyperinflation. Unfortunately for Argentina, the U.S. dollar subsequently rose in value, making Argentine goods uncompetitive in global markets. Under the pegged system, Argentines were allowed to swap pesos for U.S. dollars, resulting in a reduction in the peso's circulation at home (because the central bank could only issue pesos if they were backed by U.S. dollars) and raising the interest rate in Argentina. As a result, Argentina's export markets collapsed, economic growth slowed, and unemployment grew to double-digit levels by 2001. A severe economic crisis resulted and Argentina suddenly abandoned its currency's peg to the dollar, triggering a devaluation of 50 percent. Subsequently, Argentina defaulted on US$152 billion in debt, the largest default in the history of global financial markets at the time. Some economists point to the meltdown of the Argentinean economy in 2001 as evidence of the danger of a currency system that does not reflect economic fundamentals–artificial currency pegs are destined to fail. However, as a counter-example, Hong Kong's monetary authority along with its currency board system, has successfully maintained the ratio of HK$7.80 to $1US from 1983 until 1998 when it was pegged to HK$7.75 to $1US. Since 2005, it has been allowed to fluctuate only between

---

Box 4.2 European Monetary Union and the Euro

On January 1, 2002, 12 European countries abandoned their national currencies and adopted a single currency–the euro–as their official currency. Today, a total of 20 member states use the euro as their official currency. This was a big step towards economic integration in Europe. Germans gave up the German mark (Deutsche mark), the French discarded the franc and the Italians gave up the lira. However, some countries like the United Kingdom, Denmark, and Sweden did not join the single currency union. Then in 2020 the United Kingdom left the European Union.

One of the main economic impacts of the single currency is that national governments gave up the ability to set interest rates. Instead, the European Central Bank now establishes a single interest rate for the entire euro region. Another economic impact is the elimination of exchange-rate risk for trade within the region. The introduction of the euro also reduced transactions costs for trade between foreign countries and Europe. With the single euro, foreign firms trading with Europe no longer have to repeatedly convert receipts and expenses from one currency to the other. Multinationals that sell products throughout Europe now set only one price in the euro zone. Prior to the adoption of the euro, multinationals were constantly revising their prices across Europe, as exchange rates fluctuated.

The 2008 financial crisis and resulting economic downturn led to several eurozone member states being unable to refinance their debt. This loss of confidence in member states' economies, particularly Greece and Spain, led to a devaluation in the strength of the euro. See Figure 4.3.

HK\$7.75-7.85 to \$1US. Some say that Hong Kong has a dull currency.

As mentioned above, the fundamental economic factors that determine exchange rates include the money supply, government budgets, economic growth, relative price levels (i.e., inflation) and interest rate differentials. These economic determinants ought to establish long-term equilibrium exchange rate levels. The traditional model of exchange rate equilibrium is the **purchasing power parity** (PPP) theory. Purchasing power parity (PPP) is based on the concept that goods and services in different countries should cost the same when measured in a common currency. This implies that exchange rates between currencies are in equilibrium when their purchasing power is identical. In equilibrium, this indicates that the exchange rate between two countries should equal the ratio of the two countries' price levels for a fixed basket of goods and services. So, according to the PPP theory, $50,000 buys the same goods in the United States as $50,000 exchanged into euros buys in Western Europe. For example, a German made automobile should cost the same in the United States as it does in Germany, adjusted for taxes and transportation. If one Euro buys 1.2 dollars, then an automobile priced at 41,700 Euros in Germany should cost just over 50,000 dollars in the United States, before freight and taxes.

According to the PPP, when a country's domestic price level is increasing (i.e., a country experiences inflation), that country's exchange rate must depreciate in order to return to PPP. For example, if the inflation rate in the United States is 4% and in Europe it is 2%, then the U.S. dollar should fall by 2% against the euro in order to maintain PPP.

As an example of how a country's exchange rate may change over time relative to its long-run PPP equilibrium, consider Argentina. Argentina's currency is officially known as the Argentine Peso (ARS), but it was introduced in 1992 as the "peso convertible" when it replaced the existing Argentine peso at a rate of 1 Argentine Peso Convertible to ten trillion existing pesos (note to reader: this is not a typo). This extremely high conversion rate was a method to control the hyperinflation of the currency and make denominations more manageable.

Figure 4.5 reports the nominal and real (i.e., PPP) exchange rate for Argentina expressed as U.S. dollars per Argentinian pesos (ARS). The nominal exchange rate is the solid line and the real exchange rate is the dashed line. The real exchange rate (RER) is the nominal rate adjusted for inflation. The nominal exchange rate went from 5.25 ARS per US dollar in 2013 to about 200 ARS per US dollar in 2023, a sharp depreciation of Argentina's exchange rate. In 2018 alone the Argentine peso was down by more than 90% against the US dollar, due to a weak Argentine economy and high inflation.

Given the ongoing devaluation of the peso it is difficult to see the difference between the nominal and the real rate in Figure 4.5. Refer to Figure 4.6 for the percent difference between the two rates. This figure shows that the ARS was overvalued as much as 40% in the latter part of 2015. The ARS remained under-valued until about September 2022, and then became overvalued again due to high inflation in Argentina, which was running at about 100%. To protect themselves from declining purchasing power due to the high inflation, Argentines hoard US dollars because the official exchange rate is artificially pegged by the government and it does not reflect market conditions, especially during times of high inflation.

Argentina is a significant commodity exporter (wheat, corn, beef, soybeans, soybean oil, soybean meal, and wine) and the government's artifi-

Figure 4.5: Argentina's Real and Nominal Exchange Rate

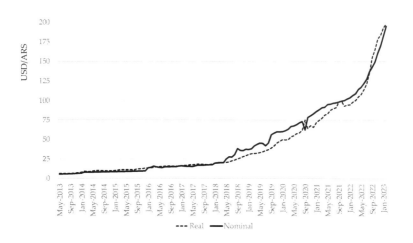

Source: World Bank, World Economics, WPI index.

cially pegged exchange rate reduces profits for Argentine exporters during times of high inflation. The government has responded to falling exports by offering several different preferential exchange rates, such as the "soy dollar", "malbec dollar", "Qatar dollar", etc. The "soy" and "Malbec" dollars allows exporters of soybeans and wine to obtain a premium exchange rate yielding more pesos to the dollar compared to the official exchange rate. The "Qatar dollar" was set up especially for Argentine football fans traveling to the 2022 World Cup. This was a good move because Argentina ended up winning the World Cup and Argentine captain Lionel Messi was voted the tournament's best player. Without the preferential exchange rate, few Argentine football fans could have afforded to travel to Qatar.

The equation used for calculating a change (Δ) in Argentina's real exchange rate (RER) is as follows:

$$\Delta RER = \Delta e \times \left(\Delta P^A / \Delta P^{US}\right) \tag{4.1}$$

where e is the nominal U.S. dollar to the ARS (i.e., Argentina peso) exchange rate, ΔP^A is the change in the general price level (i.e., the inflation rate) in Argentina and ΔP^{US} is the U.S. inflation rate. If the nominal exchange rate "e" does not change, and at the same time Argentina's inflation rate is higher than in the U.S., then the RER will increase according to the above formula, and is the case in Figure 4.5 which shows the real rate moving above the nominal rate in early 2006. Argentina's real exchange rate in the 2006-13 time period remained above the nominal rate (i.e., was overval-

Figure 4.6: Over and Under Valuation of Argentina's Exchange Rate

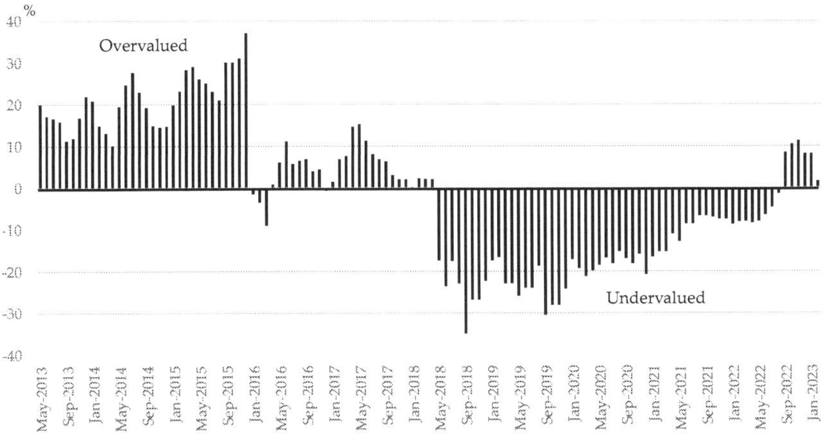

Source: World Bank, World Economics, WPI index.

ued) due to high inflation in that country. The Economist magazine stopped publishing Argentina's official inflation rate because the magazine determined the official rate was inaccurate. The website www.pricestats.com placed Argentina's actual inflation rate at least double the official rate. According to the above formula (equation 4.1) for the RER, if Argentina was to devalue its peso, then "e" would decline, and so would the RER, closing the gap between the RER and the nominal rate shown in Figure 4.5.

We see from Table 4.1 that currency futures are traded in many different countries including India, Russia, Brazil, Argentina, Korea, Japan and the United States. The largest market is in the U.S. (CME) which trades a number of different currencies such as the European Euro, Australian Dollar, Canadian Dollar, British Pound, Japanese Yen, Mexican Peso and the Swiss Franc. A popular contract traded at the ICE is the U.S. dollar index futures, based on the following weighted average formula of six currencies: Euro (57.6%) + Japanese yen (13.6%) + British pound (11.9%) + Canadian dollar (9.1%) + Swedish krona (4.2%) + Swiss franc (3.6%).

In practice, currencies deviate from their PPP rates for long time periods and therefore the PPP model does a notoriously poor job of forecasting short-term exchange rate changes. The most likely explanation is that the PPP theory is too simplistic and does not capture the importance of international capital flows. Dornbusch (1987) developed a more complicated model of exchange rates focused on asset markets to explain short-term exchange rates. His model assumes that capital will move freely among countries seeking out the highest expected return based on interest rates

Table 4.1: Some of the Top Volume Foreign Exchange Futures Contracts

Contract	Contract Size	Country Where Traded
U.S. $/Indian Rupee	1,000 USD	India (MCX-SX & NSE)
U.S. $/Russian Ruble	1,000 USD	Russia (Micex-RTS)
European Euro	125,000 Euro	U.S. (CME)
U.S. $/Brazilian Real	50,000 USD	Brazil (BM&F)
U.S. $/Argentina Peso	1,000 USD	Argentina (ROFEX)
Australian $	100,000 AUD	U.S. (CME)
British Pound	62,5000 GBP	U.S. (CME)
Japanese Yen	12,500,000 Yen	U.S. (CME)
Canadian $	100,000 CAD	U.S. (CME)
Mexican Peso	500,000 Pesos	U.S. (CME)
Swiss Franc	125,000 Francs	U.S. (CME)
U.S. $/Korean Won	10,000 USD	Korea (KRX)
U.S. Dollar Index	USD against 6 major currencies	U.S. (CME)
U.S. $/Japanese Yen	10,000 USD	Japan (TFX)

Source: Futures Industry Association

and expected currency appreciation or depreciation. The movement of capital will continue until the expected return is equalized across countries.

To illustrate this concept, assume that government bonds in Canada pay 8% interest and U.S. government bonds pay 4%. Investors might begin to invest capital in the Canadian money market (i.e., buy Canadian bonds) and the flow of capital north to Canada will expand the demand for Canadian dollars and drive up the value of the Canadian dollar. The Canadian dollar rate will continue to strengthen against the U.S. dollar until a point is reached where the market participants believe the Canadian dollar has become too strong and is likely to depreciate in the future. If the expectation of a change in the exchange rate gets to the level where the Canadian dollar is expected to depreciate by 4%, then investors would no longer view Canadian 8% bonds as a superior investment opportunity compared to the U.S. market. In other words, the Canadian/U.S. exchange rate will continue to change up until the point where the U.S. interest rate is equal to the Canadian interest rate plus the expected change in the exchange rate.

A formal representation of the (approximate) relationship between international interest rates and exchange rates is the interest rate parity condition:

Box 4.3 It's "Deflation" George, Not "Devaluation"

U.S. President George W. Bush caught foreign currency traders by surprise in early 2002. President Bush emerged from private discussions with Japan's Prime Minister in Tokyo and announced that the two leaders had talked about Japan's "devaluation" issue. Currency markets around the world reacted and the Japanese Yen immediately fell in response to George Bush's statement. Currency traders interpreted Bush's statement to mean that Japan was going to let the Yen fall in order to bolster its exports. However, after the currency markets reacted, Bush Presidential aides sheepishly corrected George's statement to indicate that he meant to say "deflation" instead of "devaluation". Deflation means falling domestic prices, something totally different than devaluation, which means allowing the value of one's currency to fall relative to other currencies.

This was a classic example of where a politician was confused over economic terminology. In this case, it cost people money, as George W. Bush's *faux pas* no doubt resulted in losses for some currency traders.

$$i_{US} = i_{CDN} + \left(e^f - e^s\right)/e^s \tag{4.2}$$

where i_{US} is the interest rate in the United States, i_{CDN} is the interest rate in Canada, e^f is the forward (or futures) exchange rate (U.S. dollars per Canadian dollar), and e^s is the spot exchange rate (U.S. dollars per Canadian dollar). The interest rate parity condition holds exactly when the rate of return on U.S. dollar deposits is equal to the expected rate of return on Canadian dollar deposits adjusted for the expected movement in the currency. Of course, equation (4.2) applies to any pair of countries, with convertible currencies. The United States and Canada are used here for illustrative purposes only.

According to the interest rate parity condition, a country with relatively high interest rates will experience an appreciation of its currency. At the same time, a country with relatively low interest rates will experience a depreciation of its currency. These expectations will be reflected in the futures (and forward) exchange rates. If interest rate parity does not hold, arbitrage will kick in and a trader could profit by borrowing in a low interest rate country and simultaneously lending in a high interest rate country. A popular currency "carry trade" before the 2008 financial crisis was to borrow in Japan and invest in Australia, where interest rates were much higher (see Box 4.4).

To further illustrate the interest rate parity condition, consider the following example. Suppose that the interest rate on a 90-day government treasury bill is 1.03% in Canada (i_{CDN}) and 0.10% in the United States (i_{US}). At the same time, assume the spot exchange rate (U.S. $ per Cdn. $) is 1.0214 ($e^s$) and the exchange rate on a futures contract price for delivery in three months time is 1.0198 (e^f). In this example, the Canadian dollar is trading at a forward discount to the U.S. dollar because the futures exchange rate is below the spot rate. Does the interest parity condition hold in this example?

Substituting the above exchange rate and interest rate figures into equation 4.2 gives:

$$0.10 \approx 1.03 + (1.0198 - 1.0214) / 1.0214 \tag{4.3}$$

$$0.10 < 1.0214 \tag{4.4}$$

Since the expected rate of return in Canada exceeds that in the United States, the interest parity condition does not hold. The U.S. investor could expect to make money by purchasing the Canadian 3-month treasury. As a result, capital would be expected to flow from the United States to Canada.

Currency Futures and Options

Currency futures began trading on the Chicago Mercantile Exchange (CME) in 1972. This class of currency futures trading has grown in importance because of globalization, the growth of foreign trade in goods and services, and the growth of foreign investment.

The CME quotes exchange rates as the U.S. dollar price of one unit of foreign currency. Sometimes, price quotes in the spot market will be the other way around; namely, the foreign currency price of one U.S. dollar. For example, if one U.S. dollar is convertible into Japanese yen (¥) at an exchange rate of ¥120/$, this means it costs 120¥ to purchase one U.S. dollar. Conversely, it costs $0.008333 to buy one Japanese yen, which is how the futures market quotes the exchange rate. Whether the home or foreign currency is in the numerator is totally arbitrary, but the CME futures price quote always has the U.S. dollar in the numerator.

Table 4.2 reports currency futures quotations for the Japanese Yen and Canadian dollar. Consider the Canadian dollar contract, traded in units of $100,000 ($Cdn) on the CME. Suppose that a trader sold one January Canadian dollar contract at $0.7881 (as reported in Table 4.2) and then the Canadian dollar subsequently strengthened to $0.7929 (i.e., the Canadian dollar became more expensive, denominated in U.S. dollars). In this case, the trader would lose $.0048 × $100,000 = $480 (before commission fees).

Box 4.4 FX Carry Trade Opportunities Come and Go

The carry trade has been a popular way to make money in the currency market. Investors take advantage of differences in interest rates by borrowing money in a low-yielding currency and investing in a high-yielding currency. As long as the exchange rate between the two currencies remains relatively constant, the investor can earn a profit by exploiting the interest rate spread. After the financial crisis of 2008, the Australian dollar was a popular currency to use as the high-yielding investment vehicle. The Australian dollar's interest rate was over 4.25% until April 2012 when the Reserve Bank of Australia reduced rates to 3.7% and then steadily continued cutting rates. These reductions in the interest rate reduced the spread between Australia's rate and the interest rates of the U.S. dollar, the Euro and the yen thus reducing the efficacy of this particular carry trade.

In 2023, the Mexican peso was relatively strong compared to the U.S. dollar as the country's relatively high interest rates attracted investors to buy pesos. The peso was a top performing currency that year. Investors could borrow in a currency with a low interest rate, like the US dollar, and then turn around and purchase Mexican financial assets offering higher rates of return. In 2023, short term interest rates in Mexico were 11.4%, compared to 4.7% in the United States.

Table 4.2: Currency Futures Quotations

	Open	High	Low	Settle	Change	Lifetime High	Lifetime Low	Open Int
Japanese Yen (CME)- ¥ 12,500,000; $ per 100 ¥								
Dec	0.8895	0.8903	0.8864	0.8885	0.0001	0.936	0.8595	217,068
Jan	0.891	0.89205	0.88835	**0.8903**	0.0001	0.905	0.875	1,733
Canadian Dollar (CME)-CAD 100,000; $ per CAD								
Dec	0.7886	0.7923	0.7873	0.7876	0.0002	0.8293	0.7286	137,196
Jan	0.7903	0.7921	0.7882	**0.7881**	0.0002	0.8111	0.7753	1,202

In Table 4.2, the Japanese yen contract is quoted in dollars per yen (i.e., the CME standard way of reporting currency values with U.S. dollars in the numerator). For example, the settlement price shown for January yen is actually $.008903/¥, because the prices in Table 4.2 are per 100 ¥. Note that the decimal point on the yen's price is moved two places to the right, in order to save ink. This convention of dropping the two zeros from the price is indicated in places like the *Wall Street Journal* by (.00) to the right of

---

Box 4.5 The Investment Biker

Jim Rogers is a writer and former currency trader. His website says that he got his start in business at the age of five, selling peanuts. As an adult, Jim states that he made a small fortune trading foreign currency futures. After he made his millions, Mr. Rogers started traveling the globe, enjoying life and looking for investment opportunities overseas. One of his first trips around the world was on a motorcycle and he wrote a bestselling book entitled Investment Biker. Jim Rogers has continued writing about his travel experiences and has published numerous magazine articles on travel and overseas investment opportunities. At the turn of the millennium, Mr. Rogers and his female companion struck out on a three-year round-the-world journey in a custom designed Mercedes-Benz. His fascinating stories about the people, the countries, and the markets visited are available on his website: www.jimrogers.com. You will find some interesting interviews with Jim Rogers on his website.

$ per yen in the Japan yen header in Table 4.2.

The CME also trades options on the underlying currency futures contracts that are shown in Table 4.2. There is active trading in options on futures for the Japanese yen, Canadian dollar, British pound, Swiss franc, and the European euro. In 2013, the CME launched a forex futures contract based on the Chinese renminbi (RMB)–also known as the yuan. Then in 2023 the CME introduced FX options on the USD/Chinese renminbi (USD/CNH). The CNH became a more important world currency after Russia invaded Ukraine in 2022, as the renminbi replaced the US dollar in Russian transactions related to oil and grain exports. China is a significant importer of these and other commodities from Russia. Before the Ukraine war the renminbi was not important in the Russian market, but that all changed once Russia was dealing with Western trade sanctions following the invasion of Ukraine.

Debt Instruments

Debt instrument (i.e., interest rate) futures have a much shorter history than commodity futures, but debt instrument contracts now dominate the futures industry in terms of trading volume. Interest rate futures are based on the same principle as any other futures market contract, but the asset is money and its price can be loosely described as the interest rate, which is the cost of borrowing money over a certain time period. Inflation erodes the time value of money and, therefore, interest rates have two components. The first component covers expected inflation, called the inflation premium, and the second component reflects the real rate of return. The expected real rate of interest is the difference between the nominal rate of interest and the expected rate of inflation. In other words, the real interest rate is the nominal interest rate adjusted for the expected erosion of purchasing power resulting from inflation. For example, with a nominal interest rate of 6 percent and an expected rate of inflation of 2 percent, the expected real rate of interest is 4 percent.

The supply and demand for money determines interest rate levels and important supply and demand fundamentals include monetary policy, fiscal policy, inflationary expectations, and international capital flows. The term fiscal policy refers to government expenditures on goods and services and to the way in which the government finances these expenditures (through borrowing or taxes). The term **monetary policy** refers to actions taken by the central government to influence the amount of money and credit in the economy.

Interest rate futures were first traded in Chicago in 1975. Futures contracts written on fixed-income Government National Mortgage Association (Ginnie Mae's) "mortgage-backed securities" were the first interest rate futures contracts launched by the CBOT. A "fixed-income security" generates a fixed income each year. The following year, Treasury-Bill (T-Bill) futures contracts were introduced on the Chicago Mercantile Exchange–CME. Treasury bond futures were then launched in 1977 on the CBOT. Interest rate futures were initially developed in the U.S., but they quickly expanded to international markets in Europe and Asia. Euribor and Euro-bond futures are successful European contracts.

The introduction of these various interest rate contracts revolutionized the futures market by introducing a vehicle to hedge interest rate risk. The futures industry's timing with the introduction of interest rate futures was impeccable. In the late 1970's, annual interest rates in the United States rose to over 20 percent and became very volatile. Prior to this, there had been a long period of interest rate stability. Financial firms that used the futures market to hedge during the period of high interest rates in the late 1970's and early 1980's outperformed their competitors, because those firms that hedged were successful in reducing the risks associated with large interest rate fluctuations. Such hedgers included banks, investment banks, insurance companies, pension funds, and bond traders. The volume of trade in interest rate futures grew dramatically in the early 1980's and has continued to expand rapidly since then. Figure 4.7 plots the U.S. prime interest rate from 1958 to 2023, which averaged 7.4% over the entire time period shown and exceeded 20% in 1981. The prime rate was held constant at 3.25% from

December 2008 (after the financial crisis) through the end of 2015.

In less than four years after its introduction in 1977, the US Treasury bond futures contract became the world's most actively traded futures contract. T-bond futures and options volume peaked in 1998 at about 150 million contracts and then began to fall as the U.S. government moved away from borrowing money through long-term debt (see Box 4.7). In 2022, about 97 million T-bond futures contracts were traded on the CBOT, each covering $100,000 in bonds. In that same year, the futures trading volume for 10 year US T-notes exceeded 460 million contracts, see Table 4.3.

The Eurodollar contract was one of the most widely traded interest financial futures contract with 394 million contracts in 2022. Eurodollars are foreign bank deposits of U.S. dollars, and the Eurodollar futures was based on the London Interbank Offer Rate (LIBOR) paid on U.S. dollar deposits in London. However the role of the LIBOR came to an end in 2023 as the U.K. Financial Conduct Authority determined that the LIBOR is no longer representative of the underlying market and economic reality. As a result, the SOFR (published by the Federal Reserve Bank of New York) has displaced the Eurodollar as the leading futures contract for managing short-term interest rate risk exposure (see Table 4.3). In 2018 the Intercontinental Exchange (ICE Europe) introduced a three-month futures contract based on "Sonia", the Bank of England's interest rate benchmark which will replace LIBOR in the UK. This contract is called the 3 Month SONIA futures.

Figure 4.7: U.S. Prime Interest Rate

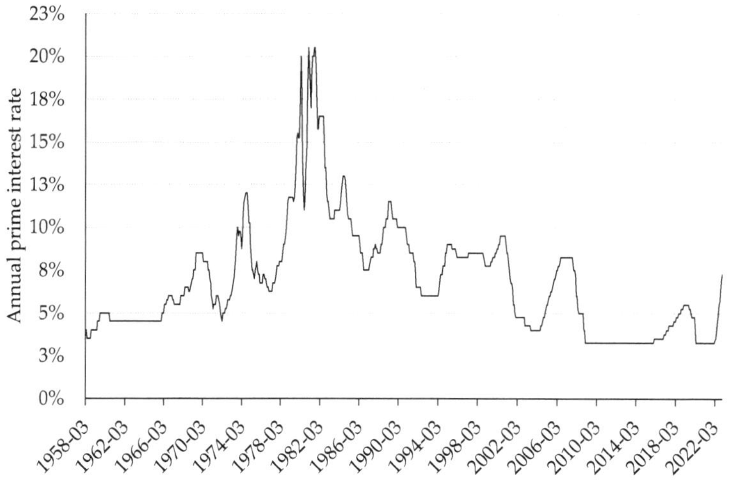

Average yearly prime rate	
2012	3.25%
2013	3.25%
2014	3.25%
2015	3.25%
2016	3.50%
2017	4.06%
2018	4.88%
2019	5.29%
2020	3.58%
2021	3.25%
2022	4.85%

Source: https://fred.stlouisfed.org/series/MPRIME.

Prior to the introduction of debt instrument futures and options, gov-

Table 4.3: Top US Financial Futures Contracts

Exchange	Category	Contract	2022 Volume Millions
CME	Equity	E-mini S&P 500	503.95
CBOT	Interest Rates	10 Year Treasury Note	462.60
CME	Interest Rates	3 Month SOFR	418.85
CME	Interest Rates	Eurodollar	394.59
CME	Equity	Micro E-mini Nasdaq 100 Index	364.95
CME	Equity	Micro E-mini S&P 500 Index	343.97
CBOT	Interest Rates	5 Year Treasury Note	326.81
CME	Equity	E-mini Nasdaq 100	176.87
CBOT	Interest Rates	2 Year Treasury Note	169.86
CBOT	Interest Rates	30 Year Treasury Bond	97.40
CBOT	Interest Rates	Ultra 10 Year Treasury Note	95.65
CBOT	Interest Rates	Federal Funds	83.83
CME	Currencies	Euro FX	61.53
CME	Equity	E-mini Russell 2000 Index	60.57
CBOT	Interest Rates	Ultra Treasury Bond	59.94
CBOE	Other	CBOE Volatility Index (VX)	52.24
CBOT	Equity	E-mini $5 DJIA	51.03
CBOT	Equity	E-micro $5 DJIA	44.93
ICE	Equity	Mini MSCI Emerging Markets	44.71
CME	Currencies	Japanese Yen	39.57
CME	Currencies	British Pound	31.24

Source: Futures Industry Association.

Box 4.6 Characteristics of Debt Instruments

- Government Debt Instruments (or "Treasuries")

    - Bills: Mature in < 1 yr.
    - Notes: Mature in > 1 yr. and < 10 yrs.
    - Bonds: Mature in > 10 yrs.
    - T-Bills are sold at a discount from face value (par) & do not pay interest
    - T-Notes & bonds generate semi-annual interest payments

- Municipal Bonds: Local Government Issues
- Secured Overnight Financing Rate (SOFR) is a secured overnight interest rate published by New York Federal Reserve

---

ernment securities (such as T-Bills or T-Bonds) were traded solely in a decentralized over-the-counter market, and prices were not highly visible to the public. The futures and options market brought increased transparency with regard to market activity. Prices and information became readily available and soon corporations, banks, and other commercial and financial institutions turned to the financial futures and options markets as a way to manage financial risk through hedging. In addition, debt instrument futures provide speculators with a market opportunity to speculate whether interest rates will rise or fall.

Reasons for increased trade volume in debt instrument futures include interest rate volatility, globalization of financial assets, and the fact that debt instruments are highly sensitive to interest rate changes (due to changes in monetary and fiscal policy, inflation, and capital flows). The debt instrument futures market is a very liquid market and there is increased awareness of hedging benefits associated with trading on this market.

As with commodity futures, interest rate futures prices (theoretically) adhere to the cost of carry model:

$$F_{t,T} = S_t \left(1 + C_{t,T}\right) \tag{4.5}$$

where $F_{t,T}$ is the futures price for delivery at time T, S_t is the spot price at time t, and $C_{t,T}$ is the net cost of carry from time t to T. Storing a financial instrument such as a Treasury Bond is conceptually the same as storing a commodity such as coffee or wheat, except that the relative importance of some storage costs (such as warehouse costs) differ. Arbitrage is also at work in the financial market to ensure that the equality in equation 4.5 roughly holds. The net cost of carry is equal to returns minus carrying charges, with interest rate futures carrying charges essentially equal to the net costs of financing. Financial futures closely adhere to the cost-of-carry model because they are highly storable, the market is competitive and there are no "seasonal" characteristics to the market as in grains.

Suppose that the equality in equation (4.5) did not hold and $F_t > S(1 + C_{0,t})$. In this case a trader could borrow money to buy the underlying financial instrument at a net cost of $S(1 + C_{0,t})$ and simultaneously sell a futures contract for price F_t. A riskless arbitrage profit would be earned through buying the spot and selling the futures contract and, as a result, futures prices would be driven down and spot prices driven up until the potential arbitrage profit approached zero as in equation (4.5).

Similarly, equation (4.5) holds for two different futures months:

$$F_{t+1} = F_t (1 + C_{t,t+1}) \tag{4.6}$$

where F_{t+1} is the futures price for delivery at time t+1, and $C_{t,t+1}$ is the net cost of carry from period t to period t+1.

Suppose June Treasury Bond futures are trading at 97-30 (which is equivalent to a contract value of $97,937) and September futures are trading at 96-29 (for a contract value of $96,906). If a trader purchases a June contract and simultaneously sells a September contract, is there an arbitrage profit opportunity? The net cost of carrying the bond from June to September ($C_{t,t+1}$) has two components, the financing cost associated with purchasing the bond and the interest paid by the bond (which is a negative cost). Suppose the 90 day T-Bill rate is 2.5%, which approximates the financing cost of holding the bond. The T-Bond futures contract specifies delivery of a 6% $100,000 bond, which returns $1500 to the holder for the June-September time period. Therefore, the net cost of financing is .025/4 × ($97,937) − $1500 = $888. Substituting into equation (4.6) gives:

$$\$96,906 \approx \$97,937 - \$888 \tag{4.7}$$

$$\$96,906 < \$97,049 \tag{4.8}$$

So, the left and right hand sides of Equation (4.7) are approximately equal, with a difference of only $143. This is a small fraction of the total value of the bond. In all likelihood, transactions costs would exceed $143, so the cost of carry arbitrage condition in equation (4.6) approximately holds in this T-Bond example. Keep in mind that this is a simplified example because it ignores the fact that the seller of a bond futures contract has both timing and quality delivery options. Therefore, equation (4.7) is only an approximation of the true and exact arbitrage condition.

When we solve equation (4.5) for the cost of carry, the result is the implied repo rate (repo is short for repurchase):

$$C_{0,t} = (F_t/S) - 1 \tag{4.9}$$

The implied repo rate in equation (4.9) is the interest rate implied by the difference between the futures and spot price. The term repo rate is derived from a repurchase agreement that is very common in financial markets. In a repurchase agreement, a financial asset owned by one party is sold to a second party at one price and then repurchased by the first party after a period of time at a slightly higher price. In other words, the second party is essentially providing the first party with a loan. The difference in the buying and selling price is the interest earned by the second party which, on an annualized basis, is called the **repo rate**.

The Term Structure of Interest Rates and the Yield Curve

The yield curve is a simple relationship that reveals an extensive amount of information about the market for debt instruments and overall government macroeconomic policy. The yield curve is the relationship between yield (i.e., the average rate of return, or the interest rate) and term to maturity. In other words, a yield curve is a graph that plots interest rates paid by bonds and short-term debt instruments as a function of time to maturity. The yield curve for Treasury debt, for example, plots yields for (default free) instruments with maturities ranging from 90 day T-Bills to 30 year T-bonds. This relationship is often referred to as the "term structure of interest rates." The yield curve is a very popular tool for investors because it provides an indication of the expected future level of interest rates and expected economic growth.

Figure 4.8 plots two US Treasury yield curves, where the horizontal axis represents the length of time to maturity and the vertical axis reports the yield on each instrument. Figure 4.8 displays the yield curve for the spring of 2022, and another for the spring of 2023. The May 2022 yield curve is represented by an upward sloping line in Figure 4.8 and the March 2023 yield curve has a portion that is downward sloping. The 2023 curve lies above the 2022 curve (as interest rates were higher in 2023). The difference in the shape between the two yield curves in Figure 4.8 is striking and it represents a significant change in short term interest rates in the one year interval due to Federal Reserve concerns over inflation coming out of the COVID pandemic.

Normally, the yield curve has a positive (i.e., upwards) slope, as shown by the May 2022 curve in Figure 4.8, because longer-term investments typically pay higher interest rates than shorter-term investments. This is due, in part, to investors' liquidity preference and the fact that longer-term investments are more risky than shorter-term investments, due to uncertainty surrounding future inflation rates.

Figure 4.8: US Treasury Yield Curve

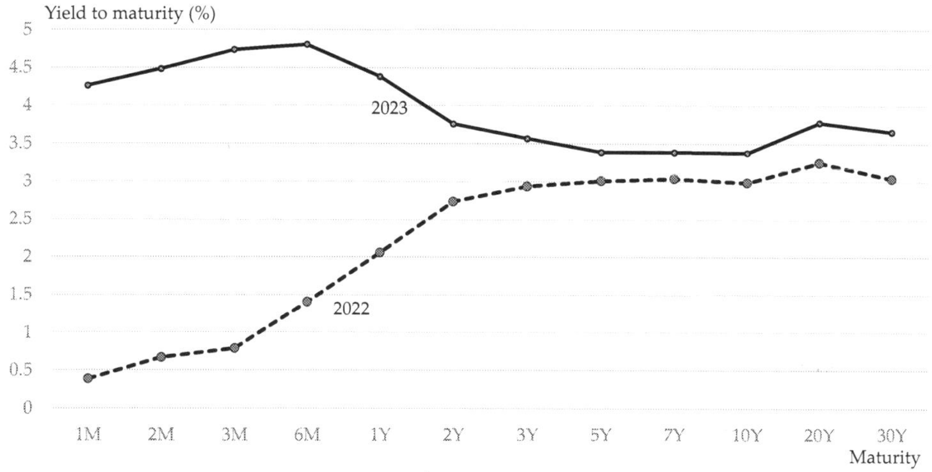

Source: U.S. Department of Treasury.

The slope (i.e., steepness) of the yield curve changes when interest rates change. The yield curve often has a relatively steep slope when short-term interest rates are low (e.g., in the spring of 2022). However, it is possible that the yield curve takes on a negative slope when short-term interest rates are high (e.g., in the spring of 2023). The downward sloping yield curve appears periodically, but its slope was most pronounced in the early 1980's when short-term interest rates were close to 20 percent and at the same time long-term bonds yielded about 14 percent. The yield curve sometimes flattens out and becomes almost horizontal, which means that investors buying long-term bonds receive no premium over shorter-term investments.

Economists have developed different explanations for the shape of the yield curve: the expectations theory, the liquidity preference theory, and the market segmentation theory. Each of these three theories offers a partial explanation for the shape of the yield curve (i.e., the term structure).

The **expectations theory** states that the shape of the yield curve is a market forecast of forthcoming spot interest rates. If investors are risk-neutral, then forward interest rates represent the market's expectations of future spot interest rates. Investors are assumed to be risk neutral because they are indifferent to the security's maturity and they are only interested in the yield. This theory assumes that the forward rate is an unbiased estimator of what the future interest rate is expected to be. This means that if the yield curve has a positive slope, then the market believes that spot interest rates will be higher in the future. This could be due to a market belief that the inflation rate is going to increase in the future. Conversely, if inflation were expected to decline in the future, then the yield curve would slope down, under the expectations theory.

According to the expectations theory, if investors can obtain a higher return on 30-year bonds, they will then arbitrage the market by selling 10-year bonds and buying 30-year bonds instead. This action will drive up the price of 30-year bonds and drive down the price of 10-year bonds. Soon market equilibrium will be reached and the return from both bonds will be equal. At this point, investors will be indifferent as to whether they hold the 10-year bond or the 30-year bond.

The **liquidity preference theory** contends that the shape of the yield curve is affected by a liquidity premium between long and short-term securities. In financial markets, a liquidity (risk) premium may be required to attract risk-averse investors to buy risky assets. For example, a government bond maturing in one year may be considered low risk by such an investor because the probability of a dramatic change in interest rates is small compared to a longer-term bond. Therefore, investors are willing to pay more for shorter-term bonds, compared to longer-term bonds. If this theory were correct, then long-term interest rates would exceed short-term interest rates by the amount of the liquidity premium.

The liquidity preference theory rejects the notion that investors are indifferent to maturity lengths. This theory maintains that investors prefer shorter-term maturities, all other things being equal, and this is why they will pay more for shorter-term bonds than for longer-term bonds. The extra amount paid is the liquidity premium. This means that buying a 30-year bond will bring a greater return than a 10-year bond, by the amount of the liquidity premium.

The **market segmentation theory** assumes that each maturity is segmented from the other maturities. Each maturity has a unique group of investors with different investment goals and horizons and these investors do not view alternative maturities as being substitutable. This theory asserts that there is a market for short-term securities, another separate market for medium-term securities, and a third separate market for long-term securities. According to this theory, spot rates are determined by supply and demand conditions in each market.

For example, banks have short-term preferences and life insurance companies have long-term preferences. These institutions prefer to make bond purchases that match their respective needs. However, they will buy bonds outside their preferred maturity range if the yield is sufficiently attractive. Therefore, according to the market segmentation theory, the yield curve is primarily determined by the interaction of these large institutions in the marketplace. The liquidity preference, market segmentation, and expectations theories all help to explain the shape of the yield curve, and no one theory dominates over time.

The yield curve provides a simple but powerful forecasting role for trades. The slope of the yield curve reflects where the markets expect the economy is heading. In fact, some traders believe that the yield curve can do a better job of predicting recessions than large scale economic models. As mentioned, normally the yield curve slopes upward with long-term rates being higher than short-term rates, due to higher risk in the long-term, especially inflation. Historically there has been a close link between the shape of the yield curve and economic growth, see Figure 4.9. As a simple rule, the steeper the upward sloping yield curve the more rapid the (expected) economics growth. In contrast, a negative sloping yield curve, with short-term rates higher than long-term ones, signals a recession around the corner.

In Figure 4.9, the interest rate spread between the 10 year and the 3 month Treasury rate is shown as the solid line. When the 10 year minus the 3 month the yield curve goes inverted, the solid line in Figure 4.9 dips below zero. In August 2006 the yield curve became *inverted* (i.e., negative slope) as short-term interest rates exceeded long-term rates. At the time this was a signal that aggregate demand in the economy was high–for instance housing prices were on fire. At the time the yield curve was signaling a recession, which officially began in December 2007, less than one and a half years later, as shown by the dashed line (representing real GDP) in Figure 4.9. Typically a recession occurs anywhere from 5 months to two years after the yield curve becomes inverted. The recession that began at the end of December 2007 lasted until the summer of 2009, and it is known as the "Great Recession." It is considered one of the most significant economic declines in U.S. history. American author Michael Lewis wrote a great book about the recession and his book is called *The Big Short*, which was made into a movie. As Lewis describes, the 2007-08 financial crisis and recession was set off by the U.S. housing bubble. However, Lewis forgot to mention that in August 2006 the yield curve predicted the meltdown.

The Federal Reserve at Cleveland maintains an informative website on the relationship between the yield curve and economic growth. To visit the site google *Cleveland Fed and Yield Curve*. The Cleveland Fed website has a nice section on using the yield curve to predict future GDP growth.

Figure 4.9: 10-Year Minus 3-Month Treasury Rate and GDP Growth

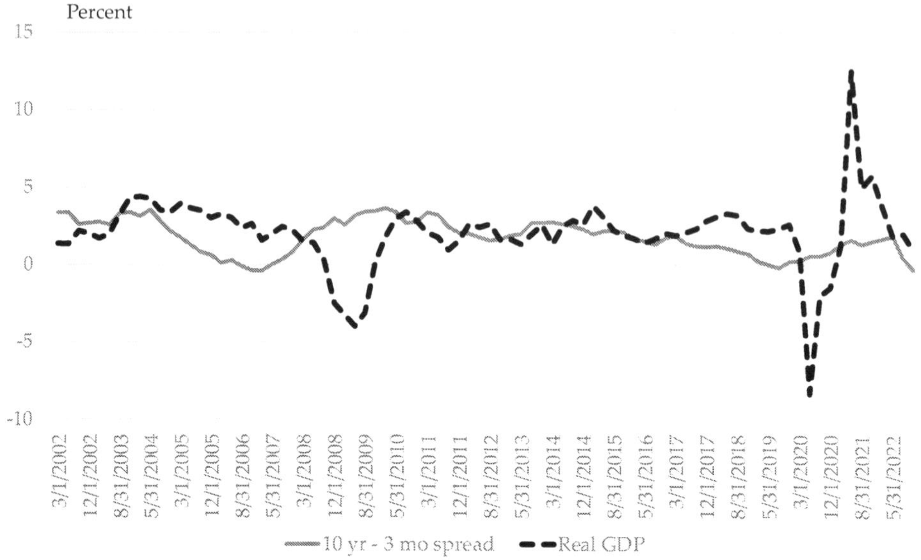

Source: Federal Reserve Bank of Cleveland.

Treasury Bond Futures

As explained above, a Treasury Bond (T-bond) is an interest-bearing cer-
tificate sold by the U.S. federal government. T-bonds are assets that earn
money with essentially no default risk because they come with the federal government's guarantee of payment. Selling bonds is one of the federal government's methods of borrowing money in order to help finance its
spending. The reason that bonds are essentially free of default risk is that
the government can always print more money in order to provide payment.
The owner of a T-bond can hold the bond for a long period of time and collect (a fixed amount of semi-annual) interest (i.e., coupon payments). Alternatively, the owner can sell the bond in the secondary market, the market in
which previously issued securities are traded, and a profit would be earned
if the price of the bond moves up. The bond's price is sensitive to interest
rate changes, as explained below. The T-bond's face value (e.g., $100,000)
is the amount to be repaid by the government upon maturity and the fixed
amount of interest paid on the bond is the coupon value. For example, a
bond with a 6% coupon and a face value of $100,000 will pay annual interest
of $6,000. Bonds, however, usually pay semiannually and in this example
the bond will pay $3,000 each 6 months.

T-bonds are long-term financial instruments. Related government
medium-term and short-term debt securities include Treasury bills (T-Bills)

with maturities of up to one year, and Treasury notes (T-notes) with maturities between one and ten years. The U.S. government is not the only institution that sells bonds. State and local (municipal) governments also issue bonds in order to raise money, as do corporations and foreign governments. In the United Kingdom (UK), government bonds are called *gilts* and the name comes from the past when the paper instruments actually had gilded edges. The German government bonds are called *bunds*—the German parliament is called the Bundestag.

Spot market bonds are traded around the world and there is no central global exchange or market for the majority of bonds that are traded in the spot or cash market. Hence, the bond market is known as an over-the-counter market, rather than an exchange market. However, bond futures and options are traded on exchanges, while the overwhelming majority of bonds do not trade on exchanges.

A bond's return comes from the fixed amount of interest the bond pays (i.e., the coupon rate) plus or minus changes in the value (or price) of the bond, which depends on the interest rate. The annual interest paid is a fixed amount, but the price of the bond fluctuates with market interest rates. Suppose that initially the market interest rate is equal to the bond's fixed coupon rate. In this case, the T-Bond would trade at its full value in the secondary market. In other words, it would trade at its **par value**. If the market interest rates rise and exceed the bond's fixed coupon rate, then the market price of the bond falls and it trades at a discount to par value. The reason the price of the bond falls is that a buyer expects to earn at least the going market interest rate and if the buyer bids the par value, then he or she would earn less than the market rate. A bond's value falls when interest rates rise and, conversely, a bond's value rises when interest rates fall. Therefore, a speculator who believes that long-term interest rates will rise is going to sell bond futures because he or she is expecting the value of bonds to fall. In contrast, the speculator expecting long-term interest rates to fall will buy bond futures, with the expectation that bond prices will rise. A measure called *duration risk* measures the sensitivity of a bond's price to interest rate changes and the higher the duration the more sensitive the price is to moves in interest rates. For example, if rates were to rise 1%, a bond with a duration of 6 years would lose approximately 6% of its value.

A bond's current yield is equal to the annual interest or coupon payment divided by the prevailing market price. For example, if a bond that is currently worth $97,000 on the secondary market has a fixed payment of $8,000 per year, then its effective yield is $8,000 / $97,000 = .0824 (or 8.24%). If the current yield rises, then the bond price falls, and vice versa.

The basic bond pricing formula is:

$$Price\ (\$) = \frac{Face\ Value}{(1+r)^t} \tag{4.10}$$

where r is yield and t is time. For example, today's price of a bond with a $1,000 face value that matures in one year with a yield of 10% is equal to:

$$Price = \$1,000/1.1 = \$909.09 \tag{4.11}$$

When there is a stream of payments the bond's price is:

$$P_{i0} = \sum_{t=1}^{M} C_{it}/(1+r)^t \tag{4.12}$$

where P_{i0} is the current price and C_{it} is the payment in each time period t.

Treasury bonds are the U.S. government's long-term bonds and they are issued with maturities ranging from 20 to 30 years. The bonds are sold by the government through auction four times a year; in February, May, August, and November. The 30 year bonds were discontinued from 2001 to 2005, and then they were reintroduced (see Box 4.7) in place of shorter term (i.e. 10-year) bonds.

The CME's T-bond futures contract calls for delivery of the equivalent of a 15 to 25-year Treasury bond with a $100,000 face value, and a 6% coupon rate. However, the government does not issue 15-year bonds and, therefore, any government T-bond is deliverable as long as it has more than 15 years to maturity. When a particular bond is delivered, the exchange applies a "conversion factor" to adjust the price to correspond to the hypothetical bond specified by the futures contract. The holder of the short futures position delivering the bond will receive a price that equals the futures settlement price times the conversion factor plus accrued interest. The CME publishes the conversion factors covering each possible deliverable bond. The conversion adjusts the different coupon rates and maturity dates to equate with the 6 percent standard. This conversion ensures that any deliverable bond will receive a fair price if delivered on a futures contract. The conversion factor is the price of the delivered bond ($1 par value) to yield 6 percent.

Table 4.4 is a table of interest rate futures quotations. The first contract shown in Table 4.4 is for Treasury Bonds. The T-Bond contract is for a $100,000 bond and bond futures are priced as a % of par, plus 32nds of a point (e.g., 131 23/32 = 131-23). The price is in points ($1,000) and thirty-seconds of a point, and each 32nd is worth $31.25, since 32 × $31.25 = $1,000. For example, in Table 4.4 the settlement price for the September contract is 131-10, which equals 131 10/32% of par value. For a $100,000 bond, this means the market price is $131, 312. So, if you buy a futures

---

Box 4.7 How many lives does the U.S. 30 year Treasury Bond have?

The 30-year U.S. Treasury bond was introduced in 1977 to finance large U.S. government deficits during the 1980s and 1990s. At the time, the government had a huge demand for long-term loans. For many years, the U.S. government's 30-year bond served as a financial benchmark. Many domestic and foreign investors viewed it as a very safe and liquid asset. Insurance companies and pension funds, with long-term liabilities, were regular purchasers of the 30-year bonds. However, in 2001, the U.S. government decided that it no longer needed the 30-year bond to meet its financing needs, and the U.S. Treasury announced that the government would no longer issue the long-term bonds. One reason the 30-year bond was abandoned was that the federal government's budget moved from a deficit to a surplus.

However, the budget surpluses did not continue and as the United States repeatedly ran budget deficits, the 30-year bond reemerged in 2006. The return of the 30-year bond was welcome by the financial industry as it provided another product for Wall Street to sell and allowed investors to lock in low long-term favorable interest rates.

---

contract at a price of 131-10 and subsequently sell at it 131-11, this equals "one full point (32/32)", which is equal to $1,000, or (32 × $31.25). Each thirty-second is worth $31.25.

Treasury Note futures contracts are based on 2-year, 5-year, or 10-year Treasury Notes. The 10 year Treasury Note futures quotation in Table 4.4 represents a contract that has a $100,000 face value. Just like the T-Bond contract, the T-Note contract is traded on points and fractions of points (i.e., 32nds) with par based on 100 points. The trading of Treasuries in fractions is based on convention and it also used to be the case that stocks were traded in fractions—this was easier for traders before the computer age. Turning back to Table 4.4, if you sold a June 10 Year T-Note futures at the settle price of 115-26, and then the market moved the up to 117-10 when you liquidated, you would have lost 1 and 16/32nds or $1,500. Below, the 3 Month SOFR futures prices are explained.

Fed Funds Futures

The U.S. federal funds rate (also known as the *fed fund rate*) is the interest rate charged by banks to other financial institutions for overnight loans. Money is moved around from bank to bank on a daily basis to ensure that

Table 4.4: Interest Rate Futures Quotations

	Open	High	Low	Settle
30 Year Treasury Bonds (CBT) - $100,000; pts 32nds of 100%				
Sep	131-23	132-08	130-14	131-10
10 Year Treasury Notes (CBT) - $100,000; pts 32nds of 100%				
June	115-145	116-080	115-010	115-260
3 Mo SOFR (CME) - $2,500 * IMM index= 100 - R				
June	95.27	95.4450	95.2400	95.3700

Source: CME.

each bank complies with "reserve requirements" established by U.S. banking laws (discussed in the next section below). The fed fund "target" rate is set by the Federal Reserve as part of official monetary policy and it applies to short term interest rates. This interest rate is an extremely important financial benchmark. For instance, Kontonikas, MacDonald and Saggu (2013) found that the stock market reacts to unexpected cuts in the fed funds rate. Cieslak, Morse and Vissing-Jorgensen (2018) concluded that information on monetary policy could actually be used to make money in the stockmarket and that valuable information about upcoming Federal Open Market Committee (FOMC) decisions had periodically leaked from the Fed.

The FOMC officially establishes the target rate, and the target is a range with an upper and lower rate, such as 4.75% to 5.00%. The rate is potentially adjusted (or left unchanged) during Federal Reserve meetings that occur with regularity about eight times per year. Prior to each meeting the fed funds futures market anticipates what the FMOC might do with regard to the short term rate.

The Fed funds futures "prices in" traders' opinions of the forthcoming fed fund rate at the time of a specific futures contract expiry. There is a corresponding options market as well. The futures contracts are traded on the CME and they are cash settled. The futures price is based on the daily fed funds effective rate for a given month. The Fed Funds Futures contract size is $5 million and the price is based on the average overnight fed funds for 30 days during the futures expiry month. The contract price = 100 − average fed funds rate, during the contract expiry month.

The fed funds futures provide the market based probabilities (i.e., traders' net expectations) of future rate movements for forthcoming FOMC meetings. An excellent website explaning the probabilities and offering up to date information on this contract is the "Fed fund watch" http://www.cmegroup.com/trading/interest-rates/fed-funds.html.

Following the 2008 financial crisis the fed fund rate was kept low (at 0.25%) until December 2015 when it was raised to 0.5%. By 2017, there were strong signs of economy recovery in the U.S. economy and the Fed continued raising interest rates. At the June 2017 meeting the FMOC raised the upper limit on the target rate to 1.25%. However, in early 2017 there was much uncertainty as to whether or not the FMOC was going to raise the rate in June 2017. Figure 4.10 shows the futures market determined chances that the U.S. Federal Reserve was going to raise the rate in June of 2017. By April that year, the probability of a rate hike (according to the futures market) reached 60%, up from less than 30% in January and February. The logic behind the calculation of these probabilities is explained below.

Figure 4.10: Implied Probability of Fed Funds being 1% to 1.25% in June

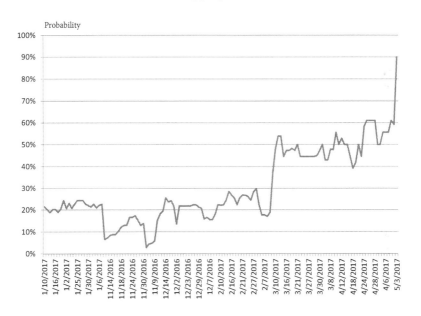

Source: Bloomberg

Figure 4.11 illustrates another example of how the futures market adjusts to uncertainty regarding Federal Reserve decisions on the benchmark Federal Funds rate. The market implied probabilities for the Fed's March 21-22, 2023, meeting are shown in Figure 4.11 on the vertical axis. Prior to this meeting the Fed Funds target rate was in the range between 4.5% and 4.75%, and at the meeting the Fed decided to raise the range to between 4.75% and 5%, a 25 *basis point* (bps) rate increase. The term "basis point" is used in finance to describe changes in interest rates. It is convenient way to quote small interest rate changes. The convention is that 1 bps is equal to one-hundredth of a percentage point, or 0.01%. This means that if the interest rate changes by 25 basis points, it has risen or fallen by 0.25% (25 bps multiplied by 0.01%).

Figure 4.11 shows how the futures market implied probabilities changed over time regarding three possible outcomes: i) holding the rate steady, ii) raising the rate by 25 bps, or iii) a 50 bps increase. As can be seen from Figure 4.11, a few weeks prior to the meeting the market implied probabilities were all over the place. In early March the market determined the probability of a 25 bps hike to be around 70%. Then this probability plunged down to just over 20%, while at the same time the probability of a 50 bps hike jumped from around 30% to close to 80% on March 8th, two weeks prior to the meeting. At this point the market apparently anticipated that the Fed would become aggressive fighting inflation and would raise the target rate by 50 bps. However the market turned swiftly and the implied probability of a 50 bps rate increase fell from around 80% to 0% in a matter of a few days. By March 13th, the likelihood of a 50 bps change was completely discounted by the market. In the last week of trading the market determined that the Fed might not change the rate at all and the implied probability of holding the rate steady went from 0% to about 45% (see the dotted line in Figure 4.11). This type of volatility prior to a Fed meeting is unusual but reflective of the difficult decision facing the Federal Reserve. Inflation was still close to 6% and the Fed has a target of about 2% inflation. To keep inflation in check the Fed would have had to raise the benchmark rate further. However on March 10, 2023, Silicon Valley Bank (SVB) went under, and this was the largest bank to fail after the 2007-2008 financial crisis. This explains why the Fed Fund market was gyrating in mid March as the market quickly started to anticipate that the Fed might not raise rates in order to prevent further bank runs and to stabilize the banking sector. In the end, the Fed went ahead and raised the rate 25 bps, apparently putting more weight on controlling inflation than on the possibility of more problems in the banking system.

An example is the best way to explain the calculation of the probability of a rate change that lies behind Figures 4.10 and 4.11. Refer to Table 4.5 which shows Fed Funds futures prices prior to a May FOMC meeting. To calculate the probability of an interest rate hike lets focus on the April and June futures. The April futures price reflects the market expectations before the May meeting and the June futures price captures traders' expectations after the May meeting. The FOMC changes the fed funds rate in increments of 0.25%, so possible changes at an FOMC meeting are either no change or a change of 0.25%. From Table 4.5 we see that the implied rate in April is 4.78% and in June it is higher at 4.925%. If we take the difference between the June and April rates that gives us the estimated change in the rate at the May meetings, which is 0.145%. We compare the 0.145% to the 0.25%

Figure 4.11: Market Implied Probability for Fed Reserve's Meeting, March 21-22, 2023

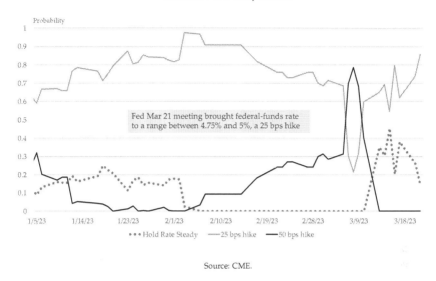

Source: CME.

Table 4.5: 30 day Federal Funds CBT - $5,000,000; 100 - daily avg

Futures Contract Month	Settle Price	Implied Fed Funds rate
Apr	95.22	100-95.22=4.78%
May	95.07	100-95.14=4.93%
Jun	95.075	100-95.075=4.925%

possible change and the ratio equals 58%, indicating a 58% probability of a rate hike equal to 0.25%. This calculation is shown in equation 4.13.

$$Probability = \Delta interest\ rate\ /possible\ rate\ hike =$$
$$= (4.925\% - 4.78\%)/0.25\% = 58\% \quad (4.13)$$

SOFR Futures

Internationally, the U.S. dollar is considered to be a reserve asset. As a result, many world residents (firms) wish to hold part of their wealth (capital) in U.S. dollars, but they do not necessarily wish to place their dollars in U.S. banks. In addition, because a large percentage of world merchandise trade is denominated in U.S. dollars, there is a large business and financial community outside of the United States that borrows and lends U.S. dollars. For example, if a wheat exporter in Kazakhstan sells a cargo of wheat to Iran, payment will most likely be made in U.S. dollars. The Iranian importer may have to borrow the U.S. dollars in the international money market and the Kazak exporter may, in turn, deposit the U.S. dollars in a European bank rather than converting the funds on the currency market into the local currency, the Tenge.

The Eurodollar futures contract was a short-term interest rate contract that was introduced in 1981, and then discontinued in 2023. It was replaced with SOFR futures. SOFR stands for the Secured Overnight Financing Rate and it is a benchmark measure of the cost of borrowing cash overnight. SOFR is based on transactions in the Treasury repurchase market (i.e., the repo market).

SOFR futures are financially settled and notional amount of each contract is $1 million. The interest rate (i.e., yield) on 3 Month SOFR futures is the compounded daily SOFR interest rate during the contract Reference Quarter, which is the interval that ends on the third Wednesday of the contract delivery month. For instance for a December contract, the contract Reference Quarter shall start on the third Wednesday of the previous September and shall end on the third Wednesday of December. The final settlement price is an index equal to 100 minus the compounded daily SOFR during the contract Reference Quarter. If the price quote on a December 3 month SOFR is 96.27 (i.e., the IMM index) that implies the implied 3 month SOFR rate is 100-96.27 = 3.73%. Therefore, as short-term interest rates rise, SOFR futures fall in price. Alternatively, when interest rates decline, SOFR futures rise in price. Table 4.6 lays out the key contract specifications for the 3 Month SOFR futures contract and more information can be obtained by referring to CME Rule Book, Ch. 460.

Table 4.6: Three-Month SOFR Futures Contract Specifications

Exchange Symbol	SR3
Exchange	CME
Price Quote	Contract-grade IMM Index: 100 minus R R = SOFR interest during Reference Quarter e.g.,: price = 95.4 means R = 4.6 % per annum
Margin/Maintenance	$1,348/1,225
Daily Price Limit	None
Contract Size	$2,500 x contract-grade IMM Index, $25 per bp
Contract Months	Mar, Jun, Sep, Dec
Trading Hours	5:00p.m.-4:00p.m. (Sun-Fri) ET
Delivery	Financially settled
Speculator Position Limits	10,000 contracts in any delivery month.
Last Trading Day	Business day immediately preceding the 3rd Wed of the next quarterly delivery month

Source CME Rule Book, Ch. 460.

In Table 4.4, the settlement (i.e., closing) price on the June SOFR futures contract is 95.37, which means the interest rate is 4.63 percent (= 100 - 95.37). For SOFR futures, a change in one tick or one basis point (one-hundredth of a percentage point) is worth $25. So, if the price of the June contract falls to 94.97 (for example), then the value of the futures contract changes by 40 basis points, or $1,000. The tick value is determined by the relationship shown in equation 4.14

$$\$1,000,000 \times .0001 \times 90/360 = \$25 \qquad (4.14)$$

In equation 4.14, $1,000,000 is the implied face value of the futures contract and .0001 represents one tick. The 90/360 ratio in equation 4.14 accounts for the fact that SOFR futures are 3 month instruments and therefore the annualized interest rate must be converted to the quarterly (i.e., 90 day) counterpart. For example, 1% of $1 million equals $10,000 for 360 days, but for a 90 day loan each 1% of $1 million equals $10,000/4, or $2,500.

Financial Swaps

In the commodity and financial markets, a swap is an agreement between two parties whereby each party agrees to initially exchange (i.e., swap) an asset and then re-exchange assets at a later date. Both parties gain from this swap arrangement. There are many analogies where two parties can both gain through swapping an asset for a fixed time period and then swapping back. For example, if a professor from UC Davis plans to visit the University of Galway in Ireland for a year, he or she might find a Galway professor who wants to spend their sabbatical in Davis. Most universities keep a listing of sabbatical homes for visiting Professors and often faculty members are willing to "swap" homes and cars with visitors. Both parties agree to swap homes and cars for a year and maybe some cash changes hands. If rental rates in Davis are significantly higher than in Galway, then the Irish professor may agree to pay the Californian an agreed amount of cash as a supplement. In any event, they both gain from this arrangement because they avoid the high transactions costs associated with finding or leasing rental property (such as search costs and realtor fees). On the Internet, there is also a very active international home exchange available to vacationers. If a New Yorker wishes to spend the summer in Italy, chances are that he or she can swap their residence with an Italian through the various home exchanges on the web.

Essentially, a financial swap is an agreement by one party to make payments to the other for an agreed period of time, and vice versa. Swaps can be used to either hedge or speculate and they are instruments that are commonly used in the financial and commodity markets. Over-the-counter swaps have been used for many years by firms exposed to commodity, interest rate, equity, or currency risk. More recently, exchange traded standardized swaps have been introduced.

The most basic interest rate swap involves an exchange of a series of fixed interest payments for a series of floating (i.e., variable) interest payments. This is called a fixed-for-floating interest rate swap, and is sometimes referred to as a "Plain Vanilla" interest rate swap. Such an exchange is beneficial to both parties as long as each has a relative cost advantage in a specific credit market. The relative cost advantage in one market is used to obtain an equivalent advantage in the other market through the swap. For instance, firm A might be in a position where it cannot obtain an attractive long-term fixed interest rate so it will have no choice but to borrow at a short term rate and then "swap" interest payments with firm B who can borrow at a more attractive long term rate. In this case, a series of payments calculated by applying a fixed rate of interest to the principal amount is exchanged for a stream of payments similarly calculated but using a floating rate of interest.

A currency swap involves the simultaneous purchase and sale of a currency for two different dates, against the sale and purchase of another currency. This is equivalent to borrowing one currency and lending in another for a given time period.

In 2001, both the Chicago Board of Trade (CBOT)–now part of the the CME group–and the LIFFE (the London International Financial Futures and Options Exchange)—now Euronex—introduced futures and options contracts based on interest rate swaps. The advantage of an exchange-traded swap is that is standardized, therefore it is easier to either buy or sell compared to the over-the-counter swaps.

Interest rate derivatives account for the largest share of the OTC derivatives market. An interest rate swap is an agreement in which interest payments are exchanged. The OTC interest rate swap market is one of the most popular financial derivatives and in recent years the trading of OTC interest rate derivatives has surged. Between April 2010 and April 2022, average daily OTC turnover of interest rate derivatives (mostly swaps) went from $2.1 trillion to $5.2 trillion - an increase of 150% (see Bank for International Settlements, www.bis.org). Counterparties in a standard interest swap agree to exchange interest rate payments on a fixed amount of principal and over a defined period of time. In a typical swap, payments by counterparty A are based on a fixed rate of interest and payments made by counterparty B are based on a floating rate of interest–the *plain vanilla* swap mentioned above. Each counterparty benefits by swapping payments, otherwise they would not enter into the contract. The fixed rate payer is the buyer of the swap and the floating rate payer is the seller.

Swap futures offer certain benefits over OTC swaps, such as trading on a margin. The CME offers 2 year, 5 year, 10 year, and 30 year maturity "floating-for-fixed" interest rate swap futures contracts (with expiry in March, June, Sept and Dec). These maturities are the most active in the OTC market. These CME interest rate swap futures contracts are deliverable, and upon maturity the futures contract converts into an OTC swap that would be cleared by the CME. The *long* has the obligation to take delivery of a cleared swap if they do not reverse their futures position prior to the delivery period. Upon delivery the long would become the "fixed rate receiver" and "floating rate payer" in an OTC interest rate swap. Unlike Treasury Bond futures the interest rate swap futures do not have a standard fixed coupon rate, instead the notional coupon is set when each new futures contract is listed.

An interest rate swap is simply a string of cash flows occurring at known future dates, so it can be valued by calculating the present value of each of these cash flows. Swap rates implicitly incorporate expectations of forthcoming short term interest rates–the SOFR.

The price at settlement will be par, plus or minus the net present value (NPV) of the swap being delivered. The NPV of the swap is equal to the NPV of fixed side of the swap minus the NPV of the floating side. Therefore the contract would trade at par as long as swap interest rates are equal to the coupon rate. However if prevailing swap interest rates are below the coupon level then the contract will have a positive NPV because investors would be willing to pay to enter into a swap where they could receive fixed payments at a rate higher than the coupon. In other words, the settlement price represents the sum of money a trader would be willing to pay or to receive to enter into the underlying reference swap.

These contracts are traded by hedgers and speculators based on their expectations regarding changes in interest rates and/or the relationships between interest rates. The price of the swap is based on the forward interest rate curve and therefore the price changes when the curve shifts up or down or the slope changes. For example, if rates fall, investors would pay a lower floating rate in exchange for the same fixed rate and the price of the swap would change. The futures contracts have a fixed and a floating rate side and the futures contract is based on the price of the swap trade. Swap futures prices are highly correlated with OTC spot market swap rates and are therefore effective hedging tools for firms that have either fixed or floating obligations. Two of the most active US swap futures are the CBOT's 2-year and 5-year Eris swaps (financially settled) and the 10-year and 5-year USD Deliverable interest rate swaps. These instruments were developed by Eris Innovations in Chicago(www.erisfutures.com).

Simple interest rate swap

Suppose there is a U.S. financial institution, called S Bank, that carries short term deposits on the liability side of its balance sheet, and it purchases bonds on the asset side. S bank does not hedge the market value of the assets on its balance sheet as the institution is a big risk taker. If S bank is unhedged, then holding mostly shorter-term bonds minimizes interest rate risk, while alternatively, holding mostly longer-term bonds maximizes interest rate risk. Duration measures the sensitivity of a bond's price to changing interest rates and long-term bonds have a greater duration than short-term bonds. Duration is measured by the number of years it will take a bond's cash flows to repay the investor the price paid for the bond. The longer the duration the more risky the bond.

Suppose that S Bank's $1 billion portfolio is mostly long-term bonds. If this bank decided that it now longer wanted to be a big risk taker, how would they hedge the interest rate risk associated with the assets on their balance sheet? Well there are a number of alternative instruments they could use for hedging, one of which is a plain vanilla interest rate swap. To illustrate one possibility, if S Bank contacts a swap dealer, they could enter into an over-the-counter (OTC) interest rate swap whereby S Bank would agree to pay the swap dealer a fixed interest rate and in return receive from the swap dealer a floating interest rate, based on a $1 billion notional amount.

Because S Bank is holding bonds they would receive a fixed rate on those bonds, and to hedge that risk through a swap they would agree to pay away a fixed yield and receive a variable yield in exchange. The $1 billion notional amount of the swap is the value upon which interest rate payments will be exchanged. Each party to the swap would pay either a fixed (i.e., S Bank) or floating (i.e., swap dealer) interest rate multiplied by the notional amount and these payments would occur at fixed periods, such as every three months, over the life of the contract such as five years.

Consider the basic swap illustrated in Figure 4.12. S Bank is no longer a big risk taker and therefore they are concerned about a rise in interest rates and an associated fall in the value of the bonds in their portfolio. They approach a swap dealer (such as JP Morgan or Citigroup) and propose a swap contract to reduce their exposure to interest rate risk. The swap dealer agrees to pay S Bank a variable interest rate payment equal to the yield on a 10-year Treasury Note, plus 25 basis points (bps). In return S Bank agrees to pay the swap dealer a fixed rate of 3% times the notional value of $1 billion. The swap specifies that every three months the swap dealer will pay the yield on a 10-year Treasury Note, plus 25 basis points, times the notional value, and on that same date S Bank would pay the swap dealer the 3%

fixed rate times the notional value of $1 billion. Both payments would be prorated from the annualized rates to interest payments over one quarter (i.e., three months). Only the net payment would change hands and the notional value is not exchanged.

Figure 4.12: Simple Interest Rate Swap

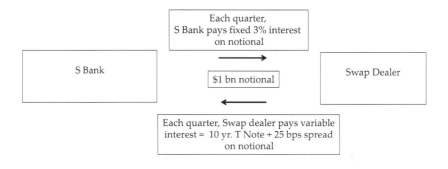

A swap is a contract in which 2 parties agree to exchange payment streams

Once entered into, the swap agreement's value will change as interest rates change. If rates rise, the Fixed Payor (in this case S Bank) will be "in the money" as the variable rates they are receiving on the swap will have increased relative to the fixed rate they are paying. At the same time the value of S Bank's underlying portfolio of bonds will have decreased as a result of higher rates. If instead interest rates decrease, the Fixed Payor (S Bank) will be "out of the money" on the swap, as their variable rate receipts will have decreased relative to their fixed payment, but the value of their underlying bond portfolio will have risen.

Equity Instruments

Futures contracts on stock market indices have been traded since 1982. There are over 80 different equity index futures contracts traded in the United States, apart from the popularity of these type of contracts in Europe and Asia. Exchanges around the world have rapidly listed new indexes in the last few years to try and accommodate investors and hedgers with complicated portfolios, made up of domestic and international equities. Stock index futures and options are not only popular with speculators, but they also provide an important instrument for hedging portfolio risk.

The most actively traded US equity index futures contracts are shown in Table 4.7. It is an understatement to observe that there are numerous futures contracts derived from stock indexes. These include the E-mini Standard

Table 4.7: Top US Equity Futures Contracts

Exchange	Category	Contract	2022 Volume Millions
CME	Equity	E-mini S&P 500	503.95
CME	Equity	Micro E-mini Nasdaq 100 Index	364.95
CME	Equity	Micro E-mini S&P 500 Index	343.97
CME	Equity	E-mini Nasdaq 100	176.87
CME	Equity	E-mini Russell 2000 Index	60.57
CBOT	Equity	E-mini $5 DJIA	51.03
CBOT	Equity	E-micro $5 DJIA	44.93
ICE	Equity	Mini MSCI Emerging Markets	44.71
CME	Equity	Micro E-mini Russell 2000 Index	32.83
ICE	Equity	Mini MSCI EAFE Index	15.29
CME	Equity	Nikkei 225 (Yen)	9.21
CME	Equity	E-mini S&P Midcap 400	3.98
ICE	Equity	FANG+ Index	2.31
CME	Equity	Nikkei 225 ($)	1.40
CME	Equity	E-mini S&P Energy Sector	0.82
CME	Equity	S&P 500 Index	0.75
ICE	Equity	Mini MSCI Emerging Markets Asia NTR	0.51
CME	Equity	E-mini S&P Financial Sector	0.47
ICE	Equity	Mini MSCI ACWI NTR Index	0.45
CME	Equity	E-mini S&P Utilities Sector	0.45
CME	Equity	E-mini S&P 500 ESG Index	0.39
CME	Equity	E-mini S&P Industrial Sector	0.38
CME	Equity	E-mini S&P Consumer Staples Sector	0.36
CME	Equity	E-mini S&P Technology Sector	0.32
CME	Equity	E-mini S&P Health Care Sector	0.32

Source: Futures Industry Association.

and Poor's 500 (S&P 500) index, the micro E-mini Nasdaq 100 Index, the E-mini Russell 2000 Index, the E-mini DJIA, and the Mini MSCI (Morgan Stanley Capital International) Emerging Markets Index. These indices are all designed to measure the performance of various portfolios of stocks on various stock markets.

These indices are weighted averages of stocks and are designed to either reflect movements in the overall market (e.g., the S&P 500) or a particular segment of the market (e.g., the S&P MidCap 400). They serve as a proxy for a specific portfolio. The futures contract on the Standard and Poor's (S&P 500) stock index was the first one traded (from 1982) and it is one of the largest volume contracts. The S&P 500 is a capitalization weighted (i.e., the weighting of each stock corresponds to the size of the company) average of 500 stocks, the majority of which are listed on the New York Stock Exchange. Alternatively, in the Dow Jones Industrial Average (DJIA),

Table 4.8: Equity Index Futures Quotations

	Open	High	Low	Settle
E-Mini S&P 500 Index (CME) - $50 × Index				
Jun	3,988.0	4,011.0	3,937.0	4,009.75
Micro E-Mini Nasdaq 100 (CME)- $2 × Index				
Jun	12,872.0	12,925.25	12,726.0	12,924.25
Mini MSCI Emerging Markets (ICE) - $50 × Index				
Jun	2,025.2	2,038.8	1,991.4	2,017.8
E-mini $5 DJIA (CME) - $5 × Index				
Jun	32,381	32,485	31,945	32,481
Euro STOXX 50 Index (EUREX) - €10 × Index				
Jun	4,118.0	4,118.0	4,032.0	4,067.0

Source: CME.

each stock is weighted by its price, which means that stocks with higher prices have a higher weights in the index. The DJIA contains 30 blue-chip stocks, representing the industrial sector.

Stock index futures are obviously settled by cash rather than by physical delivery because you cannot deliver a theoretical construct such as an index. This means that when a futures contract expires, the futures stock index equals the underlying spot market index. In Table 4.8 we find that the June futures price for the E-Mini S&P 500 Index settled at 4,009.75. To calculate the total dollar value of this contract we multiply this index by $50, because each index point is worth $50. Thus, the June contract had a total value of $200,487.

The Nasdaq 100 futures is also traded on the Chicago Mercantile Exchange and this index is based on 100 of the largest domestic, non-financial, common stocks listed on the Nasdaq Stock Market. There are two popular contracts based on the Nasdaq 100, the E-mini Nasdaq 100 and the Micro E-mini Nasdaq 100 Index. Both of these contracts have rather large trading volumes. The E-mini contract size is $20 x Nasdaq-100 Index. And the corresponding Micro E-mini Nasdaq-100 contract is one-tenth the size of the E-mini, meaning the Micro's contract value is $2 x Nasdaq-100 Index.

The Dow Jones Industrial Average (DJIA) (sometimes referred to as "the Dow") is another popular index with traders, and futures and options based on this index trade on the CBOT. The E-mini DJIA contract size is $5 x Dow Jones Industrial Average Index, and the Micro E-mini DJIA contract is $0.50 x the DJIA Index.

European stock indexes also play an important role in financial futures and options trading. For instance, the Euro STOXX 50 is composed of 50 blue-chip stocks from 11 countries in the Eurozone. The economic integration of Europe and the single currency (i.e., the euro) has made cross-border trade more efficient in Europe and has helped develop financial markets in Europe.

The role of the stock index futures in the financial community became controversial soon after the first contract was launched on the CME. Many stock market investors and politicians did not fully understand how price movements in the futures market related to the underlying stock market. For example, some investors and politicians blamed the stock market crash in October 1987 on excessive trading in the stock index futures market and allegations that the futures market was manipulated. These critics singled out portfolio insurance, a hedging technique that involves the sale of stock index futures to protect a stock portfolio from a declining market. Stock index arbitrage trading, which involves the simultaneous buying and selling of stock and stock index futures, was also thought to be a factor in the stock market plunge.

President Reagan asked Nicholas Brady (former U.S. Treasury Secretary) to determine why the stock market collapsed during October 1987. The Brady commission and other studies found no evidence to support the theory that futures-related trading constituted a major part of the October 1987 plunge in the New York Stock Exchange (see Malkiel (1988)).

Investors are constantly trying to forecast the direction of the stock market and some mistakenly look to the overnight trading in stock futures as a signal of where the New York or Nasdaq market is headed. Suppose the stock index futures market rallies during overnight and early morning trading. Does this mean that the New York stock market will necessarily open higher at 8:30am? The answer is not necessarily. Overnight futures trading establishes the market's valuation based on investor expectations on what might happen tomorrow, news that comes into the market overnight, and foreign stock market activity. This set of information could all change once the New York stock market actually opens for the day. Overnight futures trading does not necessarily point to the next day's direction in the stock market.

Spread Trading

Rather than taking an outright long or short futures position, many speculators in futures markets take a less risky approach, through spread trading. Spread trading is popular with both technical and fundamental traders. The simplest spread involves the simultaneous purchase of one futures contract and the sale of another. This could involve trading two identical futures contracts but with different delivery months, known as a calendar spread. Calendar spreads are particularly common for financial contracts.

A trader might sell a September U.S. Treasury Bond contract, and buy a December U.S. Treasury Bond contract, for example. When the spread widens or narrows, the speculator can profit by buying the cheaper contract and selling the more expensive contract. Traders also spread the same contract but on different exchanges (e.g., silver in New York versus silver in Japan). Alternatively, spread trading could involve trading two different futures contracts that are related in a way such that their relative prices have somewhat predictable patterns over time.

The objective with spread trading is to profit from an expected change in the relative prices of the two futures contracts. Rather than trying to predict absolute price changes, the spread trader is trying to predict relative price changes. There are an unlimited number of spread opportunities. In the commodity markets, examples of spread trading include cocoa/coffee spreads, wheat/corn spreads, and gold/silver spreads. In the financial markets, currency spreads are common.

Two other spreads that are common in the financial markets are the MOB and NOB spreads. The MOB spread is a Municipal bond versus Treasury Bond spread, and the NOB spread involves trading Treasury Notes versus Treasury Bonds. The NOB spread (Notes - Bonds) is a spread between maturities (i.e., medium versus long term interest rates). Alternatively, the MOB spread (Municipal bonds - Treasury Bonds) is a spread between quality levels as Municipal bonds are more risky than Treasury bonds.

Summary

The first markets that most financial traders check when they get out of bed every morning are the interest rate and currency markets. Likewise, the first markets that most commodity traders check every morning are also the interest rate and currency markets. This basic fact of a trader's life indicates that financials (i.e., currencies, interest rates and stock indexes) are pervasive in our globalized economy.

This chapter has outlined price formation in the underlying spot markets for currencies, interest rates, and stock indexes (i.e., equities). Additionally, it has traced the linkage between these spot markets and trading in financial futures and options. The workings of financial futures were explained for the major markets. Financial futures share many similar features with commodity futures, such as the cost of carry price spread relationship that ties together inter-temporal prices.

Economic integration is increasing around the globe, largely due to the efforts of the World Trade Organization and the examples set by those countries that have embraced globalization. Above average economic growth has been achieved by countries that have opened their doors to more capital flows and more trade in merchandise and services. As a result of this globalization, financial futures and options markets will continue to expand and continue to offer new and innovative products for hedgers and speculators.

Discussion Questions

1. Explain why foreign exchange rates are important to a U.S. based firm that exports final processed goods to Canada and imports raw materials from Mexico. How would changes in the Canadian and Mexican exchange rates affect the firm's sales and profits?

2. Which macroeconomic factors affect the exchange rate?

3. What have been the main economic impacts of the creation of the euro single currency zone? Describe the impacts within western Europe and for the rest of the world.

4. Explain how the British pound sterling (GBP) has performed since Brexit? How have the economies in the United Kingdom performed relative to the European Union economies?

5. Explain the macroeconomic information that is embedded in the shape of the yield curve? If the yield curve steepens during a recession, is this good news or bad news?

6. Explain why the 2007-2009 U.S. recession was called the Great Recession.

7. The Silicon Valley Bank (SVB) collapsed in march 2023 after the Fed raised interest rates. We know that when interest rates go up, the market value of long-term bonds goes down. Was the SVB simply mismanaged or were government regulations to blame? To what extent was the SVB hedged against interest rate increases?

8. Should financial futures be regulated by the U.S. Securities and Exchange Commission (SEC) instead of the Commodity Futures Trading Commission (CFTC)? What are the pros and cons of such a regulatory change?

Selected References

Cieslak, Anna, Adair Morse, and Annette Vissing-Jorgensen. 2018. "Stock returns over the FOMC cycle." https://ssrn.com/abstract=2687614.

Dornbusch, Rudiger. 1987. "Exchange Rate Economics: 1986." *The Economic Journal*, 97(385): 1–18.

Kontonikas, Alexandros, Ronald MacDonald, and Aman Saggu. 2013. "Stock market reaction to fed funds rate surprises: State dependence and the financial crisis." *Journal of Banking & Finance*, 37(11): 4025–4037.

Malkiel, Burton G. 1988. "The Brady Commission report: a critique." *The Journal of Portfolio Management*, 14(4): 9–13.

5.

Fundamental Analysis

In this chapter and the next, we introduce two general approaches to forecasting futures and options prices. This chapter discusses fundamental analysis and Chapter 6 introduces technical analysis. A fundamental analyst looks forward in time, gathering information concerning current and future supply and demand conditions, and determining what this information implies for changing market conditions and forthcoming prices. Alternatively, a technical analyst looks backward in time. He or she generates price forecasts based on historical market prices, historical volume, and open interest data. The technician has little or no interest in supply and demand fundamentals. In general, speculators are more interested in forecasting prices than are hedgers.

Fundamental analysis is more difficult and more time consuming than technical analysis because there is considerably more information to evaluate and the approaches and models used are much more complex. The use of fundamental tools requires a combination of extensive market knowledge and some knowledge of economics and statistics. Old-fashioned fundamental traders did not use formal economic models with multiple equations; instead, their models were "in their head." However their logic is consistent with economic theory, including supply and demand basics. Alternatively, technical analysis is not based on economic or financial theory.

Fundamental price forecasts are often generated using analytical tools. The same analytical tools can be applied to a number of different markets, but application requires detailed knowledge of a specific market. For example, a skilled economist can build and estimate a mathematical/statistical model of the world wheat market using the same analytical tools she would use to develop a model of the world coffee market. However, it would take a long time (e.g., weeks or months) to build either model and it would be time consuming to keep the models updated. For instance, one of the most successful commodity hedge funds in 2022, Citadel, reportedly spends large amounts of money and time on supply and demand fundamentals. Citadel is based in Chicago and the multinational hedge fund reported profits of $16 billion in 2022 (38% return), and this was attributed to profitable trades partly driven by forecasting with supercomputers focused on how weather affects energy demand.

Alternatively, technical trading rules can be generated by a personal computer, using relatively inexpensive software or simply a spreadsheet. Technical trading rules can be easily and quickly applied to a number of different markets. For example, with little or no background understanding of the wheat market, a technician could choose a forecasting approach from the family of technical procedures available on numerous websites and generate wheat price forecasts in a matter of hours. The same approach could then be easily applied to the coffee market (or any other market for that matter). Updating technical forecasts is also much easier than updating fundamental forecasts. Formal training in economics and statistics, or detailed market knowledge, is not required to become a technical trader.

These two alternative approaches to price forecasting, technical and fundamental analysis, are also used outside of the futures and options markets, such as in the equity (or stock) markets. Some investors in the stock market subscribe to forecasts generated by technical analysts, while others follow fundamental analysts. Strictly speaking, technical analysis focuses on historical price patterns in an attempt to determine where prices are headed rather than detailed stock valuation. Alternatively, fundamental analysis of the stock market focuses on price-to-earnings ratios, balance sheets and industry profitability, etc.

The fundamentalist pays attention to both the "demand" and "supply" side of the market and believes that the dynamics of the market are ultimately driven by the fundamentals. A fundamentalist tries to determine the intrinsic value of a commodity or asset, which is a long run approach to price analysis. Fundamentalist traders use different methods ranging from calculating simple ratios of economic variables (e.g., the ratio of the price of hogs to the price of corn indicates profitability of hog production and predicts the forthcoming supply of hogs) to building and estimating complex econometric supply and demand models with multiple equations. For a nice discussion of commodity fundamentals and trends in these fundamentals see (Baffes and Nagle, 2022).

Informational Efficiency of Futures Markets

There is considerable controversy surrounding the success (i.e., the profitability) of technical versus fundamental analysis. Technicians argue that the fundamental approach is far too complex to be of any benefit to the

---

Box 5.1 Sir Isaac Newton was a Fundamentalist

Sir Issac Newton (1642-1727) was one of the greatest scientists in the history of the world. He was primarily a physicist and mathematician; however, he became interested in economics in his 50s. As a result of his great mind and his fascination with economics, he was appointed Master of the British Royal Mint in 1699, a position he retained until his death.

When Newton took over the Mint, the British government was facing a perceived monetary problem due to the rising price of gold relative to silver. At the time, coins were the primary form of "money." The shilling was a coin made of silver and the guinea was a gold coin. The price of one guinea had risen from 22 to 30 shillings over a relatively short time period; the government of England was concerned with the speculative run-up in the price of gold relative to silver. Silver coins were being melted down and/or exported to buy up foreign gold, resulting in a shortage of silver coins.

Newton evaluated the problem by comparing the purchasing power of gold vis-à-vis silver across Europe. He reckoned that in England, gold was overvalued relative to silver and he argued that the laws of supply and demand (i.e., the fundamentals) would eventually solve the problem. Based on Newton's forecast, the government put a ceiling on the price of the guinea at 21 shillings, and prohibited trading at a higher price. Eventually the price of gold fell relative to the price of silver and Newton's forecast was indeed correct.

For more background on this topic, see Peter Bernstein, The Power of Gold, New York, NY, John Wiley and Sons, 2000.

---

small trader. Alternatively, the fundamentalists point out that technical trading is of no value because it is impossible to consistently predict forthcoming prices from historical prices. Fundamentalists will point out that a technical approach may work in the short run, but in the long run the market will dictate that such methods are ineffective.

At the center of the debate is the issue of whether or not the futures and options markets are informationally efficient. A very broad definition of an efficient market is one in which market prices fully reflect available information at any point in time (Fama, 1970). Alternatively, if information is costly, an efficient market is one that reflects information up to the point where the marginal benefits from trading (futures or options contracts) based on this information do not exceed the marginal costs of collecting the information.

Markets can be tested for informational efficiency and Fama has classified efficient market tests into three groups: weak, semi strong, and strong form. The information set for **weak form tests** is confined to historical market prices. **Semi strong form tests** measure the market's adjustment to historical prices plus all other relevant public information. **Strong form tests** measure its adjustment to "inside" information not available to the public. For each form of the test, if markets are efficient, the test's information set cannot be used by traders to make above average earnings. However, any test of market efficiency is a joint test of efficiency and the model of asset pricing. This means that market efficiency *per se* may not be strictly testable (Fama, 1991). As discussed below, the futures market is thought to be at least semi-strong efficient. This is supported by Park and Irwin (2010) who studied the profitability of technical trading rules in U.S. futures markets and found that technical trading does not generate profits in a consistent fashion.

Speculators who subscribe to either fundamental or technical analysis, buy and sell futures and options contracts with the expectation of making a profit. If the market is informationally efficient then predicting price changes is difficult if not impossible for these speculators, irrespective of whether they are fundamentalists or technicians. The (semi-strong) efficient market hypothesis states that today's market prices fully reflect all publicly available information. This implies that if a small speculator spends hours each morning studying the market "news" before trading, then he is wasting his time and money. If the market is efficient, then the news is reflected in the market price by the time the small speculator reads about it in the Wall Street Journal or on the Internet. These traders would not survive in the market in the long run and they would be replaced by newer speculators who had not yet learned their lesson.

In statistical jargon, if the market is informationally efficient then prices approximately follow a **random walk**. This implies that day-to-day price changes are random, so you cannot predict the future from the past. In simple terms, this means that, generally, you cannot predict whether the market will move higher or lower tomorrow based on what it did today or yesterday. The random walk theory states that:

$$P_t = P_{t-1} + e_t \tag{5.1}$$

Where P_t is the current price, P_{t-1} is the price lagged one day and e_t is an error term. Assume P_t is today's closing price on the futures market and P_{t-1} is yesterday's closing price. According to this theory, the expected value of $e_t = 0$ and e_t is not correlated with e in any other time period. If we define "E" as the expectations operator, and we rearrange equation 5.1, we find that:

$$E\left(P_t - P_{t-1}\right) = E\left(e_t\right) \tag{5.2}$$

So equation (5.2) indicates that day-to-day price changes average to zero, which is another way of saying that price changes are random. This means that the price change tomorrow (i.e., $P_{t+1} - P_t$), is independent of today's price change (i.e., $P_t - P_{t-1}$). According to this model, whether today's price change was positive or negative has no bearing on the sign of tomorrow's price change.

In an efficient market, competition among traders leads to a situation where, at any point in time, futures (and options) prices reflect both the effects of current information and events that are expected to occur in the future. In statistics, this is characterized as a "fair game" and in an efficient market the current price will be an accurate estimate of the commodity or asset's true intrinsic value. This means that it would be difficult to come up with a better price forecast to "beat" the market. If a trader did come up with a system to beat the market then, in theory, other traders would soon exploit that profit opportunity and the inefficiency would quickly disappear. In other words, a successful forecasting method would be self-destructive (Timmermann and Granger, 2004).

Prices quickly adjust to new information as it becomes available in an efficient market. Price changes from day-to-day are random because news events come into the market in a random fashion. Today the news might suggest that the market is going higher (i.e., bullish news) and tomorrow the news might be negative and suggest that the market price is going lower (i.e., bearish news).

The random walk theory asserts that price movements will not follow any patterns or trends, which means that technical analysis is less effective because past price movements cannot be used to predict future price movements. The more participants and the faster the dissemination of information, the more efficient a market should be. The debate over the efficient market hypothesis has resulted in many empirical economic studies and there is considerable evidence which suggests that most futures markets are approximately efficient but not necessarily fully efficient.

Elam (1978) developed a semi strong test of efficiency and he considered the question of whether or not profits can be earned by fundamentally trading the hog futures market. An econometric model of the U.S. hog market was estimated and used to generate price forecasts. His basic trading rule was: sell one hog futures contract if the futures contract price

Box 5.2 Commodity futures prices are not mean-reverting

In an efficient market prices are not mean-reverting, which means they can depart from their historical average price for months or years and they may or may not come back to the mean.

To illustrate this point the figure below displays daily high August temperatures for the city of Chicago in the top panel. The graph shows a mean-reverting process for the daily temperature. There would be days with unusually hot temperatures and some cool days, but the temperature would tend to come back to the mean of 83 F after a few hot days or a few cool days. If you compare that chart to the chart in the bottom panel showing wheat futures prices in August you notice the two graphs look much different. For wheat, the price trends down over the month and we see from the graph, prices do not revert to a mean like the case for the top graph in this box. Wheat prices will wonder away from the mean, following a random walk.

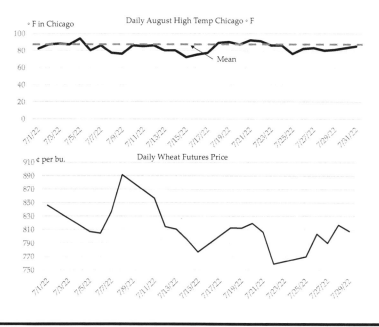

is x percent above the price level forecast and buy one contract if the futures contract price is x percent below. This rule yielded profits over the period studied and led Elam to conclude that the hog futures market is not efficient. Leuthold and Hartmann (1979) also concluded that the live hog futures market does not reflect all publicly available information and is in-

---

Box 5.3 Can the Futures Market Forecast Freezing Temperatures in Florida?

In the United States, the production of oranges for processing is concentrated in the state of Florida, which produces virtually all of the frozen concentrated orange juice (FCOJ) in the country. FCOJ futures and options are traded on the ICE.

The orange crop in Florida is susceptible to freezing temperatures from January through March in any given year. Due to the geographical concentration of production, FCOJ prices react sharply to the winter temperatures in Florida.

In a provocative research paper, Richard Roll (1984) found that price movements in the orange juice futures market could predict freezing temperatures in Florida better than the U.S. national weather service could! In other words, the futures market was found to be informationally efficient in terms of incorporating available weather information. In the winter, the best predictor of freezing temperatures in Florida is the price of FCOJ. If FCOJ futures prices were up sharply on a winter day, this could be a strong signal of a forthcoming freeze.

See Richard Roll "Orange Juice and Weather" American Economic Review; 74(5), December 1984, pages 861-80.

---

efficient.

Tomek and Gray (1970), and later Kofi (1973), were the first to test the forecasting ability of the futures market within the context of market efficiency. They argued that inventories of storable commodities provide a linkage between the spring time prices of the post harvest futures and the subsequent harvest time prices, which helps to make the futures price a self fulfilling forecast. Using the ordinary least squares technique, they estimated the coefficients of the following linear regression equation:

$$P_h = \alpha + \beta P_{fh} + e_h \tag{5.3}$$

Where P_h = cash price at harvest time, P_{fh} = planting time futures quotation for the harvest time contract, and e_h = error term. A "perfect forecast" was one for which α and β were estimated to be zero and one, respectively. In its simplest form, the efficient market hypothesis is a test that futures prices are an unbiased forecast of the forthcoming spot price.

Both studies found that the forward pricing function of futures markets was more reliable for continuous than for discontinuous inventory markets. Kofi's results clearly show that the further away from the contract expiration date the worse the futures market performs as a predictor of spot prices. Leuthold (1972) estimated equation (5.3) for corn and cattle and similarly found the futures market to be an efficient predictor of spot prices for only near maturity dates. His results for cattle show that up until the fifteenth week prior to delivery the cash price was a more accurate indicator of realized cash prices than was the futures price.

Tomek (1997) stresses that futures prices can provide poor price forecasts but still be efficient as long as their forecasts are better than any alternative, such as an econometric model. Futures prices can be considered to be unbiased because "competitive arbitrage eliminates profit opportunities based on information contained in the prices available to all market traders." If the futures market is efficient then it should be able to outforecast an econometric model.

Fama and French (1987) tested for evidence of whether or not commodity futures prices provided forecast information superior to the information contained in spot prices. They found that futures markets for seasonal commodities contain superior forecast power relative to spot prices. However, this was not the case for nonseasonal commodities. Using cointegration theory and an error-correction version of equation (5.3), Carter and Mohapatra (2008) found the Chicago hog futures market is a good and unbiased prediction of forthcoming cash prices except for distant forecasts.

What all this economic research means is that, in reality, markets are neither perfectly efficient nor completely inefficient. All markets are efficient to a certain extent, some more so than others. The reason that futures and options markets are not perfectly efficient is that these markets reflect imperfect information and reflect influences other than fundamental information. In the futures and options markets, every dollar has a vote regarding the forthcoming price and traders with imperfect information regularly "cast a vote," as do technicians with complete disregard for fundamental information. To "beat" the market, a trader must somehow use existing information in a way other than the market does or interpret existing information more accurately than the market. Another successful strategy could be based on anticipating changes in non-informational aspects of the market.

Fundamental Approach to Price Analysis

Supply and demand factors are taken very seriously by fundamental futures and options traders because supply and demand is what drives commodity and financial markets. These markets are thought to be closer to being perfectly competitive than many other markets in the economy, because there is little domestic and foreign government intervention. There

Figure 5.1: U.S. Corn Production Used for Ethanol vs. Corn Price

Source: USDA

are some exceptions to this statement in the case of agricultural commodities such as corn and sugar. The government introduces distortions to the market that can sometimes affect absolute price levels, but not so much day to day changes. For instance, U.S. energy policy mandates that close to 40% of the U.S. corn supply be converted to ethanol each year, which must be blended into the motor fuel supply. The share of the U.S. corn crop diverted to the fuel supply each year is shown in Figure 5.1. This affects the absolute price of corn, but not short-term price movements in the corn market.

Economic theory says that prices in a competitive market are determined by the interaction of supply and demand. The operations of futures and options markets do, by design, come very close to fulfilling the following requirements of perfect competition:

1. There are a large number of traders so no one trader has (too) much influence on market prices.
2. Product homogeneity is closely approached by the contract specifications.
3. Free entry and exit is closely approximated through small contract sizes and trading on margin.
4. Full information is available to everyone (in fact, futures and options markets reveal a vast amount of market information that would not otherwise exist).
5. Independence and impersonality of trading are dictated by the organization and regulation of the futures and options markets.

Fundamental traders believe that in a market so close to the competitive model described in economic theory, the key to price analysis is to interpret information concerning factors affecting supply or demand. Furthermore, the traders want to forecast the effects that this information will have on long-term price trends. Fundamentalists are not as concerned about when prices will move significantly as they are with the probability of whether prices will move in a given direction and the possible extent of such a move. If the direction of price movements can be predicted correctly, speculators can make profits and hedgers can better identify the strategy most appropriate to them. Fundamentalists know that prices are approximately random in the short term (e.g., day to-day price changes). They know there is a great deal of short-term price uncertainty, but at the same time believe there is less long-term uncertainty. Therefore, traders relying on fundamental analysis try to monitor and correctly evaluate new long term information concerning general economic factors and specific market supply and demand variables. For instance, a fundamental trader in crude oil would evaluate the market impact of new oil fields, new pipelines, the varying cost of extraction in different regions, economic growth in oil importing nations, and political developments in oil producing nations.

A fundamentalist's analysis involves determining the answers to a number of questions such as:

1. Is the current price above or below production costs?
2. What is the seasonal pattern (if any) of prices?
3. What is the current government policy and how will this affect supply and demand?
4. Are demand prospects relatively strong or weak?
5. How sensitive are prices to news events?
6. For commodities, how do production and stock levels compare to long-term averages?
7. For financials, what are the trends in general economic conditions, including inflation, unemployment, exchange rates, and retail sales?

In order to answer these (and other related) questions, fundamentalists use a variety of both quantitative and qualitative techniques. A brief introduction to examples of techniques used by analysts in commodity and financial markets is presented in the following sections.

Commodities

Futures and options markets for commodities respond to a wide array of supply and demand factors. Like financials, commodity markets have become truly globalized markets in that arbitrage is practiced around the world. For example, small farms in India can access global commodity prices on their cell phones, so they know the value of their rice and wheat and how it changes daily based on world market conditions. For traders, the only downside to the growing level of international economic integration is that it complicates fundamental analyses of markets.

Box 5.4 Trading Places

In the classic comedy movie *Trading Places*, two wealthy brothers (named Randolph and Mortimer) who are commodity traders have nothing better to do than argue with one another over whether or not environment plays a bigger role than heredity in developing a person's character. They bet that anyone could run their commodities company and so they fire their president and replace him with a homeless man. The ex-president, played by Dan Akroyd, is discredited and winds up on skid-row. Eddie Murphy plays the homeless person who takes over as president of the brokerage firm.

Once Akroyd and Murphy discover the switch played on them, they team up to teach Randolph and Mortimer a lesson. Akroyd and Murphy arrange to have advance access to the U.S. Department of Agriculture's crop report on orange juice. They then corner the frozen orange juice futures market with the advance information on the government reports and they financially break the two wealthy brothers.

Carter and Galopin ran an economics experiment, partly based on this movie. Carter and Galopin examined the value of the informational content of quarterly government reports that estimate forthcoming supplies of hogs and pigs. We assumed that a hypothetical futures trader obtains the government reports one day in advance of their release. A futures market trading rule is established which uses early access to the reports together with a priori expectations of the reports' contents. We found that the market information in the government reports is of little or no value to a futures trader in advance of the release date because this information is already incorporated in the futures price.

See Colin A. Carter and Carl A. Galopin "Informational Content of Government Hogs and Pigs Reports" *American Journal of Agricultural Economics*, (3), August 1993, pages 711-18.

Commodity futures and options prices are affected by changes in the expectations of market participants concerning a wide variety of supply and demand factors. As discussed above, efficient market studies have shown that commodity futures prices react quickly to new fundamental information factors. For commodities, important supply and demand factors include the weather, input costs, demand fluctuations, supply shocks, exchange rates, and changes in government policy.

In commodity markets a relatively small change in international trade volume can have a significant impact on price. One of the prime examples of the operation of this basic law of economics in commodity markets occurred in 1973 when Middle Eastern Arab oil producers (Iran and Arab members of OPEC) cut off exports to the U.S. to protest American military support for Israel. Even though imports from this region accounted for only about 10% of the U.S. oil supply, petroleum prices quadrupled in response to the export embargo and there were long lines for gasoline at filling stations.

Weather Patterns

The weather is more relevant for "soft" commodities such as sugar than for "hard" commodities such as copper. Weather may be the single most important influence on the supply of agricultural commodities, and it is virtually impossible to accurately predict the weather more than a few weeks out. The primary effect of weather conditions takes place during the growing season, affecting crop yields and harvest quality. Weather variables include degree days, temperature, rainfall, etc. Weather can also influence the livestock markets as things like droughts can cause ranchers to cull their herds. In addition, because weather influences the price of livestock feed (e.g., hay and corn) there is a strong indirect impact on the livestock industry.

For the heating oil and natural gas futures and options markets, the weather affects the demand side of the market. In the winter months, cold weather increases the demand for heating oil. If instead, mild temperatures are experienced during the winter, there is weak demand for heating oil. As an illustration, on January 15, 2010, the Reuters reported:

> "U.S. Demand for distillates, a fuel category that includes heating oil, was 4 percent below year-earlier levels in the four weeks ended January 8, according to the report. Temperatures are now forecast to exceed the seasonal norm, further suppressing consumption."

This story was reporting that the heating oil prices plunged with the news that warmer than average temperatures were expected to in the Northeastern United States.

The following quote from Reuters is fairly typical of news surrounding the agricultural market's sensitivity to the weather during the growing season:

> "The worst drought in more than half a century in America's corn belt has slashed the corn crop to the lowest in five years, leading to a plunge of corn supplies to the smallest in 17 years by next summer... that would result in the third year in a row of razor thin corn stocks, keeping prices at record highs and rationing demand for the world's most popular feed grain, analysts said" (Reuters, August 7, 2012).

Every year, the corn futures market is very sensitive to weather reports in June and July. Despite the well known relationship between weather and commodity supply, weather data has been of little help to analysts trying to forecast prices because it is so unpredictable. This is evidenced by Roll's (1984) study in which only three percent of frozen concentrated orange juice price movements could be explained using data from weather reports.

As noted above, livestock markets are also affected by the weather. For instance, during the same drought of 2012, unusually hot weather in the Midwest United States and rising corn prices led to reduced hog marketings as farmers responded to the increased price of feed. As a result, hog futures prices rose sharply in late July and early August.

An example of inelastic demand at work is evident in the world coffee market. Weather conditions are extremely important for many soft commodities like coffee. For example, cold weather in Brazil in July and August can harm the coffee crop in the world's largest coffee producing nation. During the southern hemisphere winter, the coffee market is usually somewhat volatile and prone to a sharp price rally on any hint of a damaging frost in Brazil. Similarly a lack of seasonal rainfall in the coffee growing region of Brazil can drive up coffee prices. In 2014, the Brazilian coffee harvest was down about 13%, and this doubled the price of coffee. World coffee production is about 150 million bags per year. As the following quote from the *Financial Times* indicates, a 10 million bag swing in Brazil's production over a two year period (about a 3.5% change in global production over a two year period) can mean the difference in coffee prices ranging between $3 and $1.50 per pound.

> Brazil is the largest coffee producer in the world, accounting for about 35 per cent of all output. Industry consensus around the 2014 Brazilian harvest seems to have settled at about 48m 60kg bags, down from the previous year's 54-55m, but the 2015 forecasts have ranged widely between 40m and 53m bags. Estimates for the cumulative Brazil supply 2014 and 2015 combined, range

Figure 5.2: Coffee Futures Prices React to Drought in Brazil

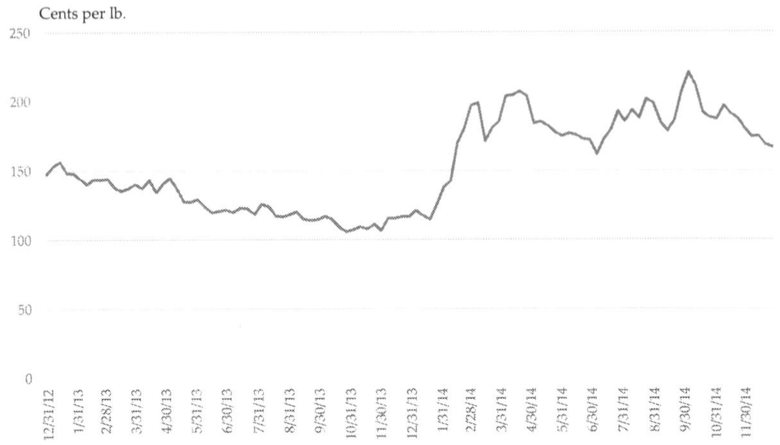

Source: Barchart.com.

from 92m to 102m bags, which is the difference between $3.00 and $1.50 per pound of coffee.[1]

The 2014 drought in south-eastern Brazil that caused a 10% drop in Brazilian coffee production and, in turn led to a 40% coffee futures price increase, is shown in Figure 5.2.

Commodity traders also watch the weather conditions in China very closely as China is the world's largest producer of raw agricultural products. For instance, China is the largest producer of wheat in the world and the second largest producer of corn, after the U.S. The degree of China's integration with world commodity is growing and China is notorious for its erratic international trade in certain commodities such as wheat, corn, oilseeds, tobacco and cotton.

For example, if China has a bumper cotton crop it could be a large cotton exporter in that particular year and international cotton prices will be depressed. However, if the weather is poor and the cotton crop suffers, then China can quickly turn and become a very large importer of cotton because China is the world's largest cotton consumer. The North China Plain is a major cotton growing area that depends on mother nature for rainfall and good growing conditions. Assessing the size of China's cotton harvest is always difficult and for this reason, small shifts in China's weather patterns impact the cotton futures market swiftly.

In 2023, Frozen Concentrated Orange Juice (FCOJ) futures reached

---

[1] *Financial Times*, Thursday, Sep 18, 2014.

Figure 5.3: Frozen Concentrated Orange Juice (FCOJ) Futures Prices

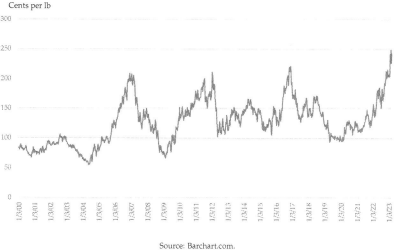

Source: Barchart.com.

record highs of $2.50 per lb. (see Figure 5.3) due to recurring weather and disease problems in Florida, which produces almost all of the FCOJ in the United States. The Florida orange crop in 2022-2023 was the smallest crop in nearly 90 years. This situation was brought on by an ill-timed holiday freeze, two hurricanes and citrus greening disease. The USDA indicated that Florida produced only 18 million 90-pound boxes of oranges in 2022/23, a 50% drop from the previous year and a 93% decline from Florida's peak output in 1998.

A growing concern for world agriculture is global warming. According to the United States Environmental Protection Agency (EPA), rising temperatures may result in grains growing more quickly and, thus, growing with a reduced yield as the seeds spend less time maturing. Other potential dangers are more extreme weather events (drought, flood etc.) that could potentially wipeout crops in certain areas as well as allowing weeds and pests to thrive in warmer climates. Any impediment to crop production will then be reflected in increased prices of crops and livestock (see Box 5.5).

Box 5.5 Climate Change and Agricultural Markets

Increased Greenhouse Gas (GHG) emissions are believed responsible for warming the earth's atmosphere-climate change. This phenomenon is an important part of the global food security equation.
Agriculture and food consumption are important drivers of climate
change because agriculture is a significant source of GHG emissions.
At the same time, the impacts of climate change on agriculture are
potentially significant, affecting crop yields, growing seasons, irriga-
tion demands, etc. But the science on climate change is uncertain, and
there is a wide range of predictions of the effects of climate change
on food production and global food security. The Intergovernmental
Panel on Climate Change has predicted mean temperatures could increase which could reduce crop yields in some countries and increase
crop yields in other countries. Similarly, the variability in temperature and rainfall is forecast to increase. Derivative markets (including
futures and options) will no doubt play a role in managing the additional market risk that could result from climate change. For more
information, see http://www.ipcc.ch/

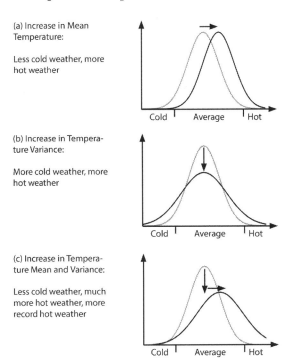

Source: IPCC Third Assesment Report, Climate Change 2001

Box 5.6 It's a State Secret

One of the most important variables in the world food equation is the size of China's grain reserves, and it is a state secret. China's State Statistical Bureau publishes an annual statistical yearbook on its agriculture and the book is about two inches thick, filled with hundreds of tables of obscure data. However, for economic security reasons, China's agricultural yearbook has no information on domestic grain stocks; this number remains a state secret in China. This presents a big problem for international commodity market analysts, because China is the world's largest producer and consumer of grain and it may hold as much as one-half of the world's grain reserves of wheat, rice and corn combined.

In an attempt to fill this huge gap in knowledge, the U.S. Department of Agriculture (USDA) and the United Nations' Food and Agriculture Organization (FAO) have periodically attempted to estimate the size of China's grain stocks. However, there is tremendous uncertainty in these estimates as some of the grain stocks are stored privately on farms in rudimentary small-scale facilities and some are stored in large state-run storage facilities that are off-limits to foreigners.

In 2001, both the FAO and the USDA suddenly revised their previous estimates of China's domestic stocks of wheat, rice, and corn. The abrupt fall in China's production in 2000 did not lead to large imports, as expected, and partly for this reason, the FAO and USDA decided that China must have been sitting on large stockpiles of grain.

With a stroke of a pen, the U.S. Department of Agriculture increased its estimate of grain stocks from 66.1 million metric tons (mmt) to 230.1 mmt–more than a tripling of the figure! That's nothing, however, as a few months earlier the FAO had revised its cereal grain stock estimate for China from 28.1 mmt to 364 mmt–nearly 13 times more than its previous estimate. The FAO's revisions for China were so large that it meant more than a doubling of its estimate of the amount of world cereal grain reserves to 640 mmt at the end of crop year 2001.

References: U.S. Department of Agriculture, Office of the Chief Economist, "World Agricultural Supply and Demand Estimates" Washington, DC, WASDE-374, May 10, 2001.

United Nations Food and Agriculture Organization, Food Outlook, Rome: February 2001.

Input Costs

Inputs are factors of production and therefore input costs affect commodity supply. The demand for an input will depend on the producer's return from employing more of the input–the marginal revenue product (MRP) of the input. It is only profitable to employ more of the input if the additional revenue exceeds the cost. As long as the MRP of an input exceeds the cost of an extra unit of the input, it is profitable for the producer to purchase and use more of the input. Alfred Marshall, the famous economist who demonstrated the theoretical power of understanding demand and supply curves, developed four main factors that determine the price elasticity of input demand. Marshall demonstrated that the (absolute value of the) elasticity of demand for an input varies directly with:

1. The (absolute value of) elasticity of demand for the product the input produces;
2. The share of the input in the cost of production;
3. The elasticity of supply of other factors; and
4. The elasticity of substitution between the factor in question and the other factors.

Many commodity markets are linked with one another in that the output of one market becomes an input for other markets. For example, corn, soybean meal, and feeder cattle are all inputs into the production of live (fattened) cattle. Therefore, the futures prices of these inputs directly affect the supply response of live cattle producers which, in turn, affects the market price of live cattle. The price elasticity of input demand plays a central role in these market linkages.

Government Policy

Some governments in rich countries have become a major factor in determining agricultural commodity prices. This is especially true in the United States, Japan, and the European Union. Agricultural policies in these areas protect their domestic farmers from global competition. Such policies can impact both the absolute price level and the volatility of prices. As a result, supply and demand shocks to the market can lead to exacerbated price impacts. This was the case with the 2012 drought.

Biofuels

The United States, Brazil and the European Union each have policies to allocate a portion of their agricultural production to be processed into fuel. In

Table 5.1: U.S. biofuels supply and disposition in 2021 (billion gallons)

	Production	Imports	Exports	Consumption
Fuel ethanol	15.01	0.06	1.25	13.94
Biodiesel	1.64	0.2	0.18	1.65
Renewable diesel	0.81	0.39	NA	1.16
Other biofuels	0.08	NA	NA	less than 1
Total	17.55	0.66	1.43	16.83

Source: Energy Information Association

the U.S., the Renewable Fuels Standard requires that about 10% of all transportation fuel sold in the country must originate from renewable sources, largely ethanol from corn. This policy actually reduces the true value of blended gasoline because ethanol has less energy per gallon, as well as increases the price of corn due to a significant portion of production being allocated to fuel instead of food. This policy experienced significant criticism in 2012 as a severe drought has lowered U.S. corn production, yet a significant portion of the crop was used as fuel, and this portion used for fuel was not sensitive to price because it was mandated by the U.S. government.

In addition, the Renewable Fuels Standard requires that a certain volume of biomass-based diesel (biodiesel from soybean oil) and renewable diesel (derived from agricultural waste products like vegetable oils and animal fats) volumes be used each year in the United States. Each year, the U.S. Environmental Protection Agency (EPA) sets required volumes. This policy has raised the price of soybeans, just as ethanol mandates have raised the price of corn (Lark et al., 2022). See Table 5.1 for the US biofuel supply and demand situation in 2012.

According to (Lark et al., 2022) the U.S. biofuels mandate has incentivized farmers to plant corn and soybeans on millions of acres of land that would otherwise have remained grassland. This land conversion released large amounts of carbon dioxide and other greenhouse gases, harming the environment. As a result and makes ethanol and biodiesel fuel is not environmentally friendly and is just as bad for the climate as the gasoline it has replaced.

U.S. farmers and the biofuel industry have vigorously and successfully lobbyied the federal government to keep increasing the mandates for biofuels, while ignoring the scientific evidence that on net biofuels do not really help to reduce greenhouse gases. Ethanol accounts for about 85% of U.S. biofuel production and biodiesel accounts for about 11%. Under pressure from lobbyists, the U.S. Environmental Protection Agency (EPA) has increased the amount of soybean oil used to produce biodiesel that then by law must be blended into the diesel supply, so much so that more than 50% of US soybean oil is now used for transport fuel. U.S. biodiesel usage increased from 0.26 billion gallons in 2010 to 1.9 billion gallons in 2020. This shift of soybean oil to the fuel supply has driven up the price of soybean oil and therefore the price of soybeans.

Brazil is the second largest producer of biofuel after the United States, but Brazil converts sugarcane to fuel instead of corn. Sugarcane is a much more efficient fuel source compared to corn. Brazil has enjoyed considerable success with its biofuel program due to its large endowment of agricultural land as well as a climate suitable to growing sugarcane, a crop that is much better suited to biofuel production than is corn. As such, Brazil is able to produce enough biofuel to satisfy domestic demand and at times it is a large exporter of fuel. To accommodate their high production of ethanol, Brazil has developed cars capable of running on a fuel mixture that contains a greater percentage of ethanol, up to 100%.

As shown in Figure 5.4, the use of corn and soybeans to fuel automobiles and trucks is costly in terms of land use. This figure shows the amount of land required per (light-duty) vehicle run on biofuel to offset equivalent gasoline GHG emissions. This Figure shows that more than 10.5 hectares of land would be required to displace the GHG emissions from one passenger vehicle burning soy biodiesel. Corn is not much better, requiring over 7.5 hectares per vehicle. The same vehicle running on sugarcane ethanol would only require about 0.7 hectares to fuel the vehicle, in order to displace the equivalent gasoline GHG emissions.

For comparison, Figure 5.4 shows the global crop- land of 0.24 hectares per person. Soybeans are a particularly inefficient source of biodiesel because soybeans crop yields are relatively low. Scientists have determined that sugarcane ethanol yields about 6,300 liters fuel/ha, compared to 3,500 liters for corn ethanol and only 545 liters of soybean biodiesel. Although it is a technical and agronomic matter to calculate how land- intensive biofuel production is, it is a matter of policy and societal choice to choose whether this is an appropriate use of land resources, and if so, how much land to thus use.

The European Union (EU) has a biofuel policy similar to that of the United States, although their renewable fuel requirement has been lower because the E.U. does not have the same abundance of farmland as in the United States. In Europe the crop-based biofuels include primarily rapeseed, palm and soy oil for biodiesel; and corn, wheat and sugar beet and sugar cane for bioethanol. The EU had a 2010 target of 5.75% of transportation fuel to be composed of renewable fuels and a 2020 target rate of 10%. Their biofuel production capacity is much lower than the United States and commodity price spikes and weather considerations caused the E.U. bio-

Figure 5.4: Land required per vehicle run on biofuel to offset equivalent gasoline GHG emissions

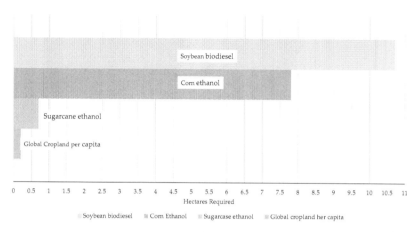

Sagar, Ambuj D. and Sivan Kartha. "Bioenergy and sustainable development." *Annu. Rev. Environ. Resour.* 32 (2007): 131-167.

fuel policy to be re-evaluated. For instance, Germany, the largest producer of biofuels in Europe, plans to phase out the use of biofuels made from food and feed crops by 2030.

Recognizing that biofuels are a failed experiment, are a wasteful use of farmland, and do not help reduce greenhouse gas emissions, in 2023 the EU banned both soybean oil and palm oil as biofuels. This was based on concerns of adverse effects on climate, biodiversity and food security of using soy and palm as transport fuels. Using these agricultural products as fuels has led to increased deforestation in Asia and Latin America. In other words, biodiesel is worse for the climate than fossil diesel. Biofuels policies also increase food prices and therefore threaten food security, especially in poor regions of the world (Fehrenbach, Bürck and Wehrle, 2023).

Seasonal price patterns

Some commodity markets typically exhibit seasonal price patterns within a production period. For some commodities, seasonal patterns occur in a high percentage of years and are somewhat consistent. For instance, U.S. corn is an annual crop that is planted in the spring and harvested in the fall. In the northern hemisphere, corn is normally planted in April and May and harvested in October and November. Once the harvest is completed, the market must ration the available supply until the following harvest and the typical pattern is that prices rise after the fall harvest. This is fundamental price behavior because economic theory predicts that prices will rise after

Figure 5.5: Seasonal Index of Wheat Prices 2010/11 to 2021/22

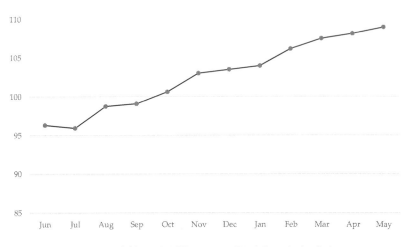

Source: compiled from USDA Wheat statistics. Price is farm price for all wheat.

harvest in order to cover the full cost of storage until the following harvest one year later. A basic understanding of seasonal price cycles offers one of the simplest approaches to fundamental analysis in commodity markets.

As an illustration, the seasonal price pattern for U.S. wheat prices is shown in Table 5.2 and Figure 5.5, for the 2000/2001 through 2011/2012 crop years. The seasonal index is computed by expressing the average price for each month as a percentage of the overall average price for the entire twelve year period. We begin with the average price in June (the start of the crop year). From Table 5.2, the price in June averaged $4.33 per bushel from 2000/2001 through 2011/2012. At the same time, the overall average price (for all months) was $4.515 per bushel. So, the June index is (4.33/4.515) × 100 = 95.9. This suggests that the price in June is 4.1 percent below the yearly average, in a normal year. The September index in Table 5.2 is 102.7, indicating that the September price is 2.7 percent above the yearly average price. Figure 5.5 is a plot of the seasonal index (i.e., the last row of Table 5.2).

We see from Figure 5.5 that, from 2000/2001 to 2011/2012, wheat prices were typically the lowest in the June to September period, just following the harvest. Wheat prices then increased seasonally from October through December, before levelling off. Prices then rose again just prior to the next harvest, with a seasonal peak in the March through May. Wheat prices tend to fall rather sharply from May through August.

Obviously, seasonal price indexes should not be relied upon alone for price forecasts, but instead should serve as a useful tool. Analysts should

Table 5.2: Monthly Average Wheat Prices: 2010/11 - 2021/22

Crop Year	June	July	Aug.	Sep.	Oct.	Nov.	Dec.	Jan.	Feb.	Mar.	Apr.	May	Average
						\$ per bushel							
2010/11	4.16	4.49	5.44	5.79	5.88	6.1	6.44	6.69	7.42	7.55	8.01	8.16	5.7
2011/12	7.41	7.1	7.59	7.54	7.27	7.3	7.2	7.05	7.1	7.2	7.11	6.67	7.24
2012/13	6.7	7.89	8.04	8.27	8.38	8.47	8.3	8.12	7.97	7.79	7.71	7.68	7.77
2013/14	7.37	6.95	6.88	6.8	6.94	6.85	6.73	6.65	6.5	6.74	6.82	7.08	6.87
2014/15	6.49	6.15	5.97	5.71	5.71	6.04	6.14	6.15	5.89	5.7	5.56	5.33	5.99
2015/16	5.42	5.23	4.84	4.72	4.86	4.86	4.75	4.82	4.61	4.4	4.46	4.45	4.89
2016/17	4.2	3.75	3.68	3.48	3.68	3.88	3.9	4.01	4.16	4.37	4.16	4.05	3.89
2017/18	4.37	4.77	4.84	4.65	4.64	4.72	4.5	4.65	4.92	5.1	5.28	5.39	4.72
2018/19	5.19	5.0	5.31	5.15	5.22	5.23	5.28	5.28	5.33	5.19	4.93	4.78	5.16
2019/20	4.81	4.52	4.34	4.26	4.45	4.39	4.64	4.88	4.88	4.86	4.85	4.76	4.58
2020/21	4.57	4.54	4.54	4.73	4.98	5.24	5.46	5.48	5.83	5.86	6.04	6.46	5.05
2021/22	6.23	6.26	7.14	7.75	7.92	8.52	8.59	8.48	9.16	9.93	10.2	10.9	7.63
12 year average	5.58	5.55	5.72	5.74	5.83	5.97	5.99	6.02	6.15	6.22	6.26	6.31	5.79
Seasonal Index	96.3	95.9	98.7	99.1	100.6	103.0	103.5	104.0	106.2	107.5	108.1	109.0	100.0

Source: https://www.ers.usda.gov/data-products/wheat-data/

not assume that seasonality alone causes price changes within a year. Seasonal price moves may be strong within a year, but if the trend is moving against the seasonal price pressure, the trend could certainly be stronger and outweigh the seasonal pressure.

There are a number of alternative approaches that can be used to calculate seasonal price patterns. The method used to calculate the wheat seasonal price pattern in Figure 5.5 is one of the simplest because the overall average price for the eleven year period was used in the denominator, in order to calculate the index. Instead, if we had reason to believe there were long-term trends in the prices, we could have used a twelve-month moving average in the denominator. With this alternative approach, the denominator would change every month.

Financials

All financial markets are influenced to some degree by a very long list of economic variables. For interest rate futures and options markets, macroeconomic variables and government macroeconomic policy are overriding fundamental factors. Stock index prices are subject to expectations concerning the general business climate. Foreign currency markets reflect the relative strengths of national economies and gaps in global interest and inflation rates. Clearly, the number of factors which might have some impact on prices in financial markets is quite large, making fundamental analysis of financials a formidable task.

Fundamental traders in the financial markets keep abreast of business cycles and the U.S. Conference Board, a private non-profit organization, publishes a well-respected measure of these business cycles. The Conference Board indicators are key factors that influence financial markets and the Conference Board groups twenty-one different economic variables into three categories: leading, concurrent, and lagging indicators: (http://www.conference-board.org/).

Leading indicators provide advance signals about the strength of the economy. They reflect expected changes in the business cycle and consequently provide an early warning system for identifying changes in financials. Concurrent and lagging indicators show the general direction of the economy and confirm or deny a trend or change in a trend implied by the leading indicators. Concurrent indicators show the degree of change that is taking place in the economy while lagging indicators show the degree of change that has taken place.

There are ten indicators that make up the Conference Board "leading indicator" index:

1. average weekly hours, manufacturing;

2. average weekly initial claims for unemployment insurance;
3. manufacturers' new orders, consumer goods and materials;
4. ISM® new orders index;
5. manufacturers' new orders, nondefense capital goods excluding aircraft orders;
6. building permits, new private housing units;
7. stock prices, 500 common stocks;
8. Leading Credit Index™;
9. interest rate spread, 10-year Treasury bonds less federal funds;
10. average consumer expectations for business conditions.

There are four variables that make up the Conference Board's "concurrent indicator":

i. personal income less transfer payments;
ii. manufacturing and trade sales;
iii. industrial production; and
iv. employees on nonagricultural payrolls.

And, there are seven components in the Conference Board's index of "lagging indicators":

I. change in CPI for services;
II. change in labor costs per unit of output;
III. ratio of manufacturing and trade inventories to sales;
IV. ratio of consumer installment credit to income;
V. commercial and industrial loans outstanding;
VI. average duration of unemployment; and
VII. average prime rate charged by banks.

The composite leading, concurrent, and lagging indexes signal peaks and troughs in the business cycle. Because they are averages, they are smoother than the individual variables that make up each index. Historically, the leading indicators have provided a reasonable measure of major turning points in economic variables such as income and employment. The Conference Board also publishes global business cycle indicators and forecasts of economic performance in a number of different nations.

Purchasing Power Parity and Exchange Rate Forecasts

As explained above in Chapter 4, the exchange rate is the price of one currency in terms of another. In international markets, relative currency values are critical determinants of trade flows and the profitability of multinational

Box 5.7 Demand for Gold and Price of Gold

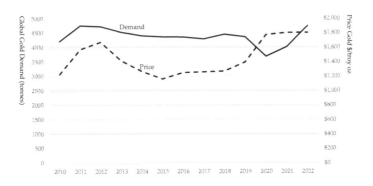

As shown in the above graph, the price of gold rose from about $1,200 to $1,800 per troy oz between 2015 and 2020. One key reason for the price increase was heightened demand for gold for investment purposes rising from 967 tonnes in 2015 to 2,416 tonnes in 2020. Investment through exchange traded funds (ETFs) peaked in 2020 at 892 tonnes, induced by the fall in the stock market in 2020 with the onset of COVID 19. The health crisis created an economic crisis and due to the heightened uncertainty gold was viewed as a *safe haven* for investors getting out of the stock market.

The graph shows total demand for gold (including investment demand, jewelry demand and industrial demand such as electronics) and the dip in total demand in 2020 was due to a 34% fall in demand for jewelry fabrication during COVID-19. The supply of gold is relatively constant from year to year compared to the demand side of the equation. In 2020 the world supply of gold was only marginally down by about 3%. The price of gold remaining relatively high at $1,800 per troy oz into 2023 can be attributed to rising inflation in the U.S. and around the globe.

Source: World Gold Council.

firms. The role of exchange rates in the economy is becoming more and more important because of increased globalization. For example, a swing in the value of the U.S. dollar vis-à -vis foreign currencies affects profits (and the competitiveness) for a large percentage of U.S. companies because of their multinational interests. Many U.S. companies earn sales revenues denominated in a foreign currency and/or they purchase inputs denominated in a foreign currency. When the revenues and costs are converted to U.S. dollars for the company's quarterly report, fluctuations in the exchange rate dramatically affect the U.S. dollar value. This is why multinationals typically hedge their exposure to currency risk in either the forward or futures market. For example, exporters of wine from Australia typically receive payment from foreign buyers in either U.S. dollars or Great Britain's Pound. The exporters convert the U.S. dollars or British Pound's back into Australian dollars and this means they are exposed to considerable exchange rate risk because costs are denominated in Australian dollars. To reduce this risk, the wine exporters typically hedge their exchange rate exposure because they are in the business of selling wine and not speculating on foreign currencies.

Foreign imports of agricultural products are also affected by currency fluctuations because most international transactions in agricultural commodities are conducted in U.S. dollars. This means that when the U.S. dollar strengthens, food imports become more expensive for these countries, and vice versa. Fortunately for developing countries, the U.S. dollar was relatively weak during the 2007-08 commodity price boom. However, the opposite was true when grain and food prices spiked again in 2012. The price of corn reached $7.11 per bushel on June 27th, 2008 and this translated into 73.5 Mexican pesos per bushel at the time. In 2012, when corn touched $7.13 again on July 3rd, the price in Mexican pesos was 94.9, almost 30% higher due to the change in exchange rate.

At the same time, speculators are attracted to the trading of currency futures and they try to predict exchange rate changes. Just like the price of any asset, demand and supply establishes values in the spot, forward, futures, and options markets for currencies.

In the short-run, such factors as interest rate differentials, economic growth rates, international capital flows, and trade balances are economic variables that affect market-determined exchange rates. However, in the short-run, the markets do not always arrive at the same currency value that an accepted economic theory would predict as being the correct long-run value. Some traders use this discrepancy to predict the intrinsic value of a currency. That is, they appeal to the purchasing power parity (PPP) theory of exchange rate determination. They use this approach to adopt a long-run strategy of trading exchange rate futures. The reasoning is that a country's exchange rate cannot remain either "over-valued" or "under-valued" indefinitely and eventually the exchange rate must return to its true equilibrium PPP rate.

As was covered in Chapter 4, purchasing power parity (PPP) is an economic theory that states that the exchange rate between two countries is in equilibrium when the "purchasing power" is the same in each of the two countries. This means that the exchange rate between two countries should equal the ratio of the two countries' price level for a fixed basket of goods and services. This is the country's "real" exchange rate. If we were interested in comparing the cost of living in the United States versus Europe, the real dollar/euro exchange rate would provide an estimate of the cost of living in the United States relative to Europe. Alternatively, from an international trade perspective, the real exchange rate is a measure of how competitive Europe is in international markets relative to the United States. If the U.S. dollar has experienced real appreciation against the Euro, then Europe has become more competitive in world markets because the U.S. price level has risen relative to the European price level.

Suppose we are interested in the dollar/euro exchange rate. Denote the dollar/euro nominal exchange rate as $N_{\$/€}$. Then we can express the "real" dollar/euro exchange rate ($R_{\$/€}$) as: $R_{\$/€} = N_{\$/€} \times (P_E/P_{U.S.})$, Where P_E is the overall price level in Europe and $P_{U.S.}$ Is the overall price level in the United States. A rise in the real dollar/euro exchange rate, $R_{\$/€}$, indicates a relative increase in European prices and this is a real "depreciation" of the dollar. A depreciation of the dollar means that there is an increase in the dollar price of the euro, and thus the dollar has become less valuable. At the same time, when the dollar depreciates the euro (measured in U.S. dollars) appreciates. Alternatively, a fall in the real dollar/euro exchange rate, $R_{\$/€}$, indicates a relative increase in U.S. prices and a real "appreciation" of the dollar against the euro. The dollar appreciates because if $R_{\$/€}$ falls, then the euro is becoming cheaper in terms of U.S. dollars. The real exchange rate therefore provides information on the real costs of acquiring foreign goods, when international prices are changing.

Comparing nominal exchange rates in the spot and futures market with PPP rates gives an indication of whether a currency is "over-valued" or "under-valued." Another term for the PPP is the "law-of-one-price." The law-of-one-price states that competition (i.e., arbitrage) will equalize the price of an identical good in two countries (adjusted for transportation costs and other transactions costs) when the prices are expressed in the same currency. When we express the exchange rate as $/foreign currency, an increase in the exchange rate is an appreciation of the foreign currency. So if the real rate is greater than the nominal rate, then the foreign currency is thought to be overvalued. According to the PPP theory, we would expect an overvalued foreign currency to eventually fall in value.

Another way to describe the real exchange rate is the currency rate that equalizes the purchasing power of different currencies by eliminating the differences in price levels between countries. In its simplest form, the real rate is the ratio of the prices in national currencies of the same good in different countries. The concept of the real exchange rate can be illustrated

Table 5.3: The Hamburger Standard

	Big Mac Prices		Implied PPP of the Dollar	Actual $ Exchange Rate	Under (-)/Over (+) Valuation Against the $US
	In Local Currency	In U.S. Dollars			
United States	$5.15	$5.15	–	–	–
Australia	A$6.70	$4.62	1.30	1.45	-10.3%
Brazil	Real 22.9	$4.25	4.45	5.39	-17.5%
Switzerland	CHF 6.50	$6.70	1.26	0.97	+30.1%
Euro	€ 4.65	$4.74	0.90	0.98	-7.9%
Japan	¥ 390	$2.83	75.73	137.87	-45.1%

Source: The Economist, 2023.
Note: The purchasing power parity (PPP) rate is the local price divided by the U.S. price (i.e., the local price divided by $5.15).

by comparing the price of a single homogeneous good between countries, such as automobiles or hamburgers. However, this does not provide an accurate measure of the real rate because only one good is used for price comparisons instead of a complete basket of representative goods.

For example, if the price of a BMW 318i automobile in the European Union is 42,000 euros and in the United States it is 45,000 dollars, then the PPP between the US dollar and European euro is 45,000 dollars to 42,000 euros or 1.07 euros to the dollar. This means that for every dollar spent in the United States, (1/1.07) or 0.93 euros would have to be spent in Europe to obtain the identical goods, if the purchasing power parity exchange rate was the same as the nominal rate. In other words if the nominal exchange rate was 1.07 euros to the dollar, and the price of a cappuccino in San Francisco cost $5, then that same cappuccino should cost around €4.70 in Dublin, Ireland. If it cost less than €4.70 in Dublin then we would say the euro is undervalued.

The Economist magazine reports local currency prices of a McDonald's Big Mac for various countries of the world, and they call it the "Big Mac Index." The Big Mac Index compares the price of a McDonald's hamburger in different countries and the PPP theory predicts that a Big Mac should cost the same in all countries, after converting the prices to a common currency.

Table 5.3 is an example of the Big Mac Index from the Economist magazine. The second column in the table reports the local currency price of a Big Mac in the United States and five other countries. A Big Mac purchased in Australia costs $6.70 Australian dollars and in Japan, the same Big Mac costs 390 Yen (¥). The price difference between the U.S. and each of these foreign countries indicates what the exchange rate should be in purchasing power parity holds.

These local prices are converted to U.S. dollars by dividing by the actual exchange rate (column five) and the results are reported in column three of the table. For instance for Australia we divide Aus$6.70 by $1.45 (Aus$ per US$) and this yields $4.62 USD. In U.S. dollars, the price of a Big Mac is $5.15 in the United States compared to $2.83 in Japan and $4.62 in Australia. The fourth column in the table is the implied PPP rate, which is the local price divided by the U.S. price (i.e., the local price divided by $5.15). For instance, if we divide the Big Mac price in Australia A$6.70 by the US price of $5.15 this gives 1.30 as the implied PPP of the US dollar. In other words, if the exchange rate was $1.30 (Aus$ per US$) and you converted US dollars to Australian dollars at this rate, then paying Aus$6.70 would be the same as paying 6.7/1.30 = $5.15 (approximately). Comparing the PPP rate with the actual rate gives us an estimate of the extent to which each currency is under- or overvalued relative to the dollar. We see from the last column in the table that the Japanese Yen is undervalued relative to the dollar by over 45 percent. Alternatively the Swiss Franc is highly overvalued at over 30 percent.

Calculating a country's real exchange rate (or the PPP rate) can be a complicated procedure given that price levels for a fixed basket of goods and services must be compared across borders. The International Monetary Fund (in Washington DC) publishes real exchange rate indices for the major industrialized countries (http://www.imf.org/). In addition, the OECD in Paris also publishes PPP exchange rates for a large number of countries: (http://www.oecd.org/). More accurate measures of PPP rates are provided in Figures 5.6 and 5.7, and these data were obtained from the OECD. Both figures plot the annual PPP exchange rate and the nominal exchange rate, from 2000 to 2022. From Figure 5.6 we see that the Canadian dollar appreciated in nominal terms relative to the U.S. dollar from around 2005 until about 2013 and then it depreciated in value. Referring to 5.7, we see that the Japanese yen depreciated in nominal terms relative to the U.S. dollar from 2012 to 2022. According to these figures, both the Canadian dollar and the Japanese yen were slightly undervalued (in terms of the U.S. dollar) in 2022. The hamburger standard in Table 5.3 gives a much different picture for the Japanese yen but remember this standard is only for one good, Big Macs. Alternatively the Real (or purchasing power parity) rates in in Figures 5.6 and 5.7 are based on a large basket of currencies.

Figure 5.6: Canadian Dollar: Nominal and PPP Rate

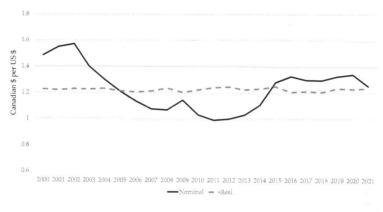

Source: OECD.

Figure 5.7: Japanese Yen: Nominal and PPP Rate

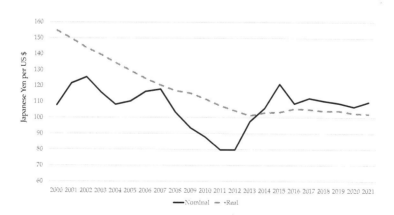

Source: OECD.

Evaluating the Fundamental Data: Further Examples

Elasticities

Any commodities trader trying to understand the price effect of a freeze affecting Brazil's coffee crop, or a drought in Australia's wheat region, must understand the supply and demand elasticities in that particular market. The price elasticities of demand and supply are both important concepts which directly link price and quantity changes. Each is calculated as a percent change in quantity (demanded or supplied) divided by the percent change in the market price:

$$E = \frac{\% \Delta Q}{\% \Delta P} \tag{5.4}$$

The price elasticity of demand measures the responsiveness of demand to a given change in price and is negative due to the "law of demand," (i.e., the inverse relationship between quantity demanded and price). The elasticity is independent of the units of measurement of price and quantity. It is related to the slope of the demand curve but it is not identical to the slope. The (absolute) demand elasticity is greater than 1.0 for goods with elastic demand and less than 1.0 for inelastic goods. In the elastic range of the demand curve, any increase of price will result in a larger-percentage decrease of quantity demanded, leading to a decrease in total revenue. So for this portion of the demand curve, what is gained in raising the price is more than offset by the loss in quantity sold. On the other hand, for the inelastic range of the demand curve, a price cut will lead to an increase of quantity demanded, but the magnitude of the percentage change is smaller which means the total revenue decreases.

The economic significance of the price elasticity of demand is that it is indicative of what is likely to happen to the price of a commodity when the available quantity changes. If there is a supply shock (say due to weather) then an analyst can infer the expected price change from knowledge of the price elasticity of demand. In addition, changes in industry revenue associated with price changes can be predicted.

The price elasticity of supply measures the responsiveness of supply to a given change in price and is positive. The cross price elasticity of demand measures the responsiveness of demand for one good to a given change in the price of a second good. The cross price elasticity is negative for complements and positive for substitutes.

Table 5.4 reports examples of demand elasticities estimated for the United States. These estimates indicate that rice has a very inelastic demand compared to say poultry or beef. Milk is less price responsive than

Table 5.4: Selected Price Elasticities of Demand for the United States

Commodity	Price Elasticity
Rice	-0.01
Beef	-0.75
Poultry	-0.76
Apples	-0.45
Milk	-0.17
Cheese	-0.33

Source: Food and Agricultural Research Institute and USDA Economic Research Service

cheese.

Often the elasticity of import demand or export supply is of more interest than domestic demand or supply elasticities, because most countries are now very open to world markets and exports and imports move with relative freedom. The elasticity of demand for imports (also referred to as excess demand) is the percentage change in the quantity of imports demanded divided by the percentage change in the price of imports. Similarly, the elasticity of supply of exports (excess supply) is the percentage change in the quantity of exports supplied divided by the percentage change in the price of exports. With increasing globalization, these trade elasticities have become more and more important. For most commodities, the domestic elasticities can differ widely from trade elasticities.

The import demand and export supply functions are generally less steep and more price responsive than either domestic demand or supply functions. In fact, the price elasticity of both import demand (ED) and export supply (ES) is larger in absolute value than either domestic demand (D) or domestic supply (S). This is shown in Figure 5.8.

In Figure 5.8, the domestic demand (q_D) and domestic supply (q_S) are shown in the left-hand panel. Without international trade, the domestic market clears at price P*. However, if we allow for international trade and the international price is different from P*, there will be either excess demand (ED) or excess supply (ES) at home in the domestic market. If the world price lies above P*, then ES is the horizontal difference between q_S and q_D, shown as the ES segment of q_T in the right-hand panel of Figure 5.8. At this relatively high price, the home country becomes an exporter because quantity supplied exceeds quantity demanded. Alternatively, if the world price is below the domestic price before trade (i.e., P*) then there is excess demand, shown as ED in Figure 5.8. The intuition is that as the price falls below P* the domestic producers move down the q_S function and domestic consumers move down the q_D function. For any given price level below P*,

Figure 5.8: Elasticity of Import Demand (Export Supply)

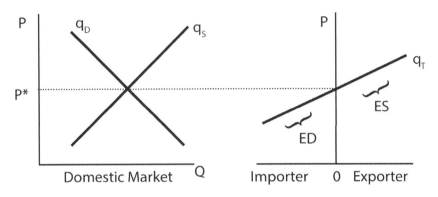

$q_D > q_S$ which means there is "excess demand" that must be satisfied by imports. The home country then becomes an importer and the quantity of imports will be equal to the horizontal gap between q_D and q_S, which can be read off the ED portion of q_T.

From Figure 5.8 We can see that for a given commodity, there will be excess supply at relatively high domestic prices and excess demand at relatively low domestic prices. Let the trade function (q_T) be equal to the difference between the quantity of domestic demand (q_D) and domestic supply (q_S) at any given price, p.

So,

$$q_T = q_D - q_S, \text{ and } q_T > 0 \text{ for } ED \text{ and } q_T < 0 \text{ for } ES \qquad (5.5)$$

Using Δ to denote a change in a variable, we can rewrite equation 5.5 as:

$$(\Delta q_T / \Delta p) = (\Delta q_D / \Delta P) - (q_S / \Delta p) \qquad (5.6)$$

or by multiplying each component of the equation by p/q_T, as:

$$\frac{\Delta q_T p}{\Delta p q_T} = \frac{\Delta q_D p q_D}{\Delta p q_T q_D} - \frac{\Delta q_S p q_S}{\Delta p q_T q_S} \qquad (5.7)$$

In elasticity form, equation (5.7) is:

$$\varepsilon_T = \varepsilon_D (q_D / q_T) - \eta_S (q_S / q_T) \qquad (5.8)$$

So, if we let $(q_T / q_D) = S$, then $(q_S / q_T) = (1 - S)/S$. This means that equation (5.8) can be expressed as:

$$|\varepsilon_T| = (1/S) \times |\varepsilon_D| + (1 - S)/S \times (|\eta_S|) \qquad (5.9)$$

Equation (5.9) Implies that $|\varepsilon_T| > |\varepsilon_D|$, since $|1/S| > 1.0$. In other words, the price elasticity of either the excess demand or excess supply is larger in absolute value than either the domestic demand or supply elasticity.

From equation (5.9) We find that import demand is more elastic:

1. The more elastic domestic demand (ε_D) is;
2. The more elastic domestic supply (η_S) is; and,
3. The smaller the market share of imports (S).

The economic intuition behind this result is that if the world price rises, then this implies a change in imports due to changes in both domestic demand and a change in domestic supply. It is the induced change in domestic supply that results in the import demand being more elastic than the domestic demand.

An example will help to illustrate why equation 5.9 is useful. We can use equation 5.9 to show that the absolute value of the price elasticity of domestic demand (ε_D) can be relatively low compared to the price elasticity of import demand (ε_T). Take beef as an example and suppose that 25 percent of domestic beef consumption is imported. For beef, let (ε_D) = -1.0 and η_S = 1.5. Thus using equation 5.9, we find that:

$$|\varepsilon_T| = (1/.25) \times |-1.0| + [(1 - .25)/.25] \times |1.5| = 8.5 \qquad (5.10)$$

So a 1 percent increase in the price of beef would induce a 1 percent decrease in domestic demand (with ε_D= -1.0), but an 8.5 percent change in the import demand for beef! The reason that the responsiveness of import demand exceeds the responsiveness of domestic demand is that the price increase also leads to a domestic supply response, which chokes off imports.

Cycles

In commodity markets, "cycles" are defined by recurring patterns in production and prices, which last more than one season (or production period). A complete cycle includes successive years of increases and decreases in either production or prices extending from one peak (or valley) to the next peak (or valley). For instance, the "hog cycle" is one of the most well known cycles in agricultural commodity markets. In fact, cyclical fluctuations in prices and production have characterized the hog industry for a number of years (Shonkwiler and Spreen, 1986).

The hog cycle is thought to have developed because of a lag in the production period, whereby current production is a function of past prices. Shonkwiler and Spreen found both a 3-year and a 7-year cycle in hogs. The

3-year cycle was found to be due to biological factors in hog production. They argued that the time lag between farrowing and rebreeding retained sows is about eight to nine months. This means that it takes about one and one-half years to expand production, which generates a 3-year cycle.

Since corn is a major component of the cost of pork production in the United States, a crude indicator of hog profitability and of forthcoming cyclical changes in production and prices is the hog-corn ratio. The hog-corn ratio is the price of hogs in dollars per hundred weight (cwt) divided by the price of corn in dollars per bushel. This ratio indicates how many bushels of corn that a hundred pounds of hogs will buy. A high ratio signals an increase in pork production and a low ratio indicates a decrease in production. Producers decide to increase their supply of hogs when the hog-corn ratio is higher than the long-run average. Similarly, when the ratio is lower than the long-term average, producers often respond by reducing hog production. The hog-corn ratio depends on the price of the product (i.e., hogs) relative to the price of the input (i.e., corn). The ratio will increase when either the relative price of corn falls or the relative price of hogs increases. This means that an increase in the price of hogs could have the same effect on supply as a fall in the price of corn. However, a limitation of the hog-corn ratio as a profit indicator is that the ratio reflects only the price of one input (corn), and it does not reflect price changes of other inputs. In addition, the ratio varies with the price of corn. This means that it takes a higher hog-corn ratio to represent a profitable situation when corn prices are low than when they are high. It may take a ratio of about 18 to 1 to be profitable when corn is $3.00 per bushel; but, at $2.00 per bushel, a ratio around 20 to 1 may be needed to generate a similar profit level, assuming non-feed costs remain stable.

The hog-corn price ratio in the United States is shown in Figure 5.9, for the 2000 to 2022 time period. During this period, the ratio averaged 15.1:1. The maximum ratio during this period was 29:7 and the minimum was 8:1. The minimum ratio was experienced in 2012 during the big drought.

As shown in Figure 5.10, high hog corn price ratios have historically led to increases in production which then bring hog prices down. On the other hand, low ratios indicate low profitability, so producers reduce hog farrowings (production), which eventually leads to tighter supplies and higher prices. Although ratios such as this are not always reliable, they are useful if combined with other techniques. A simple regression of the hog-corn price ratio on change in hog farrowings indicates that an increase of 100,000 hog farrowings is associated with an increase of 1.o in the hog-corn ratio.

Figure 5.9: Hog Corn Price Ratio in the United States: 2001-2014

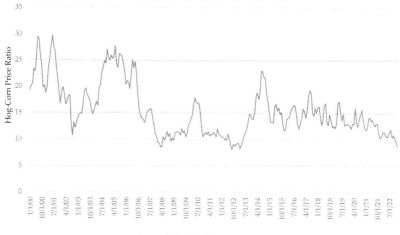

Source: USDA Feed Grains Database.

Figure 5.10: The Hog-Corn Price Ratio v. Farrowings

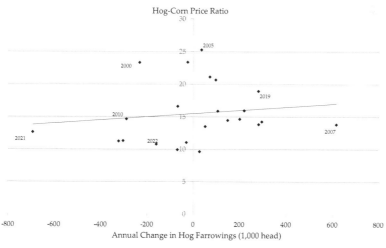

Source: USDA National Agricultural Statistics Service

Correlation

Correlation measures the degree of association (although not necessarily cause and effect) between two or more variables. Spreadsheets and regression packages available for use on microcomputers have made this technique very easy to use, even with large data sets. For example, Figure 5.11 provides the results from a simple regression of annual U.S. lumber prices (LP) on number of houses constructed or U.S. national housing starts (H): $LP = \alpha + \beta H + \varepsilon$. The dotted line through the data points in Figure 5.11 represents the estimated linear relationship between LP and H, the two variables of interest. Once the regression line has been estimated, plotting the expected housing starts and comparing that point to the regression line gives a general indication of forthcoming lumber prices. Also, if the point reflecting the current lumber price and housing starts is off the regression line, it is expected that market prices will gradually adjust so as to move back towards the line. We see from Figure 5.11 that lumber prices were unusually high in the 2020-2022 time period, during COVID 19. The problem was that supply was reduced due to lumber mill closures and at the same time demand increased as folks stuck at home during Covid started remodeling their homes, building decks, etc.

Figure 5.11: Lumber Price as a Function of Housing Starts: 2000-2022

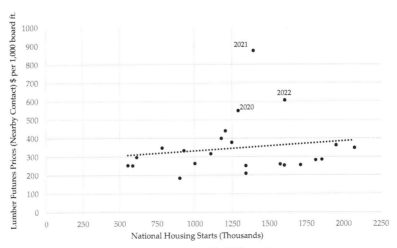

Source: Barchart.com and the US Census Bureau.

> ## Box 5.8 Globalization
>
> You can now buy a Big Mac in over 100 countries in the world! This is but one illustration of the growing integration of the world economy, popularly known as "globalization." Since World War II, the World Trade Organization has been crucial in encouraging economies to open its borders to international trade and investment. Greater interdependence among economies has raised standards of living around the world. In spite of the economic payoff from globalization it is also politically divisive, as some critics believe it threatens the environment, threatens jobs, and destroys national cultures.
>
> However, by some measures the degree of global economic integration today is not that high compared to the late 19th century, over 100 years ago. Prior to World War I, there was a similar period of globalization and the importance of international trade, measured as a share of income, was comparable to the situation today. In the late 1800s, the barriers to foreign trade were relatively low and foreign investment was very high. World trade grew rapidly with the invention of the steamship and railroad, which lowered the costs of transportation. Some economists believe that global financial markets were as well integrated in the late 1800s as they are today.
>
> *See Kevin O'Rourke and Jeffrey Williamson, Globalization and History: The Evolution of a Nineteenth-Century Atlantic Economy. Cambridge and London: MIT Press, 1999.*

Sources of information

Commodities

The Economic Research Service, U.S. Department of Agriculture, regularly publishes reports on specific commodity markets such as wheat, soybeans, cattle, cotton and coffee.

http://www.ers.usda.gov/

The U.S. Department of Agriculture's Foreign Agricultural Service gathers intelligence on foreign markets. It has market analysts stationed abroad who write attaché reports with detailed supply and demand information on conditions within foreign countries. For example, if you are looking for current crop conditions for wheat in Australia or coffee in Brazil, this is a good place to start. It is also a good source for the latest information on international trade in commodities.

http://www.fas.usda.gov/

The USDA Global Agriculture Information Network (GAIN) reports provide very useful and hard to find information on the agricultural situation and policy developments in foreign countries.

https://gain.fas.usda.gov/

The U.S. Department of Agriculture's National Agricultural Statistics Service (NASS) conducts extensive surveys of farmers and publishes reports with forecasts of supplies of food and fiber products. NASS produces the famous Hogs and Pigs report each quarter, which forecasts the U.S. pig crop.

http://www.usda.gov/nass/

The U.S. Department of Agriculture's World Agricultural Outlook Board (WAOB) provides economic forecasts on the outlook for U.S. and world agriculture. The WOAB uses remote sensing and weather to help generate its forecasts.

http://www.usda.gov/agency/oce/waob/waob.htm

The USDA's Interagency Commodity Estimates Committees prepares the World Agricultural Supply and Demand Estimates (WASDE) reports, an extremely comprehensive and invaluable source of monthly information on global agricultural supply and demand.

https://www.usda.gov/oce/commodity/wasde/

Cornell University's Mann Library has a comprehensive online collection of data and publications from the U. S. Department of Agriculture's economics and statistics system.

http://usda.mannlib.cornell.edu/usda/usda.html/

The U.S. Department of Commerce's National Oceanic and Atmospheric Administration (NOAA) provides information on current weather conditions, and weather forecasts. It is also an excellent source for historical weather information and weather links.

http://www.noaa.gov/

The Food and Agriculture Organization (FAO) of the United Nations collects and analyses information and data related to food, agriculture, forestry and fisheries. The FAO has an excellent statistical database.

http://www.fao.org/

Financials

For financial markets, U. S. Department of the Treasury is an important source of information on Treasury securities.

http://www.ustreas.gov/

The Federal Reserve System provides statistics and reports on monetary variables.

http://www.federalreserve.gov/

The Federal Reserve Bank of New York is another good site with a searchable database and research reports.

http://www.newyorkfed.org/

The University of British Columbia's Department of Commerce provides access to current and historic daily exchange rates and trend projections of the Canadian Dollar, the U.S. Dollar, and the Euro.

http://pacific.commerce.ubc.ca/xr/

The Bureau of Economic Analysis (BEA) is an agency of the U.S. Department of Commerce. This agency generates important economic numbers, including national income and product accounts (NIPA's) and gross domestic product (GDP) estimates, for the nation. The BEA also generates regional, industry, and international statistics that presents essential information on economic activity.

www.bea.doc.gov

In the private sector, Bloomberg is a news company with up to the minute and in-depth financial news and analysis, including information on interest rates and yield curves.

http://www.bloomberg.com/.

There are at least four other popular sites for financial investment information and trading techniques and tools.

http://www.morningstar.com/

http://www.TheStreet.com/

http://finance.yahoo.com/

http://www.pimco.com/

For information on European financial markets, visit the Bank of England's website.

http://www.bankofengland.co.uk/

For information on Asian financial markets, visit the Asian Development Bank's website.

http://www.adb.org/

Futures and options exchanges

All major futures and options exchanges issue statistical information on their products. The major exchanges are:

Chicago Board of Trade

http://www.cbot.com/

Chicago Mercantile Exchange

http://www.cme.com/

NYSE - Euronext

https://globalderivatives.nyx.com/

Intercontinental Exchange

https://theice.com/

Newspapers and magazines

The Financial Times (www.ft.com) and The Wall Street Journal (www.wsj.com) are helpful sources for commodity information, but are especially useful in providing financial market data. Investors Business Daily provides commodity and financial news, price quotes, and market analysis
(http://www.investors.com/).
The Economist magazine provides well researched articles on various topics related to commodity and financial markets (http://www.economist.com/). Futures magazine reports on fundamental and technical developments, plus reports on managed futures funds. Articles in this magazine offer advice on trading techniques (http://www.futuresmag.com/).

Brokerage houses

A customer's representative in a full service brokerage house is a good source for timely reports on important market changes. Also, most large brokerage houses have a futures and options research unit which issues periodic reports. These reports usually provide a summary of market events and a price forecast based on fundamental (and/or technical) factors, reflecting the consensus of the firm's analysts, brokers, and traders.

Summary

This chapter introduced fundamental analysis, one of two general categories of price analysis used by futures and options analysts and traders. The fundamental approach focuses on evaluating long run supply and demand factors in an attempt to forecast the direction of price movements. A fundamental analyst looks forward in time, gathering information concerning future supply and demand conditions and determining what this information implies for market conditions and forthcoming prices. Factors that influence the supply of and demand for commodities and financials were outlined in this chapter, as were sources of information and simple fundamental techniques. Key points made include:

- A fundamentalist tries to estimate the intrinsic value of a product, which is a long run approach to price analysis.

- There is a long running debate between the fundamental versus technical camps. This debate is not confined to futures and options markets however, as fundamental and technical approaches are also used in equity markets.

- If futures and options markets are informationally efficient, then today's market prices fully reflect all publicly available information. This means that fundamental analysis is very difficult.

- Empirical research shows that futures and options markets are not fully efficient.

Discussion questions

1. The Big Mac Index provides a rough guide to whether or not foreign currencies are at their correct level. It is based on the purchasing power parity (PPP) theory. This week, suppose the price of a Big Mac in Los Angeles California is $5.28 and in Tokyo Japan a Big Mac costs 380 Yen. If the actual exchange rate is 111 Yen per dollar, to what extent is the Japanese Yen "over" or "under" valued?

2. Suppose you heard the following two statements:

   "I do not believe in the random walk theory as an explanation of futures price behavior"

   "The futures market reacts to news quickly & soon discounts the information in the price. By the time the average trader hears the information it is already reflected in the price"

   Are these 2 statements consistent with one another? Answer yes or no & explain your reasoning.

3. List the main factors that affect exchange rates and explain why the U.S. dollar has followed its recent pattern relative to the euro and the yen. Explain what it means when there is a "strong dollar" and how are domestic and foreign firms affected by a strong dollar?

Selected References

Baffes, John, and Peter Nagle. 2022. *Commodity Markets: Evolution, Challenges, and Policies.* World Bank Publications.

Carter, Colin A, and Sandeep Mohapatra. 2008. "How reliable are hog futures as forecasts?" *American Journal of Agricultural Economics,* 90(2): 367–378.

Elam, Emmett Walker. 1978. "A Strong Form Test of the Efficient Market Model Applied to the US Hog Futures Market." PhD diss. University of Illinois at Urbana-Champaign.

Fama, Eugene. 1970. "Efficient Capital Markets: A Review of Theory and Empirical Work." *Journal of Finance,* 25(2): 383–417.

Fama, Eugene F. 1991. "Efficient capital markets: II." *The journal of finance,* 46(5): 1575–1617.

Fama, Eugene F, and Kenneth R French. 1987. "Commodity futures prices: Some evidence on forecast power, premiums, and the theory of storage." *Journal of Business,* 55–73.

Fehrenbach, Horst, Silvana Bürck, and Annika Wehrle. 2023. "The Carbon and Food Opportunity Costs of Biofuels in the EU27 plus the UK."

Kofi, Tetteh A. 1973. "A framework for comparing the efficiency of futures markets." *American Journal of Agricultural Economics,* 55(4 Part 1): 584–594.

Lark, Tyler J, Nathan P Hendricks, Aaron Smith, Nicholas Pates, Seth A Spawn-Lee, Matthew Bougie, Eric G Booth, Christopher J Kucharik, and Holly K Gibbs. 2022. "Environmental outcomes of the US renewable fuel standard." *Proceedings of the National Academy of Sciences,* 119(9): e2101084119.

Leuthold, Raymond M. 1972. "Random walk and price trends: the live cattle futures market." *The Journal of Finance,* 27(4): 879–889.

Leuthold, Raymond M, and Peter A Hartmann. 1979. "A semi-strong form evaluation of the efficiency of the hog futures market." *American Journal of Agricultural Economics,* 61(3): 482–489.

Park, Cheol-Ho, and Scott H Irwin. 2010. "A reality check on technical trading rule profits in the US futures markets." *Journal of Futures Markets,* 30(7): 633–659.

Roll, Richard. 1984. "Orange juice and weather." *The American Economic Review*, 74(5): 861–880.

Shonkwiler, J Scott, and Thomas H Spreen. 1986. "Statistical significance and stability of the hog cycle." *Southern Journal of Agricultural Economics*, 18(02).

Timmermann, Allan, and Clive WJ Granger. 2004. "Efficient market hypothesis and forecasting." *International Journal of forecasting*, 20(1): 15–27.

Tomek, William G. 1997. "Commodity futures prices as forecasts." *Review of Agricultural Economics*, 23–44.

Tomek, William G, and Roger W Gray. 1970. "Temporal relationships among prices on commodity futures markets: Their allocative and stabilizing roles." *American Journal of Agricultural Economics*, 52(3): 372–380.

6.

Technical Analysis

Technical analysis is the study of historical market prices, volume, open interest, and price volatility, usually conducted through examining price charts or computer generated buy and sell signals. Technicians, or chartists, as they are sometimes called, predict forthcoming prices from past prices, and also from price variability (i.e., volatility), volume of contracts traded, and open interest. According to chartists, examination of the history of these variables will reveal implicit signals regarding the psychology of the market. The psychology of the market may reveal the "strength" or "weakness" of a recent price move. While generating futures and options price forecasts, technicians essentially disregard supply and demand facts and figures that are related to the underlying commodity or financial asset. In other words, they ignore the economic fundamentals. Furthermore, they do not try and anticipate news events because such information is largely irrelevant to their trading system. For example, if technicians are studying price behavior in the natural gas futures market, they will not pay too much attention to winter weather forecasts even though a cold snap could shift the demand for natural gas.

The *Wall Street Journal* online provides a comprehensive and easy to use charting system for futures prices. Go to markets / market data / commodities and then select advanced charting. You can create line charts, bar charts, candelsticks, scatter plots (dots), etc. The website offers a wide range of interactive methods such as commodity channels, bollinger bands, oscillators, moving averages, momentum calculators, etc. Similar charting options are available on barchart.com. Once you select the commodity of interest on barchart.com you can click on interactive charts on the left hand side of the page, under CHARTS. There are at least 60 different technical "studies" that can be run interactively on barchart.com. These include Alligator, Bollinger Bands, Donchian Channel, Keltner Channel Exponential, Moving Average, TrendSpotter, Turtle Channel, Welles Wilder Volatility,

Awesome Oscillator, Bollinger Width, Chaikin Money Flow, True Strength Index, Wilder Accumulative Swing Index, and so on.

With inexpensive personal computers and relatively inexpensive historical data, quantitative analysis of historical market prices has grown in popularity. Most retail commodity brokers also like charting techniques because they are easy to apply and can easily make a novice sound sophisticated.

Virtually all of the charting techniques used by futures and options chartists have been borrowed from stock market chartists. With only slight modifications to charting tools pioneered in the stock market, futures and options chartists are soon up and running. Some chartists are even quick to begin selling trading advice. Charting does not require experience, knowledge, or understanding of the economics of the underlying commodity or financial asset. Rather, it requires blind faith that history will repeat itself in the way that price patterns are formed. This faith is not unlike the herd mentality that attracted "day traders" to the Nasdaq stock market prior to the tech stock crash in 2000. Meme stocks (driven by the internet, chat rooms, apps like Robinhood, and discussion boards), emerged around 2020 and are another example of herd mentality. For instance the stock price of the video game retailer GameStop Corp. (ticker: GME) shot up from less than $5 in early January 2021 to $88 by the end of January 2021, due to on-line hype. The retailer Bed, Bath and Beyond (BBBY) experienced a stock surge in 2021 as part of the meme-stock frenzy, and then the price of the stock suddenly plunged over 90%. BBBY then went bankrupt in 2023. Technical trading may indeed work for short periods of time. In other words, such systems may generate profits until they do not.

Many futures and options traders who rely on charting do not actually run the historical numbers themselves. Rather, they subscribe to professional charting services, which usually includes added services for extra costs. The professional chartists make money selling their trading systems over the Internet, through videos and books, and through mail-order courses. Most of the technical advisory services that sell futures and options trading systems have catchy titles that entice naive speculators. If you search the internet for "futures and options trading approaches," you will find several websites pitching technical advice for steep fees. Their books and software titles are often misleading as they suggest that the authors have "the" key to successful trading.

Technical trading authors write about "winning trading rules," "trading without fear," "trader's secrets," "robust trading systems," "techniques for bottom fishing," "sports psychology in trading," "Japanese candlesticks," "price filters," and "cycle analysis." There are hundreds of books available that describe winning ways to trade, following the rules of technical analysis. You can find technical trading articles by these and other authors in Futures Magazine (http://www.futuresmag.com/).

Technical traders (chartists) ignore economic fundamentals because they believe that supply and demand data are subject to too much individual interpretation and that the publicly available fundamental data are not current. With futures prices changing constantly, chartists believe that it is virtually impossible to keep up with all relevant "fundamental" supply and demand data and that long term fundamental forecasts have a very short half-life because they are too vulnerable to new information; hence, the technical focus on recent and current prices.

Technical analysts believe that the so-called problems with fundamental analysis can be avoided if, instead, you follow the "tracks in the sand" and let the market tell you when to buy and sell. They believe that by merely studying the direction and range of past price movements, information is revealed as to what other market participants are thinking. Chartists believe that trading based on fundamentals ignores the psychological mood of all other traders. They study a graph of price movements on their computer screen, in hopes of finding a recognizable pattern that indicates that a predictable price movement is underway. In addition, they compute simple statistics, that generate buy and sell signals from historical prices. In their books and courses, technicians stress trading discipline and they claim to have made large profits over extended periods of time.

The Chartist Logic

Charting is a subjective study of market price activity. A chartist attempts to anticipate the future direction of prices by appraising past and present trends and cycles. The traditional tools used in this analysis are a personal computer, access to historical data, and a graph or chart showing the movement of prices over a specified period of time. Chartists reach their conclusions by diagnosing the chart formations or patterns. They believe that they know how the pattern will further develop and play out in the market.

One purpose of charting is to measure the relative strength of buying and selling pressures. According to a chartist, if it can be demonstrated that buying pressure at the prevailing price is more powerful than selling pressure, it is logical to assume that prices will rise. If the relative strengths of the market pressures are reversed, prices are expected to fall.

The actual forecasting process consists of identifying the various patterns established by prices as they trend up or down, cycle, or move sideways. These patterns are believed to disclose implicitly the relative strength of supply and demand forces. Each chart formation has its own significance which the chartist coordinates with various other technical considerations to determine where prices are going. Chartists use primarily three sets of historical data: price, volume, and open interest.

Technical analysis provides traders with empirical, rather than theoretical, guidance in generating price forecasts. Although chartists discuss buying and selling pressures, there is little or no economics in the process. In fact, it has sometimes been described as a method of evaluating "crowd psychology." Yet, there are significant economic assumptions that are actually required to defend the logic of technical analysis. However, these assumptions are all implicit and most chartists simply ignore them.

The technical approach to price forecasting assumes that "history repeats itself," which means that the future can be predicted from the past. In particular, belief in the success of charting implies that there is no "random walk" in day to day price changes. Recall from Chapter 5 that the random walk model says that day-to-day price changes average to zero.

If price changes are random (and virtually all of the statistical evidence in academic publications suggests that price changes are close to being random), you cannot predict the future from the past. So, faith in technical trading methods implies a belief that prices do not follow a "**random walk.**" This, in turn, implies that the markets are informationally inefficient according to the usual economic definition. Recall, this issue was discussed in some detail in Chapter 5. Of course, the technicians say that random walk is nonsense. To support this view, they point out that all you have to do is look at any futures price chart and you can see how well the markets follow trends. Of course, statements like these are made *ex-post*, after the trend has been complete. Just like the old adage says, technicians have 20:20 vision with hindsight.

There are numerous methods used by chartists and they cannot all be described here. However, understanding the very basics of technical trading goes a long way to understanding this school of thought because even sophisticated sounding futures market technical methods are often simply slight variations of a basic technique that has been borrowed from the stock market. Technical proponents will go to great lengths to disguise what might be a small variation of a standard, simple technical approach. Technical methods fall into four general categories:

1. Patterns on price charts;

2. Trend following methods;

3. Character of market analysis; and,

4. Structural theories.

Each of these four categories are discussed below.

Figure 6.1: Vertical Bar Chart

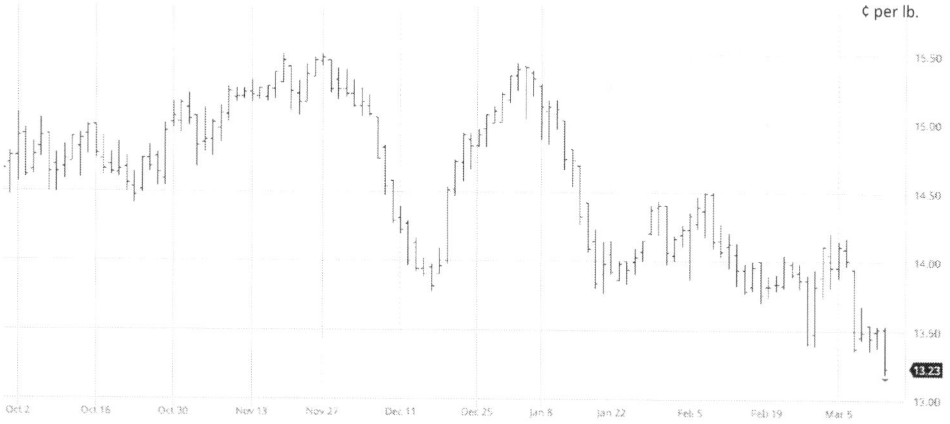

¢ per lb.

Oct 2 · Oct 16 · Oct 30 · Nov 13 · Nov 27 · Dec 11 · Dec 25 · Jan 8 · Jan 22 · Feb 5 · Feb 19 · Mar 5

15.50 · 15.00 · 14.50 · 14.00 · 13.50 · 13.23 · 13.00

Patterns on Price Charts

The study of patterns on price charts employs two types of basic charting tools: bar charts and point and-figure charts. The bar chart is the simplest to construct and easiest to interpret. It is the most popular method of reporting price and volume data. When interpreting price charts, the three main objectives of technical analysts are to:

a) identify the direction of the current trend;

b) detect when the trend is reversing; and

c) identifying entry buy and sell signals.

On a bar chart, each day (or week, or month) is represented by a single vertical line on the graph that connects the high and low prices in order to indicate the price range for the trading period. To denote the period's closing price, a horizontal bar is placed across the vertical bar on the right side of the vertical line. Figure 6.1 presents an example of a bar chart, which has time on the horizontal axis and price on the vertical axis. This chart is drawn with price data from the sugar futures market (No. 11 world sugar). This bar chart shows the open (horizontal tick mark on left hand side), the high and low (top and bottom of vertical line) and the close (horizontal tick mark on right hand side).

Point and figure (P & F) charts are used to show the direction of price changes, while ignoring any time dimension. Compared to bar charts, P & F charts generate more clearly defined buy and sell signals. P & F charts are constructed by filling in boxes with a combination of Xs (showing price increases) and Os (showing price decreases) in alternating columns, as illustrated in Figure 6.2. Price movements are depicted by either a rising column of X's or a falling column of O's.

Figure 6.2: Point-and-Figure Chart

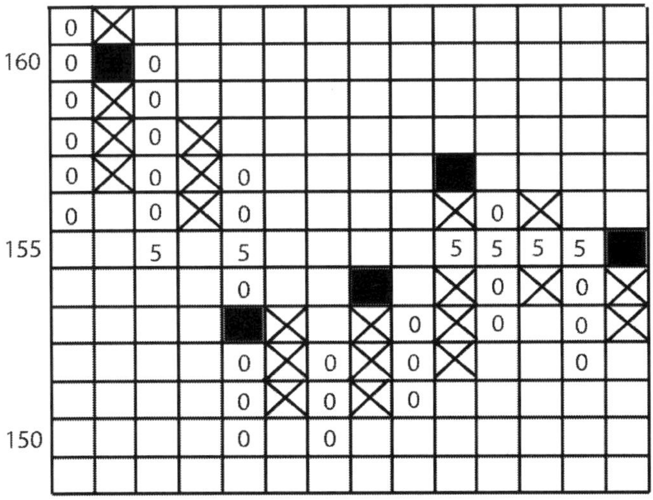

0	X											
160 0	■	0										
0	X	0										
0	X	0	X									
0	0	X	0				■					
0	0	X	0				X	0	X			
155	5	5					5	5	5	5	■	
		0			■		X	0	X	0	X	
			■	X		X	0	X	0		0	X
			0	X	0	X	0	X			0	X
			0	X	0	X	0				0	
150			0	0								

The box size is the unit price that a futures contract must move above the top of the current column of Xs (or below the bottom of the current column of Os) before another X (or O) is added to that column. The box size is arbitrary and is determined by the technician.

Once the box sizes are determined, each trend reversal creates a new column. Contrary to bar charts, time is not plotted on the horizontal axis of P & F charts. The final price square for each period is sometimes blackened.

Interpreting bar chart formations requires some imagination on the part of the technician. To make the most of the information that price charts are believed to possess, an analyst must recognize patterns as they emerge so that trades can be made before the majority of the other technical traders recognize these same patterns. Clearly, this is not an exact science. Nevertheless, this chapter will attempt to describe the basic logic used in interpreting charts. Because chartists are important players in the futures and options markets and they hold significant open positions at any given time, it is useful for fundamental traders to understand charting methods, even if little faith is placed in their forecasts. So if all chartists believe that a market price will rise, the law of self-fulfilling expectations may ensure that the

---

Box 6.1 What are Hedge Funds?

Hedge funds are private investment pools that employ sophisticated investment techniques in both asset (e.g., currencies, stocks, etc.) and derivative (e.g., futures, options, swaps, etc.) markets. These managed funds pool investors' money and they make extensive use of leverage. A leveraged fund purchases assets or derivatives with borrowed money or on margin. The term "hedge fund" is misleading because these funds do not necessarily hedge. Rather, the term refers to any type of private investment partnership. Unlike mutual funds, hedge funds are not required to register under the federal securities laws because they are not open to the public. The freedom from regulation gives hedge funds extensive latitude in their investment strategies. Some hedge funds operate from international tax havens such as Bermuda.

Hedge funds charge a management fee that is usually 1 or 2% of assets under management per year, as well as charging a performance fee as a percent of annual profits.

---

price actually does increase for a limited period of time. This could result in a small temporary bubble or market overshooting.

Bar Chart Price Patterns

A key component of many bar chart price patterns is a cluster of bars called a congestion area. This represents a sideways movement of prices on a bar chart. Identifying these sideways clusters is usually the beginning point for a forecast of a break in prices, either up or down. Congestion areas are created during temporary periods of market stability around a certain price level. These sideways movements on a bar chart (illustrated by the 3 boxes in Figure 6.3) are sometimes considered to be indicators of market equilibrium because buy and sell pressures are relatively stable for a period. Chartists believe that the longer a congestion area lasts, the greater will be the impetus for any upcoming price move, because significant buy or sell pressure may have accumulated.

Support and resistance areas are congestion areas in the middle of a trend. Chartists expect a congestion area to form whenever a trend reverses and returns to the same price range. This is expected whether the trend was originally up or down, as shown by boxes 1 and 3 in the top part of Figure 6.3. It is also believed that congestion areas often form at psycholog-

Figure 6.3: Congestion Areas

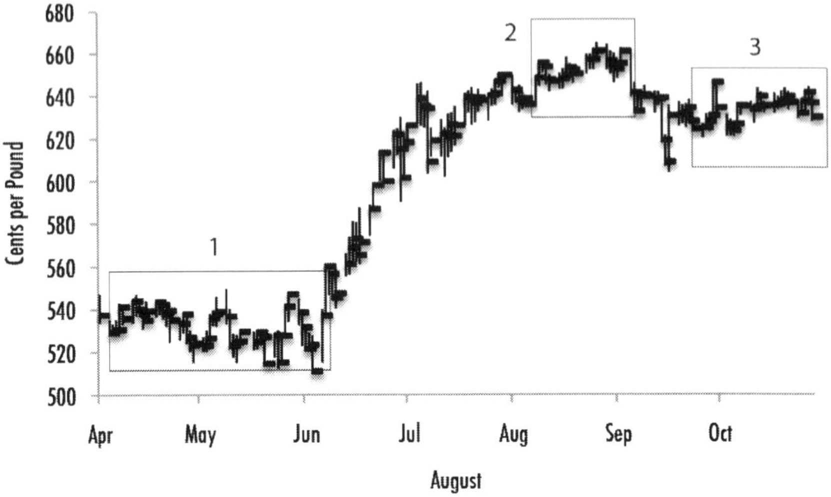

ical price levels, such as at even dollar amounts, half dollar, quarter dollar levels, and so on. This is usually attributed to the effects of large numbers of stop orders being placed at those price levels, temporarily stopping or reversing an established trend in prices.

Chartists always trade with an existing trend, never against it. This is because they believe that the key to successful technical trading is to follow a trend. The first rule of charting is that the "trend is your friend." Therefore, trend lines, such as the straight lines in Figure 6.4, receive a lot of attention from technical traders. Chartists believe that for some unknown reason, once a price trend gets started, the limits of the price fluctuations in that trend tend to remain along a straight line. When prices go through that line it is taken as an indication of a coming price reversal. To someone who does not believe in charts, the reason for this reversal may simply be the self fulfilling prophesy of technical trading. This criticism of charting will be discussed at the end of this chapter.

The basic assumption of momentum trading in the futures market is that if the is going up, it will probably keep going up; and if it is going down, it will probably keep going down. Many large hedge funds follow momentum trading rules.

Trend Following Methods Using Moving Averages

The second category of technical analysis focuses on identifying price trends using moving averages. A moving average is the average value of a contract's price over a given period of time, such as the past 10 days (i.e., a

Figure 6.4: Linear Trend

10-day moving average). Moving averages are used to smooth noisy price data, such as daily settlement (closing) prices. By charting the moving average of the settlement price, the technician can obtain a better idea of the underlying price trend. By plotting the moving average of closing prices over a specified time period, MA chartists believe that they get a good picture of the true price trend by smoothing out the effects of short-term noisy price movements that can confound the interpretation of the chart.

When using MA charts, the first thing chartists do is determine the number of days to be averaged. Any period may be chosen: 5 day, 10 day, 20 day averages, and longer periods are typically used. The longer the period used, the longer the time lag between when a trend actually changes and when a chart signals that change. This could be considered a shortcoming if it generates a buy or sell signal too late. On the other hand, it could be considered a desirable characteristic if it causes a trader to hesitate before taking action in response to short term temporary price moves that misrepresent the true trend situation.

There are a number of different ways to calculate moving averages, such as simple, weighted, smoothed, or exponential. Moving averages are typically charted against daily closing prices, and perhaps with other moving averages, to generate a buy or sell signal. Figures 6.5 and 6.6 illustrate these applications. By plotting the moving average price against the daily closing price (Figure 6.5), or another moving average (Figure 6.6), chartists believe that they can obtain a picture of the trend and an indication of when it is turning. Different types of buy and sell signals are given by the various

Figure 6.5: Vertical Bar Chart versus Moving Average

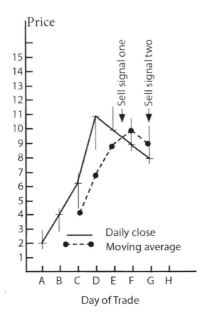

charts and combinations of methods.

Moving averages are used primarily as an indicator of long term trends. Plotting a moving average of prices alone gives a general picture of market movements, according to chartists. The moving average charts in Figures 6.5 and 6.6 combine the long term trend information with bar or other MA charts to detect short term trading signals. With all types of MA charts, a trading signal is given when lines on the chart cross. In Figure 6.5, for example, a moving average and bar chart are used jointly to find two trading signals. The first signal is given when the bar chart line falls below the upward trending moving average line. This indicates that long positions should be liquidated. The second sell signal is given when the moving average line turns down, indicating the uptrend is reversing. This would tell chartists that a net short should be initiated.

In Figure 6.6, 5 and 10 day moving averages are plotted. Notice that the 10-day moving average line is smoother than the 5-day line. The longer the time period represented by the moving average, the smoother the moving average line will be. The lower case x's in Figure 6.6 indicate when the 5 and 10 day moving average lines cross one-another. As long as the 10-day moving average line is below the 5-day moving average line, the price trend is upwards. Once the 5-day line crosses the 10-day line, this is taken as a signal that the trend has reversed itself. The buy signal (B1) in Figure 6.6 is recorded when the 5-day moving average line crosses through the 10-day moving average line from below. At this point in time, the trader goes long

Figure 6.6: Moving Averages

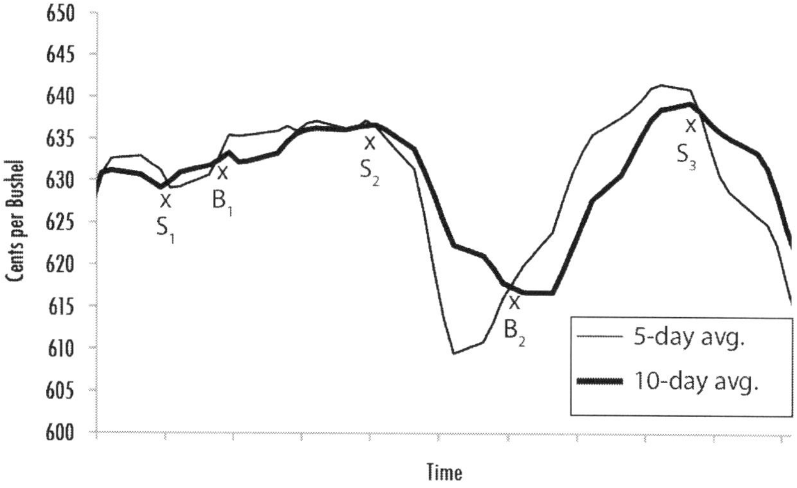

in the market and remains long until the next sell signal (S2) is generated by the moving averages. Once the sell signal (S2) is encountered, the trader reverses his or her position by going net short, and so on.

Character-of-Market Analysis Methods

Some technical analysts look beyond historical price information in making their assessments of price trends. They seek to identify characteristics of the markets which will give additional insights into what market participants are thinking. Character of market analysis, the third category of technical analysis, uses quantitative measures that are independent of price, or uses price information more subtly in making price-trend forecasts. The principal factors considered are the size of a market (open interest), its level of market activity (volume of trade), its price behavior (oscillators), and its composition (small versus large scale traders).

Open interest refers to the total number of futures contracts outstanding at a particular point in time. It equals the number of long (or short) positions being held by traders in a market. When a trader settles a position by liquidating an outstanding contract, total open interest either declines or remains the same, depending on whether or not the trader on the other side of the transaction was also liquidating an outstanding position. When a contract reaches its maturity date, by definition, all individual traders' positions in that contract must be settled and open interest declines to zero.

Chartists believe that changes in open interest, when viewed in conjunction with price changes, provides clues as to whether or not the market has

---

Box 6.2 Commitments of Traders Report

The Commodity Futures Trading Commission (CFTC) is the government regulatory agency that oversees futures and options trading. As part of their mandate, the CFTC publishes weekly reports of aggregate net open positions (i.e., long or short) of traders in the futures and options market. These are called the Commitments of Traders reports, and they are discussed in Chapter 1.

For each commodity or asset, the CFTC first breaks open interest into "reportable" and "nonreportable" positions. Only the traders with a large position (above a CFTC specified reporting level) must report whether they are commercial (i.e., a hedger) or noncommercial. For example, for corn and heating oil the reporting level is 250 contracts and for sugar it is 500 contracts. The CFTC reports open positions as a percentage of open interest. See the CFTC website for Commitments of Traders data: http://www.cftc.gov.

---

been strengthened or weakened by recent trading activity. Changes in total open interest for all futures contract months are used in the analysis. When open interest goes up and prices are rising, the market is considered technically strong due to new buying. If prices decline during a rise in open interest, the market is technically weak because short hedging or short selling is taking place.

On the other hand, when open interest declines, a chartist considers the market technically strong due to long liquidation if prices are falling. The market is technically weak due to short covering if prices are rising. Therefore, when prices and open interest move in the same direction, it indicates that the existing price trend will continue. When prices and open interest are moving in opposite directions, it is considered a symptom of possible price weakness (trend reversal) ahead. It is important to remember, however, that there are seasonal patterns to open interest (e.g., due to hedging pressure) in many futures markets. These seasonal moves must be removed from the data before open interest calculations are made by the technicians.

Volume of trade refers to the total number of futures (or options) contracts traded during a specified period of time, such as a day. It is the total number of contracts bought or sold, and each individual transaction is composed of one buy and one sell.

Volume of trade is considered to be a major structural factor influencing a market and its prices. Also, chartists believe that volume helps determine whether or not prices can be expected to continue moving in the same direction. They use total volume of trade on a given day for all delivery months combined and compare this figure with price movement. The technical rule of thumb is that prices will tend to move in the same direction as the change in the volume of trade.

Although volume of trade and open interest are related, changes in one variable cannot be used to predict the other, as explained in Chapter 1. For example, if there are only two trades during one day, volume is two, but open interest could have increased by two, decreased by two, or remained the same. If both trades established "new" positions, open interest would go up. If both trades liquidated existing positions, open interest would go down. And open interest would not change if one-half the trades established new positions and one-half closed existing obligations. A "new" position is a trade that extends a trader's net long or net short position in a particular contract month. In other words, a new position does not liquidate a previously established position.

Oscillators are a family of technical indicators based on price changes rather than price levels. An example is a 10 day oscillator which equals the current price minus the settlement price 10 days earlier. There are two basic principles behind the use of oscillators. First, users believe that a price rise or decline can become overextended if it gains too much velocity. A market rising (falling) too fast is called overbought (oversold). Second, a price trend can simply disintegrate due to a loss of momentum because everyone who wants to trade with the trend has already done so.

Both principles underlying the use of oscillators imply that there is some appropriate rate of change for prices in a market. If traders push prices at a rate that is too high, some factor such as accumulated profits or losses for traders will presumably cause those traders to react and correct the error. If this type of profit-taking behavior is prevalent in a market, using oscillators can benefit a trader by signaling the emotion level in that market. However, if prices are trending strongly in one direction due to an underlying change in the fundamentals, using oscillators can mislead a trader into thinking that the trend is reversing. Another shortcoming of this technical tool is that the subjective zones indicating an "overbought" or "oversold" market (shown in Figure 6.7) change with time and market conditions.

Other technical analysis systems based on characteristics of markets include evaluations of market composition and contrary opinion. To capitalize on this characteristic, some technical traders have developed trading rules based on market composition factors. Typically, buy and sell signals are derived from the studies of activities of large and small traders (distinguished by the size of their holdings). For example, if large traders hold short positions representing some arbitrary percentage of open interest, a sell signal is given. The logic is that large traders are assumed to be smarter

Box 6.3 Triple Witching Hour

Four times a year, futures and options traders brace themselves for a triple witching hour, when stock index futures and options and individual stock options expire simultaneously. Last minute trading volume records have been set at the New York Stock Exchange on several of these Fridays. The market always braces itself ahead of the triple witching hour.

The high trading volume concentrated into a very short period of time has significant effects on all markets involved. The volume is caused by arbitrage traders closing or "rolling over" positions into contracts which expire later. For particular stocks, the effects of these witching hours can be sizable price "bubbles" due to this technical trading. In 1986, for example, the net changes in the Dow Jones Industrial Average on each of the four triple expiration Fridays was followed by a reverse move the following Monday:

	Friday	Monday
March	-35.68	+14.37
June	+23.68	-15.28
September	-11.53	+30.80
December	+16.03	-2.67

Futures and options exchanges and regulators have tried to reduce the triple witching hour effects by shifting the expiration of some stock index futures and option contracts to the opening of trading on quarterly expiration days instead of at the close of trading. Nevertheless, regulators and legislators are likely to continue scrutinizing the witching hour controversy in an effort to reduce technical trading effects on market efficiency.

Figure 6.7: Oscillator

than small traders; therefore, taking positions favored by a significant portion of the large traders in a market is more likely to be profitable than following the crowd of small traders. This approach obviously has a number of shortcomings, the most significant being the lack of timely data concerning traders' positions. The CFTC publishes data on traders' positions (see Box 6.2).

Contrary opinion is a strategy based upon one concept: the herd mentality in the market is on the wrong side of the market. If the CFTC Commitments of Traders report indicates that most speculators are long in the market, this approach would view this as a sign that the market is overbought and is about the fall. Technicians favoring this approach use information from the CFTC concerning the open positions of large and small hedgers and speculators. When the market is overbought or oversold, contrarians see market prices as representing strong opinions supported by weak reasons. The weak reasons are that market information is well publicized and known for some time (meaning that the market has already responded). Using contrary opinion is highly subjective, even more so than some other technical analysis methods.

Structural Theories

Structural theories, the fourth category of technical methods, involve intensive study of long-term historical prices with the goal of detecting recurring market price patterns. These methods are different than simple charting because more sophisticated quantitative techniques are used in the analysis. Structural theories imply that prices follow a "blueprint" that creates patterns at irregular time intervals. The two general types of structural patterns are seasonal and cyclical. If these patterns are detected in a market, various quantitative methods are combined by technical analysts into a trading system. These systems are forecasting devices used to give buy and sell signals.

Numerous technical trading rules have been developed for measuring and predicting seasonality. These technical rules are partly based on a fundamental approach because the source of seasonality is either supply or demand driven. The distinction, however, is that technical traders view seasonal price patterns not as the result of interaction between supply and demand factors, but as systematic patterns that happen to occur with regularity.

Cycles, on the other hand, are viewed by technical traders as price patterns that occur with less regularity and without regard for seasons. The logic behind the use of cycles is that past prices are believed to contain evidence of one or more cycles that will carry prices forward. Studies of cyclical price movements have shown these patterns to be more difficult to detect than seasonality (Koekebakker and Lien, 2004). Most futures traders believe cycles are too long-term to be of use to make a profit. However, some technical traders have incorporated cyclical effects into forecasting models when long-term trends are relevant to the market and the trader's goals. See Fang (2000) for a discussion of seasonality in the currency markets. He finds seasonality in exchange rate volatility.

Elliot Wave Theory

One of the most popular structural theories is based on the Elliot wave theory. Ralph Elliot was a stock market observer and in 1942 he wrote a book with a modest title: *Nature's Law: The Secret of the Universe*. From that book and the work of supporters, the Elliot wave theory evolved. The theory is based on the belief that there is a rhythm in nature that spills over into all aspects of life, including the stock and futures markets. Elliot stressed that the rhythm is captured in the Fibonacci summation series. Fibonacci, an Italian mathematician who lived in the thirteenth century, created the series by summing the two previous numbers in the series to get the next number. The series begins 1, 1, 2, 3, 5, 8, 13, 21, 34, 55, 89, 144, and goes on to infinity.

Box 6.4 Famous Investment Bubbles

What do tulips and bitcoins have in common? Well, some would argue that the price of tulips and bitcoins have both experienced price bubbles. The tulip price bubble swept through Holland in the 17th century, and Dutch traders bought and sold tulips at incredible prices. Some tulip bulbs were reportedly traded for more than $10 million US$ in today's value. The exorbitant tulip prices were not based on fundamentals and the price spike lasted a relatively short time. The word "bourse" (which means stock exchange) is derived from the tulip mania period. In the 17th century tulips were traded at the offices of the Dutch noble family Van Bourse.

For a discussion of the most famous investment bubbles in history see Peter Garber, *Famous First Bubbles: The Fundamentals of Early Manias*. Cambridge, Mass.:MIT Press, 2000.

Elliot used the Fibonacci series to describe the "ideal" market. According to his theory, Elliot believed that a major bull market consists of five waves followed by a major bear market of three waves. He believed that a five wave bull market would consist of three "up" legs separated by two "down" legs. A three wave bear market would consist of a downswing, a rally, and a final downswing. Elliot went on to say that within the major trends are intermediate trends, and within the intermediate trends (which also contain five and three waves) are minor trends (with five and three waves). As shown in Table 6.1, the sum of waves in each uptrend, downtrend, and complete cycle all correspond to the Fibonacci numbers.

The greatest shortcoming of the Elliot wave theory, like all cycle theories, is the difficulty in determining at what point in the complex wave system a market is currently in.

In summary, the increased variety and visibility of technical trading systems in futures and options markets has raised a number of questions. Does the tremendous growth in managed futures investments imply that technical trading systems work? Why are technical trading systems so popular? Is one type of system better than the others? Questions such as these are asked constantly by futures and options traders. The answers are still being debated, but trends in responses are beginning to take shape, as explained in the next section.

Table 6.1: Principle Numbers of Elliot Waves

	Bull Market	Bear Market	Total Cycle
Number of Major Waves	5	3	8
Number of Intermediate Waves	21	13	34
Number of Minor Waves	89	55	144

To Chart or Not To Chart

Supporters of technical analysis include a majority of retail futures and options brokers and managers of futures funds. In comparing fundamental and technical analysis, technical traders' arguments center on four reasons for using their method over alternatives:

1. It is impossible for any private trader to compete with large commercial commodity and financial firms in the rapid collection of accurate and costly information. With technical analysis, a private trader can often determine whether the major commercial interests are buying or selling and then get on the same side of the market.

2. Fundamental analysis may succeed in predicting long term price moves, but it is not too helpful in the short term. With the high level

of financial leverage in futures trading private futures traders cannot afford to be wrong in the short term.

3. Preoccupization with daily news events and rumors makes it very difficult to maintain the systematic and disciplined approach to fundamental trading decisions required for successful trading.

4. Technical analysis works. For decades people have made money employing primarily technical methods. It is simple to use and the same techniques can be applied to many different markets.

The first three points all focus on the need of a trader to quickly identify what other market participants are thinking and doing. This recognizes the fact that, for speculators, futures trading is a competition between traders in which market prices are the medium, not the objective. Ignoring commissions, futures trading is a zero sum game: profits must equal losses. To make a profit, a trader must outguess other traders, which leads to a preoccupation with access to market information and crowd psychology.

The fourth reason for using technical methods is the key. Is technical analysis a profitable exercise? Several studies have tried to make an objective assessment of the performance of technical trading methods. In a survey of 95 studies of technical trading, Park and Irwin (2007) found that technical trading strategies consistently generated economic profits in speculative markets at least until the 1990's. In their survey, the identified 56 studies indicating positive results, 20 negative results and 19 with mixed results. However, they claim these results indicating the profitability of technical trading to be flawed because the studies are subject to data mining, ex-post selection of trading rules as well as difficulty in determining returns net of transaction costs. In a related study, Marshall, Cahan and Cahan (2008) report that 14 out of 15 commodities that they tested failed to generate statistically significant profits after adjustment was made for data-snooping bias. Their commodity series included cocoa, coffee, cotton, crude oil, feeder cattle, gold, heating oil, live cattle, oats, platinum, silver, soybeans, soya oil, sugar, and wheat. They tested over 7,000 technical trading rules and concluded that none of the rules can beat the market any more often than you might expect, given random data variation.

As mentioned above, using charts or other technical methods assumes that markets do not follow a random walk, rather it assumes that there are identifiable price trends. Academic research questions the grounds for such an assumption.

Critics argue that the short term success of technical methods in general, and charting in particular, can be explained as self fulfilling prophesies. The

---

Box 6.5 Can a Television Talk Show Drive Down Cattle Futures Prices?

U.S. cattlemen sued Oprah Winfrey for comments she made in 1996 on her daytime television talk show. Oprah reportedly said that her concern over Britain's mad-cow disease spreading to the United States "just stopped me cold from eating another burger!"

The mad-cow brain-destroying disease was not yet detected in the United States, but it did kill people in Britain. The lawsuit alleged that she had no right to make these comments because the U.S. was free of the disease. The cattlemen argued that cattle futures prices dropped drastically after the Winfrey television show aired.

The cattlemen had accused Winfrey and one of her guests of deliberately attacking the cattle industry and driving down futures prices through false statements. The cattlemen requested $16.5 million in damages. Eventually, the U.S. courts sided with Oprah and rejected the cattlemen's claims.

---

complaint goes as follows: a large proportion of futures traders use technical analysis as part of their decision making process. As a result, if one of the well known chart patterns begins to appear in historical prices, many traders will see it at nearly the same time. Next, because each price pattern has a specific interpretation in the chartists' logic, everyone who sees the pattern taking shape will simultaneously make the same decision as to the appropriate market response. Finally, the weight of all the orders placed by those technical traders will help create the very momentum the chart supposedly predicted; therefore, prices will begin to move through the remainder of the price pattern, picking up more momentum as additional chartists see the pattern and react in the same way as other chartists had before them.

For a trader considering the use of technical analysis, many factors must be evaluated. The relatively short amount of time required for data collection and analysis is an advantage of technical methods, according to advocates. On the other hand, accuracy of forecasts is more relevant to traders' success. Therefore, the critical factor may be whether it is a profitable exercise compared to alternative forecasting methods.

In the long run, detailed economic models whose forecasts are sold commercially do no better than futures markets in predicting forthcoming spot prices (Just and Rausser, 1981). However, traders' objectives are to forecast short run futures prices. In this regard, technical methods can aid in order placement. However, there is no reason to expect that relying only on technical systems will produce abnormal profits on average. The performance of computer guided technical trading systems has been generally poor. To improve profit performance, some additional (fundamental) information is needed to help judge the recommendations produced by a technical system. Therefore, many successful chartists are probably not "true" chartists; they are probably doing some fundamental analysis whether they like to admit it or not.

Commodity Pools and Program Trading

A commodity pool (or commodity fund) is a managed speculative futures fund similar to a mutual fund in either the stock or bond market. It pools investors' money and then trades futures contracts using these funds. Any profits from the fund's trading are returned to the investors, net of management fees. According to BarclayHedge (www.barclayhedge.com), an estimated $365 billion was invested in managed futures globally in 2022. These managed futures pools are controversial participants in the futures market because, in aggregate, they control significant speculative funds. Furthermore, BarclayHedge reports that about 80% of managed futures are controlled by systematic traders through computerized algorithmic automatic trading programs.

Most pools use technical analysis exclusively (Brorsen and Irwin, 1987) and this has generated controversy over the price effects of futures pools. For example, too much technical trading can cause price swings unrelated to the fundamentals of the market, even if the technical traders correctly forecast price trends. The economics literature also suggests that technical analysis may adversely affect price volatility.

Irwin and Brorsen (1987) studied the role of public commodity pools in a portfolio of financial assets and they found a beneficial diversification effect. Elton, Gruber and Rentzler (1989) evaluated commodity funds' performance and found that less than one-half of the funds they studied produced returns greater than Treasury bills. Additionally, the management fees and transactions costs of the funds were found to be high. Overall, they question the use of funds as an investment vehicle because they are a high risk and low return investment. Schneeweis, Savanayana and McCarthy (1991) found that commodity pools may be rational investments as stand alone investments, as additions to existing stock and bond portfolios, or as part of an optimal portfolio. Murphy (1986) found no compelling evidence that technical funds outperform a naive buy-and-hold strategy. Edwards and Ma (1988) found that a superior commodity fund could not be selected on the basis of historical performance. The research conducted on the value of funds to speculators has had mixed results, but nevertheless futures pools remain a popular investment option.

Economic research has concluded that:
- pools trade primarily in large markets;
- pools trade frequently;
- pools tend to trade when other market participants are trading (pools trading volume is correlated with total market volume); and
- almost all pools use similar trend-following methods when making trading decisions.
- pool trading is a small percentage of futures and options total trading volume, but on some days it constitutes a large share of the total volume (up to 45%).

Table 6.2 reports correlation coefficients across six different asset classes, including managed futures. This table is based on monthly data from January 2005 through August 2022. It is noteworthy that managed futures returns (captured by the Barclay CTA Index) have a very low correlation with both U.S. and foreign stocks, and a low correlation (0.05) with U.S. bonds. Commodities in Table 6.2 are represented by the S&P GSCI TR Index, and commodities are fairly strongly correlated with U.S. stocks (0.46) and foreign stocks (0.53). The correlation between U.S. bonds and commodities is -0.14. Also of interest is that compared to managed futures, hedge funds returns are more highly correlated with commodities (0.64). The correlation between managed futures and commodities is only 0.13. The bottom line with this table is that managed futures are not strongly correlated with any of the other asset classes in the table. This could be a good thing from a portfolio perspective if managed futures had reasonable returns but that has not been the case since about 2011. The average annual return of the Barclay CTA Index from 2011 to 2022 was only 1.58%.

The American International Group (AIG) established the AIG commodity index—an index of commodity futures prices—in the late 1990s. The AIG index was established in order to attract outside investors to commodity futures, as investing in the AIG index was a relatively easy way for an investor to add commodities to a portfolio. The work by Gorton and Rouwenhorst (2006) supported AIG's aim to attract investors to futures markets as Gorton and Rouwenhorst argued that commodity futures offer the same return and Sharpe ratio as U.S. equities. The underlying explanation was the existence of a risk premium in commodity futures. However, this view was not without controversy, as Erb and Harvey (2006) concluded that average commodity futures returns are not equity-like, instead they are zero. Later,

Table 6.2: Managed Futures Correlation With Other Assets

	US Stocks	US Bonds	Foreign Stocks	**Managed Futures**	Hedge Funds	Commodities
US Stocks	1.00	0.12	0.97	0.05	0.83	0.46
US Bonds		1.00	0.14	0.05	0.06	-0.14
Foreign Stocks			1.00	0.08	0.88	0.53
Managed Futures				1.00	0.23	0.13
Hedge Funds					1.00	0.64
Commodities						1.00

Data: January 2005-August 2022. U.S. stocks: S&P 500 TR, U.S. Bonds: Bloomberg US Agg Bond TR, Foreign Stocks by MSCI World Index, Managed Futures by Barclay CTA Index, Hedge Funds by HFRI Fund Weighted Composite Index, and Commodities by S&P GSCI TR Index. Source: Morgan Stanley.

Erb and Harvey (2016) argued that portfolios of commodity futures do not have equity-like returns either. The *Wall Street Journal* comes down on the side of Erb and Harvey (2016) as the newspaper reported that "investments that track broad stock indexes have become the favorite of many investors and analysts for long-term returns that are hard to beat. But index tracking hasn't done so well in the commodities market."[1]

The *financialization* of commodity futures refers to the fact that managed money (or institutional funds) investment in commodity futures grew rapidly in the early 2000s–i.e., the emergence of commodities as an asset class. Assets under management in commodities grew from less than $50 Billion in the early 2000s to over $365 Billion by 2022. A well accepted measure of the returns to these managed funds is the Barclay CTA Index. This index represents the benchmark performance of hundreds commodity trading advisers and it has been rather lackluster since about 2011, see Figure 6.8. The index in Figure 6.8 shows strong performance from 2000 to the spring or summer of 2009. Subsequently the index more or less flattened out until 2020 and then it picked up during the inflationary period of 2021 and 2022.

For 13 agricultural commodity futures markets, the Commodity Futures Trading Commission (CFTC) publishes weekly data on the relative importance of index trading in a supplemental commodity index report.[2] Trader

---

[1]*The Wall Street Journal* April 10, 2017.

[2]The CFTC explains that: "Index Traders are drawn from the noncommercial and commercial categories. The noncommercial category includes positions of managed funds, pension funds, and other investors that are generally seeking exposure to a broad index of commodity prices as an asset class in an unleveraged and passively-managed manner. The commercial category includes positions for entities whose trading predominantly reflects hedging of over-the-counter transactions involving commodity indices–for example, a swap dealer holding long futures positions to hedge a short commodity index exposure opposite institutional traders, such as pension funds." see

Figure 6.8: Barclay CTA Index

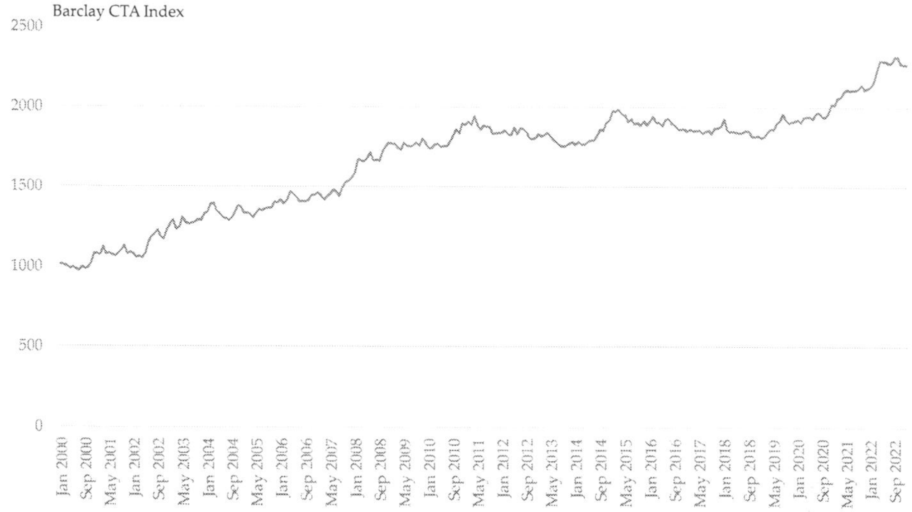

Source: BarclayHedge.

positions for six of these thirteen markets are shown in Table 6.3. The six are wheat, corn, soybeans, cotton, live cattle and sugar. The index trader position data for these six markets are summarized along with average net positions (long-short) for three other CFTC trader categories: large speculators, large hedgers, and small traders. Traders are classified as large speculators or large hedgers if they hold positions above specific reporting levels. With the exception of live cattle and sugar, the index traders were the dominant group of traders over the 2006-2019 time period. Index traders includes positions of managed funds, pension funds, and other investors that are generally seeking exposure to a broad index of commodity prices as an asset class in an unleveraged and passively-managed manner. Index traders may also include swap dealers hedging of over-the-counter transactions involving commodity indices. The index traders category is therefore typically made up of traders with long-only futures positions replicating an index.

In order to illustrate the relative stability of index traders' positions compared to large speculators and hedgers, the CFTC weekly data for corn are shown in Figure 6.9. The left-hand vertical axes in Figure 6.9 reports the

https://www.cftc.gov/MarketReports/CommitmentsofTraders/ExplanatoryNotes/ index.htm. The 13 markets included in the CFTC supplemental index report include: CBOT SRW wheat, CBOT HRW wheat, CBOT corn, CBOT soybeans, CBOT soybean oil, CBOT soybean meal, ICE cotton, CME lean hogs, CME live cattle, CME feeder cattle, ICE cocoa, ICE sugar No. 11, and ICE coffee.

Table 6.3: Average Weekly Trader Positions: 2006-2019

| Commodity | Average Net Position (Long-Short): Number of contracts | | | |
	Large Speculator	Large Hedger	Small Trader	Index Trader
Wheat	-50,610	-91,930	-14,423	156,963
Corn	46,790	-324,240	-77,324	354,775
Soybeans	34,597	-135,625	-38,051	139,080
Cotton	27,022	-103,222	5,363	70,836
Live Cattle	42,667	-124,719	-27,588	109,641
Sugar	19,885	-261,385	15,823	225,676

Source: CFTC Supplemental Index Report.

net futures positions (long minus short) for four classes of traders reported in Table 6.3. It is clear from Figure 6.9 that index traders are the largest participants in the corn market on average. Unlike other classes of traders, the overall number of contracts held by index traders from week to week does not vary much, which means it is not correlated with the price. In contrast to index traders, there is considerable variation in the large speculative positions and they switch from being net long to net short (crossing the 0 horizontal line). Large hedger positions also range widely.

In the early 2000s, investors were attracted to commodity futures as a new asset class. The investors were informed that commodities provided stock like returns, with the added advantage of a low correlation with stocks and bonds. Hundreds of billions of dollars then flowed into the commodities market. Large institutional investors generally gained long exposure to commodities through direct holdings of futures contracts as well as the use of over-the-counter derivatives and swaps. The returns to this asset class initially performed well, but then peaked in about 2012. Since then, the investment benefits have not turned out as promised. For instance, $10,000 invested on August 2010 in one of the larger commodity index funds in the United States–the United States Commodity Index Fund (USCI)–was worth approximately $8,000 in June 2022.

Summary

This chapter has introduced technical analysis, a major approach used for price forecasting by futures and option traders. Technical analysis focuses on a futures contract's price history, ignoring the fundamental factors of supply and demand. The chapter began by explaining the logic behind charting and by describing the charting process; it then introduced some of the basic quantitative approaches to technical analysis before concluding

Figure 6.9: Index Traders large share of the market: CBT Corn 2006-2019

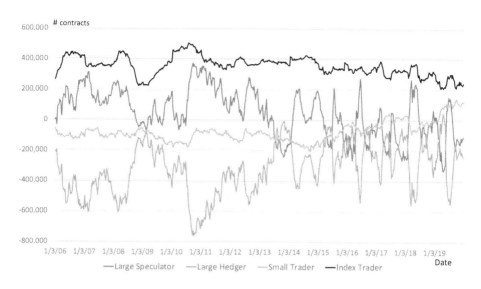

Source: Commodity Futures Trading Commission.

with a summary of the debate over the value of technical analysis. Key points made in the chapter are the following:

- Technical analysis focuses on very short term price forecasting, whereas fundamental analysis provides long term outlooks.

- Technical analysis is centered on trying to identify price trends and their turning points. It is intended to provide specific trade signals to enable the investor to trade with the trend.

- The most common charting methods use moving averages and/or high low bar charts. Patterns in the temporal charts are believed by technicians to be significant and are used in price forecasting.

- Characteristics of a futures market are quantified by some technical analysts for use in price forecasting. Open interest and volume of trade, in particular, are watched closely by these analysts when attempting to determine whether or not existing price trends will continue.

- The use of quantitative programs that run on personal computers is a popular approach to producing trading signals.

- Technical analysis can only succeed if there is no random walk in prices. Therefore, success of this forecasting approach can only be successful if the market is informationally inefficient.

- If technical analysis is profitable, economic logic suggests the profits would soon be arbitraged away by the entry of new traders.

- Managed futures funds are popular investment vehicles for speculators and the value controlled by managed futures funds exceeds $340 billion. Most of the pools use technical trading systems.

Discussion Questions

1. Why do traditional technical analysts reject the use of any statistical supply or demand data when making price forecasts?

2. What criteria should be used in selecting the type of price chart to use in technical analysis?

3. Explain how to interpret a moving average chart.

4. Compare double top (bottom) and head and shoulders top (bottom) formations.

5. Define open interest. Explain why it is significant in technical analysis.

6. How can a market become overbought?

7. Why is using contrary opinion a risky approach to market analysis?

8. What is a price channel? How can it be used by a futures trader?

9. Explain the reasoning underlying the Elliot wave theory. What is the biggest shortcoming analysts face when trying to apply Elliot wave theory in price forecasting?

10. Discuss the following statement: "The most convincing argument against the continued success of any technical trading rules (i.e., techniques) is that the process of exploiting the abnormal returns destroys the trading rule." As part of your answer, explain whether you believe this statement to be true or false.

11. Select 5 futures contracts and generate 3 technical trading rules for each contract using either barchart.com or the Wall Street Journal online. Compare and contrast the trading signals provided by the different trading rules in each of the 5 markets.

Selected References

Brorsen, B Wade, and Scott H Irwin. 1987. "Futures funds and price volatility." *Review of Futures Markets*, 6(2): 118–135.

Edwards, Franklin R, and Cindy Ma. 1988. "Commodity pool performance: Is the information contained in pool prospectuses useful?" *Journal of Futures Markets*, 8(5): 589–616.

Elton, Edwin J, Martin J Gruber, and Joel Rentzler. 1989. "New public offerings, information, and investor rationality: The case of publicly offered commodity funds." *Journal of Business*, 1–15.

Erb, Claude B, and Campbell R Harvey. 2006. "The strategic and tactical value of commodity futures." *Financial Analysts Journal*, 62(2): 69–97.

Erb, Claude B, and Campbell R Harvey. 2016. "Conquering misperceptions about commodity futures investing." *Financial Analysts Journal*, 72(4): 26–35.

Fang, Yue. 2000. "Seasonality in foreign exchange volatility." *Applied Economics*, 32(6): 697–703.

Gorton, Gary, and K Geert Rouwenhorst. 2006. "Facts and Fantasies about Commodity Futures (Digest Summary)." *Financial Analysts Journal*, 62(2): 47–68.

Irwin, Scott H, and B Wade Brorsen. 1987. "A note on the factors affecting technical trading system returns." *Journal of Futures Markets*, 7(5): 591–595.

Just, Richard E, and Gordon C Rausser. 1981. "Commodity price forecasting with large-scale econometric models and the futures market." *American Journal of Agricultural Economics*, 63(2): 197–208.

Koekebakker, Steen, and Gudbrand Lien. 2004. "Volatility and price jumps in agricultural futures prices–evidence from wheat options." *American Journal of Agricultural Economics*, 86(4): 1018–1031.

Marshall, Ben R, Rochester H Cahan, and Jared M Cahan. 2008. "Can commodity futures be profitably traded with quantitative market timing strategies?" *Journal of Banking & Finance*, 32(9): 1810–1819.

Murphy, J Austin. 1986. "Futures fund performance: A test of the effectiveness of technical analysis." *Journal of Futures Markets*, 6(2): 175–185.

Park, Cheol-Ho, and Scott H Irwin. 2007. "What do we know about the profitability of technical analysis?" *Journal of Economic Surveys*, 21(4): 786–826.

Schneeweis, Thomas, Uttama Savanayana, and David McCarthy. 1991. "Alternative commodity trading vehicles: a performance analysis." *Journal of Futures Markets*, 11(4): 475–490.

7.

Hedging

If military tension in the Middle East sends the price of crude oil higher, then this development will affect the profitability of airlines around the globe because the price of jet fuel moves up and down with the price of crude oil. Likewise, if the U.S. dollar appreciates in value this will affect the profitability of German automobile manufacturers because revenue from global car sales will be repatriated back into European euros. In both of these examples, the airline and the German auto maker could partially mitigate the effect of lost revenues by advance hedging the price of oil or the currency risk on the futures and/or options market, or with an over-the-counter (OTC) swap or option.

Hedging is an all-encompassing term that, in the futures and options market, normally refers to simultaneously holding both cash and futures (or options) positions. There are many different types of hedgers, including airlines, commodity merchants, commodity processors, exporters and importers, food manufacturers and processors, banks, fund and pension managers, industrial manufacturers, power generation companies, mining companies, farmers, etc. Because of the diversity of the underlying businesses that hedgers are engaged in, there are several different motives for hedging. This is unlike the case for speculators, whose motives are very straightforward: buy low and sell high (or first sell high and then later buy low). The traditional view is that hedgers are seeking to reduce price risk in the underlying cash market. Two other important and widely accepted explanations have hedgers either attempting to profit from expected movements in the futures-cash price spread (i.e., the basis) or endeavoring to use futures positions to diversify their portfolios made up of cash commodities and other assets.

Some of the most innovative thinking, research and writing on the subject of hedging was carried out by Holbrook Working (1962). He was the first person to challenge the traditional and naive view that hedging is a method whereby producers and merchants can reduce or even eliminate the price risk associated with owning physical commodity stocks, by taking an equal and opposite position in the futures market. He correctly pointed out that hedging is practiced for a number of other legitimate business reasons; a major one being profit maximization by anticipating favorable basis changes. Following Working, the next major reformulation of the theory of hedging was presented separately by both Stein (1961) and Johnson (1960), who cast the motives for hedging within a portfolio framework. A portfolio is a collection of financial assets like physical assets, cash, and financial derivatives.

Box 7.1 Hedging Jet Fuel

One of the first airlines in the world to hedge their jet fuel purchases was Quantas airlines in Australia. They were hedged before the Gulf War in 1990-91, which turned out to be a huge cost saving for Quantas because the war drove up fuel prices. Following the Gulf war price disruptions, several U.S. airlines started a similar hedging program, For example, Delta and Southwest airlines started hedging programs in the mid 1990s, later joined by Alaska Air. In Europe, Lufthansa, Air France, British Airways, and Ryanair typically hedge at least a portion of their fuel bills.

For most airlines, jet fuel is one of the most significant expenses. Unhedged fuel is normally 15 to 20 percent of an airline's total operating costs and the price of jet fuel is very volatile. For instance, in 2007 Southwest Airlines locked in 70% of its expected fuel use at $51 per barrel before crude oil prices reach $126/bbl. Most of Southwest's competition had only hedged 20-30% of their fuel costs and had significant difficulty competing with Southwest on fares. There is no futures or options market for jet fuel, so most airlines cross-hedge by using heating oil futures and options or OTC trades such as swaps.

The COVID pandemic was a huge setback for the world's airlines for a number of reasons, including that they had forward priced millions of gallons of fuel they didn't need and lost money because fuel prices tumbled. However, in the post-pandemic market the airline industry returned to hedging as demand for travel picked up and airline profits zoomed up.

The purpose of this chapter is to present the major theories and explanations for hedging based on the original writings of Working, Stein, and Johnson. Empirical tests of the competing theories will also be briefly reviewed. This chapter discusses hedging in both commodity and financial futures markets with futures contracts. The topic of hedging with options on futures is discussed in Chapter 9.

The concepts of hedging in financial futures versus hedging in commodity markets are very similar. Whether an oil refinery is balancing cash and futures positions in order to diversify a portfolio or a financial institution is balancing its assets and liabilities, the same economic principles apply. A primary determinant of the success of a hedge is how the basis changes during the hedging period.

Traditional View of Hedging

Hedgers are normally defined as those individuals or firms who produce, process, store, or utilize the underlying commodity, financial instrument, or asset that is being hedged. The hedger could be an airline that is exposed to fuel price risk or an automobile manufacturer exposed to exchange rate risk. Hedgers manage the risk of adverse price changes by taking positions in the futures or options market.[1] If they are long in the cash market, then they take a short position in the futures market and vice versa. Their main goal is to counter-balance price changes in the two markets against one another. This traditional view suggests hedging is carried out to reduce price risk.

In the financial markets, the largest group of hedgers includes banks and financial portfolio managers, and exporters and importers exposed to exchange rate risk. The largest group of hedgers in agricultural markets are merchants who handle, process and store the underlying physical commodity, and commodity processors who transform the commodity into an intermediate or final product. The world's four largest commodity merchants are Archer Daniels Midland Co., Bunge Ltd., Cargill Inc., and Louis Dreyfus Co., known collectively as the ABCDs of global commodity trading.

In the metals and petroleum sector, producing and processing firms also have hedging programs. The three largest global mining companies are Glencore, BHP, and Rio Tinto. At any given time, it is too risky for these mining companies, petroleum refiners (e.g., ExxonMobil, Chevron, and Shell), to hold large unhedged positions in the cash market because of potential price swings. Taking a position in the futures (or options) market opposite to the cash position allows the company to substantially reduce its exposure to this price risk.

---

[1]The focus in this chapter and in this book is on exchange traded derivatives, such as futures and options, rather than on over-the-counter (OTC) derivative trading.

Hedging Categories

In the 1960s Holbrook Working categorized alternative motives for commercial hedging in commodity futures and these motives continue to be valid today. The three broad categories are *arbitrage hedging, operational hedging*, and *anticipatory hedging*.

An arbitrage hedge is sometimes referred to as a carrying-charge hedge. Since the futures and cash price tend to converge in the delivery month, a commercial firm can "arbitrage" the two markets and earn a risk-free return from a predictable change in the basis. For instance, suppose that American Grain, Inc. has access to warehouse space in Chicago. In early April it may decide to buy wheat in the cash market for $8.25, put the wheat into storage and simultaneously sell July wheat futures at a price of $8.75. Assuming full storage costs are less than $0.50 per bushel for three months, American Grain has successfully arbitraged the markets and locked in a riskless return (of $0.50 less storage costs) for storing the wheat. Of course, any basis change will affect the outcome of this hedge, as mentioned in Chapter 3 and as will be discussed in more detail below. This type of arbitrage opportunity encourages firms to store commodities. Providing returns to those willing and able to carry products in storage is one of the many useful economic functions provided by futures markets.

Operational hedging facilitates commercial business practices by allowing firms to buy and sell on the futures markets as temporary substitutes for subsequent cash market transactions. This use of futures markets provides firms with an avenue for being flexible in day-to-day operations and reducing price risk. Profiting from a change in the basis does not figure as prominently as an objective with this type of hedge. Suppose that in April a U.S. computer firm makes a large sale of hardware to a European importer and the (forward) contract for the computers specifies delivery in August and payment in euros upon delivery. The U.S. company is exposed to the risk of an exchange rate change between April and August. However, the U.S. computer firm still has the flexibility to go ahead with the forward sale of the computer hardware because as a temporary substitute for the eventual sale of the euros in the spot exchange rate market, the firm can sell euro futures in order to reduce the exchange rate risk. Suppose that the computer hardware is worth €570,000 or approximately $712,500 if the euro is currently trading at 1.25 ($US per €). The contract specifies a price of €570,000, so if the euro were to fall in value to 1.13, the computers would only fetch about $644,100 when converted back into U.S. dollars in August. This is the currency risk facing the computer firm. It could lose $68,400 if the price of the euro drops from 1.25 €/$ to 1.13 €/$.

This example of the computer sale is an operational hedge because it facilitates the ability of the computer firm to make the forward sale to Europe, while at the same time limiting its exposure to exchange rate risk.

Anticipatory hedges involve buying or selling futures contracts by commercial firms in "anticipation" of forthcoming cash market transactions.

Box 7.2 Should Farmers Hedge or Speculate?

Typically, futures brokers, textbooks, and journal articles praise hedging and suggest that farmers should hedge. However, most farmers don't follow this advice. Despite the theoretical advantages of farmer hedging, a study by the Commodity Futures Trading Commission found that only about 7% of U.S. farmers use futures and many of them were speculating rather than hedging. This is an interesting paradox. Some of the reasons farmers give for not hedging include:

- Government programs effectively provide a price floor
- production risk is too high and a crop shortfall could lead to futures trading losses
- lack of knowledge of hedging process
- margin calls make hedging too risky
- availability of forward contracts as a better alternative
- production doesn't match size of futures contract

Actually, it is not totally surprising that so few farmers hedge and that many speculate instead. Production risk discourages hedging the full amount of the expected crop before harvest. After harvest, if a farmer expects prices to fall he simply sells in the cash market (as long as the basis isn't too wide). If, alternatively, he expects prices to rise he might sell the physical and buy futures contracts or call options instead. He is speculating with futures or options rather than the physical inventory, which makes perfect sense. It is quite possible that speculation is a better use of futures and options by farmers!

Finally U.S. government programs like revenue insurance act like a put option with a subsidized premium. With lucrative government programs, there may be no need for farmers to hedge because the subsidized government programs have removed some of the downside risk associated with low market prices.

Price expectations play an important role with this type of hedge. For example, Green Acres Inc. may have 1,000 acres planted to wheat and, before harvest, they may sell wheat futures with the expectation that prices are on the decline. It is physically impossible for the manager of Green Acres Inc. to sell the actual wheat until it is harvested and thus he is taking advantage of current prices by hedging in the futures market. In addition to price risk, this type of hedge also involves production risk–the size of the crop may fall short of expectations. A crop shortfall would result in a net loss if prices trend higher because cash market profits earned on fewer units would not totally compensate for futures losses. If there is little or no correlation between the size of Green Acres' crop and the price of wheat, then the production risk may be manageable. The anticipatory hedge may still maximize expected return even though it involves some risk. However, this correlation will depend on the commodity in question and the location of its production. For example, in an empirical study of soybean hedging, Miller and Kahl (1987) found negative correlation $(-0.3$ to $-0.8)$ between yield and price for a sample of farms in Illinois. This means that as yield falls, the price of the commodity rises.

Examples of Hedging Basics

To illustrate the process of hedging, suppose that a grain merchant–American Grain Inc.–purchases 5,000 bushels of corn at $8.00 per bushel. This merchant is now long in the cash market, which means the merchant possesses the actual physical commodity. In order to reduce the risk of a price decline and a reduction in the value of American Grain's physical stockpile of corn, American Grain takes an opposite position in the futures market. The company does so by selling (i.e., going short) a single futures contract calling for delivery of 5,000 bushels of corn at some future point in time. The simultaneous purchase of the cash corn and sale of the futures contract will place the merchant in a hedged position. If the price of corn falls, American Grain will profit on its futures position and at the same time lose on its cash position, assuming that the cash and futures prices move in roughly a parallel fashion (i.e., manageable basis risk). On the other hand, if the price rises above $8.00, American Grain will lose on its futures position but gain on the cash position. Either way, profits (losses) in the cash market offset losses (profits) in the futures market. Therefore, American Grain Inc. has hedged its inventory of corn against a price decline.

In most cases, movements of cash and futures prices are not expected to be exactly parallel. The mathematical difference between the futures and cash price, defined as the **basis**, will change over time. Examples of the

---

Box 7.3 The Texas Hedge

Texans are often "stereotyped" as being risk takers. Some believe that individuals who are not afraid of risk built the state of Texas. A real "Texan" loves risk and is therefore not very interested in hedging. However, he may still use the futures (or options) market–but to speculate and not to hedge! For example, a Texas rancher might own 200 head of cattle that he plans to sell at a later date. At the same time, for example, he might purchase five live cattle futures contracts (or buy call options for five futures contracts). This transaction is referred to as a "Texas Hedge." In reality it is not a hedge, but rather is a large speculative move. It doubles amount of risk the rancher is exposed to through ownership of the live cattle and if cattle prices trend downward his losses are double.

Table 7.1: Basis Calculations

Time Period	Futures Contract	Futures Price ($)	Cash or Spot Contract	Cash or Spot Price ($)	Basis ($)
January	May corn	6.15	Duluth spot	6.40	-0.25
January	May corn	6.15	Iowa local spot	6.20	-0.05
March	July soybeans	15.20	Illinois local forward cash	13.15	2.05

numerous ways in which a basis may change with time are given in Chapter 3. Changes in the basis ensure that the merchant cannot eliminate price risk through hedging but only reduce it. Of course, if the merchant delivers on the futures contract, there is no basis risk. Delivery on futures contracts is a relatively rare occurrence however because the making or taking of delivery is not the reason that most hedgers enter into futures trading. Alternatively, if cash and futures prices do move up and down in exact parallel fashion then the basis does not change and price risk can be totally eliminated. This is a "perfect" (or "textbook") hedge opportunity but it is rarely present in commodity markets. Some examples of basis calculations are provided in Table 7.1. Here the basis is defined as the futures price – the cash (spot) price, but the basis is often written the other way around as cash – futures. It really doesn't matter how the basis is defined (all that changes is the positive or negative sign) but the alternative conventions of defining the basis can make a discussion of the basis confusing, especially when describing the basis increasing or decreasing. With basis equal to futures minus cash in Table 7.1 both the Duluth and Iowa basis are negative numbers because the cash (spot) prices in those locations were higher than

Table 7.2: Hedging Corn: Basis Examples

Date	Futures Price ($ per bu)	Basis ($ per bu)	Cash Price ($ per bu)	Hedger's Transaction
Short Hedging Corn: An Illustration				
Dec. 1	$8.25	$0.25	$8.00	Sell One May Corn Futures Contract
Apr. 1	$7.75	$0.30	$7.45	Buy One May Corn Futures Contract
Gain (Loss)	$0.50		($0.55)	
Long Hedging Corn: An Illustration				
Dec. 1	$8.25	$0.25	$8.00	Buy One May Corn Futures Contract
Apr. 1	$7.75	$0.30	$7.45	Sell One May Corn Futures Contract
Gain (Loss)	($0.50)		$0.55	

the futures price. Alternatively for the soybeans example in in Table 7.1 the Illinois cash price is below the futures price, so the basis in this location is positive (+ $2.05).

An example of a changing basis is presented in the top panel of Table 7.2, where on December 1 American Grain, Inc. simultaneously bought 5,000 bushels of physical corn for $8.00 per bushel and sold one May corn futures contract (calling for delivery of 5,000 bushels) at $8.25. Thus, the basis on December 1 is $0.25 per bushel and once American Grain is fully hedged (i.e., the 5,000 bushels of physical corn inventories matches the size of one futures contract), its only exposure to price risk is the risk of a basis change. Being a short hedger (i.e., simultaneously holding a long cash position and a short futures position), American Grain Inc. is only concerned with a widening of the basis because this will result in a loss of revenue. At the same time, American Grain Inc. will profit from the basis narrowing. A widening of the basis means that cash and futures prices move in such a fashion that the mathematical value of the basis increases. Conversely, a narrowing of the basis implies that the cash and futures prices move in a

Table 7.3: Basis: Widening versus Narrowing

Time Period	Cash ($)	Futures ($)	Basis ($)	Basis Change
1	$8.00	$8.50	$0.50	
2	$8.00	$8.25	$0.25	Narrower
3	$8.00	$8.00	$0	Narrower
4	$8.00	$7.90	$-0.10	Narrower
5	$8.00	$7.95	$-0.05	Wider
6	$8.00	$8.25	$0.30	Wider
7	$8.00	$8.50	$0.50	Wider

way that the mathematical value of the basis becomes smaller. For example, if in Table 7.2 the futures price remains unchanged at $8.25 and the cash price increases from $8.00 to $8.10, then the basis is narrowing because the difference between the futures and cash price has declined. If, instead, the cash remains at $8.00 and the futures price rises, then the basis is widening. Examples of the basis becoming either narrower or wider are shown in Table 7.3.

Continuing with Table 7.2, on April 1, suppose that American Grain's hedge is lifted, while at the same time the physical corn is sold at the cash price for $7.45. American Grain lifts the hedge by buying a May corn futures contract, which is trading currently at $7.75. The profit on the futures transaction will be $0.50 per bushel (ignoring brokerage fees and other transactions costs). This gain will approximately offset the loss of $0.55 on the physical corn. The merchant in this example reduced a potential opportunity loss of $0.55 per bushel from holding cash corn to only $0.05, by exchanging price risk for basis risk via a short hedge. This example is referred to as a short hedge because the hedger has a short position in the futures market. The futures profit did not fully offset the loss on the cash side because the basis "widened" by $0.05 per bushel.

Alternatively, consider a long hedge in the corn market. This example is presented in the bottom panel of Table 7.2. Suppose that a cattle feeding company, Beef Barons Inc., has placed cattle on feed in early December and expects to feed them for about six months before shipping them off for slaughter. The marketing manager of Beef Barons has enough corn in storage for the first three months (December–February), but she will have to purchase an additional 5,000 bushels of corn in early March in order to finish feeding this particular herd. Obviously, a movement in corn prices between December and March will affect Beef Barons profits. Concerned about a rise in corn prices, the marketing manager buys one May futures contract at a price of $8.25, while the current cash price is $8.00. This example is a long hedge (because she is going long in the futures market)–see the bottom panel of Table 7.2. We know that corn prices fell between December 1 and March 1, as shown in Table 7.2. Cash prices fell by $0.55 per bushel to $7.45 and May futures by $0.50 to $7.75. Beef Barons lifts the hedge in March by selling one May futures contract and simultaneously purchasing 5,000 bushels of corn on the cash market. Ignoring brokerage fees, the out-come of this hedge is a loss of $0.50 per bushel on the futures transaction and an opportunity gain of $0.55 on the cash transaction. The net cost of the corn for Beef Barons is therefore $7.95 per bushel, because they paid $7.45 on the cash market and lost an additional $0.50 on the futures position. Compared to the alternative of purchasing the corn in December (at $8.00) and paying storage, the hedging outcome is more cost effective. However, if Beef Barons had not hedged at all they could have purchased the corn for $7.45 in March. This seems like the best alternative but hindsight al-ways gives a futures hedger perfect vision! The important point is that Beef Barons did not wish to risk the possibility of higher corn prices and hedg-ing provided some insurance against such an unfavorable outcome. Barons ended up buying corn for $0.05 less than the cash price in December be-cause the basis widened by $0.05 and this works in favor of the long hedge.

Long hedging in commodity markets is common place with grain mer-chants, cattle feedlots, processing firms, etc. Consider another transaction where American Grain has made a forward cash sale of soybeans to Japan at an agreed price. If the merchant has made the forward sale and does not have available inventory of soybeans on hand (i.e., is short the cash commodity), he may choose to hedge this sale by taking a long position in the futures market. The long futures position would provide interim price protection for American Grain in the event that soybean prices rise before it has an opportunity to purchase the required physical inventory on the spot market. In this example, it is evident that the hedge serves as a tempo-rary substitute for a subsequent transaction in the spot market and is thus a useful marketing tool. The initial decision by American Grain to hedge in this example is going to be dictated by the expected change in the ba-sis. If American grain feels the basis is going to narrow by a significant amount (i.e., the cash price gains on the futures) then it might attempt to buy the cash rather than going long in the futures market. But in this case the hedger would have to account for the capital and storage costs associ-ated with purchasing the cash commodity.

Choice of Market and Futures Month

In earlier chapters, we discussed the fact that for some commodities there is more than one exchange which trade futures contracts written for that commodity. For example, U.S. wheat contracts are traded on futures markets in Chicago, Kansas City and Minneapolis. The two largest wheat contracts are Soft Red Winter Wheat traded on the CBOT and Hard Red Winter Wheat traded at Kansas City. The Minneapolis exchange trades Hard Red Spring Wheat. In addition, the CME offers trading in Australian, Canadian, and Black Sea wheat futures. A hedger in wheat must first choose one of these exchanges and then choose the appropriate futures month. Hedgers may also have to decide how many contracts to buy or sell as futures contract sizes do not always match the size of the cash position.

There are also many commodities for which no corresponding futures market exists: jet fuel, lettuce, peanuts, tomatoes, sunflowers and wine. A producer and/or commercial user of these non-futures commodities might attempt to hedge in a related market where prices are highly correlated with the non-futures cash commodity price. The higher the correlation between cash and futures prices, the greater the potential for risk reduction. This type of hedging is referred to as cross-hedging i.e., placing a hedge in a related futures market. Wilson (1984) investigated cross-hedging different classes of wheat in three different futures markets. He found cross-hedging to be viable for wheat.

When choosing the exchange on which to hedge, several factors must be considered. These include:

- On which exchange is the underlying grade the closest to the grade of the product to be hedged? For example, soft wheat is not deliverable on a Minneapolis contract but it is deliverable on a Chicago contract and, therefore, a hedger of soft wheat should probably choose the Chicago market.

- Hedges are easier (and less costly) to place and lift on exchanges and contracts with relatively greater trading volume (i.e., liquid markets). In thinly traded markets, prices are more volatile and the bid-ask spread is wider, compared to liquid markets. The Minneapolis wheat market does not have the volume enjoyed by the CBOT soft red winter wheat market.

- The location of the market may be important if delivery is a viable alternative. The location of the market will also affect the basis. ICE crude oil futures are deliverable in the North Sea, whereas NYMEX crude oil is deliverable in Oklahoma via pipeline.

- The hedge should be in a futures delivery month far enough ahead to cover the entire duration of the hedge. The rule of thumb is to choose a contract which expires shortly after the date on which the hedge is lifted. This way "rollovers" from one contract month to another are avoided (which keeps transactions costs at a minimum) and correlation between the futures contract price and the cash market price is likely to be as high as possible.

Most futures markets trade contracts that stretch into the future about 12 to 18 months. In many practical applications this may not be far enough into the future. One way that is used to stretch a hedge beyond 12 to 18 months is to "rollover" short-term hedges into long-term hedges.

Consider the example of a soybean farmer who decides that current prices are at very high historical levels. He decides to sell his next three harvests at the present time and attempt to lock-in the historically high price. He expects to harvest about 5,000 bushels per year. Because soybean futures trade for only 14 months into the future, the farmer immediately sells three futures contracts for delivery in 12 months time. Next year, he sells his crop and buys back the three futures contracts. Simultaneously, he sells two futures contracts calling for delivery in 12 months time, and so on. The farmer is therefore "rolling" the hedge from one year to the next. Gardner (1989) empirically studied the effectiveness of long-term rollover hedging in soybean, corn and cotton futures. He found that multi-year rollovers have some merit as a practical hedging strategy.

Arbitrage and Operational Hedges: Importance of Basis Changes

The basis (B) was defined above as the mathematical difference between a futures price (FP) and a cash/spot price (CP): $B = FP - CP$. As discussed above and in Chapter 3, the basis may be calculated as either futures minus cash, or as cash minus futures. The cash price often refers to the price for either immediate or forward delivery at any particular terminal or local market, whereas the spot price is for immediate delivery. The cash price is sometimes referred to as the spot price and they are often used interchangeably. There can be many different bases associated with one futures contract.

Once an arbitrage or operational hedge has been placed, the hedger becomes concerned primarily with basis changes rather than changes in the absolute price level. For example, suppose a grain merchant in rural Iowa, Central Grain Co., purchased 25,000 bushels of corn on the local spot market for $6.20 in January and then subsequently sold 5 May corn futures contracts on the CBOT at $6.15. Central Grain's basis was − $0.05 per bushel when the hedge was placed (see Table 7.1) and, for the purposes of this transaction, until the hedge is lifted the company is more concerned with a change in the Iowa basis than a change in the absolute price level for corn.

One way of defining an arbitrage or operational hedge is an exchange of price risk for basis risk or, alternatively, as speculating on the basis. The reason the basis is of utmost importance is that the profitability of the hedge is largely determined by basis behavior. If a hedge is lifted at the same basis which prevailed when the hedge was initiated (a "textbook" hedge), then the hedger receives exactly the expected price prevailing on the date the hedge was initiated. This rarely occurs, however, as the basis often changes daily.

If a hedger has one unit of inventory in storage then (ignoring storage costs) the return from a short hedge from period 1 to period 2 is:

$$\tilde{R}_{S,L} = (\tilde{p}_2 - p_1) - \left(\tilde{f}_2 - f_1\right) \tag{7.1}$$

where tildes denote a random variable and:
$\tilde{R}_{S,L}$ = hedger's revenue per unit: S = short hedge; L = long hedge
$\tilde{p}_2$ = cash price in period 2
$\tilde{f}_2$ = futures price in period 2
p_1 = cash price in period 1
f_1 = futures price in period 1
B_1 = basis in period 1 = $f_1 - p_1$
$\tilde{B}_2$ = basis in period 2 = $\tilde{f}_2 - \tilde{p}_2$
The per unit return on the hedge in (7.1) is equal to the difference between the change in cash price and the change in the futures price. If there is no trend in prices the return is zero (ignoring storage costs).

Equation (7.1) can be rewritten as:

$$\tilde{R}_{S,L} = B_1 - \tilde{B}_2 \tag{7.2}$$

Any change in the hedger's revenue (i.e., any return from hedging) depends on the change in the basis. If the basis is unchanged (i.e., a "textbook" hedge), then $\tilde{B}_2 = B_1$ and the return from hedging is zero and revenue is unchanged. In this case, futures price changes exactly offset cash price changes. Alternatively, if $\tilde{B}_2 < B_1$ (i.e., the basis narrows) then the short hedgers profit from the hedge. However, there is a loss of revenue on the short hedge if $B_1 < \tilde{B}_2$.

Similarly, the return from a long hedge can be represented as:

$$\tilde{R}_L = (p_1 - \tilde{p}_2) - \left(f_1 - \tilde{f}_2\right) \tag{7.3}$$

or, rearranging terms:

$$\tilde{R}_L = \tilde{B}_2 - B_1 \tag{7.4}$$

Thus, a narrowing of the basis occurs when $\tilde{B}_2 < B_1$ and it detracts from the long hedge because equation (7.4) becomes negative. If, on the other hand, $B_1 < \tilde{B}_2$, then this outcome results in additional revenue for the hedger.

In addition, it is worth pointing out that the variance of R_S is equal to:

$$var\left(\tilde{R}_S\right) = var\left(\tilde{p}_2\right) - 2cov\left(\tilde{p}_2, \tilde{f}_2\right) + var\left(\tilde{f}_2\right) \tag{7.5}$$

From Equation (7.5) we find that the riskiness of the hedge depends on the sum of the variance of the cash price, the covariance between cash and futures prices, and the variance of the futures price. For a perfect "text-book" hedge, $var\left(\tilde{p}_2\right) = var\left(\tilde{f}_2\right) = cov\left(\tilde{p}_2, \tilde{f}_2\right)$, and the price risk is totally eliminated.

Table 7.4 shows the financial impact of a basis change on a hedger's profit. As shown in the table, a short hedger gains financially from a nar-rowing basis and loses from a widening of the basis. The impact of a basis change on a long hedger is exactly the reverse of the impact on a short hedger.

The size of the basis is largely determined by the local supply and de-mand, storage costs, transportation costs, etc. and thus it changes over time (refer back to Chapter 3 for more discussion on this point). However, basis trends or patterns within a crop year are somewhat predictable by hedgers, at least more so than are absolute price patterns. This is due, primarily, to seasonal factors in the production of many agricultural commodities and the important role of storage costs.

It is the predictability of basis changes which often induces grain mer-chants to hedge. If, for example, the basis is large and expected to decline, then the merchant will take a long cash and a short futures position. Al-ternatively, if the basis is expected to widen, this will be an incentive for the merchant to be short in the cash market (say by selling a forward cash contract) and long in the futures market. However, in practice this latter opportunity to sell a forward cash contract may not be as readily available as the opportunity to take either a long cash or spot position.

Holbrook Working was one of the first researchers to empirically study recurring basis patterns. His observations in the wheat market led him to show that the cash price is positively correlated with the basis. With this correlation, seasonal trends in the cash price provide clues as to when hedg-ing should be profitable. His theories have held in other storable markets as well, where it is often found that the basis is at its widest levels in the immediate post-harvest period, with a gradual narrowing over the course of the year.

Theoretically, the basis for storable products is easier to predict than ab-solute price levels for two major reasons. First, there is an upper theoretical limit to the size of the basis which is equal to full carrying costs and the spot

Table 7.4: Financial Impact of Basis Change of a Hedger's Profit

| Type of Hedge | Change in Basis over Hedge Period | | |
	Unchanged	Narrows*	Widens**
Short	No gain or loss	Gain	Lose
Long	No gain or loss	Lose	Gain

* Narrowing of the basis occurs when the cash price gains on the futures and the mathematical value of the basis becomes smaller.
** Widening of the basis occurs when the cash price falls relative to the futures and the mathematical value of the basis becomes larger.

and futures prices will converge during the futures delivery month as the costs of storage approach zero.

The upper limit to the basis (at the delivery point) is equal to the sum of all carrying charges such as interest, insurance, physical storage costs, etc. If the futures price rose above the spot price by more than the full carrying charges, then grain merchants would quickly arbitrage the two markets by simultaneously buying on the spot market and selling on the futures market. This would be essentially guaranteeing themselves a riskless return if the spot grain was purchased in storage in a terminal market (this is an example of an arbitrage hedge). The arbitrage mechanism would thus serve to reduce the basis down to the level equaling carrying charge costs. In theory, there is no lower limit to the size of the basis. The futures price may fall below the cash or spot price (called an inverted market) if there is a shortage of deliverable stocks (in or near the terminal markets). Since it is impossible to correct an inverted market by arbitrage, the amount of the inversion is theoretically limitless.

The second factor, which is a convergence of cash and futures, is by far the more important one, giving rise to recurring basis patterns. This relationship is shown in Figure 7.1 for a hypothetical July wheat futures contract. Suppose that, on November 1, the July futures contract was trading at $8.00 per bushel, *ceteris paribus*, this is the spot price expected to be prevailing in July. Furthermore, suppose that the spot price at the terminal delivery point (recall that this is the location specified in the futures contract) was $7.25 in November. Also, assume that the spot price at a local rural elevator was $7.00 on November 1. Under most conditions, the July basis can be expected to narrow between November and July. Once again, this occurs because the costs of storing wheat for delivery in July decline as time passes from November to July. In other words, it costs less to store wheat from March to July than it does from November to July. In Figure 7.1, this expected narrowing of the basis (shown by the shaded area) is based on the belief that the terminal spot price will gain on the July futures. The expected basis in the figure is the shaded area between the expected futures and expected spot price. The extent of the narrowing in Figure 7.1 will be approximately equal to $0.75 because, in theory, the spot and futures prices converge. They rarely converge to zero, however, because in the delivery month the spot commodity will often sell at a slight premium to futures. This premium reflects the uncertainty of the exact delivery date and exact grade associated with purchasing a futures contract and taking delivery on it rather than buying the commodity outright on the spot market.

Figure 7.1: Theoretical Basis Trend Over Time

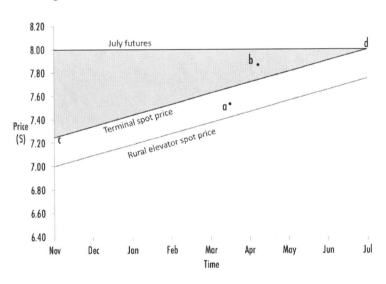

In Figure 7.1, the local or rural country basis is also shown to narrow by approximately the same extent as the terminal basis, but it will vary with local supply and demand conditions and changes in transport costs. The local basis will approach the cost of transportation from the local to the terminal delivery point, which is greater than zero. This phenomenon of the basis narrowing over time (within a crop year) is particularly acute during periods of high interest rates. This follows because the higher the interest rate the greater the storage costs.

A grain merchant operating in the terminal location in the above example will thus be encouraged to take a short futures position if the basis is larger than that which returns zero economic profit. The basis which just returns zero profit is shown by the solid upward sloping line cd in Figure 7.1. Profits are zero because the basis change covers carrying costs (as explained in Chapter 3, carrying costs refers to marginal storage costs). However, suppose that on April 1 the terminal spot price is at point "a" in Figure

7.1, which implies an abnormally wide basis. In the expectation of the basis returning to the solid trend line, the merchant would attempt to buy cash wheat and sell July futures. Several of these opportunities to hedge and profit from a basis change may arise between November 1 and July 1. Figure 7.2 displays a normal basis pattern, which trends upward, but not in a straight line. The basis pattern in Figure 7.2 would present several hedging opportunities for grain merchants.

Figure 7.2: Theoretical Basis Behavior Over Time

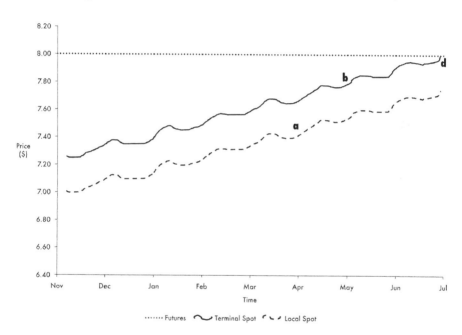

Consider the alternative point b in Figure 7.2. Here the basis is smaller than expected for May 1 and it may be expected to widen over the short-run. If, on May 1, the merchant had an opportunity to sell wheat in the forward cash market (for delivery before June 1) he would do so knowing he could simultaneously go long in the July futures. In this case, he would be expecting to profit from a short-term widening of the basis.

The inability of the storage activity to positively correlate with inter-temporal markets also periodically occurs between crop years in a storable commodity. For example, if in June, July (old crop) corn futures closed at $7.14 per bushel and December (new crop) closed at $6.78, then the fu-tures market is "inverted." This inversion of $0.36 per bushel could be a reflection of a low projected carryover of stocks from the old crop to the new crop year. As Working has shown, it is current stocks which deter-mine inter-temporal price relationships. Current stocks and inter-temporal

Figure 7.3: Inverted Market

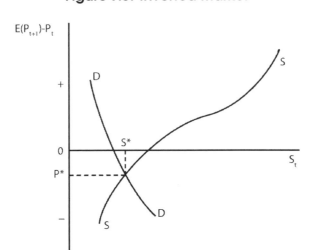

prices are simultaneously determined by the interaction of the demand for and supply of storage.

Figure 7.3 shows the demand and supply of storage, a model which was fully explained in Chapter 3. The demand for stocks (DD in Figure 7.3) relates the changes in price between the new crop period and the old crop period ($E(P_{t+1})$ - P_t) to the stocks held at the end of the old crop (S_t). The operator E ( ) denotes that P_{t+1} is the expected spot price in period t+1. Note again that the DD schedule has a negative slope. Also discussed in Chapter 3 was the net marginal cost of holding stocks, which is represented by the supply of storage (SS) in Figure 7.3. The supply of storage is the marginal cost of storage minus the marginal convenience yield.

Convenience yield refers to the benefit a firm receives from holding stocks. For example, it is important that a processing firm always maintains a certain minimum level of "pipeline" stocks. It would be costly to the firm if it periodically ran out of stocks. For low stock levels (i.e., the left hand side of Figure 7.3), the convenience yield is relatively high and it outweighs the marginal physical costs of storage such as interest, insurance, etc. This is shown by the bottom portion of the SS curve, which lies below the horizontal line showing zero difference between the inter-temporal prices. In this example, points below the horizontal line indicate that old crop futures are priced above new crop futures (i.e., an "inverted market"). For points above the line, a carrying charge price relationship exists. For example if a more normal carryover was expected in the corn example represented in Figure 7.3, then a carrying charge market would probably exist; where distant futures prices are priced higher than nearby futures prices.

In Figure 7.3, the demand for storage is positioned such that it reflects the fact that carryover stocks are relatively low (i.e., S*). In commodity markets, this is most often due to a crop failure in the current season (i.e., the "old crop" season). The position of DD gives rise to an inverted market. This equilibrium is shown by P* and S* in Figure 7.3. Note that stocks are carried out of the "old" crop and into the "new" crop, even though the expected return from storage is negative. This can be explained by convenience yield.

Figure 7.4 shows the basis for hard red spring wheat in North Dakota, Montana and Portland. In this example we are using the alternative definition of the basis, namely cash minus futures, so the sign of the basis is switching compared to the examples above. The two farming regions represented in Figure 7.4 are North Dakota and Montana, and a large share of the wheat grown in those two states is exported through Portland to markets in Asia and elsewhere. Portland is the number one U.S. port for wheat exports. The average wheat basis for the time period shown in Figure 7.4 is $1.76 per bushel in Portland, $-0.55 in North Dakota and $-0.55 per bushel in Montana. Given the way we have defined the basis here (cash - futures) this means the Portland cash price tends to be above the nearby futures price and the cash prices in North Dakota and Montana are lower than the futures price. The basis in North Dakota is more negative than in Montana, on average, because Montana is closer to Portland than is North Dakota.

Figure 7.4: Wheat Basis

Note: The basis is calculated as the cash bid price minus the nearby futures price.
Source: https://agtransport.usda.gov/Grain/Wheat-Basis-by-Location/uh4s-xysq.

Anticipatory Hedge and Production Risk

As explained above, anticipatory hedges may involve both price and pro-duction risk and expected changes in the basis are not as relevant for this type of hedge because the hedger is more concerned about an absolute price change than a change in relative prices between the futures and cash mar-kets.

The hedger's return from an anticipatory hedge from period 1 to period 2 is:

$$\tilde{R} = \tilde{p}_2 \tilde{q}_2 - h\left(\tilde{f}_2 - f_1\right) \tag{7.6}$$

where tildes denote a random variable and:
$\tilde{R}$ = hedger's revenue
$\tilde{p}_2$ = cash price in period 2
h = quantity of futures sold ($-$) or bought ($+$)
f_1 = futures price in period 1
$\tilde{f}_2$ = futures price in period 2
$\tilde{q}_2$ = hedger's production, realized in period 2
During period 1, the forthcoming cash price in period 2 ($\tilde{p}_2$), the hedger's production ($\tilde{q}_2$), and the futures price in period 2 ($\tilde{f}_2$) are all un-known. Think of period 1 as the planting period (for, say, a soybean farmer) and period 2 as the harvest period. This can easily be generalized to com-modities where there is no distinct "harvest." For example, an airline com-pany might use anticipatory hedges for its fuel purchases, and in this case the "harvest" would be interpreted as the expected fuel consumption in the next time period. Airlines have to forecast the quantity of fuel they will be purchasing, at the same time they are forecasting fuel prices.

The variance of the hedged position is:

$$var\left(\tilde{R}\right) = var\left(\tilde{p}_2 \tilde{q}_2\right) - 2h\,cov\left(\tilde{p}_2 \tilde{q}_2, \tilde{f}_2\right) + h^2 var\left(\tilde{f}_2\right) \tag{7.7}$$

This expression is more complicated than equation (7.5). In (7.7) we find that the variance of the hedge depends on the correlation between prices and production (the first term in (7.7)); the correlation between revenue ($\tilde{p}_2 \tilde{q}_2$) and the futures price (the second term); and the variability of the futures prices (the third term), and the quantity of futures sold or bought (h).

An anticipatory hedge is the type of hedge a farmer would enter into in the spring of the year if he was hedging his crop to be harvested later on in the fall. Anticipatory hedges are also common for nonstorable commodi-ties, such as live hogs or finished cattle, and the basis patterns are not as recurrent and predictable as in the case of storable commodities. Therefore, hedging to profit from basis changes is not really relevant in these markets. For example, a feedlot manager would not buy feeder cattle and sell fat cattle futures which mature after the feeding period (approximately six months) simply because of a wide basis. The feeder cattle cannot be placed in a warehouse and forgotten about! They must be fed daily and then sold for slaughter. During the feeding period the hedge cannot easily be lifted until the cattle are "finished." For the fundamental reason that the storage activity cannot provide a linkage between the current supply of feeder cattle (or any other perishable product) and the demand 12 months hence, carrying-charge markets and declining bases over time are not necessarily observed in nonstorable markets.

Hedging with Financial Futures

The tremendous growth in financial futures trading volume indicates that these instruments have economic value to an increasing number of firms. Many firms have decided that the advantages of hedging outweigh the disadvantages of not hedging. Financial firms, commercial and mortgage bankers, pension fund managers, and insurance companies all face risks associated with fluctuations in interest rates, which can be better managed through hedging. Mutual fund managers exposed to equity market risk can hedge their portfolios using stock index futures. In addition, exporters and importers can hedge foreign exchange transactions. However, there are still many firms and industries who do not share this view.

The general advantages and disadvantages of hedging with financials are similar to those for commodity futures hedging. Hedging enables firms to better manage price risk and it provides additional flexibility in the timing of cash market transactions. This section briefly explains how hedgers can use financial futures to achieve their business goals.

Hedging Exchange Rates: An Application

Volatile currency markets affect the profitability of firms that have either accounts receivable or payable in a foreign currency. Export or import companies take various strategies to cope with exchange rate uncertainty. Hedging exchange rates with futures is one such strategy and it can be viewed as a firm's attempt to lock in an exchange rate over a period of time in order to insulate the firm against an adverse move in the exchange rate.

Consider the above example of a long hedge in Japanese Yen. When foreign exchange expenditures (i.e., payables) are made after the U.S. dollar has fallen, then the cost in U.S. dollars has risen. It now costs more

Table 7.5: Long Hedge with Japanese Yen: An Illustration

Date	Cash	Basis	Futures	Hedger's Transaction
Nov. 1	$0.0127	$0.0001	$0.0128	Buy 1 June Yen Futures Contract
Mar. 1	$0.0132	$0.0003	$0.0135	Sell 1 June Yen Futures Contract
Return	($7,850)		$8,750	

dollars to buy Yen. Consider the example of a U.S. firm in the Silicon Valley that, on November 1st, orders computer components from Japan at a total expected cost of $200,000 at today's spot exchange rate of 78.74 ¥ per dollar (or $.0127/¥). Payment for the computer components is to be made in March in Yen (15.7 Million ¥). Note that the size of this Yen payment is slightly larger than the futures contract size of 12.5 million Yen. The firm ordering the computer components is concerned that the Yen will rise in value and therefore it goes long in the futures market for Yen.

As shown in Table 7.5, a long hedge is placed by buying 1 June futures contract at a price of $.0128/¥. By March 1, suppose that the U.S. dollar has fallen, as was feared by the U.S. importer. The firm now lifts its hedge by selling 1 June Yen futures contract at $.0135. The profit on the futures transaction is $8,750 (ignoring commission fees). The profit equals the futures price change (.0135 - .0128) × 12.5 million ¥: the size of the futures contract. This profit more than offsets the opportunity loss of $7,850, which the computer firm experiences on its account payable in Japanese Yen. The opportunity loss equals the change in the spot price (.0127 - .0132) × 15.7 million ¥: the actual size of the payment made. The "basis" in this example widened from $.0001 to $.0003, which assisted the long hedge. After completing the hedge, the importer's final cost of the computer components was $198,490 = (15.7 million Yen × $.0132) - $8,750 (plus minimal futures commission fees). The final cost of the computer components was about $1,500 less than the $200,000 anticipated in November.

Figure 7.5: Impact of an Exchange Rate Change on Accounts Payable

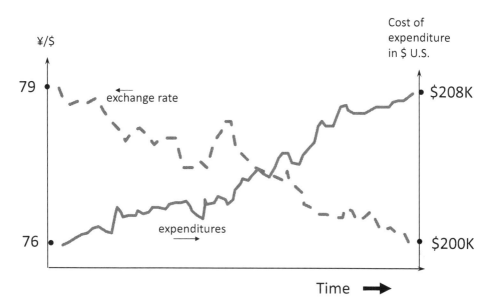

Figure 7.6: Impact of an Exchange Rate Change on Accounts Receivable

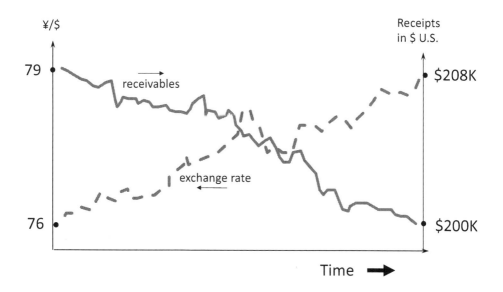

The impact of the weaker dollar on the computer firm's payables (i.e., expenditures) is shown in Figure 7.5, where the Yen/dollar exchange rate is plotted on the left hand vertical axis and the amount of expenditures or amount payable (in $ U.S.) is plotted on the right hand vertical axis. Time is represented by the horizontal axis, moving from the left to the right. The current time period (say November) is on the far left and the far right represents a subsequent time period (say March). The spot market exchange rate is shown as the dashed line in Figure 7.5, changing from about 79 Yen/dollar to about 76 Yen/dollar over the time period represented. As the Yen moves higher (i.e., the U.S. dollar weakens) the amount payable (in $U.S.) rises, as shown by the solid line in Figure 7.5. The move in the exchange rate raises the amount payable from about $200,000 to approximately $208,000. Conversely, if the exchange rate line in Figure 7.5 had a positive slope (i.e., representing a weaker Yen), then the amount payable would be shown by a line with a negative slope.

Figure 7.6 displays an alternative situation where a firm has $208,000 in receivables at the current spot Yen/dollar exchange rate. This example would represent a firm that has sold some product or commodity to Japan and will eventually be paid in Yen. In this case, if the Yen falls in value (i.e., the dollar strengthens) the dollar value of the receivables declines. Figure 7.6 depicts a rise in the dollar from approximately 76 to 79 Yen, which translates into a fall in the amount of receivables from roughly $208,000 to $200,000. A firm exposed to this type of risk would hedge by going short in the Yen futures market. Recall the futures contract is priced in $ per ¥.

Hedging Bonds: An Application

Consider an example of a pension fund manager who is motivated to preserve and expand the value of the portfolio under his or her management. Suppose the manager expects that the Federal Reserve will raise interest rates in the near term, a move that would erode the value of her portfolio because interest rates move in the opposite direction as bond prices. The portfolio manager therefore decides to try and reduce the effect of rising interest rates (i.e., bond yields) on the value of her portfolio by taking a short position in the futures market. A short bond futures position would yield a profit as interest rates rise.

Suppose it is September 1 and the fund manager is holding ten $100,000 15-year, 6 percent Treasury Bonds currently priced at 149-29, as shown in Table 7.6. A short hedge is placed by selling ten December T-bond futures contracts at a price of 148-01. By November 1, suppose that interest rates have risen as was expected by the fund manager, and she now lifts the hedge by buying back ten December bond futures contracts at 146-15. As shown in Table 7.6, the profit on the futures transaction is $15,625 (before commission fees), which partially offsets the opportunity loss of $24,375 that the hedger experiences on her inventory of bonds.

In Table 7.6 notice that the December bond futures price falls from 148-01 to 146-15, or by 1-18, which amounts to $1,562.50 per contract. At the same time, each bond held in the portfolio falls by 2-14, or $2,437.50. The basis widened from minus 1-28 to minus 1-00 (i.e., became more positive) and this detracted somewhat from the hedge.

Table 7.6: Short Hedge with Treasury Bonds: An Illustration

Date	Cash	Basis	Futures	Hedger's Transaction
Sep. 1	149-29	-1-28	148-01	Sell 10 Dec. T-Bond Futures Contracts
Nov. 1	147-15	-1-00	146-15	Buy 10 Dec. T-Bond Futures Contracts
Return	($24,375)		$15,625	

Hedging: A Portfolio Explanation

A portfolio explanation of hedging was first rigorously presented and developed by Telser (1958), Stein (1961), and Johnson (1960), who used the Markowitz (1968) foundations of portfolio management. With this approach, a hedger is viewed as holding several different cash and futures assets in a portfolio and is assumed to maximize the expected value of his utility function by choosing amongst the alternative portfolios on the basis of their means and variances.

The standard application of portfolio theory to futures markets assumes the following:

1. a risk averse hedger;
2. a fixed long cash position (e.g., some inventory in storage);
3. a short futures position is combined with a long cash position;
4. each "portfolio" of cash and futures is evaluated on the merits of its expected return and its variance;
5. a long cash position earns a higher (but riskier) return than a combined cash and futures (i.e., hedged) position; and
6. hedgers do not speculate on their price expectations.

This model is displayed in Figure 7.7 where the expected return from a portfolio comprised of hedged and unhedged stocks is plotted on the left vertical axis and the riskiness of the portfolio (measured by its variance)

Box 7.4 Metallgesellschaft Hedging Debacle

Most futures contracts expire in less than two years. Therefore, in an attempt to hedge against long-term risk, firms sometimes chose to enter into sequential short-term hedges–rollover hedging. This approach was discussed above. Rollover hedging is therefore a financial transaction where a firm attempts to use futures markets to hedge price risk far into the future (e.g. 3-10 years). The firm buys/sells futures contracts that are actively trading and then "rolls over" these hedges in the most distant futures contracts as the old contracts mature. There is considerable controversy over this hedging procedure. Some argue that rollover hedging is not a sound financial strategy because it is too risky.

The question is: Does sequential short-term hedging, or rollover hedging, serve as a beneficial mechanism for long-term hedging in commodity markets? Presently, there are several international companies that use rollover hedging.

The German based commodity firm Metallgesellschaft used this technique in the crude oil market, but encountered huge financial losses of approximately $1 billion in the early 1990s. Why those losses accumulated is still a subject of debate. Economist and Nobel laureate Merton Miller argued in a court case that Metallgesellschaft's strategy was prudent hedging. Others argued that Metallgesellschaft was speculating.

See: Edwards, F.R., and Canter, M.S. 1995, 'The Collapse of Metallgesellschaft: Unhedgeable Risks, Poor Hedging Strategy, or Just Bad Luck?', Journal of Futures Markets, vol. 15, no. 3, pp. 211-64.

---

is plotted on the horizontal axis. The risk and return associated with various combinations of hedged and unhedged portfolios are traced out by the curve UH. The shape of UH depends on the correlation between futures and cash prices. The higher the correlation, the more bowed out UH is. The expected return and variance associated with carrying the inventory unhedged is represented by point U. Point H represents the expected return and variance associated with a full 100% hedge. In the case of this traditional, full hedge, the variance of returns is the basis risk. As drawn in this example, point H is the portfolio that offers the lowest level of variance. It is important to notice that the risk at point H is non-zero.

The optimal hedge ratio represents the most desirable combination of cash and futures positions and it is chosen based on the shape of the indifference curves of the hedger. Indifference curves reflect a hedger's attitude

Figure 7.7: Portfolio Solution to the Optimal Hedge

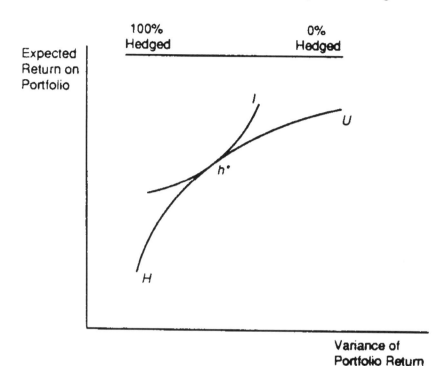

toward risk and return. In Figure 7.7 an indifference curve, labeled I, is drawn as an upward sloping convex curve, indicating that the hedger is risk averse to some degree. The hedger will have an entire set of indifference curves but only one is drawn here. All portfolios that lie on curve I are equally desirable to the hedger. Risk aversion implies that a hedger requires a higher expected return from a more risky portfolio than from a less risky one. Indifference curves for a risk-seeking investor would be drawn as concave functions with a negative slope.

In order to maximize expected utility (i.e., attain the highest possible indifference curve), a hedger will choose point h* in Figure 7.7. This point possesses minimum risk for a given level of expected return. It shows the optimal hedge in this case is less than 100 percent of stocks.

The portfolio approach to the understanding of hedging is appealing on several grounds. Most importantly, it is able to theoretically explain why an inventory position may not be fully hedged. Additionally, it explains why commodity merchant will hold a spot and futures position even if the expected return is negative, and it clearly differentiates between hedging and speculation.

Optimal Hedge Ratio

There are two standard formulas that have been developed for computing the optimal hedge ratio, that is, the optimal futures position relative to the cash position. The minimum risk hedge ratio is shown as point H in Figure 7.7. This ratio has been utilized by Ederington (1979) and others. Alternatively, there is the utility maximizing optimal ratio h*, as shown in Figure 7.7. This has been developed by Heifner (1972), Johnson (1960), and Telser (1958). If the expected profit from holding futures contracts is zero (which is typically the case because futures prices are not forecastable), then the utility maximizing optimal hedge becomes equivalent to the risk minimizing hedge ratio (Kahl, 1983). Empirical estimates of the optimal hedge ratios for commodities are often less than 1.0.

Uncertainty in production adds complexity to the Hedgers's portfolio. Rolfo (1980) notes the following:

> "While the merchant can regulate the size of his inventory, the farmer cannot accurately forecast the size of his harvest even after all production decisions have been made. Thus the farmer suffers from *both* price and quantity uncertainty."[2]

Rolfo (1980) developed a model to calculate the optimal pre-harvest futures market hedge for a producer who is subject to both price and quantity risk. His empirical analysis focuses on Ghana, Nigeria, the Ivory Coast, and Brazil, countries accounting for a large share of world cocoa production. Rolfo (1980) finds the optimal hedge ratio for these countries is < 1.0.

In any given year, the expected revenue generated by a crop (such as cocoa) depends on the expectation and historical variance of prices and production, the pre-harvest price, and the number of futures contracts or other commitments entered into prior to harvest (i.e., the hedge). Denote the expected revenue in any given year as $E(\tilde{R})$, where:

$$E(\tilde{R}) = \tilde{p}_2 \tilde{q}_2 + h(f_1 - \tilde{f}_2) \tag{7.8}$$

In the above equation $\tilde{p}$, $\tilde{q}$, and $\tilde{f}_2$ are stochastic (or uncertain) variables that represent the cash price at the time of harvest, the quantity of cocoa, and the futures price at harvest. f_1 is the pre-harvest futures price and h is the number of futures contracts or other commitments that the producer enters prior to harvest.

The cocoa producer maximizes expected utility by hedging against price and production risk. In Rolfo's mean-variance framework this task

---

[2]Rolfo (1980), p.101.

is specified mathematically as follows:

$$\max_n \text{EU} = \text{E}(\tilde{R}) - m\text{var}(\tilde{R}) \tag{7.9}$$

where m represents the degree of risk aversion.[3] The optimal hedge, h^*, is determined by taking the first-order conditions of equation (7.9) with respect to h and is calculated according to the following expression:

$$n^* = \frac{f - \text{E}(\tilde{P}_f)}{2m\text{var}(\tilde{P}_f)} + \frac{\text{cov}(\tilde{P}\tilde{Q}, \tilde{P}_f)}{\text{var}(\tilde{P}_f)} \tag{7.10}$$

As explained in Rolfo (1980) the first term on the right hand side in equation (7.10) drops out in most instances because the futures price is not forecastable. This leaves the second term in (7.10) which can be estimated by the slope coefficient in a regression equation where production revenue is regressed on price. The slope coefficient measures the increase in production revenue that is expected from a 1$ increase in price, based on the historical data.

An example of estimating the optimal hedge ratio using this approach is shown in Figure 7.8. Using annual data from 2000 to 2017, Figure 7.8 shows the scatterplot between corn revenue per acre and the corn price, for the state of Iowa. The slope coefficient for the linear regression line fit to the data in Figure 7.8 is equal to 150.24, which means it would be optimal for an Iowa corn farmer to sell futures contracts for roughly 150.24 bushels per acre. If the expected yield is around 200 bushels per acre, this implies an optimal hedge ratio equal to 75% (= 150.24 / 200).

Hedging can be viewed quite simply as the process of simultaneously choosing futures positions and underlying cash positions in order to construct a portfolio of assets. Stein (1961) and Johnson (1960), who used the foundations of portfolio management, first rigorously presented a portfolio explanation of hedging. With this approach, a hedger is viewed as holding several different cash and futures assets in a portfolio and is assumed to maximize the expected value of his utility function by choosing among the alternative portfolios on the basis of their means and variances. In a theoretical paper, McKinnon (1967) extended this concept and used a mean-variance objective function for the producer. In this framework, the objective function is: $\theta = EU(\Pi) - (\lambda/2)V(\Pi)$, where $EU(\Pi)$ is expected utility of profit (Π), $V(\Pi)$ is the variance of profit, and λ is the absolute risk aversion coefficient. McKinnon (1967) focused on the hedge decision (rather than the production decision) and calculated the optimal hedge ratio assuming minimum risk hedging.

---

[3] Note that $\text{var}(\tilde{R}) = \text{var}(\tilde{p}_2\tilde{q}_2) + h^2\text{var}(\tilde{f}_2) - 2h\text{cov}(\tilde{p}\tilde{q}, \tilde{f}_2)$.

Figure 7.8: Optimal Hedge Ratio Example: Corn

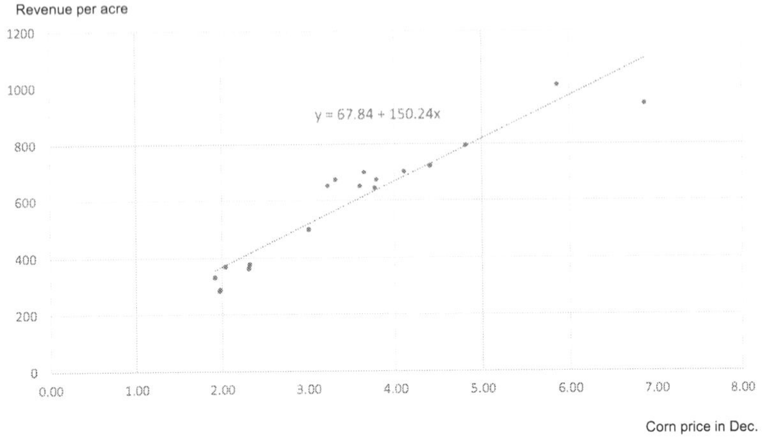

Source: Data obtained from USDA *Feedgrains Yearbook*.

Using an expected utility maximization framework, but focusing on the production decision (rather than the hedge decision), Danthine (1978) incorporated the possibility of buying and selling futures contracts into the model of the competitive firm under price uncertainty. In the Danthine model, production is not risky and it is assumed there is no basis risk. He demonstrated that planned production responds positively to the current futures contract price and that changes in the subjective distribution of futures or spot prices do not lead to changes in production decisions. The firm copes with price uncertainty by participating in the futures market, where a certain price is substituted for an uncertain one, while optimal production is unaltered. The futures price is the driving force affecting producer production decisions. With a futures market, production decisions are shown to be independent of both the producer's degree of risk aversion and price expectations, and they are separable from the producer's "portfolio problem" (i.e., just as under the Markowitz separation theorem). The optimal hedge in the Danthine type model depends on the degree of risk aversion and the probability distribution of the forward price.

Anderson and Danthine (1983), showed that the "separation" result in Danthine (1978) does not hold when either output or the basis is random. For example, when basis risk is present, changes in the subjective distribution of the forthcoming spot price lead to changes in the production decision.

Anderson and Danthine (1983) modified the McKinnon (1967) model to allow for the simultaneous determination of hedging and production decisions. In a mean-variance framework and with price, yield and basis risk, the Anderson-Danthine optimal hedge result is:

$$\frac{h^*}{E(q)} = \frac{\rho(s,f)\sigma(s)}{\sigma(f)} + \frac{\rho(q,f)\sigma(q)/E(q)}{\sigma(f)/E(s)} + \frac{F - E(f)}{\lambda E(q)\sigma^2(f)} \qquad (7.11)$$

where h^* is the number of futures contracts ($h* > 0$ indicates a short hedge); s, f, and q are random variables representing the spot price at harvest, harvest time futures price, and quantity produced, respectively; ρ is the correlation coefficient; σ is the standard deviation; F is the planting time futures price; and E is the expectation operator. The first term on the righthand-side in equation (7.11) represents the effect of basis risk on the optimal hedge. From the first term, the higher the correlation between the spot price and futures price at harvest, the larger the optimal hedge, *ceteris paribus*. The impact of yield risk is captured by the second term, where we find that the higher the correlation between harvest time futures price and production, the higher the optimal hedge. The numerator in the third term represents the extent to which futures prices are thought to be biased estimates of forthcoming spot prices. If there is no perceived bias, then this speculative component of the hedge ratio is zero.

Some firms prefer forward contracting to direct hedging with futures or options contracts. Forward contracts are a substitute for futures contracts, as both provide an opportunity to reduce price risk. However, from the firm's perspective, neither financial tool dominates the other as there are pros and cons of using one versus the other. Perhaps the one key distinguishing feature is the absence of basis risk with forward contracting (Miller, 1986). As above, using the mean-variance framework, the first order conditions for forward contracting are:

$$\frac{q^*}{E(q)} = 1 + \frac{\rho(q,f)\sigma(q)/E(q)}{\sigma(s)/E(s)} + \frac{G - E(s)}{\lambda E(q)\sigma^2(s)} \qquad (7.12)$$

where q^* is the quantity contracted and G is the cash forward contract price. Miller concluded that the absence of basis risk does not necessarily lead to higher levels of forward contracting relative to direct hedging with futures. This is true both theoretically and empirically.

Hartzmark (1988) has empirically tested the portfolio theory of hedging using Commodity Futures Trading Commission (CFTC) weekly data on cash and futures positions held by large commercial hedgers. He specifically tested for risk minimizing behavior in wheat and oats by comparing cash and futures positions with risk-minimizing positions. Hartzmark found that the firms he studied adjusted their cash and futures positions in accordance with one another and that they did not adapt their expectations to changing market conditions. He therefore concluded the firms acted as though they were risk-minimizers. In a related paper, Peck and Nahmias (1989) came up with much different results. They analyzed quarterly cash and futures market positions for a number of U.S. flour mills aggregated together. They calculated the recommended hedging strategies from portfolio theory (optimal and minimum-risk hedges) and compared it to actual behavior. Their results show little statistical relationship between either the optimal or the minimum risk ratios and actual hedge ratios. From this, Peck and Nahmias concluded that the portfolio model has little practical relevance. As pointed out by Hartzmark, Peck and Nahmias use more aggregate data than Hartzmark, and they analyze small long hedgers, compared to Hartzmark's sample of large short hedgers.

Castelino (1992) estimated minimum variance hedge ratios for wheat, corn, T-bills, and Eurodollars. He found a stronger linkage between cash and futures prices for wheat and corn compared to T-bills and Eurodollars. In other words, the basis risk was higher for interest rate futures contracts compared to grain futures. Castelino estimated the extent to which the optimal hedge ratio varies over time and found the time dimension associated with the optimal hedge ratio was more important for financial futures than grain futures. Time varying hedge ratios make sense in the business world because the factors that determine the optimal hedge ratio (see equation 7.11) are not constant over time. For instance, the correlation coefficients and price and quantity expectations in equation 7.11 are changing over time.

Hedging with Futures versus Options

Hedging with options on futures will be described in Chapter 9. Sakong, Hayes and Hallam (1993) compared hedging with options versus futures. They set up a standard hedging model with both price and production uncertainty, and they find that the introduction of production uncertainty alters the optimal futures and options position and almost always makes it optimal for the producing firm to purchase put options. Event risk has long been one of the standard reasons for hedging with options rather than futures (see Feiger and Jacquillat, 1979). Stoll and Whaley (1985) explain:

> "options not only provide insurance against price risk that is conditional on an event (receiving the bid, having a successful harvest, making the loan, making the stock offering) but also avoid any penalty if the event does not occur (the bid is rejected, the harvest is poor, the loan is not taken down, or the stock issue

---

Box 7.5 Silicon Valley Bank Unwinds its Interest Rate Hedges and then Collapses

California's Silicon Valley Bank (SVB) was a publicly traded bank that was focused on serving technology and venture capital firms. In 2023, the collapse of SVB was a significant event in the history of U.S. finance. It was the second largest U.S. bank failure, behind Washington Mutual's collapse in 2008, during the financial crisis at that time. SVB was the nation's 16th largest bank, and it literally failed overnight in March 2023—actually it took 36 hours. There are different theories as to why the bank failed but the explanation is quite simple—a lack of proper risk management. The bank invested in long-term US treasury bonds and those bonds fell in value when interest rates moved higher in response to inflation. Treasury yields moved significantly higher over a short period in mid-March 2023, and SVB was caught unhedged.

SVB did not have a chief risk officer for most of 2022 and this may be the reason it did not hedge its exposure to rising interest rates. The bottom line is that SVB did a horrific job of risk management. After all, if you invest in government bonds and then interest rates rise, you lose money. This is no different than a commodity merchant who buys corn and then prices fall, they lose money. However most commodity merchants learned 150 years ago the importance of hedging risk. Surprisingly SVB was not applying basic risk management practices. What is even worse is that apparently SVB had some hedges in place in December 2021, but these hedges were unwound by the bank as of December 2022. This type of incompetent management would no doubt sink a commodities firm and unlike SVB, an incompetent commodity merchant would not get bailed out by the government.

---

is not sold). It is in this sense that options provide protection against both price and quantity risk and are, therefore, a better hedging tool than futures contracts in some cases" (p.229)

Lapan, Moschini and Hanson (1991) compare hedging with options versus futures with nonstochastic production. First they show that if futures prices and options premiums are unbiased, options are a redundant hedging device. Then they go on to demonstrate that if prices are symmetrically distributed and if futures prices are biased, then options may be useful.

Commodity Swaps

The foregoing discussion in this chapter has assumed the commercial hedger is focused on either a single risky payment on the input side or a volatile price on the output (i.e., receipt) side. In these cases, there may be a single purchase of an input (e.g., corn for an ethanol manufacturer) or the single sale of an output (e.g., gasoline for an oil refinery) that is at issue. Above, we have also discussed the importance of production uncertainty, which means the final volume purchased or sold is unknown at the time the hedge is initiated.

In practice firms looking to hedge price risk may encounter a stream of risky payments or a stream of risky receipts. These payments or receipts could be hedged individually as discussed above, or hedged collectively with a single transaction–a commodity swap. A commodity swap is essentially a forward contract or a series of forward contracts that provide for an exchange of payments over time between two parties, according to some pre-specified rules. The simplest swap is a forward contract settled either with a single payment or with physical delivery.

Consider the basic swap illustrated in Figure 7.9. Assume that in early October an oil refinery (depicted on the left side of Figure 7.9) expects to produce 42,000 gallons of gasoline that will be sold and shipped in late November. At the same time, a downstream gasoline blending station (wholesaler) expects to purchase 42,000 gallons of gasoline in November, in order to supply its retail customers. In October, the oil refinery is concerned about a falling price of gasoline before the late November spot market sale, and the blending terminal is concerned about a rising price of gasoline before its late November spot market purchase.

In order to manage their respective price risks, suppose the refinery and the gasoline wholesale terminal enter into an over-the-counter (OTC) swap

Figure 7.9: Simple RBOB Swap Example

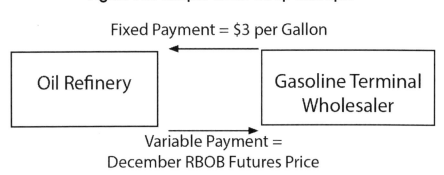

Fixed Payment = $3 per Gallon

Oil Refinery   Gasoline Terminal Wholesaler

Variable Payment = December RBOB Futures Price

on October 1st. The swap specifies that the gasoline terminal will pay $3 per gallon to the refinery on the last business day in November, and on that same November day the oil refiner agrees to pay the gasoline terminal the settlement price of the December gasoline (i.e., RBOB) futures, a variable price. The swap volume is 42,000 gallons, which is the same size as one gasoline futures contract. This November swap will expire at the end of November. For simplicity we ignore basis (futures-cash) fluctuations.

Suppose gasoline prices then fall after the swap agreement is made and by the end of November the price of December gasoline futures is $2.50. In this case, the oil refinery would sell the 42,000 gallons of gasoline into the spot market, receiving $2.50 per gallon. At the same time the refinery would receive $3 per gallon from the terminal wholesaler (times 42,000 gallons) and then pay back the wholesaler $2.50 (the December futures price), earning $0.50 per gallon, to supplement the $2.50 fetched in the spot market. The final net price received by the refinery would be $3.00 per gallon ($2.50 from the spot market sale plus $0.50 profit from the swap contract).

If instead, the price of gasoline rose to $3.50 by the end of November, the oil refinery would receive $3 from the terminal and would simultaneously pay the terminal $3.50, to fulfill the swap. The loss of $0.50 on the swap would be offset by $0.50 per gallon gain in the spot market when the refiner sells the spot gasoline for $3.50, up from $3. Irrespective if price of gasoline goes up or down, the net price received by the refiner is $3 and the net price paid by the gasoline wholesale terminal is $3. This is an example of a simple OTC swap that is settled financially, rather than through physical delivery. Of course, it could easily be re-structured for physical delivery if the refiner delivers the gasoline directly to the terminal site and the terminal pays $3 per gallon, the price fixed in early October for delivery in late November. The example in Figure 7.9 illustrates the essence of a commodity swap–two parties exchange a fixed price (the $3) with a variable price (the December futures price in late November) for the commodity.

Swaps are commonly traded as OTC contracts between a buyer and a seller (called the counterparties) and they are most often settled financially, rather than through physical delivery. But due to increased government regulation of swaps, it is becoming more common for swaps to be cleared by a central clearinghouse. For many cash settled swaps, commodity exchanges (e.g., CME) provide clearinghouse services to eliminate counterparty risk. For instance, the CME offers (cash settled) trading in energy products like the WTI Crude Oil calendar swap futures, RBOB gasoline calendar swaps, and agricultural products like the corn, wheat, and soybean calendar swap futures. Interest rate swap futures are also traded on the CME. These products allows for "clearing" of swap trades by the exchange, ensuring the financial integrity of OTC swap transactions through elimination of counterparty risk. Most commodity swaps are based on the nearby corresponding commodity futures prices and the daily swap price is identical to the corresponding futures contract until the delivery month, when the swap price typically becomes an arithmetic average of the daily futures prices in the delivery month.

For each swap, for marking-to-market and settlement purposes the exchange uses the futures prices for the nearby month after the swap's maturity (e.g., outside the maturity month, the November swap settles at the December futures price). During the maturity month, each swap is settled at the monthly average of the nearby-month futures settlement price. For example a November swap is settled in November at the monthly average of the December futures price during the month of November.

Dual Payment Swap

Expanding on the above example in Figure 7.9, suppose the oil refiner aims to fix the selling price of a certain volume of RBOB (abbreviation for Reformulated Regular Gasoline Blendstock) gasoline each month for the next two months while a wholesale gasoline terminal, a buyer of RBOB gasoline, is also interested in managing the risk of a fluctuating RBOB prices over the same time period. The oil refiner and the gasoline terminal could manage the gasoline price risk by entering into a commodity swap similar to the one discussed above. The oil refinery could guarantee the price received for its RBOB gasoline for the next two months and the terminal could at the same time lock in the RBOB gasoline purchase price for the next two months. Suppose the two parties agree on a RBOB gasoline price of $3.00 per gallon for each month. The swap could be settled by physical delivery, whereby the oil refiner makes two separate deliveries of RBOB gasoline to the gasoline terminal operator in each month and separate payments are made with each delivery.

Alternatively, the swap could be settled financially with the first variable payment set equal to the November futures price at the end of October, and the second variable payment set equal to the December futures price at the end of November (see Table 7.7). For example, by October 31st, if the November futures price of RBOB gasoline has fallen to $2.50 per gallon then the gasoline terminal pays the oil refiner the difference between $3.00 and the futures price, and the terminal operator then turns around and purchases its RBOB gasoline at the cash price ($2.50).

If by November 30th the cash price rises to $3.50 when the second delivery is made, then the oil refiner pays the terminal the price difference and sells its RBOB gasoline in the cash market. No matter what the cash price of RBOB gasoline is at time of delivery, the effective price paid by the ter-

Table 7.7: RBOB Commodity Swap Table

Date	Spot Market Price	Oil Refiner's Swap Position	Wholesale Gasoline Terminal's Swap Position
Sep. 1	$3.00	Agrees to pay November RBOB futures settlement price on last business day in October	Agrees to pay $3.00 on last business day in October
Sep. 1	$3.00	Agrees to pay December RBOB futures settlement price on last business day in November	Agrees to pay $3.00 on last business day in November
Oct. 31	$2.50	Pays Gasoline Terminal $2.50 November futures settlement price	Pays Refiner $3.00
Nov. 30	$3.50	Pays Gasoline Terminal $3.50 December futures settlement price	Pays Refiner $3.00

minal is $3.00 and the effective price received by the oil refinery is $3.00. As above, we are ignoring basis risk in this example. A swap dealer may come between the oil refiner and RBOB gasoline terminal and the dealer would earn a fee for being the counterparty to each principal (the merchant and the ethanol plant).

In the above example the initial swap price ($3.00 per gallon) would not be listed by the exchange, because it is an over-the-counter (OTC) trade. However if the parties decide to clear their swap on the exchange then the oil refiner would be assigned short swap futures positions and the gasoline terminal would be assigned long futures swap positions in RBOB gasoline swap futures. Their respective swap futures positions would be marked-to-market each day. This would eliminate counterparty risk. A November CME swap trades until the last business day in November and its settlement price is equal to the arithmetic average of the next futures contract (December) price during November.

Airline Commodity Swap Example

CFTC data showed that during calendar years 2021 and 2022 swap dealers were net long in the WTI crude oil futures market. During part of 2021 their net short positions exceeded 500,000 contracts. Some of these futures positions could represent hedged positions. Recall that a swap dealer is a firm that deals in commodity swaps and then, in turn, may use the futures markets to manage the risk associated with its swaps transactions. The counterparties to the swap dealers may be speculative traders, like hedge funds, or traditional commercial hedgers. Let's consider two examples where the swap dealer's counterparties are commercial hedgers.

Consider the basic swap illustrated in Figure 7.10. Assume that in mid October an oil company such as state-owned Pemex in Mexico (depicted on the left side of Figure 7.10) expects to produce 1,000 barrels of oil that will be sold and shipped in mid May. Pemex is concerned about a fall in the price of oil between October and May and therefore they approach a swap dealer (such as JP Morgan in New York or HSBC Bank in London) and propose a swap contract to reduce their exposure to oil price risk. The swap dealer agrees to pay Pemex a fixed payment of $100 per barrel in May and in return Pemex agrees to pay the swap dealer the June futures price in mid May. Ignoring basis risk, if both spot and June crude oil futures prices then subsequently dropped to $80 per barrel by May, then the swap dealer loses $20 on the swap (i.e., they have to pay Pemex $100 per barrel and Pemex pays them $80). Alternatively, if spot and futures prices increase to $120 by May then the swap dealer would make $20 on the swap. At $120 oil Pemex would lose $20 on the swap but would be able to sell their physical

Figure 7.10: Swap Example Where Swap Dealer Goes Short Futures to Hedge Swap Contract

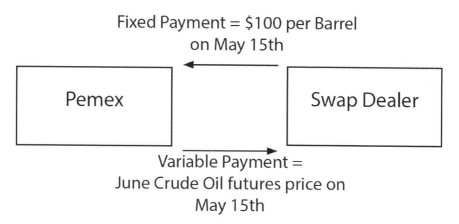

oil for $120 in the spot market, earning a net $100 per barrel. No matter whether the price rises or falls, Pemex fetches $100 per barrel. However, the swap dealer will lose in a falling market and therefore they may decide to offset their risk by going short in the June crude oil futures market. In Figure 7.10 the swap dealer would go short futures to hedge the swap.

Consider an alternative over-the-counter (OTC) swap on October 15th, depicted in Figure 7.11. In this example, a major airline (Singapore Airlines: SQ) is concerned about the rising price of fuel and decides to enter into a commodity swap to hedge their risk. The swap specifies that on May 15th the swap dealer will pay to SQ the settlement price of the June crude oil futures, a variable price, and on that same day SQ would pay the swap dealer $100 per barrel, a fixed price. The swap volume is 1,000 barrels, which is the same size as one futures contract. For simplicity we ignore basis (futures-cash) fluctuations, as above.

Suppose oil prices then fall after the swap agreement is made and by the middle of May the price of June crude oil futures is $80 (i.e., is down $20). In this case, SQ would buy the fuel equivalent of 1,000 barrels of oil in the spot market, for $80 per barrel. At the same time SQ would lose $20 per barrel on the OTC swap, because the swap dealer would receive the pre-determined $100 per barrel from SQ and then pay back $80 to SQ (i.e., the June futures price in mid May). The final net price paid by SQ would be the equivalent of $100 per barrel ($80 paid in the spot market sale plus $20 loss from the swap contract).

If instead, the price of oil rose to $120 by mid May, the SQ would pay the fixed swap payment of $100 per barrel from the swap dealer and would si-

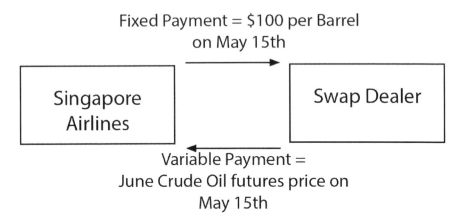

Figure 7.11: Swap Example Where Swap Dealer Goes Long Futures to Hedge Swap Contract

multaneously receive from the swap dealer $120 (the variable futures price), to fulfill the swap. The gain of $20 on the swap would be offset by higher price paid in the spot market when SQ goes to purchase fuel in the middle of May.

The example in Figure 7.11 illustrates this swap: the parties exchange a fixed price (the $100) with a variable price (the June futures price in mid May) for the commodity. In this example the swap dealer would go long futures in order to hedge their OTC position. The swap dealer would want to be long futures because if oil prices rise they would lose money on the swap, which would be offset by holding long futures. Alternatively if oil prices fell the swap dealer would make money on the swap, and this would be offset by a loss on their long futures position. The gain (loss) on the swap would be offset by a loss (gain) in futures, which is the idea behind hedging, balancing one position against another.

Summary

This chapter has introduced the economics of hedging commodities and financials through the use of the futures market. The basic fundamentals and theoretical explanations of hedging have a wide application. A coffee importer in New York may use the futures market for the same reasons and with the same objectives as a major San Francisco bank. Commercial motives for hedging commodities are arbitrage hedging, operational hedging, and anticipatory hedging. Three different explanations of hedging activity were covered. These theories include hedger's desires to reduce price risk, profiting from basis movements, and diversifying a portfolio. Whenever market price shocks occur, firms become more interested in hedging. They then develop a hedging program and tend to stick with it. This has been the experience recently in the markets for petroleum, minerals, interest rates, agricultural commodities and currencies.

Discussion Questions

1. Explain some of issues associated with hedging on a futures market located in a foreign country.

2. Discuss factors giving rise to an inverted futures market for a storable versus non-storable commodity. What are the implications for a hedger?

3. Is convenience yield an important component of the basis for financial futures or is it a concept that is mostly applicable to commodities?

4. Using Figure 7.7, discuss the conditions under which the utility maximizing hedge ratio (h*) would be equal to the risk minimizing hedge ratio (H).

5. Compare the IRS definition of a hedger with the CFTC definition.

6. It is currently the beginning of December and you have just been hired as an operations manager at small gold mine in Nevada. The mine is expected to extract 700 troy ounces of gold this month. It will ship the gold to San Francisco and receive payment in $US when the gold is delivered on February 1st. Your boss has informed you that she is concerned about price risk regarding the value of gold and that your task is to hedge against that risk. The current spot (i.e., cash) price for gold is $1,700/troy ounce in San Francisco and the February New York futures price is $1,718/troy ounce. In the table below indicate whether you go long or short futures and the number of contracts required for the hedge. You plan to lift this hedge on February 1st when you receive payment in the cash market in San Francisco. Assume that on February 1st you lift the hedge; with the cash price at $1,685 and February futures trading at $1,708. Assume brokerage fees of $25 per contract. Remember the gold futures contract size is 100 troy ounces.

    (a) Calculate the outcome of this hedge.
    (b) What is the final price received for the gold in $ per troy ounce?
    (c) Was the basis change favorable or unfavorable to the hedge?

7. Answers to question 6.

Date	Cash Price	Basis	Futures Price	Hedger's Transaction
Dec. 1				
Feb. 1				
(Gain/Loss)				

Date	Cash Price	Basis	Futures Price	Hedger's Transaction
Dec. 1	$1,700	$18	$1,718	Sell 7 Feb. Gold Futures Contracts
Feb. 1	$1,685	$23	$1,708	Buy 7 Feb. Gold Futures Contracts
(Loss)	$(1,700-1,685)$ *700 =-$10,500			($1,718-$1,708)*700 =$7,000 Now account for brokerage fees $7,000 − 7*$25= $6,825

- Final Price Received = (($1,685 * 700) + $6,825)/700 = $1,694.75/troy ounce.
- Unfavorable basis change.

Selected References

Anderson, Ronald W., and Jean-Pierre Danthine. 1983. "The time pattern of hedging and the volatility of futures prices." *The Review of Economic Studies*, 249–266.

Castelino, Mark G. 1992. "Hedge effectiveness: Basis risk and minimum-variance hedging." *Journal of Futures Markets*, 12(2): 187–201.

Danthine, Jean-Pierre. 1978. "Information, futures prices, and stabilizing speculation." *Journal of Economic Theory*, 17(1): 79–98.

Ederington, Louis H. 1979. "The hedging performance of the new futures markets." *The Journal of Finance*, 34(1): 157–170.

Feiger, George, and Bertrand Jacquillat. 1979. "Currency option bonds, puts and calls on spot exchange and the hedging of contingent foreign earnings." *The Journal of Finance*, 34(5): 1129–1139.

Gardner, Bruce L. 1989. "Rollover hedging and missing long-term futures markets." *American Journal of Agricultural Economics*, 71(2): 311–318.

Hartzmark, Michael L. 1988. "Is Risk Aversion a Theoretical Diversion?" *Review of Futures Markets*, 7: 1–26.

Heifner, Richard G. 1972. "Optimal hedging levels and hedging effectiveness in cattle feeding." *Agricultural Economics Research*, 24(2): 25–36.

Johnson, Leland L. 1960. "The theory of hedging and speculation in commodity futures." *The Review of Economic Studies*, 27(3): 139–151.

Kahl, Kandice H. 1983. "Determination of the recommended hedging ratio." *American Journal of Agricultural Economics*, 65(3): 603–605.

Lapan, Harvey, Giancarlo Moschini, and Steven D. Hanson. 1991. "Production, hedging, and speculative decisions with options and futures markets." *American Journal of Agricultural Economics*, 73(1): 66–74.

Markowitz, Harry M. 1968. *Portfolio selection: efficient diversification of investments.* Vol. 16, Yale university press.

McKinnon, Ronald I. 1967. "Futures markets, buffer stocks, and income stability for primary producers." *Journal of political economy*, 75(6): 844–861.

Miller, Stephen E. 1986. "Forward contracting versus hedging under price and yield uncertainty." *Journal of Agricultural and Applied Economics*, 18(2): 139–146.

Miller, Stephen E., and Kandice H. Kahl. 1987. "Forwarding Pricing when Yields are Uncertain." *Review of Futures Markets*, 6: 21–39.

Peck, Anne E., and Antoinette M. Nahmias. 1989. "Hedging Your Advice: Do Portfolio Models Explain Hedging?" *Food Research Institute Studies*, 21(2).

Rolfo, Jacques. 1980. "Optimal hedging under price and quantity uncertainty: The case of a cocoa producer." *Journal of Political Economy*, 88(1): 100–116.

Sakong, Yong, Dermot J. Hayes, and Arne Hallam. 1993. "Hedging production risk with options." *American Journal of Agricultural Economics*, 75(2): 408–415.

Stein, Jerome L. 1961. "The simultaneous determination of spot and futures prices." *The American Economic Review*, 51(5): 1012–1025.

Stoll, H. R., and R. E. Whaley. 1985. "Futures markets: their economic role." , ed. Anne Peck, Chapter The new options market. American Enterprise Institute.

Telser, Lester G. 1958. "Futures trading and the storage of cotton and wheat." *Journal of Political Economy*, 66(3): 233–255.

Wilson, William W. 1984. "Hedging effectiveness of US wheat futures markets." *Review of Futures Markets*, 3: 64–79.

Working, Holbrook. 1962. "New concepts concerning futures markets and prices." *The American Economic Review*, 52(3): 431–459.

8.

Options Markets

Recall that options on futures are financial derivatives that provide the holder with the right, but not the obligation, to buy or sell a futures contract at a predetermined fixed price (i.e., the "strike" price) on or before a specific date. They are similar to stock options and investors in the equities market can buy or sell stock options for almost any major stock (i.e., security). For instance, if an investor believed that Tesla Inc. (TSLA) was a good buy, rather than purchasing the stock outright, she could purchase a call option, which would give her the right to buy the stock at a certain price (i.e., the strike price). The call option would subsequently increase in value if there were an increase in the price of the underlying Tesla stock.

Options on futures are bought and sold on the same exchanges that trade the underlying futures contracts. Options provide an investor the opportunity to profit from changes in the price of the underlying futures contract without having to buy or sell the actual futures contract itself. The buyer of an option has the choice (or opportunity) to buy or sell a futures contract and the seller of an option provides the buyer with that opportunity. For example, the buyer of a "call" option purchases the right (by paying a "premium") to hold a long position in a futures contract. If the call option buyer chooses to exercise the option, they acquire the futures contract at a predetermined price (i.e., the strike price). Alternatively, the buyer of a "put" option purchases the right to a short futures position. The option has an expiry month that corresponds to the futures contract month of expiration and the various strike prices are set by the exchange. For example, both call and put options for a specific futures contract, say May 2025 natural gas, will have numerous strike prices, ranging below and above the current futures price of the May contract.

Options are a derivative security because their value depends on the underlying futures contract. Like futures contracts, options provide a form of price insurance for commercial traders engaged in hedging. At the same

---

Box 8.1 Military Aircraft Options

The C-17 is a huge cargo aircraft used extensively by the United States Air Force to deliver troops and cargo, for military peacekeeping and humanitarian missions. The C-17 aircraft was manufactured by Boeing, under contract with the U.S. Air Force. It is a very versatile aircraft and can takeoff with a payload of about 170,000 pounds and land on short air-fields if necessary. However, this plane is not cheap, with each costing approximately $370 million.

In an effort to save the U.S. taxpayers some money, the Air Force established a type of options contract with other users of C-17s. Under this arrangement, Boeing sold new C-17 planes to private air cargo companies (such as Federal Express), under the stipulation that the U.S. Air Force could use the private fleet of C-17s in times of emergency. In return for the "option" to access the aircraft in time of need, the Air Force provided the private buyers of the planes an initial fee plus annual payments. The Air Force reports that it saves several billions of dollars of taxpayers' money under this arrangement.

---

time, they provide speculators with an opportunity to profit from price movements in the underlying commodity or financial asset.

This chapter covers the basic concepts of options written on futures contracts. It focuses on the important relationship between options prices (i.e., the premium) and the underlying futures prices, and discusses factors that impact this relationship. The basics of the theory behind options on futures pricing are outlined in this chapter and some examples are provided to illustrate the speculative use of options on futures. Hedging with options on futures is covered in the following chapter.

Options on futures contracts have rapidly emerged as an important risk-management and trading tool. As explained in Chapter 1, options written on futures contracts received formal governmental approval for trading on organized exchanges in the United States in early 1987. However, commodity options have a very long history that goes back two centuries. Options (or privileges) were actively traded in the U.S. grain markets as far back as the 1860s and they continued to be traded until the 1930s. The U.S. Congress then chose to ban commodity options trading in 1936 for two main reasons. The first was that option (or privilege) trading was unregulated at the time and thus periodic trading abuses and defaults arose. Secondly, options were partially blamed for the excessive volatility and eventual collapse of commodity prices in the early 1930s. During the period in which they were banned in the United States, commodity options traded actively in London for such commodities as coffee, sugar, cocoa, copper, silver, and tin. During the ban on U.S. options trading, several firms specialized as intermediaries between their American customers and the London options markets.

What is an Option on Futures?

There are some important differences between futures and options contracts. First of all, for the buyer of an option, the risk involved in options trading is much different than that involved in futures trading. The holder of a futures contract has the obligation to either deliver, or accept delivery, of the underlying asset or financial instrument (or cash settled for nondeliverables). This obligation must either be "met" or "offset" by the owner of a futures contract. It is most often offset by the holder entering into an equal and opposite futures position, rather than through delivery or cash settlement.

In contrast, the owner of an option has the "right," but not an "obligation" to either buy or sell the underlying futures contract. For example, a buyer of a Treasury bond futures contract must either accept delivery or sell an offsetting futures contract before contract expiration. On the other hand, a buyer of a T-bond "call" option can either exercise her right and obtain a long position in T-bond futures, or sell her option at the prevailing market price (i.e., the premium). Alternatively, if the market has moved against her, she will choose not to exercise the option and simply let it expire worthless. The basic differences between futures and options contracts are outlined in Table 8.1.

As shown in Table 8.1, an options contract gives the buyer of the option considerable flexibility and limited risk relative to the buyer of a futures contract. Of course, the catch is that the option buyer has to pay an upfront premium to the option seller, so there is no free lunch. For the buyer of either a put or call option, there are no margin calls because the premium is the maximum amount they can lose no matter what happens to the underlying futures price and the premium is paid "upfront" at the time the option is purchased. In order for the options buyer to earn a profit, the futures price must be above (for a call option) or below (for a put option) the option's strike price by more than the amount of the premium paid.

However, if the futures price is not above the strike (for a call option) or not below the strike (for a put option) the buyer can still recover a portion of the premium through either exercising the option or selling it. The premium paid by the buyer is a "fixed" cost and the buyer might decide to either exercise the option or sell it, even if a "profit" is not assured. In

Table 8.1: Basic Differences Between Futures Contracts and Options on Futures

Alternative Positions	Trader's Rights	Trader's Obligations	Margin Required
Futures contract buyer		Accept commodity or financial asset at contract price	Yes
Futures contract seller		Deliver commodity or financial asset at contract price	Yes
Put option buyer	Sell futures contract at strike price		No
Put option seller		Buy futures contract at strike price	Yes
Call option buyer	Buy futures contract at strike price		No
Call option seller		Sell futures contract at strike price	Yes

Note: For nondeliverable futures contracts traders agree to offset their position at the cash price during the expiry period.

those cases where a portion of the "fixed" cost (i.e., the premium) can be recovered, the option buyer might well decide to cut his or her losses by either exercising the option or selling it. In contrast to the buyer's limited risk, the seller of an option must post margin calls because their potential losses are high. The risk taken on by the options seller is very similar to the risk exposure experienced by the holder of a futures contract.

To reiterate, an option is a contractual agreement to either purchase or sell a futures contract at a pre-established price, and within a specified time period. There are two types of options–puts and calls. A **call option** gives a buyer the right (but not the obligation) to purchase a futures contract at a specified "strike price" within a specified period of time (before the expiry date). A **put option** gives a buyer of the option the right (but not the obligation) to sell a futures contract at a specified price within a specified period of time. The seller (writer) of an option receives a premium, which is the amount paid by the buyer of the option in return for the right to control a futures contract. The premium is the price of the option, thus it fluctuates with the supply and demand for the option itself. The holder can exercise an option on a futures contract at any time during the life of the option (see

---

Box 8.2 American versus European Style Options

- European Style Options: can be exercised only at expiration.

- American Style Options: can be exercised at any time prior to expiration.

Calls and puts on futures contracts are classified as either "American" or "European" style options, depending on when they can be exercised. Compared to European options, American options give the buyer more flexibility because an American option can be exercised or offset at any time prior to expiry. In contrast, European options can only be offset or exercised during the expiry month. These terms do not necessarily indicate where the options are traded because American options are traded on European exchanges, and vice versa.

As examples, CME Group corn, lean hog, and gold options on futures are American style options. Most of the CME foreign exchange (FX) futures options are European style. At the same time, the CME trades both American and European style crude oil and natural gas options.

Box 8.2). The seller of a put (call) option is obligated to buy (sell) a futures contract at the strike price, if the buyer decides to exercise the option.

A few examples will help to illustrate these basic concepts. Consider Table 8.2, where representative futures options prices are reported for options written on corn and gold futures contracts. The top panel of Table 8.2 reports corn option prices. On the day in question, the purchaser of a call option in corn would have four different "strike" prices to choose from, ranging from $7.90 to $8.20 per bushel. The exchange determines the range of strike prices available for trading. Normally, the strike prices are set so that they are spaced evenly around the price of the underlying futures prices, with fixed price intervals separating each strike price. For example, the corn strike prices are 10 cents apart. If the underlying futures price moves considerably, then new strike prices will typically be added to the list of strike prices by the exchange because options traders will be interested in trading options at these new strike prices.

Referring to Table 8.2, if the option buyer chooses $8.10 as the appropriate strike price then she would pay 41.88¢/bushel for the right to purchase one December corn futures contract at a strike price of $8.10/bushel. The buyer may exercise this right any time before the month of December.[1] The

---

[1]Options will typically expire in the month prior to the futures delivery month.

Table 8.2: Examples of Futures Options

Strike Price	Premiums					
	Calls			Puts		
	October	December	March	October	December	March
Corn: Chicago Board of Trade, 5,000 Bushels (cents per bushel)						
790	25.63	50.38	68.63	20.13	44.88	62.13
800	21.00	46.00	64.25	25.50	50.50	67.75
810	16.88	**41.88**	60.13	31.38	56.38	73.63
820	13.63	38.25	56.25	38.13	62.75	79.63
Gold: COMEX, 100 Troy Ounces (dollars per troy ounce)						
	September	October	December	September	October	December
1650	17.40	36.10	65.80	0.30	18.70	46.10
1655	12.40	33.20	63.10	0.50	20.80	48.40
1660	7.40	30.40	60.50	1.50	**23.00**	50.80
1665	2.40	27.80	58.00	1.50	25.40	53.30

total premium the buyer pays to the seller of the option is $2,094 ($0.4188 per bushel × 5,000 bushels–the size of the contract) and this is paid up-front at the time the option is purchased. If the price of corn falls and the buyer chooses not to exercise the option then the buyer's total loss is limited to $2,094 (plus brokerage fees). However, if the price of corn rises and the buyer exercises her option, then she will acquire a "long" futures position at the option strike price of $8.10. At the same time, the exchange clearing-house will (randomly) assign a "short" futures position to a trader who has previously sold an identical "call" option with the same underlying futures contract and the same strike price. The clearinghouse assigns the short futures position to one of the option writers because for every buyer in the futures market there must be a seller. Recall that instead of exercising her option, the option buyer could also reverse her position by selling an option with the same strike price and delivery month.

Suppose that after the buyer has purchased the call option, the price of December corn futures increases to $8.60/bushel and she decides to exercise her option. Upon exercise, the exchange clearinghouse gives her a long position in December corn at $8.10 and; at the same time, assigns a call writer a corresponding short position in December corn at $8.10 (i.e., at the strike price). The long and short futures positions are marked to market (up to $8.60) by the clearinghouse and the original call writer (who now is short December corn) is assessed a margin call. The original call buyer can immediately liquidate her futures position for a (gross) return of $0.50/bushel (= $8.60 - $8.10) or; alternatively, hold onto the long futures position. Similarly, the original writer of a December call can directly liquidate his futures position (for a loss of $0.50/bushel) or, instead, hold onto the short futures position with the expectation that the upward price trend might reverse itself.

Turning to the gold example in Table 8.2, consider the buyer of a put option. If the purchaser chooses a strike price of $1,660 per ounce and an October expiry date, the premium paid in order to purchase the option from the seller is $23.00/oz., or $2,300 for one put option as the contract is for 100 ounces. The holder of this option has the right to acquire a short position in October gold futures at a price of $1,660. If the price of gold falls prior to the month of October and this option is exercised, then the holder obtains a short futures position from the exchange clearinghouse. He must then liquidate his futures position in order to capture the full revenue available to him at the time. Of course, if the premium increases in value, he could

---

Options on December corn futures, for instance, expire in the third week of November. For a calendar of CME expiry dates see http://www.cmegroup.com/tools-information/calendars/expiration-calendar/.

also sell a October gold put option and his return would equal the change in the value of the premium, minus brokerage fees.

Option Payoffs

A call options buyer's possible profit and loss combinations are shown graphically in Figure 8.1. For comparison purposes, Figure 8.1 also depicts a payoff line for a holder of a long futures position. For ease of exposition, the current futures price is assumed to be equal to the strike price. The options payoff line is depicted as the kinked line and the futures payoff line is the straight 45 degree line, with an arrow at each end of the line. Profits (losses) are shown on the vertical axis and the underlying futures price at time of contract expiry (or at time of exercise) is shown on the horizontal line. When either an option or futures contract is purchased, profits (losses) accruing to the holder largely depend on the extent to which the futures price moves in a favorable or unfavorable direction (assuming the option is not canceled by an offsetting trade in the options market). The expected profit from a long call position is:

$$E\left(\pi_L^C\right) = Max\left[-PR, (FP - SP - PR)\right] \tag{8.1}$$

where E is the expectation operator, PR is the option premium, FP is the underlying futures price, and SP is the strike price.

On the left-hand side of Figure 8.1, the options payoff line lies below the horizontal axis (denoted by 0 profit) by the amount of the premium. This

Figure 8.1: Long Futures vs. Call Options Payoff

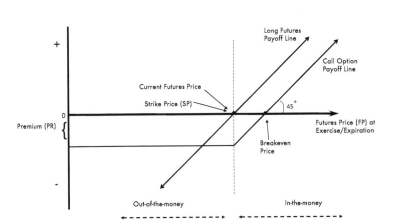

premium is the maximum loss to the holder of the option and is given by the vertical distance between the horizontal axis (shown as 0) and the flat portion of the kinked option payoff line. As the underlying futures price increases, we move to the right side of the graph and the option payoff line becomes kinked at the strike price. Additionally, the call option payoff line crosses the horizontal axis at the futures breakeven price. It is kinked at the strike price because once the futures price moves above the strike price, the option can be exercised for a monetary return. In other words, the option becomes "in-the-money." The option could be "in-the-money" but the return could still be less than the premium paid. However, once the futures price rises high enough, the monetary return exceeds the premium. This is the point referred to as the breakeven point. The breakeven futures price can be solved by setting expected profits in equation 8.4 to zero, or:

$$E\left(\pi_L^C\right) = (FP - SP - PR) = 0 \tag{8.2}$$

and therefore the breakeven futures price equals:

$$FP^B = SP + PR \tag{8.3}$$

In Figure 8.1 the futures payoff line is drawn for the holder of a long futures position. It is the 45° line crossing the horizontal axis at the current futures price, which is assumed to be equal to the strike price (in this example), in order to simplify the graph. Comparing the two payoff lines in Figure 8.1 helps illustrate the risk/reward characteristics of options versus futures. The futures payoff line shows large potential profits if the futures price rises above the current level, and large potential losses if the futures price falls. In contrast, the options payoff line shows large potential profits if the futures price rises above the current level, but limited losses if the futures price falls. Losses to the holder of the call option are limited to - PR. When the futures price rises, the call option payoff line is everywhere below the futures payoff line by the amount of the option premium. The maximum profit for a call option depends on the difference between the futures price and the strike price, minus the premium.

Now let's turn to Figure 8.2 where we depict the payoff line for the holder of a put option. For comparison purposes, Figure 8.2 also has a payoff line for a short futures position, and it is assumed that the current futures price equals the strike price. The expected profit for the holder of a long put position is:

$$E\left(\pi_L^P\right) = Max\left[-PR, (SP - FP - PR)\right] \tag{8.4}$$

where the variables are as defined above. Equation (8.4)–the payoff equation for the holder of a long put, is very similar to equation (8.1)–the payoff equation for the holder of a long call. In both cases, the maximum loss is the premium (i.e., -PR). The maximum profit for a call (put) depends on the difference between the futures (strike) price and the strike (futures) price, minus the premium.

Figure 8.2: Short Futures vs. Put Options Payoff

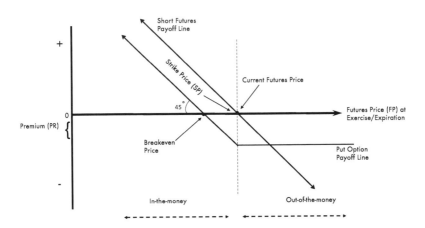

Again, the flat portion of the options payoff line (on the right-hand side of Figure 8.2) lies below the 0 horizontal line by the amount of the premium. If the futures price remains relatively high (i.e., stays to the right hand side of Figure 8.2) and is above the strike price, then -PR is the loss incurred by the put option holder. Once the underlying futures price falls to the level of the strike price, the option moves "in-the-money" and this is the point where the payoff line becomes kinked. For the put option, the breakeven price is found by setting expected profits equal to zero:

$$E\left(\pi_L^P\right) = (SP - FP - PR) = 0 \qquad (8.5)$$

and therefore the breakeven futures price equals:

$$FP^B = SP - PR \qquad (8.6)$$

Option payoff possibilities are perhaps best illustrated by some real-world examples. Turning to Figure 8.3, let us presume that a trader expects long-term interest rates to fall and to capitalize on this expectation, she buys a March Treasury Bond call option at a premium of 3-50 with a strike price equal to 150-00. The call option premium is 3-50/64ths, or $3,781 ($15.62 per 64th), and suppose the underlying March futures price is 149-01. In

Figure 8.3, the payoff line is kinked at the strike price of 150-00 and the breakeven futures price is 153-25 (= SP + PR). Note that the T-Bond futures price is quoted in 32nds and the options prices are quoted in 64ths.

The call option depicted in Figure 8.3 is "out-of-the-money" to the left of the strike price, where the payoff line is flat and where the FP<SP. The option is "at-the-money" where the SP=FP, and it is "in-the-money" to the right of the strike price, where the FP>SP. We can say that this option is out-of-the-money because the underlying FP = 149-01, is less than the strike price of 150-00.

Figure 8.3: T-Bond Call Option Example

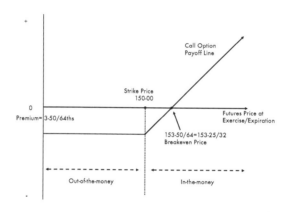

Figure 8.4: Japanese Yen Put Option Example

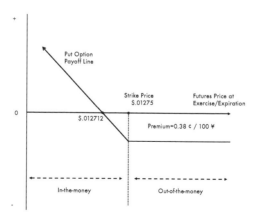

Box 8.3 Off-Exchange Agricultural Trade Options

In 1984 the U.S. government permitted the trading of commodity options, as long as trading was conducted on organized exchanges. In 2000, the Commodity Futures Trading Commission (CFTC) went one step further and lifted a long-standing government ban on the trading of off-exchange agricultural options, which had been in place since 1936. The new rules were introduced following a change in U.S. farm policy that exposed farmers to greater price risk. The 1996 U.S. farm bill, known colloquially as the Freedom to Farm Act placed more reliance on the free market. The new farm legislation reduced the use of government programs that were designed to dampen fluctuating commodity prices. The Freedom to Farm Act separated government payments from production and prices, and eliminated annual production controls for the major crops. As a result of their increased exposure to the market, farmers have a greater need for risk management instruments.

The off-exchange agricultural options are called "trade options." The CFTC limits trade in these options to commercial producers or users of the commodity, to avoid off-exchange speculative trading in commodity options. The CFTC decided to allow off-exchange trading in order to increase the supply of option contracts available to farmers. Off-exchange options are non-standardized and this may allow farmers to hedge more precisely, as the off-exchange contracts can be tailored to individual situations. They are essentially "over-the-counter" derivatives.

In Figure 8.4, the payoff chart is drawn for a trader who purchases a Japanese Yen put option, with the expectation that the U.S. dollar is going to strengthen in value, thus decreasing the $/¥ exchange rate. The trader therefore buys a September put option at 0.38¢/100¥ with a strike price equal to $.01275/¥. The premium is thus equivalent to $475 (= ($.000038/¥) *12.5million ¥). In order to draw the payoff chart, let us assume that the underlying March futures price is $.01271/¥ , which means that the option is currently in-the-money. The payoff line in Figure 8.4 is kinked at the strike price and it crosses the horizontal axis at the breakeven futures price of $.012712 (= SP-PR). Notice that yen futures are quoted in $/¥ while options prices are quoted in ¢/100¥.

Option Pricing Structure

The buyer of an option is exposed to much less price risk than the seller (writer) of the option, so their risks are asymmetrical. The buyer's risk is limited to the premium paid at the time of purchase, whereas the seller's downside risk is proportional to the potential price movement of the underlying futures contract. This is unlike futures trading where the buyer's and seller's risks are symmetrical.

Generally speaking, an option's premium consists of two components, intrinsic value and time value:

$$Intrinsic\ Value + Time\ Value = Premium \qquad (8.7)$$

The intrinsic value refers to the amount by which an option is currently in-the-money. An option is in-the-money if there is some revenue which can be immediately realized by exercising the option. This revenue is derived from a gap between the option strike price and the futures contract price. Theoretically, a premium should never be less than the intrinsic value. For a call option, the intrinsic value (per unit) is the amount that the futures price is currently above the strike price. The option buyer can acquire the futures contract at the lower strike price (through exercising the option) and then immediately turn around and sell the futures contract at the higher futures price. Alternatively, for a put option, the intrinsic value is equal to the amount by which the futures price is below the strike price. If an option is out-of-the-money it has no intrinsic value and its premium consists solely of time value.

Essentially, "in-the-money" means the same thing as intrinsic value. If an option has intrinsic value, then it is worth exercising. The relationship between the strike price and underlying futures price determines whether or not an option is "in-the-money." This is shown in Table 8.3.

Time value represents the amount of money buyers are willing to pay for an option with the expectation that the underlying futures price will change favorably to cause the option to increase in value. Of course, time value also reflects the return that sellers are willing to accept for writing an option. Therefore, time value is simply the market's assessment of that part

Table 8.3: In and Out of the Money

Term	Call Option	Put Option
In-the-money (has intrinsic value)	Futures >Strike	Futures <Strike
At-the-money	Futures =Strike	Futures =Strike
Out-of-the-money (no intrinsic value)	Futures <Strike	Futures >Strike

of the option's value based on the possibility that its intrinsic value may increase in the future.

Given the general definition above, it follows that time value (T) may be determined by subtracting intrinsic value (I) from the total market price of the option (i.e., its premium, P). Thus, $T = P - I$, which means that the time value is the amount by which an option's premium exceeds its intrinsic value. Options are sometimes referred to as a decaying asset because the time value decreases with time, becoming zero when the option expires.

For example, the possibility of a July soybean futures contract increasing by $1.00/bu. in the six month January to June period certainly exists because weather events alone that time of year could send soybean prices soaring. However, the possibility of the same contract increasing $1.00/bu. a few days prior to the expiry of the contract is very unlikely because there is little time for big surprises in the market just before expiry. A call option buyer might be willing to pay a $0.30/bu. premium in January for an out-of-the-money option with a strike price $1.00 higher than the January price of the June futures contract, since there is a five or six month period during which the option could move into the money. Likewise, the writer of that out-of-the-money option might be willing to accept $0.30/bu. as a premium. However, with a few days left until expiry, the buyer would not be willing to pay such a high premium, nor would the option writer demand it for an option so far out-of-the-money. This concept of the decaying value of an option is shown in Figure 8.5. Basically, this figure illustrates the idea that, *ceteris paribus*, the more time an option has remaining until expiry, the larger is its premium.

Figure 8.5: Decaying Value of an Option

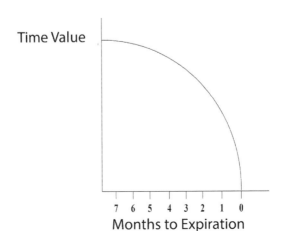

Months to Expiration

Table 8.4: Options Premium: Maximum and Minimum Price

	Call	Put
Maximum Price	Futures Price	Strike Price
Minimum Price	Max [0, (Futures Price - Strike Price)]	Max [0, (Strike Price - Futures Price)]

The theoretical boundary prices for call and put options are shown in Table 8.4. For a call option, the maximum premium is the futures price, because even if the strike price was zero, no rational buyer of an option would pay more than the futures price. At the same time, the minimum price is the current intrinsic value. Alternatively, for a put option, the maximum price is the strike price. It would be irrational to pay more than the strike price for a put option, because this is the maximum intrinsic value even in the unlikely event that the futures price went to zero. Of course, the minimum premium for a put option is its current intrinsic value.

The information in Table 8.4 is shown graphically in Figure 8.6 and 8.7. Using crude oil futures options as an example, Figures 8.6 and 8.7 display the (theoretical) possible range of option premiums for a call and put option, respectively. Suppose that for both the call and put option the strike price is $99.50 per barrel. In both Figures, the shaded areas give the range of possible option prices. The most likely options prices are shown along the price paths A and B in both figures. In Figure 8.6, the maximum value of a call option is the futures price itself and so the left-hand side of the shaded area is a 45° line that rises with the futures price. Alternatively, the minimum price is the intrinsic value, which is either 0 or the futures price minus the strike price, in the case of the call. This means the bottom portion of the price border follows the 0 horizontal axis until the futures price hits the strike price (moving to the right). The bottom portion of the border becomes kinked at the point where the futures price equals the strike price and then the option price border rises along the lower 45° line as long as the futures price continues to increase above the strike price.

The theoretical maximum price that a call buyer would pay for the crude oil option depicted in Figure 8.6 is an amount equal to the futures price. Suppose the futures price was $75 per barrel. In this case, the maximum revenue from exercising that option is $75 per barrel for the trader who buys a call option. So, even if the strike price were 0 the buyer would never pay more than $75 for the premium, as long as the futures price was no greater than $75. If the futures price rises to $100, then the maximum price paid would rise to $100. In a competitive options market, the actual premiums paid would be much less than the theoretical maximum and therefore the

Figure 8.6: Call Option: Minimum & Maximum Prices

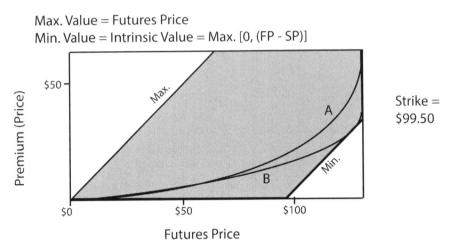

Max. Value = Futures Price
Min. Value = Intrinsic Value = Max. [0, (FP - SP)]

Strike = $99.50

Futures Price

Note: Either price path A or B depends on volatility & time to expiry

most likely premiums are shown along the curved lines A and B. If volatility decreases, then the price path might fall from line A to line B. In other words, premiums would fall, *ceteris paribus*. As time to expiry declines, the premium also falls (moving from line A to line B) because of the declining time value.

Figure 8.7: Put Option: Minimum & Maximum Prices

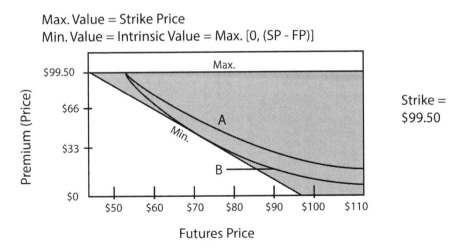

Max. Value = Strike Price
Min. Value = Intrinsic Value = Max. [0, (SP - FP)]

Strike = $99.50

Futures Price

Note: Either price path A or B depends on volatility & time to expiry

Figure 8.7 depicts the range of theoretical prices for a put option and suppose the crude oil put also has a strike price of $99.50 per barrel. For a put, the maximum premium is equal to the futures price, so the top portion of the theoretical price border is a horizontal line at $99.50.

No rational trader would pay more than $99.50 for the put option in this example, because $99.50 is the maximum revenue that could be earned if the option is exercised, even if the futures price falls to zero. The minimum price is the intrinsic value, which is shown by the left-hand 45° line as the price border. If volatility increases, then the put option price would rise for a given futures price and the price path would shift from the curved line B to that labeled as A in Figure 8.7.

Market Pricing of Options

To gain a basic understanding of option pricing, it is useful to look at some market-generated data on option premiums to help illustrate the concepts discussed so far in this chapter. Refer to Table 8.5. Understanding the option premium data in Table 8.5 is facilitated by first computing the intrinsic value, if any, for each option. To review, call options will have intrinsic value only if the current futures price is above the strike price for that option, whereas put options will have intrinsic value only if the strike price is above the current futures price. The time value of each option may then be computed by subtracting the intrinsic value from the option premium. Those options that are in-the-money (IM) are shaded in Table 8.5.

Table 8.5: Market Determined Options Premiums: A Cotton Example

S.P.	Cotton Options: 50,000 lbs (¢/lb)					
	Calls			Puts		
	Mar	May	July	Mar	May	July
73	5.47	6.05	8.06	1.54	2.12	3.34
74	4.81	5.42	7.46	1.88	2.49	3.75
75	4.20	4.84	6.90	2.26	2.90	4.18
76	3.57	4.30	6.36	2.63	3.36	4.64
77	3.09	3.80	5.85	3.15	3.86	5.00
78	2.68	3.35	5.38	3.73	4.41	5.65

Underlying Futures: Mar 75.09, May 76.41, July 77.09

In Table 8.5, the 76¢ call option on the July cotton futures contract is trading at 6.36¢ per pound. This option has intrinsic value because the strike price of 76¢ is below the current July futures price of 77.09¢. The underlying futures prices are shown at the bottom of Table 8.5. The intrinsic value is therefore equal to 1.09¢ per pound (=77.09¢- 76¢). With a premium of 6.36¢ per pound and intrinsic value of 1.09¢ per pound, it follows from equation (8.7) that the time value on that option must be 5.27¢ per pound. Alternatively, the March call option with the 76¢ strike price has no intrinsic value because the strike price of 76¢ exceeds the current March futures price of 75.09¢. The entire 3.57¢ premium for this option is therefore time value.

The May put option in Table 8.5 with a 78¢ strike price has substantial intrinsic value since it gives the buyer the right to sell a futures contract at 78¢ that can be immediately purchased at the current futures market price of 76.41¢. With a premium of 4.41¢ and intrinsic value of 1.59¢ (= 78¢ - 76.41¢), the time value is 2.82¢ for this option. In contrast, the 75¢ strike on the March put option has no intrinsic value, rather its entire 2.26¢ premium is time value. This option has a total premium of $1,130 (=2.26¢× 50,000 lbs.).

Notice that for the March call in Table 8.5, the premium for the 73¢ strike is 5.47¢ per pound. For the 78¢ strike, the premium is much lower–only 2.68¢ per pound. Actually, for the March call, the option premiums (in ¢ per pound) fall continuously from the 73¢ strike to the 78¢ strike (from 5.47¢ down to 2.68¢). Why do these premiums decline as we move from the lower to the higher strike prices? The answer is that the premiums fall largely due to the change in intrinsic value as the strike prices increase from 73¢ to 78¢. For call options, the intrinsic value declines with higher strike prices and therefore the premiums decline.

As another example, observe that for the 77¢ calls, the premiums rise as we move along the row from March to July options. The premiums are 3.09¢, 3.80¢ and 5.85¢ for the March, May, and July calls with a 77¢ strike, re-spectively. What explains this phenomena of rising premiums as the expiry month becomes more distant? For the 77¢ strike price, the March premium is 3.09¢ and the July premium is almost double at 5.85¢. This increase in premiums for the same strike price but for more distant maturity months is largely due to the role of time value.

Option Traders

An option's premium will respond to changes in a number of underlying factors. The most important factors include time to maturity, volatility of the underlying futures price, and the price of the underlying futures con-tract. At the most basic level, the relationship between the futures price and the option premium is shown in Table 8.6. A call option's premium is positively related to the price of the underlying futures contract. That is, if the futures price goes up, the call option's premium also goes up. If the futures price falls, then generally the call option's premium falls. Alterna-tively, a put option's premium is inversely related to the price of the un-

Table 8.6: Relationship Between Futures Price and Options Premium

	Underlying Futures Prices	
	Declines	Increases
Call Option Premium	Declines	Increases
Put Option Premium	Increases	Declines

derlying futures contract. The basic objective of the option trader is to sell the option for a higher premium than the premium paid, or alternatively, to profit from exercising the option. This underscores the importance of understanding how changes in futures prices affect the call and put option premiums.

Put Option Buyer

As a speculator, a put option buyer expects futures price will fall. Alternatively, as a hedger, the put option buyer wants to purchase some protection from the consequences of the futures price falling below the strike price. The bearish expectation of falling prices is shown in the top right hand panel of Table 8.7. As indicated earlier, a put option premium is composed of only time value if the futures price is equal to or above the strike price. A put option buyer can therefore only realize a net gain if the intrinsic value rises by more than the sum of any decline in time value plus the opportunity cost of the premium and brokerage charges. There is an absolute upper limit on the net gain that a put option buyer may realize. The worst outcome for a put option buyer is that the option has no intrinsic value near the end of trading and the option is allowed to expire with no remaining value. Therefore, a put option buyer knows at the time of purchase that the maximum possible loss is composed of the premium paid for the option plus brokerage fees. This relationship is depicted in Figure 8.8. When exercising a put option, a buyer profits by the amount the option is "in-the-money," less the premium paid and brokerage fees.

Table 8.7: Option Traders' Positions and Their Price Expectations

	Call Option	Put Option
Buyer (holder)	Bullish	Bearish
Seller (writer)	Neutral to slightly bearish	Neutral to slightly bullish

Figure 8.8: Risk-Reward Structure of a Put Option

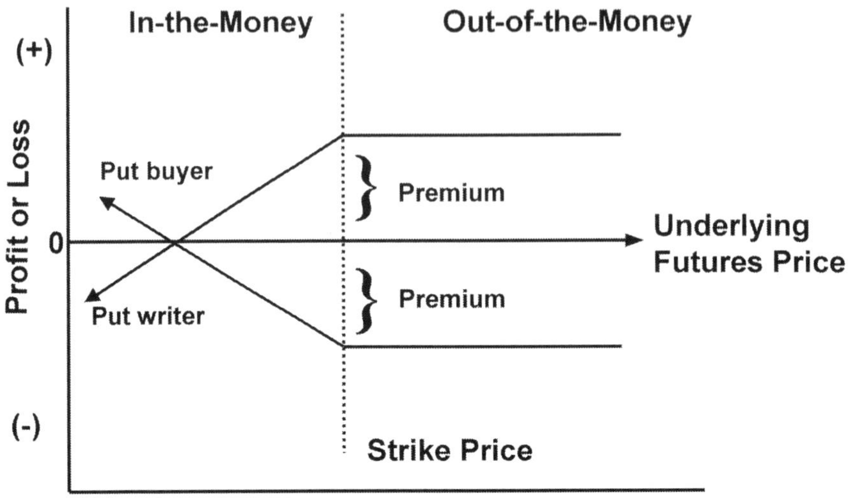

Put Option Seller

A put option seller is neutral to slightly bullish on prices (see Table 8.7). The seller receives the full premium immediately when the option is sold, less brokerage charges. The total amount of a premium is the asset's "price," normally quoted in dollars per unit, times the number of units specified in a futures contract. Also, at the time a position is opened by a put option seller, the seller must deposit in a margin account the amount of the premium plus a sum of money similar to the margin that buyers and sellers of futures contracts must maintain. If the premium on a put option rises, option sellers must, in general, deposit additional margin money equal to this adverse change in the value of the option position. The clearinghouse sets these rules. If the premium declines after a put option seller opens a position, the seller will be allowed to withdraw from the margin account an amount generally equal to the decline in the premium.

A put option seller has the best possible outcome when an option is allowed to expire with no value to the option buyer. In this case, sellers keep the entire premium, less brokerage costs. This shown on the right-hand side of Figure 8.8, where the put option is out-of-the-money. The maximum gain for a put option seller is limited to the net amount received in total premium at the time of sale. The worst possible outcome for a put option seller occurs when there has been a very large drop in the futures price and the option buyer closes the position by either selling the option in a offsetting transaction or by exercising the option. In the latter case, a put option seller must bear the full cost of acquiring a long futures position at the strike price and subsequently offsetting it at a lower price. The maximum loss for a put option seller is limited to the total value of the associated futures contract (which requires the futures price going to zero). Of course, the total net gain or loss is also a function of interest earnings from holding the premium, minus the margin deposit and brokerage fees during the period an option position is open.

Call Option Buyer

Figure 8.9 depicts the risk/reward structure for a call option. A call option buyer knows at the time of purchase that the limit to her possible loss with an option is composed of the premium paid for the option plus brokerage fees. As a speculator, a call option buyer expects that the futures price will rise or, alternatively, as a hedger, she wishes to buy some protection from the consequences of the futures price rising above the strike price. As indicated earlier, the premium on a call is composed of only time value if the futures price is equal to or below the strike price. If speculating, a call option buyer realizes a net gain if the intrinsic value rises by more than the sum of any decline in time value. The worst outcome for a speculative call option buyer occurs if the option has no intrinsic value at the end of trading and is allowed to expire. This is shown on the left-hand side of Figure 8.9, where the call option is out-of-the-money.

Call Option Seller

A call option seller knows when opening a position that she will be paid the full amount of the premium immediately, less brokerage fees for the option sale. Also, at the time a position is opened, a call option seller must make a deposit in a margin account. If the premium on a call option rises, option sellers must, in general, deposit additional margin equal to this adverse change in the value of the option position. If the premium declines after a call option seller opens a position, the seller will be allowed to withdraw from the margin account an amount generally equal to the decline in premium.

Just as described above for puts, call option sellers have the best possible outcome when an option is allowed to expire with no value to buyers; sellers keep all the premium, less brokerage costs. The maximum gain for a call option seller is limited to the net amount received in total premium at

Figure 8.9: Risk-Reward Structure of a Call Option

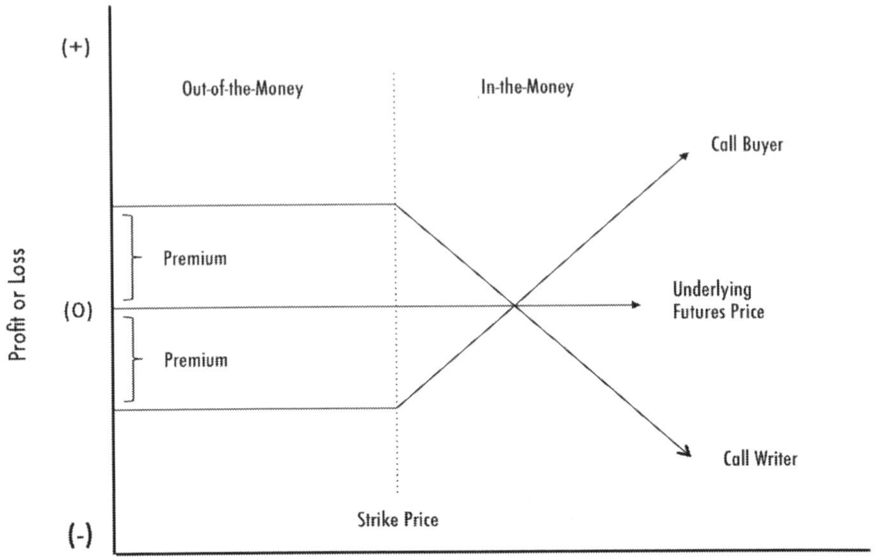

the time of initial sale. The worst possible outcome for a call option seller occurs when there has been a very large rise in the futures price and the option buyer makes an offsetting transaction or exercises the option. The maximum loss of a call option seller is unlimited theoretically. As long as futures prices rise, every dollar increase in total contract value represents a dollar lost to call option sellers. These relationships are depicted by the kinked arrows in Figure 8.9.

The above discussion surrounding Figures 8.8 and 8.9 implicitly assumed that options were held until the date of expiry. This simplifies the presentation. It is also possible to either offset or exercise an American option before the date of expiry (see Box 8.2). The results of this alternative trading strategy do not materially differ from those presented in Figures 8.8 and 8.9. For instance, if the intrinsic value increases to the point where it is profitable to exercise, the buyer of an option can choose to exercise the option at any time before expiry. Alternatively, he could sell the option for a higher premium than he initially paid. Traders usually take the second approach because selling an option enables both intrinsic and time value to be captured, exercising an option captures only its intrinsic value.

Speculation with Options on Futures

There are pros and cons associated with speculative trading in options, as compared to futures. The pros include:

(a) the limited risk associated with buying an option;
(b) the absence of margin calls when buying an option; and
(c) a greater number of investment opportunities and a higher degree of flexibility provided by options.

As a result, options are an attractive investment alternative to most traders and they provide risk/reward opportunities not available with futures. For example, options allow an investor to enter into a trade with an expected positive profit even if his price expectations are neither bullish nor bearish but "neutral" instead. Many investors also spread options and/or combine futures and options positions. All of these advantages are not costless, however, since those who sell options must be paid for the risk they incur and therefore they collect the option's premium. This is the downside of speculating with options rather than futures. There is nothing equivalent to the upfront premium when speculating with futures contracts.

Putting some numbers on payoff graphs helps to understand the impact of a futures price change on both the buyer and seller of an option. For illustrative purposes, consider both a call and a put option on July ICE world sugar futures with premiums (prices) prevailing during the month of March shown in Table 8.8.

Table 8.8: Illustrative Sugar Options Prices: Contract Size 112,000 lbs

	Premium	Strike Price
July Call	$0.0304/lb.	$0.175/lb.
July Put	$0.0039/lb.	$0.175/lb.

Note: Assume that the underlying July futures contract is trading at $0.1970/lb.

Using the prices in Table 8.8, the potential profits/losses of going long versus going short in either a put or call are graphed in Figure 8.10 against changes in the underlying sugar futures contract price. For simplicity, all brokerage fees are ignored in this example. The shape of the profit/loss lines for calls are mirror images of those for puts. The northwest panel (Panel a) of Figure 8.10 displays the potential profit for the buyer (at the time of expiration) of a call option. This can be represented by:

$$\pi_L^C = FP - SP - PR = intrinsic\ value - premium\ paid \qquad (8.8)$$

where FP is the futures price, SP is the strike price and PR is the premium. If the option is "out-of-the-money" then the payoff is negative and equals π_L^C = -PR. Otherwise as the option moves into the money, π_L^C = FP - SP -

PR. Going long in the July sugar call option will be profitable for a trader as long as the futures price is above the breakeven amount of $0.2054 (= $0.175 + $0.0304) at the time the option expires. The potential profit is theoretically unlimited as futures prices could increase dramatically, even though a huge price change has a very low probability.

Figure 8.10: Options Payoff at Expiration

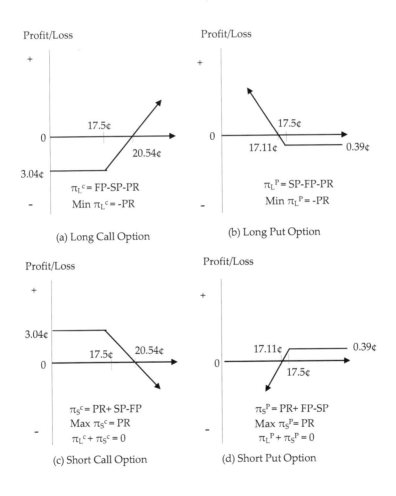

(a) Long Call Option

$\pi_L^c = FP-SP-PR$
Min $\pi_L^c = -PR$

(b) Long Put Option

$\pi_L^P = SP-FP-PR$
Min $\pi_L^P = -PR$

(c) Short Call Option

$\pi_S^c = PR+ SP-FP$
Max $\pi_S^c = PR$
$\pi_L^c + \pi_S^c = 0$

(d) Short Put Option

$\pi_S^P = PR+ FP-SP$
Max $\pi_S^P = PR$
$\pi_L^P + \pi_S^P = 0$

In Panel c of Figure 8.10, the profit/loss opportunities for a short seller of a July sugar call option are depicted. The maximum profit available to the seller is the premium, which is $0.0304. This represents a total of $3,404.80 because the sugar futures contract calls for delivery of 112,000 lbs. This profit potential begins to erode very quickly if futures prices rise above the strike price of $0.175, the point at which it becomes worthwhile for the buyer of the call option to exercise her right to obtain a long futures position. The expected profit for the holder of a short call position is given by:

$$\pi_S^C = PR + SP - FP = premium\ receieved - intrinsic\ value \qquad (8.9)$$

for FP ≥ SP - PR, and π_S^C = PR, otherwise.

This becomes a large negative number if at expiry FP > (SP + PR) by a large margin. Recall that PR and SP are both constant after the option is sold, so the path of FP is all important.

Now consider the expected profits for a long and short put option on world sugar, shown in Table 8.8. First, Panel b of Figure 8.10 represents the payoff situation for a long put position. An investor would purchase a put if she expected futures prices to fall. In the example shown here, the premium paid is $0.0039/lb., or $436.80 for an option on a 112,000 lb. sugar contract. This premium is relatively low because the underlying July futures price was $0.1970/lb. at the time of the option purchase. The seller of the option is willing to accept a small premium because he believes that there is only a small probability that the price of sugar will fall from $0.1970 to $0.1750 (or lower), between March and July. As long as the futures price remains above $0.175 it will not be worthwhile for the long position to be exercised so an option holder would simply let the option expire. The put buyer recovers her premium and begins to reap a profit if the futures price is less than $0.1711 (= 17.5¢ - 0.39¢) when the option expires. The expected profit for the long put option position is given by the following equation.

$$\pi_L^P = SP - FP - PR = intrinsic\ value - premium\ paid \qquad (8.10)$$

for FP ≤ SP - PR, and π_L^P = -PR, otherwise. This becomes a large positive number if SP > (FP - PR) by a large amount.

Finally, Panel d shows the profit/loss opportunity for a short put option. In this case, the maximum profit is $436.80 ($0.0039/lb × 112,000 lbs). At the same time, the holder of the short put is exposed to a large potential loss if sugar futures prices fall below $0.1711 lb. The expected profit equation for the short call holder is:

$$\pi_S^P = PR + FP - SP = premium\ receieved - intrinsic\ value \qquad (8.11)$$

for FP $\leq$ SP - PR, and π_S^P = PR, otherwise, which is positive, if FP > (SP - PR).

Speculative Trading Strategies

There are a large number of potential option strategies available to speculators. Many of them are quite complex and offer varied risk/return opportunities. The more basic strategies will be discussed here, concentrating on strategies based on price expectations, with some limited discussion of price volatility factors. These strategies focus on expectations concerning the underlying futures price at expiration, rather than on more complex factors.

Basic Call Option Strategies

If a speculator has strong bullish price expectations, a straightforward strategy is to purchase a call option. The more bullish the expectation, the better it is to purchase an option which is far out-of-the-money. This provides tremendous leverage in an up market, with relatively little downside risk because the premium paid is so low. Once a call option is purchased, the holder may choose (a) to exercise it and obtain a long futures position, (b) offset the position by selling the option, or (c) allow the option to expire.

If a speculator has strong price expectations that range from neutral to bearish, a reasonable strategy is to sell a call option. In-the-money call options provide maximum possible returns for the short trader who is very bearish. For a trader who has neutral to slightly bearish expectations it is generally advised that she sell out-of-the-money options with a relatively high strike price.

Basic Put Option Strategies

If a speculator is very bearish towards the market, a reasonable thing to do is purchase a put option. The more bearish the expectation, the better it is to purchase an option far out-of-the-money. This strategy gives a speculator maximum leverage.

Alternatively, a short put is the correct trade for a speculator who has strong neutral to bullish price expectations. If the trader's expectations are very bullish, maximum profit is obtained by selling a put with a strike price that is far in-the-money. Conversely, for a neutral to weakly bullish expectation the best approach is to sell a put with a strike price that is far out-of-the-money. A mildly bullish trader may sell a put which is at-the-money.

Basics of Spread Trading

The goal of spreading options, just as with futures spreads, is to profit from relative price movements of the two contracts. One of the simplest spreading strategies involves choosing two call options with the same expiry month but different strike prices and going long in one and simultaneously short in the other. Or alternatively, going long in a put and short in a put at the same time. These type of spreads are often referred to as vertical spreads.

Figure 8.11: Vertical Bull Spread Payoff at Expiration

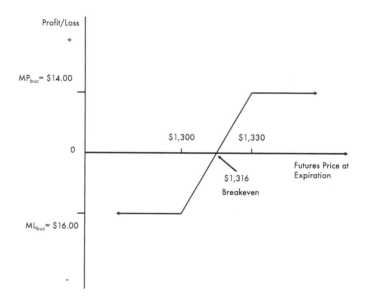

Consider a vertical bull spread for the October gold call options reported in Table 8.9. The trader entering this spread expects prices to rise somewhat. The spread, illustrated in Figure 8.11, might involve buying the $1,300 strike at a premium of $49.20/oz ($4,920 in total for 100 oz.) and simultaneously selling the $1,330 strike at a premium of $33.20/oz (or $3,320 in total). The long call premium (PL) is higher than the short call premium (PS) and the difference (ML_{buc}) is the maximum loss that can be incurred from the spread; in this example it is $16.00/oz. (or $1,600 in total). The maximum profit (MP_{buc}) equals the difference between the strike prices, $SP_h - SP_l$, less the maximum loss ML_{buc}. Thus, $MP_{buc} = SP_h - SP_l - ML_{buc} = \$1,330 - \$1,300 - \$16.00 = \$14.00$.

The break-even point for this spread is equal to $SP_l + ML_{buc}$, which is

Table 8.9: Gold Futures Options Premiums (100 Troy Ounces, $ Per Troy Ounce)

Underlying Future Prices; Sept $1,311.60, Oct $1,311.30, Dec $1,310.00

Strike Price	Calls			Puts		
	September	October	December	September	October	December
1280	49.4	61.4	79.9	18.3	30.4	48.5
1290	42.4	54.9	74	21.2	33.8	52.2
1300	36	49.2	68.2	24.8	37.6	56.2
1310	30.1	43.2	62.8	28.9	42.1	60.7
1320	24.7	38	57.3	33.6	46.7	65.3
1330	20.1	33.2	52.2	38.9	52.2	70.4

Figure 8.12: Vertical Bear Spread Payoff at Expiration

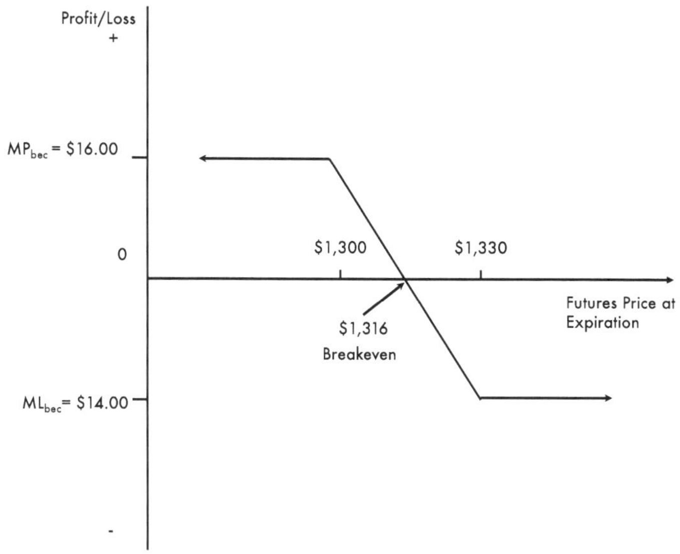

$1,300 + $16.00 = $1,316.00. By accepting a limit on the profit side, a spread trader gains a limit on the loss side of the spread.

A bull vertical spread involves buying an option with a relatively low strike price and selling an option with a relatively high strike price. Conversely, a bear vertical spread entails selling an option with a relatively low strike price and buying an option with a relatively high strike price. The options trader is bearish in this case. The payoff is exactly opposite that of the bull spread discussed in the previous paragraph. The maximum profit, MP_{bec}, is equal to the net premium received, which is $PL - PS$. In the example of October gold options discussed above, this equals $16.00 per ounce. The maximum loss, ML_{bec} is equal to the difference between the strike prices, less the net premium received, which equals $14.00/oz. This payoff diagram is depicted in Figure 8.12. The break-even point is equal to $SP_l + MP_{bec}$, which is $1,316.00.

A vertical call bull spread is more common than a vertical put bull spread, however both spreads work much the same way. Both profits and losses are limited. For a bull put spread the maximum loss, ML_{bup}, is equal to the difference in the strike prices, less the net premium received. The maximum profit, ML_{bup}, is equal to the net premium received. The break-even point is equal to $SP_h - MP_{bup}$.

An opposite strategy involves trading a bear put spread, which means buying a put with a relatively high price and selling a low priced put. The maximum loss is the net premium paid, and the maximum profit is equal to the difference in the strike prices less the maximum loss. The break-even price is equal to $SP_h - ML_{bep}$.

Horizontal Spread: S&P 500 Index Options

An alternative trading strategy used by some speculators in options markets is spreading positions in two contracts with different delivery dates, called a horizontal spread. In a spread between options contracts expiring at two different times, two separate markets are involved, so two sets of supply and demand factors are relevant to the results. The key to such a trade, therefore, is to understand the economic relationship between the two markets.

An example of a horizontal option spread involves the E-mini S&P 500 options contracts traded on the CME. The goal of the trade is to take advantage of the different rates at which the time value of the two options decreases. Selling an at-the-money option that has at least a month before it expires, and buying another option with the same strike price but with a few additional months before expiry establishes the spread. The options can be either calls or puts, but either two puts or two calls must be used together to create this particular spread.

For example, suppose it is mid March and a speculator examines the June and September at-the-money calls. If the S&P 500 index is around 4280, options with a strike price of 4280 would be approximately at-the-money. Suppose that the June 4280 call is currently trading at 34.00 points (or $1,700) at $50 per 1 index point. The speculator would sell the June call and, at the same time, purchase the September 4280 call. Assume that the September call is trading at 148.00 points (or $7,400) when it is purchased. The opening spread is therefore 148.00 - 34.00 = 114.00 points, or $5,700.

Two months later, suppose that the spot market for the S&P 500 index is unchanged at around 4280. The speculator sees that the June 4280 call option still has no intrinsic value and that its time value is decreasing rapidly as its expiration dates approaches. With a few days before the June option expires, the June 4280 call is trading at 10.00 points (or $500). The September 4280 call has no intrinsic value either, but it still has three months before it expires so its time value of 80.00 points ($4,000) exceeds that of the June call. As a result, the speculator closes the spread by making offsetting trades: a June 4280 call is purchased and a September 4280 call is sold. The closing spread is 80.00 - 10.00 = 70.00 points, or $3,500. The speculator has benefited by the change in the spread: 114.00 - 70.00 = 44.00 × $50 (the value of each point in the E Mini S&P 500 index) equals a profit (before brokerage fees) of $2,200 per spread (one contract of each option). The cost to open this spread is the financing cost of the difference in premium paid for the September option ($7,400 per contract) and premium received from selling the June option ($1,700), or $5,700 per spread.

Option Straddles

Option straddles are similar to option spreads, but are traded for different reasons. Whereas spreads use either two calls or two puts (one long and one short), straddles combine one put and one call (both long or both short) for the same underlying futures contract. Unlike spreads, profits from straddles are earned from changes in absolute prices, not relative prices. As a result, straddles combine some aspects of basic option strategies and spread trading. This is illustrated in the following example.

An options speculator who expects the price of cattle to change, but who is not confident about the direction of the change in absolute prices in the short-run may choose to trade cattle using an option straddle. One strategy is to create a long straddle by simultaneously buying one put and one call, both at-the-money and with the same expiry date. Suppose that the underlying cattle futures contract is currently selling for $125 per hundredweight, and both options purchased have a $125 strike price. As shown in the top half of Figure 8.13, the net effect of buying a call and a put is a maximum loss equal to the sum of the two premiums paid (assumed to be $2 per hundredweight for each option in this example). The maximum loss is incurred if the underlying futures price does not change during the period the straddle is held. However, if the price of cattle futures either rises or falls one of the options will be in-the-money. If the price rises or falls by $4 per hundredweight (the total premiums paid), the profits on the option in-the money will cover the premiums on both options. Large price changes will produce profits net of premium costs.

As shown in Figure 8.13, the long straddle (panel a) is a limited-risk strategy while a short straddle (panel b) is a very risky trade. A short straddle on the cattle market in the previous example generates outcomes which are opposite to those of a long straddle. The bottom half of Figure 8.13 indicates that a speculator would profit from this short straddle only if the underlying price of cattle does not change by more than $4 per hundredweight (cwt). Also, $4 per hundredweight is the maximum profit available, while potential losses are virtually unlimited. In general, the limited risk of long straddles make them more popular than short straddles, but traders planning to hold positions only a brief time may find short positions appealing in some markets.

Figure 8.13: Examples of Option Straddles in Live Cattle Futures

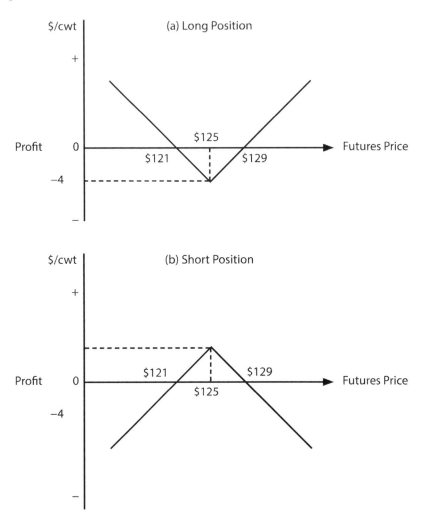

Options Pricing in General

The most accurate way to describe option pricing is to say that prices, usually known as "premiums," are determined by supply and demand for a particular option at a particular point in time. Supply and demand factors, and therefore option premiums, are influenced by:

1. The relationship of the strike price to the underlying futures price.
2. The time remaining until the option expires.
3. The volatility of the price of the underlying futures contract.
4. Prevailing interest rates.

The market equilibrium for a call option is illustrated in Figure 8.14. Suppose this option is out-of-the-money. The demand curve intersects the vertical axis at the existing futures price, which is the maximum price that any trader would pay for a call option. The demand curve slopes down because there is a negative relation between the number of options contracts that traders are willing to purchase and the price (i.e., the premium). If the premium is relatively low, more options will be purchased, *ceteris paribus*.

Figure 8.14: Market Equilibrium for a Call Option

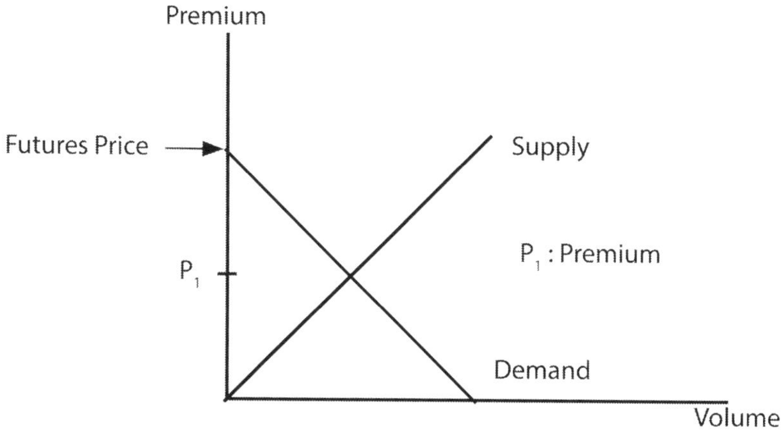

The supply curve is upward sloping, as the greater the premium the larger the number of option contracts traders would be willing to write. The intersection of the supply and demand curves will determine the premium at any given point in time. The supply and demand functions will shift and/or rotate with changes in the four factors mentioned above. For example, if the underlying futures price increases, the demand curve in Figure 8.14 will shift outward to the right and the supply curve will rotate inward to the left, resulting in a new equilibrium with a higher premium.

The demand curve would shift (and not rotate) because the futures price establishes the point where the demand curve intersects the vertical axis. This means that if the futures price increases, then the demand curve's vertical intercept shifts upwards and the entire demand curve shifts out.

At the same time, when the futures price increases the supply curve rotates to the left because the call option is moving closer to being in-the-money and this concerns the writers (i.e., suppliers) of the call options. If the futures price rises sufficiently, the call option will move in-the-money and the option will be exercised, which is a bad outcome for the option writer. Therefore, for a given volume of options, the writers' require a higher premium if the futures price increases, *ceteris paribus*.

Think of the following example: If Australian Sugar Corp. buys a call option that gives it the right to buy an October sugar futures contract at $0.20 per pound and the current futures price for the same futures contract is $0.21/lb, Australian Sugar should be willing to pay at least $0.01/lb, less transaction costs, for that option. The option might be worth more than its $0.01 intrinsic value (meaning that it has some time value) based on Australian Sugar's expectations that the intrinsic value might become larger than $0.01 sometime before the option expires. In turn, no one would be willing to sell this option unless they were to receive its full intrinsic value because, otherwise, a buyer might immediately exercise the option or close it with an offsetting transaction. Additionally, option sellers would rationally attempt to obtain sufficient payment for time value to compensate them for the premium risk they have accepted. The required time value is based on their assessment of prospects that additional intrinsic value will be captured before the option expires, their risk preferences, and the cost of capital. In other words, time value represents the market's offer of return for the risk accepted by options sellers.

Figure 8.15: Market Equilibrium for a Put Option

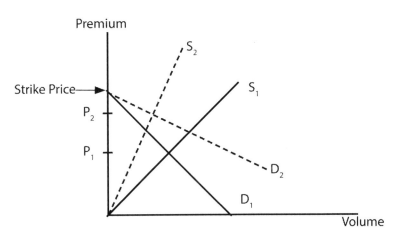

In Figure 8.15, the market equilibrium is represented for a put option that is out-of-the-money. The maximum premium is the strike price and therefore the demand curve intersects the vertical axis at this price. Initially, the equilibrium premium is shown as P_1 where the solid supply (S_1) and demand (D_1) curves intersect. Now, suppose that the futures price declines. As a result, the demand curve rotates rightward from (D_1) to (D_2) as options buyers are now willing to pay a higher premium for any given volume of options contracts. The reason the buyers are willing to pay more is that when the futures price declines, the put option is closer to being in-the-money. In other words, the expected payoff rises with a decline in the futures price (refer back to equation 8.4).

At the same time, when the futures price declines, the supply curve in Figure 8.15 rotates to the left (from S_1 to S_2) as writers of these put options now offer the same volume of put options but at higher premiums. The intersection of the new demand and supply curves occurs at premium P_2, which is higher than P_1, because as the futures price falls, the options' premium rises. This graph illustrates the delta effect for put options, which is discussed in the next section.

Delta (δ)

A major concern of option traders is determining how responsive the option premium is to changes in the price of the underlying futures contract. For example, if the November crude oil futures price increases from $92.00 to $93.00 per barrel, how much will the premium for a $93.00 November call option change?

The relationship between the price of an underlying futures contract and an option premium is measured by an option's delta. The delta, which lies between zero and one, is equal to the ratio of the price change of the option over the price change of the futures contract (i.e., $\delta = \Delta P / \Delta F$).

The delta value normally depends on the extent to which the option is either in-the-money or out-of-the-money. See Table 8.10 for the general relationship between an option's delta and whether or not an option is in-the-money.

Table 8.10: Range of Option Deltas

	Delta
In-the-money	0.5 to 1.0
At-the-money	0.5
Out-of-the-money	0 to 0.5

Generally speaking, options that are deep-in-the-money have delta values which lie close to one, which means that there is almost a one-to-one relationship between a change in the underlying futures price and the option premium. For instance, if the S&P Index futures contract for June delivery is trading at 4295, an option to buy a June S&P Index contract for 4250 is worth at least 45 index points. This option is deep-in-the-money and thus has a delta value near one. If the price of the June contract rises to 4300, then the premium will also increase by about 5 index points.

If an alternative call option on the same June futures contract had a strike price of 4340, then it would be deep-out-of-the-money (i.e., no intrinsic value) and its delta value would be near zero. In this case, a 5 point rise in the price of the contract would only translate into a small rise in the option premium, such as 1 index point. An at-the-money option on the June contract would have a strike price of 4295 index points and its delta would be approximately 0.5.

Time Value: theta (θ)

Since time value reflects nothing more than the market's expectations concerning the prospects of an option having additional intrinsic value sometime before it expires, time value is affected by the amount of time remaining before expiry. A buyer would be willing to pay a higher premium, and a seller would insist on a higher premium, the longer the trading period remaining because this means that there is a greater probability that the option will take on increased intrinsic value. In practice, it appears that time value declines by very small increments per unit of time early in the trading period, while later in the trading period time value declines at an increasing rate as the last day of trading approaches. After trading has ended, an option has zero time value. This decline in an option's time value with the passage of time is frequently referred to as time decay of the premium (refer back to Figure 8.5). Therefore, $\theta = \Delta P / \Delta T$.

Some option buyers will close their option position just before the rapid decline of time value begins and, in this way, recapture a large proportion of the original premium paid for an option, whether that option has intrinsic value at that time or not. However, if an option is far out-of-the-money at the time the option position is closed, it will have very little premium to recapture even if the option has not yet reached the period of rapid time-decay.

Options farther in- or out-of-the-money have declining time value because the options have progressively lower probability of taking on additional intrinsic value. An option that is far out-of-the-money will be of little interest to buyers. The seller of such an option expects that she will not sustain a loss on the option and is willing to sell at a low premium. Alternatively, an option that is far in-the-money will have relatively little time value because, to reach the in-the-money position, the price of the futures contract would have already experienced substantial price change. Hence, there is a reduced probability that the option will take on increased intrinsic value before trading ends.

Price Volatility: lambda (λ)

An options buyer would be willing to pay a higher premium if the associated futures contract has recently experienced a high level of price volatility, because high volatility increases the probability that an option will have more intrinsic value sometime before its trading ends. In the same manner, option sellers would insist on receiving higher time values for options with higher price volatility due to the higher probability that intrinsic values will increase causing them to lose money on the position.

For given levels of volatility, premiums would be higher as the price of the associated futures contract goes higher. This is true because a given level of volatility applied to a higher futures price means that potential gains and losses in holding an option position will be higher. In such a case, buyers like Australian Sugar Corp. are willing to pay higher prices and sellers demand higher premiums for their increased risk.

An example of the relationship between volatility and time to expiration for silver futures is provided in Table 8.11. Looking down the columns, we see that as volatility increases, the call option premium increases. For example, with 40 days to expiration, as volatility rises from 15 percent to 35 percent, the premium rises from 24.8¢ to 50.8¢. The decaying time value is also clearly shown in Table 8.11 by looking across the rows. For a given volatility level, as the time to expiration is shortened from 40 to 10 days, the premium for the call option drops off.

Figure 8.16 provide an example of historical volatility of the British pound (£). This was calculated as the standard deviation of percent price changes of nearby futures. Volatility varies by both month and year. Figure 8.16 also displays the fact that the 2016 Brexit vote in the United Kingdom–a referendum to leave the European Union resulted in extreme volatility in the foreign exchange market.

From the perspective of a speculator, when volatility increases, the option's value rises and when volatility decreases the option's value falls. Therefore, rising volatility works to the benefit of speculators who are

Table 8.11: Time to Expiration versus Volatility Change (Silver Futures = $34.00, Interest Rate = 3%)

Volatility	Time to Expiration		
	40 Days	20 Days	10 Days
15%	24.8¢	21.1¢	12.9¢
25%	36.2¢	26.6¢	16.2¢
35%	50.8¢	32.0¢	26.4¢

Figure 8.16: Historical Volatility of GBP: £

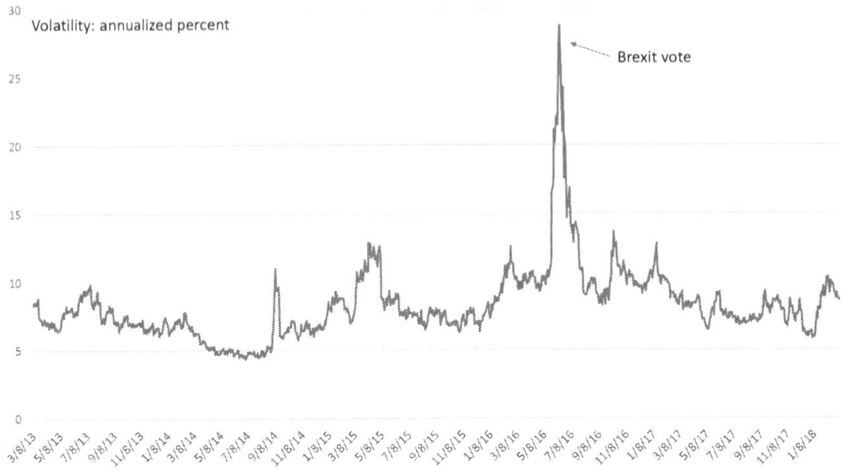

Source: Bloomberg.

"long" options and to the detriment of investors "short" options.

Most speculators who trade options on volatility expectations calculate what is referred to as the implied volatility of an option. That is, they calculate the volatility expectations which are currently built into an option's premium. Using an options pricing model or a simple spreadsheet program, they calculate implied volatility as a function of the premium, strike price, underlying futures price, term to expiration, and interest rates. Their trading is then based on whether they believe the implied volatility is too high or too low.

Whether the implied volatility is judged either too high or too low is often based on a comparison with historical volatility. For example, a trader may check historical prices and find a "normal" yearly price range for silver futures, using annual percentage changes as a yardstick. The addition and subtraction of the annual percentage change from the current futures price gives a range of expected prices for the year. Like with the Black-Scholes formula, this assumes that returns are distributed normally and that commodity prices are distributed log-normally. For example, if the futures price is $34.00 per ounce and the speculator calculates the historical volatility to be 10 percent, then, using a normal probability distribution table, the implication is that she is 68 percent confident that silver futures prices will be in a range of $30.60 to $37.40 during the year.

Alternatively, the normal probability assumption can be used, for example, to calculate the probability that a long call option holder will lose his premium. This is the probability that, by expiration, the market will be trading at or below the strike price. Similarly, the chances of earning a profit can be calculated by determining the probability that the expiration price will be above the strike price by at least the amount of the premium. Suppose that July silver futures closed at $33.50 while the $34.00 call closed at $0.75, with an implied volatility of 10%. Assume that there are 120 days to expiration. What is the probability that the buyer of this call will make a profit? In other words, what is the probability that the futures price will reach $8.4 before expiration? The following formula can be employed:

$$N = \frac{\ln(P/C)}{v\sqrt{d/365}} \tag{8.12}$$

where
P = the "target" futures price level
C = current futures price level
v = futures price volatility
d = days until expiration

The result gives $N = 0.64$, which corresponds to 0.739 on the cumulative normal probability distribution table. This means there is an 73.9% chance the futures price will be at or below the breakeven price of $34.75 before expiry. It also means there is a 100% - 73.9% = 26.1% probability that the market will be at or above the breakeven price.

Price projections are very important for both producers and users of commodities. As indicated elsewhere in this book, futures prices provide an estimate of forthcoming prices and can serve as a pivoting point for production, supply chain management, storage or budgeting decisions. However, a price projection is just a single point. What if a farmer wanted to know the probability of the price of a commodity being lower than a certain level? For example, a corn farmer might require a certain price to break even, that is, not to experience losses. Just as an example, suppose the farmer needs a $5.20 per bushel price to achieve this. In this case, he might wish to buy some form of insurance against price dropping beyond the $5.20 per bushel mark. He will harvest his corn in October and November and is therefore interested in the December price. The insurance will be more expensive the more likely it is for a price to fall beyond $5.20 per bushel. But, how can the insurer, or the farmer know that probability? The actual probability is nearly impossible to know, however, thanks to the options and futures market it is possible to infer the probability the market participants are assigning to such an event.

The pricing of options relies on the basis that the future price of an asset is uncertain, and given that uncertainty it has a distribution of possible prices it can take. By looking at market data such as the price of different options at different strikes, an analyst can infer the market implied distribution for a certain maturity. An example of this is provided by Sherrick and Schnitkey (2018) from the Department of Agricultural and Consumer Economics at the University of Illinois. You can find their interactive price distribution tool at http://farmdoc.illinois.edu/cropins/price-distribution.html. They compute the implied probability distribution for the price of corn and soybeans at different maturities. So, back to our example, what is the probability of corn prices falling below $5.20 per bushel by December? The market assigns a probability of just over 50% of that happening.

Figure 8.17 shows that market prices indicate there is about 25% chance that the expiration price for the December corn futures will be below $4.57 – or alternatively, there is a 35% chance that harvest price will be above $5.58. Additionally, from looking at Figure 8.17, it can be inferred that with a 90% chance, according to market expectations, the price of corn will be between $3.80 and $7.09 dollars per bushel in December. This gives farmers and traders much more information, not only can they infer that the median of the price distribution for the December contract is $5.19 per bushel, but they can also get a sense of how volatile prices are expected to be. To do this, all you have to do is compute the interquartile range, i.e., the difference between the 75th percentile and the 25th percentile. In this case, that is $1.33 per bushel.

Figure 8.17: Corn Price Distribution

Probability Below	Price at Expiration
5%	$3.80
15%	$4.27
25%	$4.57
35%	$4.83
45%	$5.07
50%	$5.19
55%	$5.32
65%	$5.58
75%	$5.90
85%	$6.32
95%	$7.09

Enter Price to Evaluate: $ 5.20

The implied distribution indicates that there is a 50.33% probability that the price will be below $5.20 at expiration.

Source: http://farmdoc.illinois.edu/cropins/price-distribution.html

Bloomberg also offers a commodity forecast monitor (Bloomberg code: XLTP XCFM) that provides futures price distrbutions similar to that shown in Figure 8.17. Using this tool, Figure 8.18 shows the cumulative probability distribution for WTI crude oil prices during the expiration month, and these price forecasts were made about 250 days prior to expiration. When Figure 8.18 was generated the futures price was about $58.8 per barrel. From Figure 8.18 we find that the market (futures and options combined) was indicating about a 10% probability that crude oil prices would fall below $44.85 per bbl. before contract expiry. There was a 50% probability that the futures contract would expire at a price below $58.8 the futures price prevailing when the forecast was made. Although difficult to read from Figure 8.18, the Bloomberg monitor forecast a 19.7% chance of a 20% price increase, versus a 14.85% chance of a 20% price decrease. In other words the market was slightly more optimistic that crude oil prices would go 20% higher versus 20% lower. In other words the probability distribution (not shown) was skewed to the right.

Figure 8.18: Cumulative Probability of WTI Crude Oil Prices at Expiration

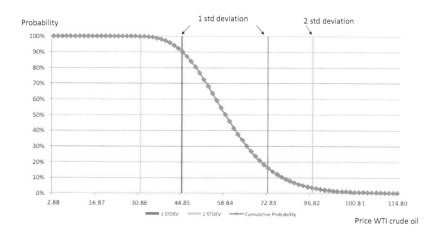

Source: Bloomberg Commodity Forecast Monitor XLTP XCFM.

Interest Rates: rho (ρ)

Higher interest rates are expected to discourage options buyers and encourage option sellers to add to their option positions. These incentives arise because buyers will pay a premium at the time an option position is opened, and if there is any price gain it occurs only after the option has taken on increased intrinsic value. Therefore, a buyer must impute the time-value of up-front money paid in the form of a premium as a cost of holding an option position. An option seller receives the premium when an option position is opened and holds those funds until the position is closed or is left to expire. This assumes the seller can deposit a Treasury Bill with the brokerage firm in order to satisfy margin requirements. An option seller may invest money received as premiums during the time a position is open, and will derive somewhat greater benefits from this as interest rates are higher. While theory and logic says that option premiums should decline with rising interest rates, other variables held constant, in practice premiums are rather insensitive to changes in interest rates. The relationship between interest rates and the options premium is: $\rho = \Delta P / \Delta i$.

The Black-Scholes Model

Figures 8.6 and 8.7 above show the range of possible options prices (i.e., premiums). The options prices vary with the strike price, the underlying futures price, volatility, and other less important factors. The mathematical formula that captures this pricing relationship is known as the Black-Scholes model. Black and Scholes (1973) derived a stochastic partial differential equation explaining the price of an asset and then solved the equation to obtain the Black-Scholes formula for the price of the option on that asset. The 1997 Nobel Prize in Economics was awarded to Myron Scholes for the development of this options pricing model. Fischer Black passed away in 1995. He would undoubtedly have shared in the prize had he still been alive.

The mathematical-economic model they developed was appropriate for the pricing of stock options (i.e., options on equities) and it therefore required modification to be directly applicable to the pricing of options on futures contracts or options on physical commodities. The principal difference is that stocks usually pay dividends while futures contracts do not. In 1976, Black published a model modified for commodity contracts.

The Black model of option pricing is really based upon "European" options, which may be exercised only at the end of trading for the option, rather than "American" options which may be exercised at any time prior to the end of trading. Since the Black model does not allow for the possibility of early exercise it tends to slightly under-value in-the-money options. Models (such as the one by Cox, Ross and Rubinstein (1979)) have since been produced that are directly appropriate to American options, but these models are much more complex and produce estimates of option premiums that are very similar to those produced by the Black model. Keep in mind that a number of options on futures traded on the CME are European style options. You can find the list of American versus European style CME options at: https://www.cmegroup.com/trading/files/strike-price/strike-price-listing-and-exercise-procedures-table-cme-cbot.xlsx.

In order to calculate an option premium estimate with the Black-Scholes

Table 8.12: Factors Affecting an Option's Price

Factor	Measure	Comments
Change in option premium associated with a change in underlying futures price	Δ (delta)	Lies between 0 and 1. Approximately equal to 1 for deep in-the-money options, near 0 for deep out-of-the-money options, close to 0.5 for the at-the-money options.
Rate of change in Δ	γ (gamma)	Lies between 0 and ∞ Approximately 0 for deep in-the-money or deep out-of-the-money options.
Time	θ (theta)	Lies between 0 and the total value of the option. Declines as option nears expiry.
Volatility	λ (lambda)	Lies between 0 and ∞. Declines as option nears expiry.
Interest rate	ρ (rho)	Lies between 0 and ∞. Usually is near 0.

model, five variables are required. The variables (as discussed above) are as follows:

1. current price of the associated futures contract,
2. option strike price,
3. days to option maturity,
4. volatility of the associated futures contract price, and
5. the interest rate on a relatively safe investment.

The factors influencing an option's premium are summarized in Table 8.12, and four of these factors are directly measurable. However, volatility is not directly observable and must be estimated. Table 8.13 provides an example of historical volatility in the wheat futures market, calculated from the standard deviation of day–to–day logarithmic historical price changes over the most recent 60 days for the nearby contract. Notice in Table 8.13 wheat futures prices tend to be more volatile during the months of May–August when there is uncertainly over the wheat yields.

Table 8.13: Historical Monthly Volatility (%): Wheat Futures Prices

Month	2013	2014	2015	2016	2017	Average
Jan	20.5	15.1	29.2	23.3	25.7	22.8
Feb	18.9	21.6	28.4	20.4	26.6	23.2
Mar	23.7	28.9	29.6	20.1	24.7	25.4
Apr	27.9	29.4	30.5	25.9	23.8	27.5
May	27.9	27.4	32.5	28.8	25.7	28.5
Jun	22.9	22.9	36.5	31.6	29.4	28.7
Jul	18.6	27.2	37.5	27.8	32.3	28.7
Aug	18.7	30.0	34.5	26.3	34.8	28.8
Sep	18.2	30.0	27.7	27.7	29.1	26.5
Oct	18.0	23.4	27.1	29.1	24.7	24.5
Nov	15.2	23.5	26.2	26.6	20.8	22.4
Dec	12.5	28.7	24.4	27.4	21.3	22.8
Average	20.2	25.7	30.3	26.3	26.6	25.8

Source: Bloomberg HVOLWHEA. Calculated from standard deviation of day to day logarithmic historical price changes over the most recent 60 days for the nearby contract.

If the Black-Scholes model is assumed to be accurate, the options premium can be inserted into the formula in order to solve for the implied volatility as in Figure 8.19, an illustration from the WTI crude oil market.

Figure 8.19: Historical and Implied Volatility for an at–the–money WTI Call Option

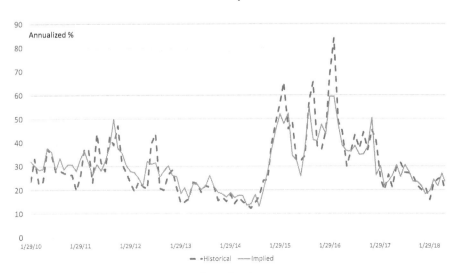

Source: Bloomberg.

As explained above, holding everything else constant, the change in the price of an option with respect to the underlying futures price is referred to as the option's delta (Δ), where $\Delta = \partial P/\partial F$. The price (premium) of the option is denoted by P and F is the price of the underlying futures contract. The change of an option's price with respect to time is measured by theta (θ), thus $\theta = \partial P/\partial t$ where t represents time. Gamma (γ) measures the rate of change of an option's delta with respect to the price of the underlying futures price, so $\gamma = \partial^2 P/\partial F^2$. The rate of change of an option's price with respect to the volatility of the futures price is lambda, λ. This means that $\lambda = \partial P/\partial \sigma$, where σ is the standard deviation of the futures price. Finally, the rho (ρ) of an option is the rate of change of an option's price with respect to the interest rate, $\rho = \partial P/\partial i$, where i is the interest rate.

Research comparing market options prices with predicted prices from the Black-Scholes model shows that the model is a very good approximation of what futures options markets actually discover in the way of premiums. Professional options traders (principally option sellers) use either a formal option pricing model, such as the Black-Scholes model, or they (implicitly) have in their minds a good approximation of these formal models so that they can judge successfully when premiums available offer them a good profit opportunity. Of course, there are many reasons why the theoretical premium value may differ from the observed market value. These include:

1. Effects of trading liquidity;
2. Different volatility expectations among traders;
3. Differences between borrowing and lending rates; and
4. Distributional characteristic of the underlying futures prices that do not conform to theoretical expectations.

Online, there are a number of sites that provide Black-Scholes "greek" calculations with the Black-Scholes model embedded behind the calculations. One such example is barchart.com. Once you go to barchart.com select a commodity such as WTI crude oil. This page will show you the futures prices. Click on "options quotes" near the top right hand side of the page, select the relevant expiry month, and then over on the left hand side of the page click on "volatility & greeks" under the Options heading. Your output will look similar to Table 8.14, except there will be entries for all of the various strike prices.

Put-Call Parity

Referring to Table 8.15, we see that the premium on a July sugar call option with a 19.5¢/lb. strike price is 1.68¢/lb. The July put option with the

Table 8.14: Volatility and Greeks: WTI Crude Oil. Underlying Futures Price $59.26 and 250 days to Expiry

Option	Premium	Implied Vol.	Delta	Gamma	Theta	Vega
$60 Call	$4.27	24.03%	0.51	0.0332	0.06	0.19
$60 Put	$5.68	24.02%	-0.48	0.0333	0.06	0.2

same strike price is 1.02¢/lb. Given that the two options are linked to the same strike price and futures contract month, is there any expected relationship between the put and call option prices of 1.68¢/lb and 1.02¢/lb, respectively? If nothing else was changed in Table 8.15, but the July put option premium was raised to 2¢/lb., instead of 1.68¢/lb., would there be a riskless arbitrage opportunity? The answer to both questions is yes because of the put-call parity relationship . It is a fundamental pricing relationship that exists between the price of a put and call option, with an identical strike price and expiration date.

Table 8.15: Sugar Options: 112,000 lbs (¢/lb)

Strike	Calls			Puts		
Price	June	July	October	June	July	October
19.5	1.01	1.68	1.83	0.35	1.02	1.13
20.0	0.71	1.43	1.58	0.55	1.27	1.38
20.5	0.49	1.21	1.36	0.83	1.55	1.65
21.0	0.32	1.02	1.16	1.16	1.86	1.96

As discussed above, with regard to the Black-Scholes formula, the same set of principal factors determine both put and call premiums. These factors are the strike price, the price of the underlying futures contract, the estimated price volatility, the time to expiry, and the interest rate. With these common factors, it is therefore intuitive that a predictable relationship exists between puts and calls–the *put-call parity relationship*.

To illustrate the put-call parity relationship, we assume that the option expiry date is the same as that of the futures contract. In other words, assume a European-style option. The put-call parity formula is then:

$$(Call\ Premium - Put\ Premium) =$$
$$(Futures\ Price - Strike\ Price)\ /\ (1 + r\ (t/360)) \tag{8.13}$$

where r is the annualized risk-free interest rate and t is the number of days until expiry. This equation says that the difference between the call and put premiums is equal to the difference between the (present value of) the current underlying futures price and the options' strike price. Given a call premium, its strike price, time to maturity, and underlying futures price, we can use the put-call relationship to solve for the matching put option premium, or vice versa.

If the put-call parity relationship does not hold, then there are riskless arbitrage opportunities for an options trader to make a profit. This means that traders' arbitrage will force the put-call parity relationship to (approximately) hold. The hypothetical purchase of a put option and simultaneous sale of a call option, with the same strike price and expiration month, can be used to demonstrate this parity relationship. The simultaneous purchase of a put and sale of a call actually creates a synthetic short futures position. This means that the synthetic short futures position could be combined with a long futures position to create a riskless arbitrage portfolio.

We know that the value of an option at expiration is equal to its intrinsic value, so at expiration, the expected value of the long put is:

$$E\left(EV_L^P\right) = Max\left[0, (SP - FP)\right] \tag{8.14}$$

and, for the long call, the expected value is:

$$E\left(EV_L^C\right) = Max\left[0, (FP - SP)\right] \tag{8.15}$$

where $E\left(EV\right)$ is the expected value at the time of expiry.

If, at expiry, the $FP < SP$, then the put option is in-the-money and the buyer of the put earns $SP - FP$, while if the $FP > SP$, then call option expires in-the-money and the writer of the call option earns a negative profit equal to $SP - FP$. Thus, upon expiration, the payoff to a combined long position in a put option and a short position in a call option is $SP - FP$, meaning that $E(\Pi_L^P) - E(\Pi_S^C) = SP - FP$, which is the put-call parity formula, evaluated at $t = 0$. However, $SP - FP$ is also the expected payoff to a short position in the underlying futures contract, sold at a price SP. Thus, buying a put while selling a call with the same strike price and expiration date just replicates the return to a short futures position (i.e., it creates a synthetic short futures position).

We can illustrate the put-call parity formula with the aid of the sugar example in Table 8.16. Suppose that the underlying July futures price is 20.16¢/lb., the riskless interest rate is 4%, and there are approximately 180 days remaining to expiry. Then, the put-call parity relationship for this example is:

$$(1.68 - 1.02) \approx (20.52 - 19.50) / \left[1 + (0.04 \times 180/360)\right], \text{ or } 0.66 \approx 0.66$$

This result verifies that the two July sugar options prices have the correct relationship. It also implies that the expected arbitrage profits would be approximately zero if a trader pursued a strategy of buying the underlying futures contract, selling the call option, and simultaneously buying the put option.

This result is illustrated in Table 8.16 and Figure 8.20. In Table 8.16, the price of the futures contract at expiration is shown on the left hand side of the table. The three middle columns in the table show the respective profits or losses accruing to each of the three positions: long futures, long put, and short call. In Table 8.16, the arbitrage strategy net profit is shown in the column on the right hand side.

No matter where the futures price settles (either above, below, or at the strike price), the arbitrage strategy will generate a profit of $0. If the futures price settles at 9.5¢/lb., then the profit from the long futures position is $1,097.60 (for one 112,000 lb. sugar contract). There is a corresponding loss of $145.60 from the long put position and a loss of $952 for the short call position. These three figures sum to zero. As we move down the table, we see that for alternative futures prices at expiration, the result is exactly the same, with net profits equal to zero. This example ignores the time value of money, which appears in the put-call parity relationship, but which is not very empirically important in this formula.

Table 8.16: Expected Profits and Losses from a Hypothetical Arbitrage in Sugar: 112,000 lbs (¢/lb)

Price of Futures Contract at Expiration (¢/lb)	Expected Profit from Long Futures Position 20.16 ¢/lb	Expected Profit from Long Put Position 1.02 ¢/lb & Strike = 19.5 ¢/lb	Expected Profit from Short Call Position 1.68 ¢/lb & Strike = 19.5 ¢/lb	Net Profit
21.5	$1,500.80	-$1,142.40	-$358.40	$0.00
21	$940.80	-$1,142.40	$201.60	$0.00
20.5	$380.80	-$1,142.40	$761.60	$0.00
20	-$179.20	-$1,142.40	$1,321.60	$0.00
19.5	-$739.20	-$1,142.40	$1,881.60	$0.00
19	-$1,299.20	-$582.40	$1,881.60	$0.00
18.5	-$1,859.20	-$22.40	$1,881.60	$0.00

Figure 8.20: Expected Payoff from a Hypothetical Arbitrage Trade in Sugar: 112,000 lbs (¢/lb)

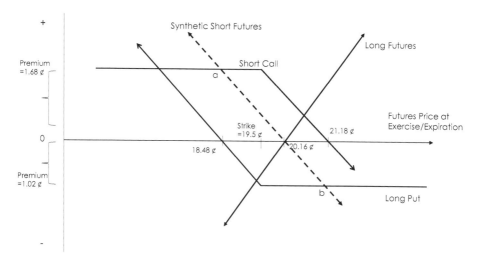

Figure 8.20 shows the arbitrage strategy in graphical form. Combining a short call, long put, and long futures position will generate a net gain of zero, irrespective of where the underlying futures price settles at expiry. For example, if the futures price happens to settle at the strike price (19.5¢/lb), then the loss on the futures position is equal to 0.66¢/lb (= 20.16-19.5); the loss on the long put is 1.02 ¢/lb. (i.e., the put premium); and, the gain on the short call is 1.68¢/lb. (i.e., the call premium). So the net gain is zero.

In Figure 8.20 the long put and the short call positions create a synthetic short futures position (shown by the dashed line sloping donward from the left). Point a in Figure 8.20 represents the price point 18.48¢/lb where the return on the short call is 1.68¢/lb and the return on the long put is zero. Therefore the combination of the two options (i.e., the synthetic short futures) must go through point a. At this point the trader is adding a zero return on the long put to a 1.68¢/lb return on the short call. Similarly, point b represents the price point where the return on the short call is zero and the return on the long put is -1.02¢/lb. If we draw a line through points a and b we have drawn the payoff line represeting the combination of the short call and the long put, which is a (synthetic) short futures payoff. This dashed line crosses the futures price line at 20.16¢/lb, because it is 45 degree line and if the price increases from point a (18.48¢/lb) by 1.68¢/lb then we have 20.16 ¢, as 18.48¢+ 1.68¢= 20.16¢.

Strictly speaking, the put-call parity relationship described here applies only to European style options. The relationship does not exactly apply to American style options because an option holder may exercise the option before expiration. However, in practice the empirical importance of this distinction is not very significant.

Summary

This chapter has introduced the reader to call and put options on futures contracts, with examples drawn from the commodity and financial markets. We built on the previous chapters on the fundamentals of futures markets. The focus here was on developing a basic understanding of how the market participants price both call and put options on futures. Traders who sell options are constantly adjusting the price (i.e., premium) they are willing to accept as market volatility, futures prices, and time to option maturity changes. Buyer and seller motivations were discussed and examples were provided of speculative strategies for trading options on futures.

Option payoff charts were utilized to explain the important relationship between futures prices and options prices. The fair market value of call and put options was discussed with an intuitive explanation of the factors underlying the famous Black-Scholes model of options pricing. The important factors include the strike price, the underlying futures price, days to expiry, and price volatility. Within the options market, there are also important relationships among put and call prices and some of these price parity relationships were explained with examples. We also learned how the options and futures market prices can be used to generate a forecast of the distribution of forthcoming prices, which allows us to place a probability on a certain percentage price move in one direction or the other.

Discussion Questions

1. Compare and contrast the commitments taken on by a futures contract seller versus a buyer of a put option.

2. Compare and contrast the commitments taken on by a futures contract buyer versus a buyer of a call option.

3. A March cotton call option has a strike price of 60 cents per pound. The underlying futures price is 58.69 cents per lb. and the premium is 1.57 cents. One cotton futures contract is 50,000 lbs.

   The intrinsic value is _____(cents/lb) _____($ per contract).

   The time value is _____(cents/lb) _____($ per contract).

4. A June Treasury Bond put option with a strike price of 102-00 points has a premium of 5-30. The underlying futures price is 97-06. Recall that T-Bond options are quoted in points & 64ths of 100% while T-Bond futures are quoted in points & 32nds of 100%.

   The intrinsic value is _____(pts.& 64ths of 100%) _____ (per contract).

   The time value is _____ (pts. & 64ths of 100%) _____ (per contract).

5. Assuming zero transactions costs, does the put-call parity relationship hold exactly for the May put and call with a strike of $7.20? Answer yes or no & show your calculations. If the answer is no, indicate how far off the relationship is.

6. Given the corn options market information, draw the expected payoff chart for:

   a) Short July put with a $7.00 strike.

   b) Long May call with a $7.10 strike.

   Note: Carefully label both diagrams and on each diagram shown the maximum profit and maximum loss, breakeven prices, etc.

Corn Options (5,000 bu): Option Premiums are in Cents per Bushel

Strike ($ /bu)	Apr Call	May Call	Jul Call	Apr Put	May Put	Jul Put
6.80	36.875	44.625	45.000	0.375	8.125	26.500
6.90	27.375	37.625	39.750	0.875	11.125	31.250
7.00	18.625	31.250	34.875	2.125	14.750	36.375
7.10	11.125	25.625	30.625	4.625	19.125	42.125
7.20	6.125	20.875	26.750	9.625	24.375	48.250
7.30	2.875	16.750	23.250	16.375	30.250	54.625

Underlying Corn Futures Prices:

Delivery Month	Price ($/bu)
May	$7.17
July	$7.00
September	$5.85
December	$5.61

Selected References

Black, Fischer. 1976. "The pricing of commodity contracts." *Journal of financial economics*, 3(1-2): 167–179.

Black, Fischer, and Myron Scholes. 1973. "The pricing of options and corporate liabilities." *Journal of political economy*, 81(3): 637–654.

Cox, John C., Stephen A. Ross, and Mark Rubinstein. 1979. "Option pricing: A simplified approach." *Journal of financial Economics*, 7(3): 229–263.

Sherrick, B, and G Schnitkey. 2018. "Implied Probabilities for Corn and Soybeans Prices in 2018." *farmdoc daily*.

9.

Hedging with Options

Commodity boom and bust cycles raise interest among hedgers in the use of more sophisticated risk management tools such as options (Power et al., 2013). One reason is that hedging with options provides commercial traders with many alternatives not available in a futures only hedging program. Although the use of futures versus options on futures provides similar risk management benefits, they differ in terms of cost, and there are significant differences that make hedging strategies unique for each instrument chosen. Table 9.1 sets out some of the fundamental differences between hedging with *options on futures* versus *futures*. Basically, a trader enjoys substantially more versatility when it chooses to hedge with options rather than futures only. For instance, options come much closer to providing traditional price insurance than futures because either a floor or a ceiling price can be established with options. However, options are not necessarily superior to futures as a hedging tool in many instances, largely because trading options requires the buyer to pay an upfront premium to the seller. Also, futures and options are not mutually exclusive in the development of hedging strategies; in some cases, a complex strategy that uses both futures and options may be ideal.

In a general sense, hedging with options (or futures for that matter) involves the management of risk through the use of derivative contracts in order to balance a portfolio. This strategy is common in commodity markets for both inputs and outputs (such as copper, sugar or crude oil) or in the financial markets for interest rates or exchange rates (such as Treasury Notes or the Euro).

In this chapter some very basic option hedging strategies are discussed. Some of the strategies are then compared to futures hedging methods. In this way, the reader should gain a basic understanding of both the mechanics of hedging with options and the factors that affect whether options strategies provide a hedger with a superior strategy compared to futures.

Table 9.1: Pros and Cons of Hedging with Futures versus Options

Futures	Options	
	Buyer	Seller
• Unlimited risk on long and short futures position	• Limited risk with purchase of a put or call	• Unlimited risk with the sale of a put or call
• Margin calls with a long or short position	• No margin calls with purchase of a put or call	• Margin call with sale of a put or call
• Establishes a "locked-in" price but it may vary with basis risk	• Establishes either a "floor" or "ceiling" price which may vary with basis risk	• Establishes either a "floor" or "ceiling" price which may vary with basis risk
• Limited number of hedging strategies	• Multiple hedging strategies	• Multiple hedging strategies
• No premium is paid	• Synthetic futures can be created	• Synthetic futures can be created
	• Premium is paid	• Premium is received

Basic Option Hedging Strategies

There are four basic hedging strategies associated with the use of options: two involve going either short or long a *put option*, and two involve being either short or long a *call option*. These four strategies are specified in Table 9.2. To illustrate the basic difference between option and futures hedges, consider the simplest case in which a commodity producer might be long in the cash market and, therefore, seeks protection against a steep price decline. He would buy a put option and thus establish a price floor. However if prices should suddenly rise, this producer does not have to forego all of the financial gain from the higher cash price. In contrast, with a short hedge in the futures market, profit opportunities from a higher cash price are foregone. For simplicity in the following examples, the basis is assumed to be constant and zero. Also, the returns to option positions are based on the premium adjusted for the intrinsic value of the option at expiration.

Long Cash: Basic Option Hedge

As an example of a long put hedge, consider a commercial sugar trader who has a storage facility and who believes sugar prices are going higher.

Table 9.2: Basic Hedging Strategies: Options versus Futures

Cash Market Position	Futures Hedges	Options Hedge	
		Puts	Calls
Long	Short	Long	Short
Short	Long	Short	Long

She has purchased 112,000 pounds of physical sugar (the quantity in one futures contract) on the world market at a price of 20¢ per pound in June. Her intention is to sell the sugar in late September. However, the volatile sugar market is subject to weather and political effects, and the trader is concerned about her exposure to a sudden price decline. In order to hedge her position, she may elect to buy an at-the-money put option based on an October sugar futures contract for a premium of 0.55¢ per pound and a strike price of $0.20 per pound. The trader's expected returns are shown in Figure 9.1. In effect, with the long cash and long put, she has a bullish position and has established a synthetic call (see the dashed line in in Figure 9.1).

Figure 9.1: A Long Cash Position and a Long Put Hedge

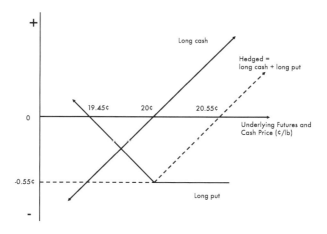

Any loss on the long put is equal to 0.55¢ (i.e., the premium) minus the intrinsic value. Figure 9.1 shows that the *long put* reduces the final return on the sugar inventory by 0.55¢ per pound (the amount of the premium paid) if futures prices go up and stay up. If the futures price stays higher than the strike price $0.20 per pound then the intrinsic value of the option is zero. As a result, the dashed line for potential outcomes for the hedged position is below the line for unhedged outcomes for all prices above 19.45¢ (the strike price minus the premium). Nevertheless, returns on a hedged position do increase with rising futures prices, unlike the outcomes from a short futures hedge. On the other hand, if prices decline the *put* has intrinsic value equal to the strike price minus the futures price, which keeps the hedged outcome (dashed) line in Figure 9.1 flat. The net return will be 19.45¢ no matter how far prices fall.

If instead of being outright bullish, suppose the trader was neutral to slightly bullish. In this situation she might still take a long cash position at 20¢. But, being of the belief that prices might not increase by much, she sells an in-the-money 19¢ call option at the same time and collects the premium, equal to 2.5¢ per pound. She now has some cushion if prices do not fall too far below 20¢, because she will not lose money as long as prices remain above 17.5¢. If prices remain above 19¢ she is guaranteed a profit equal to 1.5¢ per pound. The unlimited gains in the long cash position exactly offset the losses in the call option trade for any price above 19¢ per pound. This hedging strategy is depicted in Figure 9.2.

Figure 9.2: A Long Cash Position and a Short Call Hedge

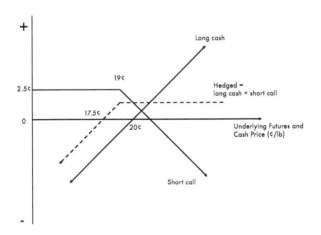

Short Cash: Basic Option Hedge

Alternatively, consider the purchase of a call option for a commercial trader who has a short position in the cash market. Suppose, the sugar trader becomes short in the cash market by making a forward sale (at a fixed price) to an importer without having the required sugar inventory to meet the forward delivery commitment. In this case the sugar trader profits if prices fall (because she can purchase the needed sugar at a price below that for which she has sold it), but is exposed to a loss if prices suddenly rise. She can hedge against an unexpected price rise. Suppose the forward sale was for 112,000 pounds at a price of 24¢ per pound. As a hedge the trader may elect to purchase an at-the-money July $0.24 call for 1¢. In essence, she has created a synthetic put with the short cash and long call positions. The trader's expected returns are graphed in Figure 9.3. By hedging she has given up one cent per pound of potential return if prices decline, but she is guaranteed not to get caught paying a much higher cash price if prices rise.

Figure 9.3: A Short Cash Position and a Long Call Hedge

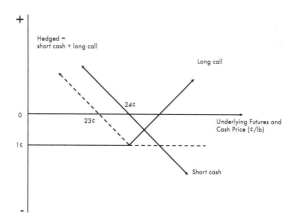

If instead of being outright bearish the trader is neutral to bearish and enters into a short cash position in a similar fashion as above, the hedge would involve selling a put option. Assume the short cash position is at $0.24, and an at-the-money $0.24 put is sold for a premium of 1¢. Thus, the sugar trader makes a profit as long as prices remain below $0.25. This situation is depicted in Figure 9.4. The trader loses money only if prices rise above $0.25, whereas in the unhedged short cash position, losses are incurred as soon as prices rise above $0.24.

In each of these basic option hedging strategies an important question is whether to choose an option which is "at", "out of", or "in-the-money". The answer really depends on how much protection the hedger wishes to purchase. The basic rule is that more price protection costs more and less price protection costs less! For example, in the situation depicted in Figure 9.1, the hedger is basically bullish. An out-of-the-money put option will require much less premium, but its low delta means it will also provide

Figure 9.4: A Short Cash Position and a Short Put Hedge

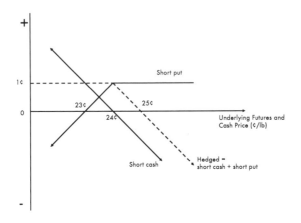

less protection on the downside. A deep-in-the-money option may offer protection at lower cost (because it has relatively less time value in its premium), but requires a much larger deposit initially; although the intrinsic value portion will be recaptured, paying the large premium may strain the hedger's cash flow while the option is held.

Delta Hedging

As discussed in Chapter 8, an option's delta (δ) is a measure of the change in the option's premium relative to a change in the underlying futures price. An at-the-money foreign currency option, for example, which has a delta of 0.5 means that for every $0.01 change in the currency futures price, the option will change in value by $0.005. A long call delta implies that if currency futures price rise by $0.01, the premium will also rise, but only by $0.005. Alternatively, for a long put option, a $0.01 rise in the currency price implies the option's premium will fall by $0.005. Short put deltas are denoted by a positive number and short call deltas by a negative number. For deep-in-the-money options the delta is near 1.0 and for deep-out-of-the-money options the delta is near zero. Of course, it is also important to remember that the delta value is not a constant and it may fluctuate with underlying price changes and as the option approaches expiry. Towards expiry, the delta of an out-of-the-money option approaches zero and the delta of an in-the-money option approaches 1.0.

Since the object of hedging is to offset a loss in the cash market with a gain in the options market, the delta is an important factor in a hedging program. A neutral hedge ratio is the reciprocal of a delta and it is a measure of how many options contracts must be held in order to offset price changes in the underlying cash market (assuming either a constant basis or a favorable basis change). For example, a hedger who is long 40,000 pounds of beef in the cash market and wishes to offset the price risk must purchase or write 2 at-the-money 0.5 delta options to neutralize his cash position. If the delta is 0.25, four options would be required, assuming the optimal hedge ratio for beef is 1.0.

However, optimal hedge ratios are not necessarily equal to 1.0. This means the "neutral" ratio must be converted by the appropriate hedge ratio in order to derive a more effective option hedge. The option hedge ratio

---

Box 9.1 How an Airline Uses Call Options to Hedge

As mentioned in Chapter 7, all of the nation's top airlines have turned to hedging in order to try and better manage wildly fluctuating fuel prices. A jump in fuel prices can quickly turn a profitable quarter into red numbers because fuel is the second most important expense for airlines, after labor costs. By hedging, the airlines are able to manage some of the fuel costs and some airline companies have reported that they saved hundreds of millions a year through hedging. United, Delta, Southwest, and American all have hedging programs. It leaves these companies to do what they are best at–providing transportation. They are not commodity speculators.

At least one major U.S. airline uses call options to hedge. It buys heating oil call options, as a type of cross-hedge because the price of heating oil and jet fuel is highly correlated. The airlines' goal is to protect itself against sharp fuel price increases but still benefit from price declines. Of course, the downside is the option premium expenses that can also run into the hundreds of millions of dollars for a single airline.

For airlines, it is a long-term hedging program and they try to hedge in and around the long-term average price of fuel. This means they purchase a lot of call options when fuel prices are relatively low and their hedge ratio varies over time depending on price expectations. In early 2018 Bloomberg reported that European airlines such as Lufthansa, East-Jet and Ryanair had each hedged more than 75% of their fuel needs for fiscal year 2018 and beyond. It was reported that Norwegian Air planned to hedge only about 27% of its fuel purchases in 2018.

(OHR) is therefore:

$$OHR = FHR \times NR = FHR \times \frac{1}{\delta} \qquad (9.1)$$

where FHR denotes the desired futures hedge ratio and NR the neutral ratio. For instance, in the beef example above suppose that FHR = 0.8 and NR = 4. This implies that 3.2 or approximately 3 options contracts would be required for the hedge.

An option's delta is a function of the underlying commodity price and time, therefore it changes over time. To account for changing deltas, an optimum hedge must be rebalanced over time. This leads to a dynamic hedging program.

Comparison of Alternative Hedging Strategies

Put options represent an alternative method of establishing a forward price for a firm's inventory and/or output. Producers can also establish a forward price for products by either signing a forward pricing contract with a local buyer or hedging the commodity on the futures market. The forward contract is similar to the futures hedge, except it has no basis risk.

The example discussed below illustrates how put options compare to cash marketing and forward pricing of oil. It is assumed that on June 1 a producer—Wildcat Inc.—is considering the pricing of 5,000 barrels of crude

---

Box 9.2 Mexico's Oil Hedging Program

Mexico is one of the world's largest producers of oil and revenue from oil exports is extremely important to the Mexican government. Oil makes up approximately 15 percent of Mexico's export earnings and the state oil company Pemex accounts for more than 30 percent of the government's revenue. In order to stabilize this revenue, Mexico often hedges its future oil sales for up to one year in advance through the use of options. The Mexican government's oil hedging program has transitioned from one of establishing a floor price through the purchase of put options to a more complicated hedging strategy involving buying puts at a high strike price and simultaneously selling puts at a lower strike price. By simultaneously buying and selling puts at different strike prices, Mexico reduces the cost of the total option premiums paid for hedging. But at the same time this "spreading" strategy exposes Mexico to financial losses if there is a significant drop in the price of oil.

oil that it plans to produce during the fall. If Wildcat decides to simply wait until November 1 to price the oil, it has selected a cash marketing strategy.

Forward pricing locks Wildcat in at a specific price. If prices go down and it has forward contracted at a higher price, the forward pricing decision would be profitable. However, if cash prices increase significantly, Wildcat would not benefit from the price increases because it had already sold forward. Further, if Wildcat's production falls short, but has already been contracted (at a lower price), it might have to purchase oil to meet the delivery requirements of the contract. This potential loss is extremely unattractive from a risk management perspective, because when the firm has short production volume its net profit is likely to be either very small or negative particularly if local cash prices are negatively correlated with the quantity supplied (i.e., if production shortfalls imply higher cash prices). To pay a competitor for every contracted barrel not produced could mean financial problems. To control this type of financial risk, Wildcat may limit the percentage of expected future production that it forward contracts.

Put options are an attractive marketing alternative because they have the ability to partially overcome both of these limitations to forward contracting. First, a put option establishes a floor price, but leaves open the possibility for a producer to at least partially benefit from upward price movements. Also, if Wildcat has a production shortfall, the firm would not have to go on the open market and purchase physical oil. The firm's maximum loss per unit is the put option premium, not the price for an entire barrel of oil. The following two cases examine how a decrease or an increase in crude oil prices affect the outcomes of alternative hedging strategies.

Case 1: Crude Oil Decreases in Price

On June 1, Wildcat Inc. is confronted with three marketing strategies: cash marketing in the fall when the oil is ready to sell, forward contracting in June, or purchasing a put option in June. Table 9.3 summarizes the prices per barrel under each alternative. The basis assumption is that futures and cash prices move perfectly together. Using the cash marketing alternative, Wildcat does nothing in advance to establish a price. If forward contracting, it signs a contract with a refinery for $91.50 per barrel for delivery on November 1. If it selects the put option alternative, it could buy five put options on the November futures contract (1,000 barrels each), traded on the New York Mercantile Exchange. Suppose on June 1 the November futures contract is trading at $92.00 per barrel.

Assume Wildcat must pay 70 cents per barrel for a $92.00 November put option. This means it has paid 70 cents per bbl. to have the right to sell the November crude oil futures contract at $92.00 per barrel. In buying the put option it is important to realize that Wildcat is not buying price protection directly on the physical commodity. Rather the price protection is indirect through the futures market. This relationship between the futures market and local cash market must be fully accounted for if options are going to be used effectively.

Now jump ahead to November 1. Wildcat Inc. had a good production volume and has sufficient oil to sell. Cash oil prices dropped to $90.00 a

---

Box 9.3 What are Hedging Losses?

The popular press sometimes refers to "hedging losses" as a cause of concern for stockholders of corporations that have a hedging program. For example, Australia has several world-class mining companies and these companies rely on export markets for sales of gold, zinc, etc. A weak Australian dollar (AD) is good for these export-oriented mines because the metal exports are priced in the stronger U.S. dollars (USD). When export revenue in USD is converted back to AD, the amount of AD generated rises as the AD weakens. Australian mutual fund managers with offshore investments also hedge the AD for essentially the same reasoning as the mining companies.

The AD fell almost continuously from $0.79 (USD) in late 1996 to $0.50 (USD) in late 2001. During this time period, the Australian mines were benefiting from the weak AD but, at the same time, they were nervous about a turnaround in the AD and they kept expecting a reversal.

To protect themselves against a possible rising AD, several Australian mines hedged the exchange rate, using futures, options and forward markets. This was an attempt to "lock-in" the existing exchange rate. However, AD continued to fall in value relative to the USD. Consequently the mines "lost" money in their futures and options market positions and these losses offset corresponding "gains" in the spot market. The mines no longer continued to benefit as much it from the falling AD, because they hedged against its rise. The futures and options losses were reported to shareholders, stock prices fell, and the Australian newspapers were full of stories about "hedging losses." Of course, these weren't losses at all because they were offset by gains in the spot market. "Hedging losses" is an oxymoron. The same thing happened in 2017 when fuel prices fell and airlines reported "hedging losses." The press viewed this in a negative light, not understanding the importance of the long-term approach to hedging.

Table 9.3: Comparison of Cash Marketing, Forward Contracting, and Put Option Marketing Strategies*

	Marketing Strategy		
	Cash Marketing	Forward Contracting	Put Options
Cash Crude Oil Price Decreases from $91.50 on June 1 to $90.00 on November 1			
1. Cash price received on November 1	$90.00	$91.50	$90.00
2. Plus premium for put option sold on November 1	N/A	N/A	+$1.60
3. Minus premium for put option bought on June 1	N/A	N/A	-$0.70
4. Total revenue per barrel	$90.00	$91.50	$90.90
Cash crude oil price increases from $91.50 on June 1 to $93.00 on November 1			
1. Cash price received on November 1	$93.00	$91.50	$93.00
2. Plus premium for put option sold on November 1	N/A	N/A	+$0.10
3. Minus premium for put option bought on June 1	N/A	N/A	-$0.70
4. Total revenue per barrel	$93.00	$91.50	$92.40
N/A - Not available			
* Producer forward contracted with refinery for November 1 delivery for a price of $91.50 per barrel. The basis is 50 cents per barrel. The put option has a $92.00 per barrel strike price.			

barrel and the November futures contract is now trading for $90.50. There has been a drop of $1.50 per barrel in both the cash and futures market. The success of each alternative strategy can now be evaluated.

The lowest return would accrue to the cash marketing strategy. The firm would only receive $90.00 per barrel. The best strategy would be forward contracting with the refinery for final price of $91.50.

The put option strategy would require Wildcat to sell its oil to the refinery for $90.00. Offsetting the drop in the cash market, however, is the profit from the put option that was purchased in June. Assume Wildcat was able to obtain a premium of $1.60 by selling its $92.00 November put option back to the market. What accounts for the price increase in the put option? Remember that the put option represents the right to sell the November futures contract for $92.00. If the November crude oil futures contract is trading at $90.50 on November 1, the right to sell the contract at $92.00 definitely has increased the intrinsic value of the option. The profit from the put option transaction would equal the $1.60 premium received minus the 70 cents that Wildcat paid for the put option. The net price received by Wildcat with a put option, therefore would be $90.90 (cash price plus options profit). This is an intermediate price between the price received from either cash marketing and forward contracting.

Case 2: Crude Oil Increases in Price

Assume that Wildcat, Inc.'s marketing options and prices are the same on June 1 as in Case 1. However, instead of initially declining, cash crude oil prices increase in the local cash market to $93 per barrel from $91.50 and the November futures contract price increases from $92 to $93.50 on November 1, as shown in the bottom half of Table 9.3. In other words, both prices increased by $1.50 per bbl. The best strategy in this case is cash marketing—with the firm selling its oil at $93 to the local refinery. The former preferred strategy, forward contracting in Case 1 above, would return a price of only $91.50 and is the worst strategy in this scenario.

The option trading strategy means the firm would deliver its oil to the local refinery for $93.00, but offsetting this price is a loss in the put option transaction. With the November futures contract trading for $93.50 per barrel, the right to sell contracts at $92 would not be valuable. Assuming that some other trader would be willing to buy Wildcat's put option for 10 cents, the net price received by Wildcat would equal $92.40. The loss in the options market is 60 cents (the 70 cents paid for the option minus the 10 cent selling price). Unlike forward contracting, the put option allowed Wildcat to benefit from the price rise. However, again the option strategy is second best in hindsight.

Can a put option strategy ever be the worst marketing alternative? Yes, this would happen if crude oil prices change very little during the hedging period. For example, if oil prices stayed at $91.50 per barrel in the cash market and $92 for the November crude oil futures contract between June 1 and November 1. Both the cash marketing and forward contracting strategies would result in prices of $91.50. The option strategy would result in Wildcat receiving $91.50 a barrel in the cash market, but the put option would be sold for less than was originally paid due to its decreased time value. This loss would lower the price received by Wildcat to a level below that from the two other marketing alternatives. In the final analysis, however, numerous factors can impact on the ranking of puts as a strategy, such as basis risk, as described below.

Additional Factors Affecting the Ranking of Puts as a Marketing Strategy

In the cases above only the absolute level of prices in the futures and cash markets have been varied. Among the other factors to consider when selecting a hedging strategy are the basis, transaction costs and "insurance" premiums. As explained above, basis is the futures price minus the local cash price. In the case studies above, basis was assumed to be constant at -50 cents or "50 cents under" the futures contract. For example, during the initial decision period of June 1 the cash market price was $91.50 and the futures market price was $92.00. The basis equaled $92.00 minus $91.50 or 50¢.

In order to use commodity options effectively, a hedger must understand the futures basis for his or her marketing location. If a basis "widens," the local cash market has become weaker relative to a specific futures contract. For example, the basis widens if the local cash price falls and the futures price remains constant. A narrowing basis implies that the local cash price has become stronger relative to the futures contract. This would occur if the cash market price increases and the futures contract price does not change.

Since cash marketing and put options do not establish a cash price for a future delivery date, these marketing strategies suffer a decline in revenue when the basis widens, but they gain revenue when the basis narrows. A forward pricing contract does establish a future cash price so the producer's cash price is not affected by a change in the local basis because the basis was implicitly locked in with the forward contract. This means that with forward contracting, a producer does not benefit from a "narrowing" of the local cash basis. It is also important to note that increasing or decreasing volatility can affect the deltas so price protection will also change with volatility.

Selling a Call Option

In selling a call option, a hedger has sold to another trader the right to buy a futures contract at a specific price. The hedger receives the option premium. However, "shorting" a call is more risky than buying a put for a hedger who is long in the cash market. With this strategy, a hedger limits his upside potential and at the same time leaves himself exposed to downward price movements. Yet this strategy is appropriate when expectations are for prices to be relatively stable or slightly higher.

In selling calls, several basic points must be remembered. Due to the risk of this type of transaction, a hedger will be required to have a mar-

**Table 9.4: Sample of Put and Call Option Premiums for Cattle
(June Futures Contract Price: $126.50 per 100 Pounds)**

Strike Price	Call			Put		
	Premium	Intrinsic Value	Time Value	Premium	Intrinsic Value	Time Value
$124.00	$4.20	$2.50	$1.70	$1.80	$0	$1.80
$126.00	$3.15	$0.50	$2.65	$2.60	$0	$2.60
$128.00	$2.25	$0	$2.25	$3.70	$1.50	$2.20

gin account and be subject to margin calls. The original margin equals the option premium plus the margin required on the futures contract. If the option premium increases, the producer will be required to deposit additional margin money.

To illustrate hedging by selling calls, assume in March there is a rancher with fed cattle he knows will be ready to deliver to the market in May. He is considering using an option strategy. In this example, the cash price for his local market is assumed to be $1.00 under the Chicago Mercantile Exchange's June futures contract, which means the basis equals $1.00. He is confronted with the option prices per 100 pounds (hundredweight: cwt.) specified in Table 9.4. He notes that the time values of the puts are as follows: $1.80 for the $124.00 put, $2.60 for the $126.00 put and $2.20 for the $128.00 put. Since he is planning to deliver the cattle at the end of May, he expects to lose most of the time value component of the premium. Remember, the time value disappears rapidly once the option approaches expiration. The loss of the time premium is an expense to the put owner. He decides that this price insurance is too expensive given his expectations concerning prices.

Instead of buying a put, he decides to short (sell) a call. In selling a call, he will receive the premium but will be required to place the premium in a margin account, along with margin money for the underlying futures contract. If the option increases in value, he will have to place additional money in his margin account. However, if the option premium declines, he will be able to withdraw funds from his margin account. When he wants to liquidate his option position, he will have to buy the call option back, unless it is going to expire worthless.

The rancher must now decide which call option to sell. To assist in this decision, he completed a set of calculations given in Table 9.5. He has estimated that the futures contract could trade in a range of $118.00 to $133.50 per hundredweight. The June futures is currently trading at $126.50 per cwt. After subtracting the expected basis of $1.00 from the June futures

Table 9.5: Calculation of Total Revenue Received When Shorting Different Calls: Current Futures Price is $126.50

Description	Future Market Price When Call Option is Repurchased				
	$118.00	$123.00	$126.50	$130.00	$133.50
Adjust for the basis*	$1.00	$1.00	$1.00	$1.00	$1.00
Local cash price	$117.00	$122.00	$125.50	$129.00	$132.50
Analysis of Selling $128.00 Call					
Revenue from selling call	$2.25	$2.25	$2.25	$2.25	$2.25
Cost of buying call back	$0.00	$0.00	$0.00	$2.10	$5.55
Total revenue from strategy	$119.25	$124.25	$127.75	$129.15	$129.20
Analysis of Selling $126.00 Call					
Revenue from selling call	$3.15	$3.15	$3.15	$3.15	$3.15
Cost of buying call back	$0.00	$0.00	$0.65	$4.05	$7.53
Total revenue from strategy	$120.15	$125.15	$128.00	$128.10	$128.12
Analysis of Selling $124.00 Call					
Revenue from selling call	$4.20	$4.20	$4.20	$4.20	$4.20
Cost of buying call back	$0.00	$0.00	$2.60	$6.05	$9.53
Total revenue from strategy	$121.20	$126.20	$127.10	$127.15	$127.18
* Estimated and actual bases are assumed to be identical in this analysis.					

contract, he established the cash price for his cattle for five price levels. The cash prices were projected to range from $117.00 to $132.50 per cwt. The next step is to establish the profits and losses for each of the call options at the different futures contract prices. The revenues will equal what he will be able to sell the call for to a call option buyer. The cost of a call option in each transaction equals the option premium he must pay to buy back the option. His gross profit or loss on the call option transaction equals the revenue from selling the option minus the cost of buying the option back.

If the option strike price is greater than the market price, the call option will expire worthless. No one will exercise an option that requires the buyer to pay a higher price than the futures price. For example, if the futures contract price is $120.00, the $126.00 call option will expire worthless because it would be cheaper to buy the futures contract on the exchange than to exercise the call option at the specified strike price. In Table 9.5 the hedger entered a zero for the buyback price for the situations in which the option would expire worthless.

On the remaining options he calculated the intrinsic value of the call option at a specific futures contract price and added some expected time value. Even though he is planning to buy the call option back on the day prior to expiration, he expects the in-the-money options to have some time value. If the futures contract price is $130.00, the $126.00 call will have $4.00 of intrinsic value ($130.00 minus $126.00). The rancher assumed there would be $.05 of time value when he buys the $126.00 call option back. Therefore, the option premium would equal $4.05 (the time value plus intrinsic value.)

His total revenue from the strategy would equal the projected cash price for the cattle sold, plus the gross profit or loss in the call option transactions. This amount represents the total revenues he would have available to offset transaction costs, margin account expenses and the cost of production. To simplify the example, the transaction costs, margin expenses and production expenses were not included in the example.

In examining Table 9.5, the hedger notices that no single call option is the best strategy in all the price scenarios. The $128.00 call would be the best option when futures prices run up to $133.50, since his total revenue is $129.20. But this total revenue is less than the projected cash price of $132.50. If the futures contract price drops to $118.00, his best strategy would be the $124.00 call with a total revenue of $121.20, which is greater than an estimated cash price of $117.00. What explains the pattern of these specific rankings?

If prices increased, the $128.00 call would allow the rancher to benefit from the fact that the option was initially out-of-the-money and the price would have to increase by $1.50 before the option took on intrinsic value. In addition, the producer would benefit from $2.25 in time value contained in the $128.00 call option when he sold. This time value eroded as the futures price went above the strike price. Only after the intrinsic value of the option became greater than its lost time value did the rancher have to pay more for the option in May than he sold it for in March.

If prices declined, the $124.00 call allowed the rancher to benefit from the fact that the strike price was lower than the futures contract price when he sold the call. The option had $2.50 in intrinsic value and $1.70 in time value for a total premium of $4.20. As the futures price dropped, the level of intrinsic value also decreased. In this case, only after the futures price decline totally offset the total premium received by the rancher did his total revenue begin to fall below the original cash value per unit, $125.50.

Selecting which call option to sell is based on futures contract price expectations. Producers must establish a marketing plan based on a specific price expectation and have plans for situations when prices move against their position. As indicated in this discussion, the size of the time premium is an important factor in determining strategies. Large time premiums make selling calls attractive, while small time premiums increase the attractiveness of buying puts for a hedger who is long cash. A systematic scheme for ranking the basic options hedging strategies for inventory holders is presented in the next section.

Ranking Alternate Strategies

With calls and puts, a hedger must select between using in-the-money, at-the-money, or out-of-the-money options. Each of these options represents a distinct strategy based on a specific price expectation. Presented in Table 9.6 are rankings of the eight strategies under five basic price scenarios: major price decline, moderate price decline, no change in price, moderate price increase, and major price increase. For each price scenario, a ranking is given to the eight different strategies with the first being the best strategy and the eighth strategy being the worst. Included in the table are cash marketing and forward contracting, compared to options strategies for a long hedger.

An implicit assumption of the table is that there is no uncertainty in the hedger's production and total production in the industry. If prices and the production level of the hedger are uncertain, the ranking of the marketing alternatives may be different from those present in Table 9.6. For example, if the hedger's output is below what is planned, and a significant number of other producers experience this decline in production, the price of the commodity will rise. Such a situation makes the put option more attractive because of its ability to allow the hedger to benefit from upward cash price movements. In the same manner, a production increase implies lower

Table 9.6: Ranking of Alternative Marketing Strategies Under Five Basic Price Change Scenarios for a Hedger Long in the Cash Market

Ranking of specific strategy	Changes in Futures Price				
	Major price decline	Moderate price decline	No change in the price	Moderate price increase	Major price increase
First	Forward contracting	In-the-money call	At-the-money call	Out-of-the-money call	Cash Marketing
Second	In-the-money put	At-the-money call	Out-of-the-money call	Cash Marketing	Out-of-the-money put
Third	At-the-money put	Out-of-the-money call	In-the-money call	At-the-money call	At-the-money put
Fourth	Out-of-the-money put	Forward contracting	Cash Marketing	In-the-money call	In-the-money put
Fifth	In-the-money call	In-the-money put	Forward contracting	Out-of-the-money put	Out-of-the-money call
Sixth	At-the-money call	At-the-money put	Out-of-the-money put	At-the-money put	At-the-money call
Seventh	Out-of-the-money call	Out-of-the-money put	In-the-money put	Forward contracting	In-the-money call
Eighth	Cash Marketing	Cash Marketing	At-the-money put	In-the-money put	Forward contracting

Note: The Hedger is long in the cash market and therefore sells call options and buys put options in this example.

prices and the downward price protection of the put becomes more important. Keep in mind that Table 9.6 deals only with changes in the price level, ignoring changes in production levels.

A key conclusion from Table 9.6 involves the competitiveness of puts as a strategy. In none of the price scenarios would buying a put be the best strategy, and the highest rank achieved by any put strategy was third. Why? Because time value is a deteriorating asset. The decline in time value is a cost to the buyer of a put option. If the expectation is for a major price decline, the best strategy is forward contracting. However, if the time value is large, selling call options may provide a significant source of price protection. Table 9.6 clearly indicates that the task of price risk management by producers requires careful consideration of price forecasts. But the most important contribution of options may be their ability to provide hedgers with a middle ground in marketing. One does not have to trade away all the potential of improved prices to avoid some of the price risk associated with product marketing.

Summary

This chapter has discussed the pros and cons of hedging with options versus futures. Hedging with options has both advantages and disadvantages. It involves basis risk in the same way as hedging with futures does. Options clearly enlarge the hedging opportunities available to commercial firms.

Four basic hedging strategies were analyzed in this chapter. These are:

- Long cash and either long puts or short calls
- Short cash and either short puts or long calls

Alternative hedging strategies were compared and it was demonstrated that price expectations play an important role in the choice of the appropriate options contract.

Discussion Questions

1. What two option hedging strategies can a producer currently holding an inventory use to protect against a reduction in that inventory's value?
2. Which of the two strategies discussed in Question 1 is the least risky? Explain your answer.
3. Under what circumstances should a hedger choose an out-of-the-money option?
4. Why is basis less important in hedging with options than in futures hedging?
5. Describe what happens to an option's delta as the contract approaches its expiration date.
6. How is an option's delta used in hedging?
7. In general, what is the advantage of using options to hedge, compared to futures contracts?
8. When product prices are expected to be stable over the period a hedge is to be held, why are short option strategies generally favored over long option strategies?
9. If options used by a hedger expire worthless, is that hedger worse off than he would have been if he had not hedged? Explain you answer.
10. If a hedger exercises options purchased, is that hedger better off than he would have been if he had not hedged? Explain your answer.

Selected References

Power, Gabriel J., Dmitry V. Vedenov, David P. Anderson, and Steven Klose. 2013. "Market volatility and the dynamic hedging of multi-commodity price risk." *Applied Economics*, 45(27): 3891–3903.

Glossary

Add-on rate Add on rate=discount/face value x 360/t

Algos Technical traders who follow algorithmic trading rules.

American Option Options that can be exercised on or any time before the expiration date

Anticipatory hedge An anticipatory hedge involves buying or selling contracts by commercial firms in anticipation of forthcoming market transactions.

Appreciation When a currency experiences appreciation, it's value increases. If the U.S. dollar were to appreciate, for example, it would take more of another currency to purchase $1. Appreciation is the opposite of depreciation.

Arbitrage Attempting to profit by exploiting price differences of identical or similar financial instruments on different markets or in different forms.

Arbitrage hedge Sometimes referred to as a carrying charge hedge. An arbitrage hedge is possible because the futures price and cash price converge in the delivery month. A risk-free return can be earned by arbitraging the two markets.

Arbitrageurs A sub-classification of speculators that try to make a profit by taking very short positions in the market to take advantage of market anomalies.

Ask The price that a seller is willing to accept.

At the money In options, when the strike price equals the price of the underlying futures.

Bar chart Bar charts are used by technicians to report price and volume data. Each day (or week or month) is represented by a single vertical line on the graph drawn connecting the high and low prices to indicate the price range for the period's trading.

Basis point A basis point is also referred to as a tick. It is one-hundredth of a percentage point. Each tick is worth $25.

Basis The principle measure for linking cash and futures prices for storable commodities. Calculated as futures price-cash price or cash-futures.

Bear Vertical Spread A bear vertical spread involves selling an option with a relatively low strike price and buying an option with a relatively high strike price.

Bearish A trader who is bearish expects prices to fall.

Bid The price that a buyer is willing to pay.

Black-Scholes The Black-Scholes formula prices call options using factors such as volatility, interest rates, strike prices, stock prices and time to expiry.

Board of directors The board is elected from the membership and manages the affairs of the exchange. The board enforces the bylaws of the exchange and arrives at management decisions when necessary.

Breakaway gap Breakaway gaps, as seen in bar charts, signal the beginning of a move. They occur when a stock that's been moving sideways breaks out of the base with such power that a gap is created in the price chart.

Breakeven Price For a call option the breakeven price is equal to the strike price plus the premium. For a put option the breakeven price is equal to the strike price minus the premium.

Broker A person or firm that handles futures and options trades on the floor of the exchange for a nominal commission fee.

Bull Vertical Spread Bull vertical spreads involve buying an option with a relatively low strike price and selling an option with a relatively high strike price.

Bullish A trader who is bullish expects prices to increase.

Butterfly Option Spread A strategy aimed at taking advantage of differences in time value erosion in markets with relatively stable prices. This spread is created by buying one in-the-money call option, buying one out-of-the-money, and simultaneously selling two at-the-money options, all with the same expiration date.

Buyer The buyer of a futures or options contract is the holder of the contract.

Buying pressure Buying pressure occurs when more stocks, futures or options are being bought than sold. The price will therefore increase.

Call Option Buyer As a speculator, a call option buyer expects futures prices to rise. As a hedger, protection from price increases is obtained by buying a call option. The maximum loss possible is the premium plus brokerage fees. There is no limit on the gain.

Call Option Seller A call option seller is neutral to slightly bearish. The most a call option seller can profit is the premium less brokerage fees. The loss is theoretically unlimited as futures prices can continuously rise.

Call option A call option gives the buyer of the option the right but not the obligation to buy the underlying asset at a specified price.

Carrying charge market Also known as contango. A typical inter-temporal price pattern that occurs when the prices for futures contracts with later maturity dates are higher than prices for those contracts with earlier maturity dates.

Carrying-charge hedge Sometimes referred to as arbitrage hedge. An arbitrage hedge is possible because the futures price and cash price converge in the delivery month. A risk-free return can be earned by arbitraging the two markets.

Cash delivery Cash delivery applies mostly to commodities. In this case, the seller delivers the actual product to the buyer.

Cash prices Also known as spot prices. Cash prices refer to the actual market for the physical commodity underlying a futures or options contract.

Cash settlement Cash settlement applies mostly to financial contracts. In this case there is no delivery of the financial instrument.

Ceiling price A ceiling price can be established with hedging, which will create a maximum price that one will have to pay for a commodity.

Channel systems The goal of a channel system is to look for a price breakout outside the range of past prices. The channel is defined by two trend lines drawn on a vertical bar chart.

Chartist Also referred to as technicians. This term referring to those who use technical analysis.

Clearinghouse The clearinghouse consists of a subgroup of members from the exchange. It financially guarantees all contracts on the exchange and manages the financial settlement of a contract.

Combination systems Combination systems include trading two systems simultaneously.

Commodity A homogenous good or product that is not differentiated by place of production or by the firm producing it

Commodity fund Also referred to as a commodity pool. A commodity fund is a managed speculative futures fund similar to a mutual fund in either the stock or bond market. It pools investors' money and then trades futures contracts using these funds.

Commodity Futures Trading Commission Abbreviated as CFTC, it is the United States federal government agency that regulates and oversees the futures industry.

Commodity pool Also referred to as a commodity fund. See definition above.

Common gap A common gap is formed in a market with small trading volume.

Congestion area The area on a bar chart that contains a cluster of bars is referred to as a congestion area. Congestion areas are created during temporary periods of market stability around a certain price level.

Contango Also known as carrying charge market. See above definition.

Contrary opinion A technical trading system based upon the concept that the crowd is wrong.

Convenience yield The convenience yield refers to the benefit (the convenience) of holding an inventory. It is one possible explanation for the theory of normal backwardation.

Convertible currencies Currencies that can be exchanged for another country's currency in the open market.

Cross hedging Occurs when one wants to hedge against a commodities price movement but there is not a futures contract in that commodity available. The hedger then hedges in another type of futures whose price movements are similar to those of the commodity they are hedging.

Cross price elasticity Measures the responsiveness of demand for one good to a given change in the price of a second good. This number is negative for complements and positive for substitutes.

Cycles Recurring patterns in production and prices that last more than one season.

Cyclical Something that happens periodically, i.e. on a regular basis.

Delivery month Indicates the month during which the futures contract expires.

Delta Effect For put options the effect of delta is that as the futures price falls, the options' premium rises. The delta effect on call options is that as the futures price rises, the premium rises as well.

Delta Delta measures the relationship between the price of an underlying futures contract and the option premium. The delta is equal to the ratio of the ratio of the price change of the option over the price change of the futures contract. Delta lies between zero and one.

Demand for storage An element in the theory of price storage. The demand for storage is downward sloping.

Depreciation When a currency experiences depreciation, it's value decreases. It is the opposite of appreciation.

Derivative Securities whose value depends on an underlying asset. Futures and options are both examples of derivatives.

Discount rate The interest rate used in discounting future cash flows.

Discount A bond is sold at a discount when it is traded at a price that is less than its par or face value.

Double bottom A technical chart pattern that shows a drop in price, then a rise, then another drop to the same price level.

Double top A technical chart pattern that shows a rise to high price, then a drop, and then another rise to the same high price.

Duration A measure of the sensitivity of a bond's price to interest rate changes.

Efficient A market is efficient when stock, futures, and options contract prices fully reflect all available information at any point in time.

Elasticity of demand Measures the responsiveness of demand to a given change in price. It is negative.

Elasticity of supply Measures the responsiveness of supply to a given change in price. It is positive.

Elasticity The percent change in quantity (demanded or supplied) divided by a percentage change in the market price.

Elliot wave theory This theory is based on the belief that there is a rhythm in nature that spills over into all aspects of life, including stock and commodity markets. This rhythm is captured in the Fibonacci summation series.

Eurodollars Deposits of U.S. dollars in foreign banks or foreign branches of U.S. banks.

European Option An option that can only be exercised on the date of expiry.

Exchange rate The rate at which one country's currency can be converted into the currency of another country.

Exchanges Organized futures and options markets where futures and options contracts are traded.

Exercise price Also known as the strike price. It is the pre-established price that the buyer of a call option can buy a commodity at (or the price the buyer of a put can sell at).

Exhaustion gaps Exhaustion gaps, as seen in bar charts, signal the end of a move. They are associated with rapid advances and declines.

Expectations theory A possible explanation for the shape of the yield curve. This theory states that the shape of the yield curve is a market forecast of the forthcoming spot interest rates.

Farmgate prices Prices received by farmers at the point of production.

Fibonacci summation series This series is created by summing the previous two numbers in the series to get the next number.

Filter systems A system used by technicians that indicate trade signals given by trailing stops.

Fiscal policy The governments expenditures on goods and services and the way in which the government finances these expenditures (through borrowing or taxes).

Flexible exchange rates Also known as the floating exchange rates. When using flexible exchange rates, supply and demand determine the value of a currency and currency's value fluctuates accordingly.

Floor price A minimum price that will be received. Created through hedging.

Forward contract A forward contract is a contract calling for the future delivery of an item or service at a specified price and at a set time period.

Fundamental trader Fundamentalists focus on evaluating long-run supply and demand in attempt to forecast the direction of price movements.

Futures contract An obligation to buy or sell a specific quantity and quality of a commodity or financial instrument at a certain price in a specified future date.

Futures curve A plot of futures prices against the month of maturity

FX The abbreviation for foreign exchange.

Gap A space on a bar chart between the high price of one day and the low price of the next day, or vice versa.

Globalization A term that describes a growing trend towards internationally integrated markets and the free movement of goods, services, and factors of production.

Hard commodities Hard commodities are the class of commodities that are mined or extracted from the earh, including copper, gold, iron ore, and oil.

Head and shoulders formation Patterns resembling the head and shoulders outline of a person that are used by technicians to chart price trends.

Hedging Participating in the futures or options markets to neutralize the effects of commodity or financial price risk. Individuals who hedge are referred to as hedgers.

Horizontal Spread This spread is created by spreading positions in two contracts with different delivery dates.

Implied Volatility Implied volatility is the volatility expectations currently built into an option's premium.

Index futures Futures contracts based upon indices such as the S&P 500. These contracts are cash settled.

Interest rate parity The relationship between international interest rates and exchange rates.

Inter-temporal Inter-temporal is across time. It is one of the dimensions to commodity price relationships.

In-the-Money An option is in the money if there is some revenue that can be realized by exercising the option. If an option is in the money then it must have intrinsic value.

Intrinsic Value The difference between the premium and the time value. A call option will have intrinsic value when the current future price is above the strike price of the option. A put option has intrinsic value when the strike price is above the futures price.

Inverted markets Occurs when futures contracts on the nearer months are trading at a price premium to the more distant months.

Law of demand If supply is held constant, an increase in demand leads to an increased market price, while a decrease in demand leads to a decreased market price.

Law of one price The law of one price says that there is one price for a commodity, the cash price of the underlying asset, and all other prices are related to that price through storage and transport costs.

Leverage The use of financial instruments such as debt or margin to magnify the the potential gains (and potential losses) of an investment.

Liquidity preference theory A possible explanation for the shape of the yield curve. This theory states that the shape of the yield curve is affected by a liquidity premium between long and short-term securities. It maintains that investors prefer shorter-term maturities and will pay a liquidity premium for shorter-term bonds.

Liquidity premium According to the liquidity preference theory, it is the extra amount that investors will pay for shorter-term bonds over long-term bonds.

London Inter-Bank Offered Rate (LIBOR) The 90-day deposit rate on U.S. dollars traded between banks in London. The LIBOR is the yield on Eurodollar futures.

Long call A long call gives the buyer of the option the right but not the obligation to buy the underlying asset at a specified price (See call option buyer).

Long hedge A long hedge is taken when one currently holds a short cash position and seeks protection from prices rising by taking a long position in futures or options.

Long put A long put gives the buyer of the put the right but not the obligation to sell the underlying asset at a specified price (See put option buyer).

Long A long position in the futures market entitles one to buy the underlying asset.

Margin call An investor will receive a margin call when the market has moved unfavorably against the investor. The investor must then deposit additional funds into the account to bring the balance back up to the original margin deposit.

Margin deposit A good-faith deposit an investor must deposit into their account when buying or selling. If futures prices move adversely, the investor must deposit more money into the account to meet margin requirements.

Market segmentation theory An explanation for the shape of the yield curve. This theory states that there are separate markets for short-term, medium-term, and long-term with securities and spot rates are determined by supply and demand conditions in each market.

Market A place or situation that puts sellers and buyers in communication with each other.

Momentum Trading A type of algorithmic computer trading approach that is based on a defined set of rules. These technical rules follow price trends and hold onto winning trades and exit losing trades.

Monetary policy Refers to actions taken by the central government to influence the amount of money and credit in the economy.

Moving averages A technical analysis term meaning the average price of a security over a specified time period. Used in order to spot pricing trends by flattening out large fluctuations.

Naked option Also known as uncovered options. Naked options are those in which a speculator has sold options for underlying futures contracts, which the writer does not hold at the time.

Neckline The neckline is a part of the head and shoulders formation. It is formed during the correction of a price advance that represents the head.

Net cost of storage The net cost of storage is a function of 3 components: physical costs of storage, a risk aversion factor, and convenience yield. Net cost=physical cost of storage + risk aversion - convenience yield.

Neutral hedge ratio The reciprocal of a delta. It is a measure of how many option contracts must be held in order to offset price changes in the underlying cash market.

Non-storable Commodities are considered non-storable if they cannot be held onto and used in future time periods.

Open interest The number of open futures contracts for which a trader remains obligated to the clearing house because no offsetting purchase of sale has been made yet. Open interest can either be the number of open longs or the number of open shorts.

Operational hedge Operational hedges facilitate commercial business by allowing firms to buy and sell on the futures markets as temporary substitutes for subsequent cash market transactions.

Optimal hedge ratio The optimal hedge ratio represents the most desirable combination of cash and futures positions and it is chosen based upon the shapes of the indifference curves of the hedger.

Option hedge ratio The option hedge ration is equal to the futures hedge ratio x neutral ratio. It is also equal to the futures hedge ratio x 1/delta.

Option Straddles This position is taken by either going long (a long option straddle) or short (a short option straddle) in both a put and a call.

Options An option gives the buyer the right, but not the obligation, to exercise the option and take possession of a futures contract at a predetermined price. There are two types of options: calls and puts.

Oscillators A family of technical indicators based on price changes rather than price levels. The indicator moves up and down or wavelike within a price range.

Out-of-the-Money If an option is out of the money there is no intrinsic value and the premium therefore consists solely of time value. A put option is out of the money when the futures price is greater than the strike price. A call option is out of the money when the futures price is less than the strike price.

Overbought A market that is rising too fast.

Oversold A market that is falling too fast.

Over-the-counter swaps Financial swaps that are bought and sold without going through an exchange.

Par delivery A par delivery point is a cash market where no deductions (premiums) are taken from (added to) the futures contract price upon settlement.

Par value Also referred to as face value. A bond trades at par when the coupon rate is equal to the interest rate.

Payoff Line A line that graphically shows the profits/losses to futures and options contracts as the futures price changes.

Pennant In technical analysis, a chart pattern which occurs when the trading range formed by successive highs and lows narrows over time.

Point-and-figure (P&F) A chart used by technicians which plots price movements only, without measuring the passage of time.

Position limit To deter market manipulation, the CFTC establishes a maximum number of contracts that a speculator may hold.

Premium The premium is the price paid for the right to buy or sell and options contract.

Price Inelastic If a commodity is price inelastic, it's price is insensitive to changes in supply and demand.

Price of storage theory This theory is used to explain the pattern of inter-temporal price relationships among futures contracts for storable commodities. It predicts that inter-temporal price relationships are determined by the net cost of carrying inventory.

Price seasonality Price seasonality occurs in markets that exhibit seasonal price patterns.

Price volatility Price volatility is represented as lambda. Price volatility increases the probability that an option will have more intrinsic value before expiry.

Privileges Privileges are an older form of futures. They are very similar to modern futures with the major difference being that privileges were normally of a shorter duration.

Purchasing power parity (PPP) theory This theory is based on the concept that goods and services in different countries should cost the same when measured in a common currency. If goods do not cost the same then the country's currency is either under or over valued.

Put Option Buyer As a speculator, a put option buyer expects prices will fall. As a hedger, the put option buyer seeks protection against prices falling below the strike price. The maximum loss is the premium plus brokerage fees. There is no limit on the gain.

Put Option Seller A put option seller is neutral to slightly bullish on prices. The most a put option seller can profit is the premium less brokerage fees. The maximum loss is limited to the total value associated with the futures contract which requires the futures price falling to zero.

Put option A put option gives the buyer of the option the right, but not the obligation, to sell the underlying asset at a specified price.

Put-Call Parity The put-call parity relationship is (Call Premium - Put Premium) = (Futures Price-Strike Price)/(1 + r (t/360)) If this relationship does not hold, there will be arbitrage opportunities. This relationship only applies to European options.

Random walk The Random Walk implies that day-to-day prices are random and future prices cannot be predicted.

Real rate of interest The difference between the nominal rate of interest and the expected rate of inflation.

Repo rate Repo is short for repurchase. The repo rate is the interest rate implied by the difference between the futures and spot price.

Reserve requirements In the U.S. the Federal Reserve Bank requires that financial institutions hold a certain percentage of the deposits they hold in reserves.

Resistance area Congestion areas in the middle of a trend. Resistance is the inverse of support. It can be found at a previous high.

Risk premium The risk premium is the financial reward that an investor earns for holding more risk than average.

Roll over hedging Roll over hedging is used when a futures or options contract with the desired time frame is unavailable. Therefore to hedge, the hedger takes either a long or short position, closes the position at expiry then opens another position and again closes the position at expiry. The hedger repeats this until the desire time frame to hedge is covered.

Round bottom A formation produced by the gradual reversal of a price trend.

Round top A formation produced by the gradual reversal of a price trend.

Runaway gaps A runaway gap in a bar chart is approximately the midpoint of a price move.

Seasonal pattern Any systematic function in prices within the crop or marketing year.

Seasonal A product is seasonal when there are variations in business or economic activity that recur with regularity as a result of changes in climate, holidays and vacations.

Selling pressure There is selling pressure when there are more financial instruments or commodities being sold than bought. This will therefore drive prices down.

Semi-strong efficient If a market is semi-strong efficient then prices reflect all publicly available information. An investor cannot make higher than average returns using historical data or public information.

Short call An individual who shorts a call sells a call option (See call option seller).

Short hedge A short hedge is taken when one holds a long cash position and at the same time takes a short position in the futures market.

Short put An individual who shorts a put sells a put option (See put option seller).

Short A short position in the futures or options market entitles one to sell a futures contract or an option.

Sideways movements Sideways movements on bar charts are created during temporary periods of market stability around a certain price level.

SOFR SOFR stands for Secured Overnight Financing Rate, an overnight interest rate published by the New York Federal Reserve. SOFR futures are the most widely traded futures contract in the United States.

Soft commodities Also known as "softs." Soft commodities are typically agricultural products, including tropical products like coffee, grains, oilseeds and livestock.

Sonia The Sterling Overnight Index Average (SONIA) is a widely used interest rate benchmark by the Bank of England. The ICE has a three-month futures contract based on Sonia.

Speculating Speculators participate in the futures market with the sole intention of making a profit. Individuals who participate in speculating are referred to as speculators.

Spot prices Also known as cash prices. The spot price is the present price of a commodity that is bought and immediately delivered in the cash market.

Spread trading Spread trading involves taking simultaneous (long and short) positions rather than taking an outright long or short futures position.

Storable A commodity is storable if it can be stored to use in future time periods.

Strike price Also known as the exercise price. This is the predetermined price that the underlying asset is bought or sold at.

Strong form efficient If a market is strong form efficient then private information is fully reflected in prices. The implication is that an investor cannot make higher than average returns using historical, public or private data.

Supply of storage Refers to the supply of commodities as inventories.

Supply The total amount of a good or service available for purchase; along with demand, one of the two key determinants of price.

Support area Congestion areas in the middle of a trend. A support is a price at which buyers step in and arrest a decline. Support is typically found at a level where a bottom was formed during a previous decline.

Swap An agreement between two parties whereby each party agrees to initially exchange an asset and then re-exchange assets at a later date. Swaps can be used to either hedge or speculate and they are instruments that are commonly used to foreign currency and bond markets.

Synthetic call This call is created by simultaneously holding a long cash position and purchasing an in-the-money put option.

Synthetic put This put is created by simultaneously holding a short cash position and purchasing a call option.

Technical trading Technical trading or technical analysis focuses on futures contract's price histories to predict tomorrow's prices.

Technicians Also referred to as chartists. This term referring to those who use technical analysis.

Texas hedge A Texas hedge is not actually a hedge but is instead a large speculative move that increases risk.

Theory of normal backwardation This theory explains how positive carry markets have price differences between the contracts that are insufficient to cover full costs of storage. This theory says that hedgers must compensate speculators for assuming the price risk associated for holding futures contracts.

Theory of price of storage This theory developed by Holbrook Working says that inter-temporal price relationships are determined by the net cost of carrying stocks.

Thin market situation A thin market is one that is inactive or illiquid. In such a market the volume of trading is small, there are relatively few transactions per unit of time and price fluctuations are high relative to the volume of trade.

Time Decay This term refers to how the time value of an option decays as expiry approaches.

Time Value Time value is represented as theta. Time value reflects the market's expectations concerning the prospects of an option having intrinsic value before expiry. It is the premium minus the intrinsic value.

Tradable Goods are tradable if they can be consumed away from the point of production.

Trading system Trading systems are forecasting models used to give buy and sell signals. These are based upon seasonal and cyclical patterns detected in the market.

Uncovered option Also known as naked options. These options positions are those in which a speculator has sold options for underlying futures contracts that the writer does not hold at the time.

Vertical Spreads An option strategy involving the simultaneous purchase and sale of options of the same class and expiration date but different strike prices.

Volume The number of contracts traded over a given time interval.

Weak form efficient If a market is weak form efficient then past prices contain no information about forthcoming prices and price changes are random.

Writer The writer of an option is the person selling the option.

Yield The average rate or return or the interest rate.

Yield curve The yield curve is the relationship between the yield and term to maturity.

Index

Made in the USA
Las Vegas, NV
08 August 2023

75827029R00227